This People Israel

This People Israel:

The Meaning of Jewish Existence

Leo Baeck

Translated and with an Introductory Essay by
Albert H. Friedlander. Union of American
Hebrew Congregations, New York

This translation was initiated as a special project of the
Union of American Hebrew Congregations.

Published in German under the title
Dieses Volk: Jüdische Existenz. Copyright © 1955, 1957
by Europäische Verlagsanstalt.

Published simultaneously in Canada by Holt, Rinehart and Winston
of Canada, Limited.

Editor's Note: In this publication of *This People Israel*, Book One and Book Two correspond to Volume I and Volume II respectively, published separately in the original German edition.

This edition is published in co-operation with
Holt, Rinehart and Winston, Inc.

Library of Congress Catalog Card Number: 64-14367

First Edition

Designer: Ernst Reichl
Printed in the United States of America

ACKNOWLEDGMENTS The translator acknowledges his great indebtedness to all who have shared in the task of bringing Leo Baeck's words to the English-speaking public. The credits belong to many, of whom only a few can be singled out: Eugene B. Borowitz, whose initiative originated this project and whose constant guidance is evident on every page; Arthur A. Cohen, whose personal friendship and perceptive editing were a bulwark to both translator and translation, and who spent countless hours in shaping the final form of this work. I must also thank Mrs. Ruth Berlak, Rabbi Baeck's daughter; Dr. Max Kreutzberger and the Leo Baeck Institute; Evelyn Friedlander; Seymour Barofsky; the Religion Department of Columbia University; and the Union of American Hebrew Congregations for their assistance.

CONTENTS

Introduction

Some men stand above the flow of time. They are touched by all the events of their era, are in the midst of its movements, organizations, and ideas, and all of their actions proclaim the spirit of their times—and yet a curious objectivity, residing within them, turns their existence into something twofold: it is lived as the constant encounter with the contemporaneous, and as the unremitting struggle to view life *sub specie aeternitatis*. Such men are rare, but they exist in every age, for no age could exist without them. They are needed to proclaim the oneness, the totality that underlies the diversity of existence. Rebels, prophets, and sometimes rabbis, they supply vision; for where there is no vision the people perish. In our day, one of these men was Leo Baeck. He taught a vision that encompassed "history and anticipation, task and mystery, the apparent and the invisible, both earth and heaven. It contained all because it knew the relationship of all, because it knew of the unity revealed in all." Thus Baeck spoke of the poetry of divine legislation, of the essence of Judaism, which was his message to our day.

Leo Baeck (1873–1956) was one of a number of figures produced by a German-Jewish community that seemed to be moving toward a renaissance, a golden age of creativity. The names of Hermann Cohen, Martin Buber, and Franz Rosenzweig come to mind and invite comparison. In that group, we must recognize Hermann Cohen as the foundation upon whom all the others built, Baeck included. Yet it must be affirmed that Baeck stands solidly alongside Buber and Rosenzweig. His teachings precede, complement, and fulfill theirs. Baeck's magnum opus, *The Essence of Judaism,* was published in 1905, long before Buber and Rosenzweig became the spokesmen of their age. And Baeck's final work, *This People Israel,* appeared half a century later, transcending and reconciling much of Rosenzweig and Buber. It does not do so consciously, but rather as the end product of an encounter between Judaism and German culture that began in the days of Mendelssohn and ended in the nights of Auschwitz and Theresienstadt. It is also a summation of rational and mystic trends that, in asserting the dynamism of an ancient faith, clashed in creative strife within the Jewish community. More than anything else, though, this book is the actualization of the life of Leo Baeck. To plumb its meaning fully, we must come to know Baeck. In Jewish tradition, a scholar was often identified by the title of his chief work: A man, his book—they were the same. As we turn to the one, we encounter the other.

The book of Leo Baeck's life was opened in Lissa, a border town in Posen where Eastern and Western European culture commingled. Amos Comenius had founded the *gymnasium* Leo Baeck attended. Rabbi Akiba Eger had left his imprint upon the Jewish community of Lissa, afterward guided by Baeck's father. On the one side, there were the strong tensions between Poles and Germans, between Catholics and Protestants; on the other, a warm and human atmosphere of small-town life. The young boy learned to walk carefully between warring ideas; he learned to love his fellow man, and he acquired a piety in which a love for God and for His teachings fell into a pattern somehow reminiscent of the *haside ashkenaz*—the Jewish mystics of the Middle Ages. All these were pathways that had to bring him into the way of life that was a family tradition: Leo Baeck became a rabbi.

The liberal seminary in Berlin ordained Baeck, but the more conservative Breslau institution also left its imprint upon him. Just as significant, Baeck received his Ph.D. from the University of Berlin. He was a completely modern rabbi: pastor and preacher, scholar and teacher, as much at home in the secular as in the religious disciplines of learning. New tensions filled an ancient calling. Baeck's life was balanced between the dynamism of an utter sharing and complete loneliness, of working for others and of creating within himself. His life combined concentrated contemplation and study of the past with the widest opportunities of realizing its values in the present and in the future. The dimensions of a rabbi's life can take on such proportions that many falter and fail. It is the few, men like Leo Baeck, who fill all aspects of it and validate the rabbi's place in society. By their actions, life itself becomes sanctified, and the Pharisaic vision of the holy grows within the community and the ancient promise of a "kingdom of priests and a holy people" re-enters society and the world.

Baeck's first pulpit was in Oppeln, in Upper Silesia, where he served for ten years, from 1897 to 1907. While there, he published *The Essence of Judaism* (1905), and became known as a brilliant and passionate spokesman of Judaism. In 1907, he moved to Düsseldorf; and he was called to Berlin in 1912, to a post he held until 1942. When World War I broke out, he volunteered as an army chaplain and served on the Western and Eastern fronts before returning to Berlin. This is significant, as significant as his early work for the Central *Verein*, the major association of German Jews that proudly asserted its German culture and heritage. Baeck truly "represented" German Jewry—both the majority and the minority. In his first year as a rabbi (1897) he was one of the very few men who did not join in the national rabbinical association's condemnation of the First Zionist Congress. Twenty-five years later, he became the president of the rabbinical association. A short time after that (in 1924), the presidency of the B'nai B'rith order came to him. All segments of the Jewish community had come to believe in him and to trust in his leadership. He always saw both sides of an argument; this understanding did not lead him into meaningless compromise, but toward a reconciliation on a higher plateau of truth. When Hitler's decrees of 1933 created second-class citizenship for Germany's Jews and all dreams of a common culture were smashed, the newly formed Ghetto turned to Leo Baeck and asked him to be its leader as the president of the *Reichsvertretung der Juden in Deutschland.*

II

Plato would have philosophers be kings. But mankind will not have it so. There is a mass distrust of the intellect. And so the leaders of a community, more often than not, are chosen for the success they have obtained in the market place, for the so-called "practicality" that men can understand. Occasionally, that pattern is broken, and then that very fact bespeaks the greatness of an individual. The historian Jacob Burckhardt once wrote: "According to the proverb, 'no man is indispensable.' But the few who are so nevertheless are great" (*Weltgeschichtliche Betrachtungen*).

Leo Baeck was one of the few. When he was chosen to lead the German Jew as he descended into the Vale of Tears, it was a proper—indeed an unavoidable—choice. What Louis Marshall for some represented to America, what Weizmann was to British Jewry—that was Leo Baeck in Germany. Bruno Italiener, in his deeply moving tribute, shows us the reason:

They chose their greatest rabbi . . . for with that sense for the future which long suffering seems to have bred within us Jews, they felt that this time of need required a man who would not only strive to meet the arch-enemy with the weapons of worldly wisdom. It had to be a man wearing the armor the prophets wore when, in the name of the just and holy God, they called the rulers of their time to battle within the lists; a man who drew his full strength out of his living belief in God, out of his impassioned love for the Jewish people.

Baeck was a man of God, and he represented God's people.

The *Reichsvertretung* was the representative body of a Jewish community within an invisible jail that steadily moved closer toward becoming a death chamber. Here were gathered the Jewish leaders who had to sit down at the conference table with their Nazi jailers and had to fight for their lives—or at least for time, so that some lives might be saved. Someday the diplomatic history of the *Reichsvertretung* must be written, so that the achievements of men like Otto Hirsch and Leo Baeck, of women like Cora Berliner and Hannah Karminski, can be evaluated properly. As long as the Nazis tried to conceal their crimes under the cloak of legality, the *Reichsvertretung* leadership fought for every possible concession for their people. When legality was gone, they interposed their own lives between oppressor and victims. Time and again, Leo Baeck refused offers from abroad that would have brought him into safety. He was not to be separated from his flock. As late as 1939, he could take a group of children to England—and return to the death trap of Hitler's Germany. This was the moral leadership of Leo Baeck, the actualization of the essence of Judaism in a life that instructed by both precept and example.

The presidency of the *Reichsvertretung* also involved practical politics. The administrative work of a complex organizational network of Jewish life came to involve Baeck. Under his presidency, millions were spent annually in clearly defined fields: emigration, economic help, charity, education, and culture. And while the Jewish community was united against their oppressors, internal differences between Zionists and non-Zionists, organizations, institutions, and congregations created countless crises that were adjudicated by Leo Baeck. They were not always clearly resolved, but differences were never permitted to split apart the Jewish community. The Jews remained one people, and their leader was Leo Baeck.

Darkness descended, and with it came death for six million Jews. Cities of slaughter arose around Nimrod's furnaces, and names of infamy came to be muttered in the world: Auschwitz, Bergen-Belsen, Dachau. Leo Baeck continued to lead his people, to teach and to preach. Five arrests later, he too was in a concentration camp. Here, over-efficiency betrayed the oppressor. One Rabbi Beck, a saintly aged teacher, died in Theresienstadt, where Baeck had been sent. Word went out that *the* Rabbi Baeck had died. (They still could not understand that it was not with one man they had to contend, but with *this people Israel!*) Now he was only one number among many—187 894; by a miracle, it was one of the few not drawn in the grim lottery of death.

What did Baeck do in the concentration camp? The answer is a simple one: A rabbi is a teacher, and Baeck continued to teach his people. Late at night, the prisoners would crowd into one of the barracks and listen to Baeck lecture on a variety of subjects. They would listen—and they ceased being numbers and once again became human beings. In the daytime, Baeck would walk around the camp, and peace and comfort walked with him. A first-hand account gives us clear insight into those days:

> The most memorable personality in the Council of Elders was Rabbi Leo Baeck . . . who was universally respected among all prisoners and regarded with ever higher esteem for his readiness to help. He never withdrew from the camp, but it did not seem to exist near him; none of its filth could touch him. Peace emanated from him. He could be gentle . . . but could also speak with zealous anger, for he knew the demands of the hour, knew of the fateful failings to which he and everyone else in the framework of history was subject. This oppressed and saddened him, but could not break him. For he always held himself ready for new tasks; tenaciously, bravely, he never refused them. He knew that he was a witness to the fact that there still had to be a different world from this "ghetto." Incorruptible, he saw weaknesses and corruption in his

surroundings. He exerted his influence against them, particularly through the purity of his own example. . . . He was a shining beacon in the salt tear ocean of despair.*

Baeck survived the concentration camp; more than the biblical span of eighty years was granted to him so that he might teach his people. But as the author of *The Essence of Judaism* walked through the dark valley, the idealistic vision of the teachings of Judaism merged with the existential reality of the Jewish people. And a new book emerged, the recapitulation of all his days and nights: *This People Israel: The Meaning of Jewish Existence.* It was written in the concentration camp, a bundle of pages that had to be concealed again and again. It was a very personal expression, but it had to testify before men and bear witness. Now it is here to speak to us.

III

The book confronting us is the end product of fourscore years of living experience. But it is also based on the experience of a people that looks back on almost four thousand years of existence and development. As a professor of homiletics in Berlin and in Cincinnati, Baeck taught his students how to relate themselves to the classic sources of their heritage and how to give them modern forms of expression. The authentic rabbi is part of the chain of tradition transmitting the bibilical word and transmuting it for every generation. Baeck's special field was midrash, the rabbinic interpretation of the Bible during the first centuries of the common era. Reacting to a developing Christianity and to an all-pervasive Hellenism, midrash strove to preserve the essence of biblical thought and to secure its authority for all ages. The rabbis were never blind to the contemporary influences of Greek and Christian thought. They knew that what was good would be compatible with the essence of Judaism and would be absorbed—and what was

* H. G. Adler, *Theresienstadt 1941–1945* (Tübingen, 1955), pp. 249-50.

inimical would be eliminated. The biblical word lived within them and reacted to their environment. And this penetration of the changing environment by the divine word was Leo Baeck's ultimate concern.

Baeck wrote as a rabbi interpreting the Bible, and the book before us must be understood, first of all, as a midrash for our times. A midrash takes a divine word and explores its meaning to the fullest extent possible. This is a religious exploration; it is not philological, it is not historical—in the Midrash, Moses can study in the school of Akiba. *This People Israel* is a modern midrash, as Baeck was a modern rabbi, and all of its pages are in consonance with the scholarly disciplines. Yet it would be a mistake to read it as a history, or to lose oneself within philological excursuses. It must be understood as theology, as midrash, as a religious quest that seeks out the meaning of the divine word. "This people which I formed for Myself, That they might tell of My praise" (Is. 43:21), was the biblical word that cut into the dark night of Theresienstadt and came to Leo Baeck. In that time and place, it needed exploration. And out of that exploration came this modern midrash.

This people Israel stands in a special relationship to God—the *peshat*, the simple meaning of the biblical word, is unmistakable. Leo Baeck had learned it as a youth, and it had brought him into the rabbinate. He had explored all aspects of this relationship. With the clarity of thought that was his inheritance from Hermann Cohen, he came to know its structure; with the poetry of the law derived from the Midrash, he saw it as a ladder reaching from earth to heaven. And just as the rabbis of the Midrash came to their clearest definition of Judaism responding to the challenge of Christianity, so the young Baeck had achieved his classic delineation of the relationship of Israel to God when he wrote *The Essence of Judaism* in answer to Harnack's *The Essence of Christianity.*

Harnack's work had gone back to those days of the Midrash and of the Gospels. He had affirmed the early Christian texts as the purest source, as the only true expression of Christian faith to which the believer would return, sloughing off the mistakes acquired since the time of Jesus and inherited from before the time of Jesus. Baeck did not answer with a point by point rebuttal. Instead, he presented a different concept on the essence of religion: a vision of "classic" Judaism as against "romantic" Christianity, a picture of a dynamic living faith that shattered Harnack's framework and established a world in which there was room for both faiths. But the differences between them were vast—the difference between the faith that places an intermediary between man and God, and the faith that confronts man continually and directly with the moral decision, with God's commandment and God's mystery. Harnack had seen Christianity as a process commencing with the tremendous creative period of the Gospels, a vision soon lost but eventually to be reclaimed in all its purity. By contrast, Baeck saw no single flowering of vision in Judaism. He saw the essence of Judaism as the conquest of time, as the great chain of tradition in which each generation confronts tradition and experiences a rebirth of creativity that adds to that tradition. And each generation *must* respond to God's command; faith and action are inseparable, and the categorical imperatives of the moral life reach into every time and into all areas of existence. All men are God's partners in the creation of a better world; and a basic optimism affirmed a goodness resident in man that could lead to greatness. All of this was part of Israel's relationship to God: it had heard the divine commandment and had experienced the Mystery; and every generation had to give its response.

The vision of *The Essence of Judaism* is reaffirmed in *This People Israel.* The intervening fifty years have left their mark. The emphasis has shifted from that rational idealism that centered on theological structure to a passionate awareness of this people Israel whose daily life gave testimony to those beliefs. But their "twofoldness"—Baeck's favorite term—is preserved in both visions; faith and action cannot be separated. It is only that the young scholar was closer to the concepts; the aged rabbi was closer to the people he had led. Footsteps along that way: In 1933 (in *Pathways in Judaism*) Baeck wrote:

The constant unity of life endured: *the people,* which lives in its religion and through its religion (and everyone uproots himself when this religion is weakened within himself, and everyone separates himself when he gives up this religion); and the *religion,* which speaks to all men and is to exist as universal truth for all men and which, nevertheless, exists on earth only through this one people and must therefore be lost from earth when this people dies.

Religion as universal truth exists beyond time, but the people who affirm it live in the ebb and flow of history. By 1938 (in the preface to *Out of Three Millennia,* a book immediately destroyed by the Nazis, who recognized in this abstruse scholarly tome a dangerous foe) Baeck presented an outline of Jewish history which is at the core of *This People Israel:*

Three great times encompass the intellectual history of Judaism: the time of the Bible; following that, the time of penetration, the "midrash," which constantly takes hold of the Bible and ever anew emanates from it . . . and finally this new time seen so far only in its beginnings, extending the ways of a newly awakened strength of faith . . .

In 1955, the pages written in the concentration camp went out to the world as *This People Israel: The Meaning of Jewish Existence.* The road from essence to existence, from nineteenth-century optimism to twentieth-century existentialism, had been followed to its logical conclusion.

IV

The Talmud tells of four rabbis who entered *Pardes* (Paradise): Ben Azzai died, Ben Zoma became insane, Elisha b. Abuya turned apostate; Akiba entered in peace and left in peace. *Pardes* signifies the divine word, and the name is an acrostic for the four methods of interpretation: "*P*eshat," the straightforward interpretation; "*R*emes," the allegorical one; "*D*erush," the homiletic approach; and "*S*od," the esoteric, mystic interpretation. In times of darkness, Jews have often turned to mystic speculation, placing its veil between themselves and bleak reality. But the darkness of Theresienstadt could not force Baeck out of reality; it could not crush him, or turn him away from Judaism. Baeck was fashioned in the mold of Akiba. *This People Israel* is an interpretation of the divine word which blends the four aspects of midrash into one. The emphasis on the mystery is ever present, but it is never experienced without the clear and unequivocal commandment. The allegory of Israel representing all of humanity carries within itself homiletic exhortations that had a profound impact in postwar Germany wherever this book was really read.

How did God form this people, "This people," as God said, "which I formed for Myself, That they might tell of My praise"? Our midrash from the concentration camp turns to consider the work of God. First, there was the covenant, coming from beyond time and entering into time to create this people. Other peoples have placed their origin into the hands of the gods, but none had the eschatological vision of Israel which equated the beginning and the end of its days. The covenant entered time with the divine "Thou shalt." Israel listened, and it learned who it was and where it was going.

But, continues Baeck, this people also had a beginning in time and history—the Exodus. A covenant people cannot be enslaved, cannot have masters other than God. Jewish history here becomes an allegory for all of history, and the exodus exists both within time and outside of time. From the exodus we move to the revelation, which shows Israel its way in the world.

Baeck's final category of contemplation is land: the desert of Sinai and the soil of Canaan. He knew that God also reveals Himself in nature. And there are countless passages in the Bible that bear the imprint of the desert. Israel was molded by the desert: puritanism, a stubborn streak of independence—these come out of the desert. But the harvest seasons of the land also touched this people. Canaan took hold of this people, and it became holy soil to Israel. More than that, it becomes the place of actualization, where the word of God can become the act of man. And Israel, formed by God through covenant, exodus, and revelation, can now proclaim God's praise by realizing His commandments in the land of promise. And this is true for every people, for every time and place: "not only Israel, but all men"—that is the final word of this midrash from the concentration camp.

The first part ends here. If it seems almost too clear and lucid, too much removed from the anguished reality out of which it was created, we can only view this as a victory achieved both by Baeck and Israel against that environment. *This is what Baeck saw in the concentration camp.* All of the squalor and pain, all of the degradation and suffering, could not extinguish the divine spark that had been placed into this people. With each reading of this book, one becomes more aware of the hidden power and passion concealed behind the simplest phrases. The stench of burning flesh was there, was cruelly real. But the timeless Word of God was also there; and it was the ultimate reality.

The second part of *This People Israel* was finished only a few days before Leo Baeck's death (November 2, 1956, in London). Returned to life, immersed in the everyday world once more, Baeck listened to his own words from out of the valley of the shadow of death. And he realized that the work was unfinished, that history goes on. He had outlined the eternal foundations of Jewish existence. Now he had to show the progress of this existence through life itself, its self-realization in history. For "this people had traveled through the history of humanity, century after century, millennium after millennium. Its very history became divine guidance for it."

Once more, a biblical word speaks the great truth that must be explored: "Till Thy people pass over, O Thou Who Art, Till the people pass over that Thou hast gotten" (Ex. 15:16). The text is clear. This people Israel has safely passed through the sea, will pass through all stormy seas of persecution in the years to come. The manner in which Israel met the challenges of each age is again a proclamation of the timeless categories of God's creativity that had fashioned this people to proclaim God's praise.

The 1938 time-scheme of three great ages covering four thousand years of Jewish history has been maintained. The second book is divided into five parts. The first part, "Growth and Rebirth," deals with the age of the Bible, the period viewed most closely by the concentration camp midrash, from its beginnings to its renewal and rebirth in Babylonia. The next three sections cover the Jewish Middle Ages, in which the Bible penetrated into all areas of Jewish existence: "The Way and the Comfort," "Prayer and Learning," and "The Kingdom of God." The last section, by far the longest in the book, covers the most recent days. Significantly enough, it is entitled "The Hope," a magnificent hope in which the image of God is rediscovered in man and in which Jewish optimism is vibrantly affirmed. On the whole, this second part makes easier reading. The sweep of history carries the reader along, and there are marvelous vignettes of movements and of men—of Marranos and Hasidim, of Spinoza, of Zunz, and of Graetz. Judaism's creative encounters with other cultures, the rise and fall of empires round about this people Israel—all of it is examined by a scholar with a profound knowledge of the history of culture. But again, it must be kept in mind that this is not history per se. In the many aspects of Jewish history, we find the timeless categories of theological existence: the divine mystery and the divine commandment that speak to everyone.

In their Bible translation, Buber and Rosenzweig reminded this generation that the Bible was not intended as a text to be read: it was the spoken word to which one listened. *This People Israel* is an exegesis of that word. As such, it is not a sacred text that enters the world from beyond time; it is the personal exposition of a man who lived in our time and expressed our needs and moods. But he spoke out of a unique tradition that entered time through the covenant, and with all the authority of a personal witness. More than reading this book, therefore, we must listen to it: It is a personal communication to each of us.

V

Leo Baeck's style is almost legendary. He wrote as he preached, and each and every word was used with the utmost caution and precision. Fritz Bamberger once pointed out that "an essential quality of Baeck's thought-process is reflected in his tendency to hypostatize adjectives, participles, and verbs into nouns. A noun is better defined, more substantial, closer, if I may venture that far, to a Platonic idea than the fluid, moving adjective, verb or participle." Walter Kaufmann, the finest translator of Baeck, also emphasizes Baeck's use of substantive concepts treated as entities and played off against counter concepts antithetically. Style and content are combined in Baeck's writing—the "twofoldness" is evident in all. These difficulties have been kept in mind in the attempt to let the text speak to the reader. Translation, at best, is flawed communication, but it opens a door between an author and his larger public. And if the author is a Leo Baeck, love of wisdom, love of Torah, and love of man enter through that door.

The memory of a winter morning lingers with me, when Dr. Baeck and I walked through the snow-covered woods surrounding the Hebrew Union College. Dr. Baeck was in a communicative mood that morning and spoke with fervor and intensity on many topics. At one point, his thoughts turned to the lives of those German-Jewish children who had found a refuge in America. "There is a special obligation for that generation to transmit the greatness of European Jewry's culture to America," said Baeck. He felt that the richness of the European heritage, blended with the dynamism of the American community, might well re-create what the forces of darkness had destroyed. And he expressed his hope and confidence for the future. In completing this labor of love, I do not discharge the obligation placed upon me, but I begin to fulfill it. May the reader, in his encounter with Baeck, discover his own obligation.

Albert Hoschander Friedlander
Columbia University

June, 1964

This People Israel

Dedicated to the life and memory of my wife

This people which I formed for Myself,
That they might tell of My praise.
Isaiah 43:21

BOOK
One

PREFACE TO BOOK ONE

This book was written during dark times. In the days when the annihilation of Jewish life had been announced and was being actively pursued, the writer felt impelled to render an account of this Jewish life, this Jewish people.

The first chapters of this book were written in the writer's old house; those following were written in the concentration camp, on any scrap of paper that came to hand, whenever a quiet hour was to be found. When the liberation came and the war ended, the bundle of pages which had been hidden repeatedly had become a very personal possession. By itself it told of the miracle of survival.

But the events have become history, and the experiences of that time have been transmuted into spirit. The present called and asked, and all the days were to answer. It thus seemed that, after all, this book should speak before men and bear witness. May it then make its way to them.

Leo Baeck

I

The Covenant

The Inner and the Outer World

Every people, particularly in its youth, wishes to possess the account of its beginning; its legends and poems sing of it, and many peoples desire to be descended from gods and heroes. But it is unique that one people found its special origin, its foundation, in the origin of all origins, in the foundation of the universe. Coming forth from the precincts of the eternal and the infinite, the revelation of the One who exists behind all multiplicity assigned to it the task of life. The world beyond spoke of the beginning and the essence of this people, and proclaimed to it the conditions and the goal of its history. Out of all peoples, only the people of Israel experienced this in its youth and preserved it for all time. God, the One and Eternal, the Creator and Ruler, had become central to all that Israel experienced, and He was therefore the measure for all its action and striving. In Him, Israel had the explanation for its special life. The word which He had spoken, the demand He had made, had increasingly become to this people the constant and only answer whenever it desired to inquire about the meaning of its particular fate. To this people, its beginning thus became an idea. In a sense it knew itself as a people emerging out of the beyond, as a people of metaphysical existence, a people brought into existence by a revelation of God and on behalf of a revelation of God.

Ever since men began to reflect, ever since they began to search for reasons and relationships in what they experienced and observed, and philosophy and religion began to develop, they came to understand that human life moves in two spheres. At times this insight was obscured; at times it was clear. Life disclosed itself to them from without, through the senses, and was quantified by measuring, weighing, and counting. Life also opened itself to them from within, through feelings and desires which became doubts, certainties, and decisions. At times men turned outwards; at times they harked within. Intellectual developments were carried by both spheres through the centuries. In both realms, certain proprieties, relationships, and anticipations have become knowledge: from without, certainty comes through rationality, through measuring, weighing, and building; from within, something different, the unmeasurable, the unweighable, the irrational, shows the way.

Men who reflect are at times more capable of entering the one sphere, at times more capable of penetrating the other. The same division is found in the talents of peoples. It is the characteristic genius through which the Jewish people defined its uniqueness that it constantly refined its knowledge; it attempted and succeeded in understanding both spheres. It understood them not only in terms of their own specific actuality, but also, above all, in terms of the relationships existing between them. The Jewish spirit has always sought to grasp the oneness of all of reality. All reality, whether unfolding itself in one sphere or in the other, expresses one great unity to the Jewish spirit. It comes from the One God, is created by Him, and reveals Him. Only the One God exists, and therefore there is only one order, no matter how manifold its appearances, how contradictory its representations. The natural and the spiritual, the external and the internal, cannot be separated from one another if they are to become known. They arise from the One. They are His creation, His revelation.

The rational and the irrational do not contradict one another here; they are related. They cannot be understood without each other. The irrational is the root of the rational, the predicate of its existence and its validity; and the rational is an expression of the irrational, a form in which the irrational reveals itself. An irrational reality that sought to be self-validating would remain formless and void of development; and a rational reality, limited to itself, would ever remain without solid foundation, without deep security. The unity of the rational and irrational was always recognized in the Jewish spirit, even though the ways and means of expressing this unity in a definite fashion took time to develop. But once begun, the forms which it unfolded were ever fresh and new.

This people Israel came to have a particular understanding of this view of reality through its history, and was persuaded by it. Its history is something clear to this people, a clear way, a clear task, a clear commandment; but it rises out of the world of the mystery, out of the supernal unity, out of the deepest foundation of everything that is.

In this perspective Israel received the form of its spiritual being. Little was given to it by way of external security or protected days. In place of such, it received inner security and certainty. It knew that the root of its being is in the One and Eternal, that the integrity and meaning of its life emanates from this source. He alone had become Israel's great certainty. A *beyond* sustained the moment; that which had been was the foundation of what Israel was becoming. Because it found its source in Him, Israel was often considered rootless by those who wanted to draw their strength from the terrestrial; and, at times, Israel was accounted godless and atheistic by those whose powers and deities had established their altars upon the earth. For this people, history—its own and that of all peoples—developed out of final causes. Historical consciousness was first of all knowledge of the One God, and, at the same time, a knowledge of the beginning and the totality of all men, of humanity. What it experienced in itself became a testimony and an instruction that reached far beyond its own boundaries. Israel could thus appear to be without history to those peoples who had entrapped themselves in self-contemplation and regarded only their own soil and surroundings as having the power to speak to them of history's meaning.

The Task of Existence

The religion of this people, in which its genius matured, in which alone it could flourish, is marked by a unique concept: human existence elevated into the realm of the task and the chosenness of man. Everything given to man in his existence becomes a commandment; all that he has received means "Thou shalt!" The word "life" acquired a different content from that which it received in other cultures. Not only the conduct of individual life, but the form of communal life in which the individual participates, is converted into a matter of personal decision. Man is born both into individual life and into communal life, without his willing it and without any action on his part. Man, with his own will and actions, with the self given to him by God, stands amidst both his lives and makes them into his task. They are now the meaning which God has assigned for him. Because he was born, they became the place in which he lives, they are the path he walks, the way which God commands him; and it is also God's ways that are to radiate outward from this place. Human existence becomes a task assigned by God. By the fulfillment of God's commandment a people must truly become itself. It must make itself into a people. In Israel this task was fully experienced and exhibited. The idea of the beginning of the people and the idea of God's choice cohered as one. This people was given a direction. It had been chosen by the One, the Eternal; and the One, the Eternal, was to renew the choice. It could only understand its existence and its history as God's mission among men.

One verse therefore became almost a title for this people, a motto for its beginning: "Thou hast avouched Him-Who-Is this day to be thy God. . . . And He-Who-Is hath avouched thee this day to be His own treasure . . ." (Deut. 26:17–18).* It is thus that Moses, the servant of Him-Who-Is, spoke to this people whom he was the first to form. A poetic prophet later found a tender personal expression by which to let God address the people:

And I will betroth thee unto Me for ever;
Yea, I will betroth thee unto Me in righteousness,
    and in justice,
And in lovingkindness, and in compassion.
And I will betroth thee unto Me in faithfulness;
And thou shalt know Him-Who-Is.

Hosea 2:21–22

The knowledge of God and the knowledge of self became a unity that remains indivisible in this people. Whether Israel lived through bright or dark days, it always knew who was above it and who was before it. It was embraced by the "everlasting arms" (Deut. 33:27), the *brachia sempiterna.* Its history thereby assumed the kind of meaning that signifies greatness.

At this moment its history is a history of millennia, and under-

* *Er, der ist,* Baeck's rendering of the Tetragrammaton, usually given in English as "Lord," I have translated throughout as "He-Who-Is." Otherwise, biblical quotations are taken from *The Holy Scriptures According to the Masoretic Text: A New Translation* (The Jewish Publication Society of America: Philadelphia, 1917), except where Baeck's translation of Scriptures, which is always his own, requires, in context, a different rendering. [Translator]

standably it comprehends a diversity of times and persons. At some times and in various places the people were few and their achievements small. The saying that the corruption of the best is the worst corruption—*corruptio optimi pessima*—was a palimpsest of many a line of this history. Nonetheless, someone who views the whole becomes aware of what might almost be termed a sublimity. That great trait, that trait of ultimate loyalty toward the Eternal and His word, remains in constant evidence. Through each of the many centuries, no matter how this or that person in the House of Israel acquitted himself, despite every divergent way, including wrong ways and detours, the idea that Israel had to be a people before God continued to shine clearly. It is for this reason that the existence of Israel has historic value.

Only as a people of meaning could, and can, this people Israel be. Only thus can it exist before God and before itself. It can consider its history only from the perspective of God. It is to be a people in relation to God, not simply a people in relation to other peoples. One of its historians, in the days when its individuality was first brought to view before the world, Flavius Josephus, created the word theocracy. This people's constitution is founded in God's commandment; it is to be a people that is predisposed to God, one that in all its development, its wandering, in all of the ebb and flow of history, must remain within its relationship toward the One-Who-Is. Israel is not only to be a people within history, but the people of history. And with the desire to be this, it becomes at the same time the people of humanity. As it cannot and may not think of itself without God, it cannot see itself without all of humanity. Universal history and Israel's particular history become one. "I will . . . give thee for a covenant of the people" (Is. 42:6; 49:8). This people stands on earth within a covenant that encloses all people and is valid for everyone.

Its ways have led it, perhaps had to lead it, through days and even epochs in which it was fated to seek humanity and not to find it. A foreign world confronted it, bitter and hard, cold and cruel, a world of injustice, of incomprehension, of blasphemy. A moral chasm, a spiritual abyss, seemed to have opened up; Israel lived alone. When it looked about, it could not see where humanity dwelt. For the sake of humanity it had to feel separate from the many peoples. To the author of the Book of Daniel, the father of the apocalypse, the great kingdoms, the rulers of might and culture once appeared in the form of wild animals; he saw only his people in the likeness of human beings.

In such days, when this people meditated concerning the future of humanity, it could look only toward its own future. It had no other choice. If it had no future, humanity had none. And when it looked about for a way which would lead to a time of humanity, the idea of judgment had to awaken within it, the idea of the avenging, eternal judgment which alone would create a place for humanity. For the sake of humanity, this idea had to come to life. For only if the punishing judgment of God would fall on all of these masters and servants of blasphemy, only then would those lands once again become pure and free and wide, so that humanity would be able to live there. It is anger, often fiery anger, which speaks here, but humanity's yearning and conscience seek expression in it. It contains more true humanness than is found in many a sweet song of man. The soul of a people of humanity wrestles here. At this point the call "for a covenant of the people" has captured the soul.

The word covenant (*berit* in Hebrew), which now confronts us, has a consistent emphasis within the sacred scriptures of Israel. The book became the Bible, the book of humanity, and with it this word, covenant, assumed its place among the great words of humanity. Following the period of Alexander the Great, at a time when East and West sought to find each other, the Bible was translated into Greek; and this word was reproduced by a Greek expression which belonged in essence to legal terminology. It could and did happen in the Greco-Christian world that the word became a juristic-theological concept with all of the formality and occasional artificiality of such a concept. But in the Bible the word is elemental, alive, filled with a germinating and unfolding meaning. Through the religion of this people, a unique power developed within its language, enabling it to unfold new and living content out of archaic words. A language of religion and of humanity developed. In it, the word covenant, too, was taken far beyond it beginnings.

In the inscriptions of old Arabian tribes, the Sabeans and the Minaens, this word was already used as a general term indicating the relationship of a tribe to its deity, a contract between them, binding upon both parties. But in the language of the Bible it was lifted into the sphere of revolutionary meaning. It became a characteristic religious word, one of those words in which the idea of the great interrelatedness, the great unity of all, of mystery and ordered certainty, seeks to express itself. The God-given order was to find expression in this term—the here and the beyond, the near and the far, earth and heaven. This order is equally a covenant, for man and his free will are introduced into the covenant so that the *berit* might become the rule of man's domain. Poetry dared even the bolder image that the covenant was also a decision of nature to recognize and to accept this order.

Whatever its linguistic origins, the word *berit* entered the Bible. Through the religious power which it contains, the word became the expression of this order. It is the expression of that which is to endure because God has made it part of the beings and forms which He has created, the condition for their unity and interrelatedness, the prerequisite for reality itself. This makes it possible for a psalm to parallel the word *berit* with: "The word which He commanded to a thousand generations" (Ps. 105:8); and, then, with the word "statute" (Ps. 105:10). Later, the old Aramaic translation of the Bible, more concerned with the inner content than with the outer form of the word, translated *berit* as *kayama*, the established, the firmly founded, the enduring, the existing, indicating that which is above all change, above all that comes and goes.

The closest approximation to the meaning of the word *berit* is the word "law." Or, we could say that the concept of law (no matter how it has been developed in other languages) has here been given in the Hebrew a more vigorous, more inclusive sense, a more dynamic content. A comparison will clarify this. In the Greek language the word "law," *nomos*, indicated something functional within a totality, an effectively forming and defining force. To the Romans, the word "law," *lex*, indicated, rather, something organic, constructive, the great coordination, the secure structure of human relations.

In the Bible, the idea of law, as suggested by the word *berit*, encompasses the idea of the living creation through the One, and the living revelation of the One, the idea of the beyond entering the present. Law, creation, revelation—all are fused in a single word.

What is law? In it and through it, all endures that has been created and revealed; that is, this creation, this revelation. Law is the continually active order of creation and revelation, which find in law their ever-new and yet ever-identical expression. Ground and appearance are related through the law. The law is that in which and through which the changing and the abiding, the visible-audible and the invisible-inaudible, the rational and the irrational, are one. In the world of nature it confronts us as the cosmos which is simply there; in the human world it confronts us as a cosmos which, ever again, ought to come into being. Law, creation, revelation, they are the same, they are God's "covenant." The word "covenant" first signified a contract. The contract became the law in which creation and revelation find expression. Above, below, before and after, all that comes and goes is that which is and remains, the covenant of the One.

That this *berit* lives, that it binds and rules eternally and everywhere, has become the faith of Israel. Ever again it has ascertained this. All comes from the One and is oriented toward the One—law is established by the One God. He has established it in the universe and among men. Nothing is outside this enduring covenant, nothing exists without it—this became the particular certainty of Israel within an encompassing metaphysical certainty. The law of this people endures—this people is called by the One God to the law so that the law might become its life and its future. Within the covenant made with the world and all its creatures, there is God's covenant with this people and its history.

Prophets experienced the certitude of God and His covenant. This certitude went forth from them and became the experience of their people, and afterward an experience for the peoples of the world. Within every thing, therefore, there exists an inner reality—unique, one, concealed, unfathomable, infinite, eternal—which is its foundation. It is the all-embracing, so that no one and no thing can exist beside it or outside it. No one may suppose that he exists only for himself or within his own realm. Man is always in this oneness and of it, lost in it and yet facing it. He is seemingly embraced, seen, and heard by it, and can never elude nor evade it. He is never able to make his way solely on his own, nor can he be related only to himself. He is always recognized, he is taken, he is held. Always and everywhere, man is encompassed by an eternal certainty, embraced by the arms of eternity. He is therefore never forsaken and never lost, nowhere alone, nowhere condemned forever. He is never surrendered or wholly abandoned to anyone. Rather, he is always supported by the One, the unfathomable. At all hours, in all places, this was the living experience. We human beings can therefore strive toward the nearness and the power of this Incomprehensible, Eternal One. We can aspire toward union with it, yearn for it, and trust in it. This eternal *I* that speaks to us, this I of all I's, from which all emanates, is that which creates all, determines all, beholds all, analyzes all. This I is for all at once the enduring *Thou*, a Thou of all Thous. Everyone can look to it, call to it, can elevate himself to it, and can bring his anguish and fears to it. The eternal, infinite covenant is sealed.

Anyone who has fully experienced how he has come to be, how he is sustained, how he is guided, cannot fail to see something else. He learns that simultaneously a demand is affirmed that can no longer be ignored. The direction has been shown. He has been given a task, and with it, a promise has been granted him. Out of the concealed, the distant, the beyond, out of the unique, the One, out of the eternal, infinite I, the inexorable *Thou shalt* reaches every man, quite intimate, quite clear. He now becomes Thou, named thus by the One. To everyone, wherever he might be, the word of the One God comes as a command, and simultaneously as a promise.

The Law and the Commandment

The experience of the One revealed to Israel that a commandment confronts man. It is always the same commandment, because it is the commandment of God. Yet it is also always new, because it is the commandment of each and every hour. Man is to fulfill it; a purpose is set before him. As long as he lives, he is on the way; as long as he lives, the way lies before him. Fulfillment itself can be found only at the end of the way. Man can only direct his vision toward it, for man is finite. But that is the great design, man's answer to the limitations of human existence. Wherever a man travels on the right way, achievement is already his, for he fulfills there and then a commandment of God.

God demands from man, and with this the greatest has already been given to him. God has awaited him, and with this the greatest has already been assured. It is a paradox that God's will can be realized through man. The Eternal's everlasting will can be, and is to be, the will of mortal man. What is demanded is the pledge; the commandment is the promised possession. Through the fulfillment of the commandment man becomes an I out of God's I: I by the grace of God. The individual becomes a personality, becomes a chosen one. The language of the Bible attempts to express this by saying that man is made in the image of God. Every *Thou art* is also a *Thou shalt*. Man is the image of Him who is the eternal, infinite I. Through God, man becomes I, his particular self, someone special within the world. He is that because he is someone to whom God calls "Thou," someone called forward by God and addressed by Him. God says to him, "Thou," and thus makes him I. From the eternal I, through the "Thou shalt," a particular uniqueness enters into his life and makes him conscious of his I. Now he can also speak to God, can say to Him, "Thou art my God."

The law becomes a reality by the fact that man realizes it. He now shares the law, shares God's covenant. This vision of decision, this moral imagery given to this people to take along its way, went forth from it to all the world. And because such an experience existed, because an historical decision grew out of it, this people, throughout the process of having to become I, possesses a clear beginning and a clear way. It always learned anew in order to know the covenant. It always had the living experience of this totality, the one, the decisive. It always held to the truth that every final condition and limitation, every true demand and certainty, is rooted in a metaphysical reality, in a world beyond the terrestrial. It understood this beyond, this domain of the eternal and the unending, because it was able to comprehend how the beyond entered into the here and now as the creation and the revelation of the One. It comprehended how the beyond, as the foundation that supports all, as the order which determines all, lives in all that changes and moves. Thus was it experienced: there is something permanent in everything, *one* standard is given for all, *one* law sealed into all. A covenant exists and endures.

This covenant is God's covenant with Noah and his descendants. "Noah was in his generations a man righteous and whole-hearted; Noah walked with God" (Gen. 6:9). He alone survived the destruction of a world that had become corrupt and had been destroyed to clear it for a renewed creation. This covenant, within the new humanity, is also the covenant with the father of this people, Israel, with Abraham, and with his descendants. God had spoken to Abraham: "Get thee out of thy country, and from thy kindred, and from thy father's house . . . and be thou a blessing . . . and in thee shall all the families of the earth be blessed" (Gen. 12:1–3). God had "Known him, to the end that he may command his children and his household after him, that they may keep the way of Him-Who-Is, to do righteousness and justice" (Gen. 18:19).

The covenant with the world and with the human race is, logically and theologically, first in the order of experience; psychologically, however, the covenant with Noah was within Israel from the very beginning. The sense of humanity and of the world as universe was experienced by this people as its own history.

The Bible as the Book of the Covenant

The Bible strives to exhibit this covenant, this law. The Bible is then by definition the book of the covenant. Understanding this, the religion which in the course of time emerged out of the religion of this people, and then separated from it, named the book that was to bear witness for it the book of the "New Covenant." Sentence by sentence, in ever-new poetry, the idea of the covenant, of law, found its expression. God said to Noah and to his sons with him:

"And as for Me, behold, I establish My covenant with you, and with your seed after you; and with every living creature that is with you, the fowl, the cattle, and every beast of the earth with you . . . neither shall there any more be a flood to destroy the earth." And God said: "This is the token of the covenant which I make between Me and you and every living creature that is with you, for perpetual generations: I have set My bow in the cloud, and it shall be for a token of the covenant between Me and the earth. . . ."

Genesis 9:9–13

The law for Abraham and his descendants follows later:

He-Who-Is appeared to Abram, and said unto him: "I am God Almighty; walk before Me, and be thou whole-hearted. And I will make My covenant between Me and thee, and will multiply thee exceedingly. . . . And I will establish My covenant between Me and thee and thy seed after thee throughout their generations for an everlasting covenant, to be God unto thee and to thy seed after thee. . . . And ye shall be circumcised in the flesh of your foreskin; and it shall be a token of a covenant betwixt Me and you . . ."

Genesis 17:1–11

In the law fixing the terms and intentions of this people's life God affirmed:

> Now therefore, if ye will hearken unto My voice indeed, and keep My covenant, then ye shall be Mine own treasure from among all peoples; for all the earth is Mine; and ye shall be unto Me a kingdom of priests and a holy nation.
>
> Exodus 19:5–6

This same law is then witnessed and attested: "He-Who-Is said unto Moses: 'Write thou these words, for after the tenor of these words I have made a covenant with thee and with Israel.' . . . And he wrote upon the tables the words of the covenant, the ten words" (Ex. 34:27–28).

Within this framework the rhythmic law through which, week after week, creation and legislation seek to become one within the soul of this people—the law of the Sabbath—is enjoined: "Wherefore the children of Israel shall keep the sabbath, to observe the sabbath throughout their generations, for a perpetual covenant. It is a sign between Me and the children of Israel for ever . . ." (Ex. 31:16–17).

The law is a way to the future, uniting the beginning and end, Israel with all of humanity, so that the covenant becomes a covenant with all the nations. It commences with the same "and as for Me" as did the law of the world. It seeks to enfold all that can be uttered: this, beyond which no further "and" can exist; this "I," which stands as the foundation, as the beginning and the end of all. Thus, the word goes forth to Israel:

> And as for Me this is My covenant with them [that is, with the peoples of the West and of the East], saith He-Who-Is. My spirit that is upon thee, and My words which I have put in thy mouth, shall not depart out of thy mouth, nor out of the mouth of thy seed, nor out of the mouth of thy seed's seed, saith He-Who-Is, from henceforth and for ever.
>
> Isaiah 59:21

The covenant with all peoples, the hour for all humanity, is founded upon the spirit which ought to be in this people. Therefore, what was asked of this people was once a beginning, but is now a goal.

Thus saith He-Who-Is: If My covenant be not with day and night, if I have not appointed the ordinances of heaven and earth; then will I also cast away the seed of Jacob, and of David My servant, so that I will not take of his seed to be rulers over the seed of Abraham, Isaac, and Jacob; for I will cause their captivity to return, and will have compassion on them.

Jeremiah 33:25–26

For this is as the waters of Noah unto Me;
For as I have sworn that the waters of Noah
Should no more go over the earth,
So have I sworn that I would not be wroth with thee,
Nor rebuke thee.
For the mountains may depart,
And the hills be removed;
But My kindness shall not depart from thee,
Neither shall My covenant of peace be removed,
Saith He-Who-Is that hath compassion on thee.

Isaiah 54:9–10

Many such verses occur throughout the Bible. A new poetry, a poetry of the covenant and of the law, was created through them. It tells of that which is human and of this world. At the same time it speaks of that which reaches beyond the human and this world. Yet, in order to speak of that which is beyond, it needs no myths; it does not even enter the domain of the myth. The mythical remains bound to the earth; it merely enlarges the terrestrial or exaggerates the human. Biblical poetry, on the other hand, is different. It is the contradiction of myth, since it moves beyond the here and now. It does not lose the present; however, it brings it together with the beyond. It comprehends history and opinion, task and mystery, the visible and the invisible, heaven and earth. It embraces all because it comprehends the interrelation of all, because it knows the unity which reveals itself in everything. Only in poetry, this poetry of the law and of the covenant, could this express itself.

The Bible speaks with an exalted perception. For the first time, the exalted found its total expression. The covenant has been established so that, through it, creation might continue; it has been commanded that, through it, man might endure within creation. Because the covenant exists, the power of creation and the power of revelation remain in the world and with man. The one covenant endures, the one law of the One God. Nature and morality thus share *one* origin, *one* root; they emerge out of the One. Together they are the covenant, the law of the One God.

Man as God's Servant

Under the covenant, every single human being stands before God. Here, everyone takes his stand beside others. No one stands beneath or above anyone else. Moses began with these words when he bade his final farewell to his people:

> Ye are standing this day all of you before Him-Who-Is your God: your heads, your tribes, your elders, and your officers, even all the men of Israel, your little ones, your wives, and thy stranger that is in the midst of thy camp, from the hewer of thy wood unto the drawer of thy water; that thou shouldest enter into the covenant of Him-Who-Is thy God—and into His oath—which He-Who-Is thy God maketh with thee this day.
>
> Deuteronomy 29:9–11

Words come from God to man. Man is given the appointment and the promise of guarding and realizing the covenant so that it might endure through him. The law is prescribed by God, and man can and should "enter into it" only by choice. With man, through man, it becomes the commandment, the decisive essence, of existence.

The law comes from God, but with each and every hour it becomes the task of man. In the world of the visible it is manifest under the aspect of constraint and necessity; within man it becomes the possibility, the way, freedom. It realizes itself in the world of humanity through the existence of the man who fulfills it, upholds it, keeps it. The covenant has been entrusted to historical man. He is obligated under the law, and at the same time he is its master. Through the covenant, the law, the world exists. But within the world of man it exists first and only through him; he creates its existence. In a century of change, the poetic word of a teacher of this people spoke out: "When God made the covenant with the people at Sinai and the people accepted the covenant as its own, then and only then did the world, which had been chaos, receive its foundation." The law that enters the will of man causes a universe to come into being. The old Aramaic translation expressed the same when it translated "the righteous is an everlasting foundation" (Prov. 10:25) as "the righteous is the foundation of the world." Or, to marshal another quotation from that period:

> He who strives early and late to make the true law a reality is a partner of God in the work of creation. It is said of God's work "And it was evening, and it was morning, a day . . ." And it may be said of the faithful judge: "It was morning and it was evening, a day . . ."

The judge in his court continues in the manner that God has begun and established.

Therefore, this people knows no higher or nobler term within its Bible than the words, "servant of the Lord." This designation it applied to itself, to its prophets, to Moses, the foremost of the prophets, and to all its followers and the community of the future. This phrase, "servant of the Lord," suggests the ideal that all might share in helping the covenant to become the witness for all men.

The Law and the Mystery

The religion of this people, the mother of religions, has often been called the religion of the law. And, in fact, the law is essential within it, but its total meaning is revealed only in something deeper, something paradoxical. The law may appear to men within the measured boundary of our space, in the limitation of our days. Yet with it comes the awareness that the same law, always and everywhere, arises out of the infinite, out of eternity. Only out of the experience of the eternal mystery, of infinity, of the beyond, can the experience of the law emerge. One cannot be without the other. Behind the law, imperative and commanding, is the mystery surrounding God the Eternal.

Through the law, since God has given it and man fulfills it in his sphere, man can approach the Eternal One. But the true discovery of the law, and thus of God's nearness, is only possible to man if he discovers the mystery at the same time. We cannot experience God Himself; but this people first made the discovery that we are able to experience the eternal mystery that surrounds God, and the eternal law rising out of the mystery. Through both of them man is led into the kingdom of God, so that he may "walk in all His ways" and "cleave unto" the Eternal, his God (Deut. 11:22).

The law reveals its fundamental meaning at this point. But it is not self-sufficient. The law assumes its meaning because it is the revelation of the Eternal, the *word* of the One God. Its power and its permanence rise out of the mystery. For that reason, every commandment is inseparably united with the utterance: "I am He-Who-Is thy God." Only with the presentation of this utterance does the totality speak to us. For example, "Thou shalt love thy neighbor as thyself . . ." is quoted often, yet one frequently omits the mysterious and decisive sentence establishing its foundation: "I am He-Who-Is" (Lev. 19:18). When the second sentence is omitted, the first is left without roots. Only the two together are the truth, the commandment, the covenant of the Eternal One.

The strongest, most unconditional expression of the commandment is the intention of the covenant. At the same time, nothing can comfort more, nothing can give more confidence than this knowledge that the law expresses the covenant, this revelation of the Eternal and Unending, this testimony of Him who forms and determines all. The law, the covenant, is "as true as heaven and earth, as true as day and night, . . ." according to the prophet. Upon understanding this, men experienced the embrace of the universe. They knew themselves to be contained by that which never ceases, never abandons, that which is above all, before all, and will be after all is gone. The most assured certainty of the lasting and the enduring reached them through the law. And it was such a personal experience that they had no better word for it than love, faithfulness, eternal, unending love and faithfulness. Covenant and love are thus united; the two words become as one. God is He "Who keeps the covenant and love" (Deut. 7:9, etc.).

Ethical Monotheism

Ethical monotheism has been a favorite term used to emphasize the unique character of the religion of Israel. It is useful, but incomplete. There is more to the character of this religion than its teaching of the *One* God and His law, more than its monotheism and its ethics. Rather, its uniqueness reveals itself in that the will of the One God is recognized as the focal point from which understanding and thinking, acting and hoping, receive their structure. Everything proceeds from the One God; everything returns to the One God. He is the focus of all that is, and all that shall be. It is precisely this theocentricity which allows monotheism to achieve its character and its completeness. Thoughts have their greatest meaning, and the determined action is turned into the right path, when they are directed toward the One God. This alone lets searching and thinking, deciding and acting, express a relationship to ultimate reality. Life, even though pursued within narrow boundaries, acquires character and style, and the touch of greatness. Life is preserved; its melody does not become a monotone.

If this monotheism is called ethical, there are, as indicated, good reasons for this. This religion pushes right action into the foreground. It had the living awareness that human thought and cognition also express a moment of the will. If they are to remain honest, an open will is the first requirement. Right action is the path for right thinking, more so than the opposite. The sentence with which the people had answered the revelation at Sinai, "All that He-Who-Is hath spoken will we do, and obey" (Ex. 24:7), was early given a special emphasis (it was even treated as "one of the mysteries of the higher world," to use the hyperbolic language of an early rabbi): first the action and then through it and upon it the hearing, the understanding. Right action, in which man ascertains more and more the idea of the right and with it God, this acting "in God's ways," this coming toward God, is not only morality, but also "the beginning of wisdom."

God as the Foundation of All Action

Israel challenged the Socratic and Stoic thesis that right thought is automatically followed by right action. It can be observed that often a contrast exists between teaching and life, between spirit and action. One is satisfied with thought, and forgets the commandment or deems oneself released from it. Moreover, thoughts are obedient, flexible, and patient. The commandment of the right action is less elastic, and often appears to be inflexible. Upon that condition it assures will of its right direction and leads to uprightness of thought. This uprightness of direction is the first demand, and it is a demand for thought and action. It is directed through the one focal point which determines all.

Thus, one does not begin with man—a concept peculiar to pagans; he is not the measure and the commandment for all. But everything gains its foundation from the One God, everything takes its path toward Him. That is what this religion calls *faith.* Faith is the fulfillment of man's relation to the covenant; it forms the unity and the steadiness which he gives his life. Man becomes pious when he experiences himself as being of God, and brings himself to God, so that now no part of his life can exist without this one focal point, without this union. As an ancient prayer says, his "heart" is "made one" (Ps. 86:

11), made one in the One God. Faith is therefore not a commanded faith—"Thou shalt believe" would sound strange in this context—but it is a commanding faith. It is not a demand to accept truth without question; it is not surrendering oneself to an overpowering emotion; it is neither orthodoxy nor ecstasy. It is the choice of one's stand and the way. Its first expression is not in what can be felt nor in what can be conceptualized, but in the decision. It does not mean a simple profession of faith in God, but the will toward God. It is the all-embracing will to the One, to that which is within and above the terrestrial, to the present and, at the same time, to that which is beyond the present. It is the will to what is more than everything that is merely there.

Faith can never become an escape for man nor an evasion of the commandment. Its meaning can find no better expression than the sentence found in one of the wisdom books of this people: "If thou wilt, keep the commandment. Faith is performing His will" (Sirach 15:15). Therefore, to believe in God means at one and the same time to love God, for love itself means to be at one, to be certain.

"Hear, O Israel, He-Who-Is our God, He-Who-Is is one. And thou shalt love Him-Who-Is thy God, with all thy heart, and with all thy soul, and with all thy might" (Deut. 6:4–5). In these words this people speaks to itself; these words are its prayer and confession. To possess God as the One, to remain united with him forever and everywhere, to accept God's covenant as one's own—here is the belief in God, the love of God. Individuals within this people, and then the people itself, came to experience this. Because of it there was a constantly renewed union with the categorical commandment and with the categorical certainty. Reflection upon the faithful and unique Creator and Ruler allows sensitivity to the absolute to grow in the soul. Through the "Thou shalt," the "Who am I?" is answered in the hour when man questions himself; and the "Where am I?" is answered when man seeks himself in his coming and going. All that may occur—past, present, and future—gains an inner union through the knowledge of the absolute. Man could now master finitude, this precarious time, this evanescent structure. He could, as an old usage says, "come to possess his eternity within an hour."

This people Israel wanted to live as the people of the covenant. In its best days, it always chose that way. It wanted to be the people of a mission, a mission from the One and Only who alone can establish such a mission. Therefore, as long as this people remains true to itself, there is no place within it to differentiate, let alone to contrast, its consciousness as a people and its religious consciousness. This, in itself, shows it its place and its way on earth. It was to be the people of the covenant amidst the peoples, among whose strivings and envy it was to remain. It was to serve to reveal to humanity God's covenant with it, what God's law and His mystery have expressed. Through this people, too, humanity shall come to experience God. Its prophet could therefore say: "a covenant of peoples," a mystery and a law for the peoples. To be a people of the covenant, to stand as "testimony" of another world before the eyes of this world, before its own unbelief and its belief—in this the people sought to discover the meaning of its life; in this it possesses the meaning of its history. And in this way it found its foundation in the foundation of the All.

II

The Exodus

The Exodus: Beginning of Historical Existence

In the mystery and the commandment of God, in the covenant which it had sealed, this people discovered its foundation. It confronted itself as the people of such a groundwork because it had heard the call. It knew when and why its being had entered history, and where the way commenced that had been assigned. It recognized itself as an historical people, even as it thought of itself as a metaphysical people. It named one day as the one on which it was chosen by God as "a nation from the midst of another nation" (Deut. 4:34), and appointed to a destiny.

Clans and tribes had come out of the East, into the land of the Nile delta, had entered into the service of Pharaoh as mercenaries, *Ivrim* ("Hebrews"); and then in the course of time they had been made slaves. On one special day they had been released into freedom; on another day they had been saved from the cavalry of Pharaoh by being brought safely across a parted sea. They had become an historical people. One man, Moses, child of this people and child of the Egyptians, had shown the way. The word of the Eternal One had gone out to him. He had wakened the Hebrews and, led by him, they went forth from Egypt to find themselves as he had found himself, that they might become the people of God as he had become the "man of God."

With the exodus of this people, its national history commences: toward this event the way of its ancestors had been leading, and to this event in order to gain a better understanding of its present and its future. It looked to the exodus and found in it the certainty that just as it arose, so will it endure. The certainty of this beginning accompanied it through the centuries. The remembrance of this exodus is celebrated by the first of its feasts, in the season of spring—that a springtime of existence should renew itself, year after year, within its soul. Nature and history here became one. Century after century, with the beginning of the Passover, these people sit together at a festive evening meal, as if in a confessional celebration, and recite: "We had been slaves unto Pharaoh in Egypt, and He-Who-Is, our God, led us forth with a strong hand and outstretched arm; and had not the Holy One, blessed be He, brought our fathers forth, we and our children and our children's children would still be slaves unto Pharaoh in Egypt." History and religion became one.

In the deepest and most serious sense, the exodus of Israel from Egypt was the beginning of this people's history. It signified not only a beginning in time but a beginning of life. This people did not march out; rather, the Eternal One led it out, that it might become His people. Thus had God, the Eternal One, once called to the fathers of this people: to Abraham, whom He commanded, "Get thee out of thy country, and from thy kindred, and from thy father's house, unto the land that I will show thee. And I will make of thee a great nation, and

I will bless thee, and make thy name great" (Gen. 12:1–2); to Isaac, whom He commanded, "Sojourn in this land, and I will be with thee, and will bless thee" (Gen. 26:3); and to Jacob, to whom the word went, "Thy name shall be called no more Jacob, but Israel; for thou hast striven with God and with men, and hast prevailed" (Gen. 32:29).

This exodus is also a law, a covenant, "the covenant of their ancestors" (Lev. 26:45). Therefore the great commandment of the covenant, the Ten Commandments, commences with the sentence which speaks of the exodus from Egypt: "I am He-Who-Is thy God, who brought thee out of the land of Egypt, out of the house of bondage" (Ex. 20:2). Revelation and the beginning of history are conjoined. The essence and the origin of this people are conceived of as one. Because idea and history came together, this people could maintain an inner connection with its beginning. In the Passover celebration of the evening meal of its spring festival, this people could say to itself: "Generation after generation shall consider itself as though it had gone forth from Egypt." The people saw its way from the beginning to the present, and from the beginning to the future.

Israel learned through its history to understand humanity. The idea which is revealed to it in its history gives evidence of the wholeness of history, and both illustrates and determines the continuity of law and event. For though each event is particular, so, too, is the law which holds sway over it always and everywhere the same. History never became for Israel the mere account of times nor the mere account of relationships between peoples. Israel saw history as the law of a higher will, as the moral law—it encountered a commanding legislation, entering history out of the eternal, infinite beyond. This legislation therefore applies to all; it sets before everyone the commandment of God, the enduring moral task.

Therefore, the twofold is alive in Israel's history: there is an awareness of the depths of the past in which distant events merge with the mystery; and there is the sense of the endlessness of the effect, through which the individual historical event reaches out into the mystery of the future. The interrelationship of the two exists through the enduring "Thou shalt" which goes out to the peoples of the world through the commandment of God. History, thus, is God's blueprint. It is a path that can be freely walked by all, for the unique potency of every people is included within it.

The great pathos of history finds its expression in this view. The peoples are placed before God. Each has its possessions. Each has its dominions and its days. Each has its will and its spirit. Each has its possibility. They can go the way of the covenant to the goal, the near one or the far, this way of law and consummation. But they often depart from it. Then, they strive only after some gain or profit, after some importance and power, and they think that they are creating history. Thus do "the peoples labour for the fire, and the nations weary themselves for vanity" (Hab. 2:13; cf. also Jer. 51:58). They are all subject to one law—the devisings of a beyond work within them; they are instruments of a logos, of an eternal architect of history.

The Time of Wandering

God led forth not merely this one people, but all of them, when their time came, one from here, the other from there; to all of them the great possibility was given. As far back as our view of the past can still discern clear outlines, this possibility began with wandering. The first book of the Bible tells of it. The first step into the world, the time before actual history, is this time of wanderings. Everywhere, clans and tribes wandered as nomads, their herds indicating the way, or as warriors, driven by avarice for the possessions of others. At times they came here, at times they went there. Often, they were both nomad and warrior. Actual history begins when clans or tribes relate themselves to a smaller or larger landscape. They do so by cultivating it, and thus accept the obligating, binding concept of the enduring boundary. The boundary around their domain and the boundaries within that domain, the boundary stones and stakes are, in a sense, the first law that is given. The clans and tribes now have their land. In it they can prepare their ways. They have become a people. Their time becomes history.

To acquire history, to possess history, is the task of every people.

When a people discovers within itself an idea, a determining, genuine thought, when it then clings to it, the time of its great history commences. Little peoples, too, more than great peoples, have gained great history; world history commenced with them.

Many tribes remained without history. A fear of the boundary existed within them, and they only desired to keep moving; they remained infantile, or at least juvenile. Ultimately, amidst the peoples and the established boundaries, there remained no more room for them and they ceased to exist; or they continued to exist like animals in the process of extinction. They did not go beyond mere possibility; they are without history.

This theme permeates the Hebrew Bible: history is the realization of the possibility given human groups and communities. Such possibility has been granted to all. In many places on earth many peoples, in many ways, prepared the soil of history. No people can make the claim that it alone has history. Amos, the first prophet after a considerable lapse of time whose speeches are preserved for us, said of himself what all the prophets, each in his way, experienced: "He-Who-Is took me from following the flock, and He-Who-Is said unto me: Go, prophesy unto My people Israel" (Amos 7:15). Amos said this in order that he might then admonish his people: "Are ye not as the children of the Ethiopians unto Me, O children of Israel? saith He-Who-Is. Have not I brought up Israel out of the land of Egypt, and the Philistines from Caphtor and Aram from Kir?" (Amos 9:7)

God led them out: that is what is given. How they continued from there and continue now is in their will; it is determined by their decision. Every people received its talent and its day; but this one sustains, as well, its particular moral obligation. Thus Amos was able to say to Israel: "Hear this word that He-Who-Is hath spoken against you, O children of Israel, against the whole family which I have brought up out of the land of Egypt, saying: You only have I known of all the families of the earth; therefore I will visit upon you all of your iniquities" (Amos 3:1–2). This is the law of history, the law for every people.

One can speak of a prophecy of history here, and one may see in it an essential feature of this people. This people already achieved an individuality in becoming, before all others, a history-writing people. In the lands which surrounded Israel, only the events of the day were recorded, and only the pomp of war and victory was proclaimed. Meanwhile, this people was the first, even before the Greeks discovered their genius, to have created masterpieces of historical writing. History is truly recorded here, with the power of structure, with the joy of presentation, with an insight into the content of the event, and with a feeling for the dramatis personae. Actually this was but one intellectual trait among many. It remains an indication, nevertheless, of how intensely the *essential* addressed this people, even in its youth. Its complete individuality reveals itself in this other fact: its constant inner relationship with history and its law. Without the vision which sees each day of history as part of a totality, Israel would have been unable to become conscious of itself and to articulate its own spirit.

The more this people became certain that human existence is determined by a higher order, the more its receptivity to its calling and the courage to assume its special existence was enhanced. Israel acquired from its moral will the strength to face the fact that it would always be a minority and therefore it would be exposed to the assaults of history more than other communities. A change within the historical situation, an historical pressure, had a stronger, more immediate impact upon it than upon others. There was almost never a time in which this people could feel the comfort of having arrived, in which it could experience completely the security of the present.

Toldot: The Unity of History

In terms of this vision and prophecy which looks backward and forward simultaneously, nothing exists solely for itself. Everything has its predecessor and its successor, its ancestry and its direction. The words, "thy father," "thy children," are characteristic of this manner of thinking. A separation of the epochs, an internal division, would be considered strange. As much as this religion wishes to be part of the living present, as much as it always means a specific "thou" in a given "now," so much does it also see the individual and the people as existing within the sequence of the generations, within the constancy of the law. For this reason, Israel could never enjoy the serenity which issues from self-satisfaction. It is significant that already in the Bible the words were coined, "from generation to generation," "all days," "the whole earth," "all peoples." Within the law, times and nations are connected; law only knows relationship and totality. What the Greeks called *historia*, "investigation," here was called *toldot*, "generations."

The forms in which this awareness of history expressed itself changed. In the beginning, there was the historical which brings the peoples before God, that they might hear the word of the law. Later there followed an historic apocalypse, the poetic pattern, which sees the events fulfilling themselves in another world that they might then be concretized in this world. A mysticism of history also arose, and it spoke of human actions, of creative men who bring the Divine Presence, the Shekinah, down to earth, and of destructive men who force God away from the earth. It also taught that there are spheres between God and the creation, moral and spiritual spheres, cosmic fields of force in which man by his striving could ascend to God and in which unity and contradiction could be reconciled. Beside this existed a philosophy of history which sought to exhibit creation and history as set into the same order. It spoke of historical periods as if they were to be considered history's days of creation, from the beginning of all days down to the ultimate Sabbath of the world, to the time of fulfillment after all division, after all dispute.

The Tension Between the Particular and the Universal

This manner of thinking seems contradictory, since it culminates in the particular as well as the universal. Tension, in fact, exists between the two. Israel, on the one hand, clung to its particularity and its uniqueness. Moreover, the knowledge concerning its individuality and its will to preserve it never wavered, was never permitted to waver. An old prayer dared to speak to the One and Eternal: "And who is like Thy people, like Israel, a nation one in the earth" (2 Sam. 7:23). This verse became rooted in the soul of the people, for it always took the answer of God into itself—a sometimes punishing, sometimes promising answer which is meant solely for Israel. But Israel heard with equal force and equal acceptance that the One God, who "called the generations from the beginning" (Is. 41:4), also addresses all peoples, warning them, encouraging them. It comprehended that destinies are apportioned in equal measure to all peoples: to the one which wanted to hear God's word, and to the other which wished to remain deaf to it.

The tension between the particular and the universal prepared the soil. The soul of this people was plowed in it, so that the seeds of historical understanding scattered by the times could grow and develop in it. Often this soul experienced its difference painfully; but it grasped with all the more certainty a coming communality, an *allness*. It emphasized, often reaching the intensity of defiance, that which belongs solely to itself; all the more unbendingly, nevertheless, it clung to that which unites all by the very nature of its function. It could not be within the one without possessing the other.

That is a law of the soul. Only one who is someone special possesses the sense of the encompassing, of the whole. The more profound the personality, the more it can unfold; the more certain a man is of his particularity, the stronger is his comprehension of the totality. Without the strain for difference, without the pain and the tragedy of such struggle, a universalism would be shadowy or empty. Such universalism, which is supposed to be an obligation, would stand as a nonbinding, merely conceptual configuration. Because this people clung to its individuality, universalism could become a task and a commandment for it.

There stands before us that which has become characteristic of this people: everything which emanates out of the mystery enters the sphere of the moral. The experience of the soul is vital here, for genuine individuality can only develop and genuine universalism can only form itself in the moral sphere. Upon the foundation of the moral, difference and community find one another; here they come to be one internally.

It is also the way of history that difference and unity come to terms with one another. History is formed through such coming to terms. History is thus also a will to justice and a readiness to strive for it. For justice, too, above all is this one thing: the bringing together of particularity and of community. Where there is striving for justice, history builds. Without it, history becomes destruction, builds up what will break down, heaps ruins upon the earth, strives for nought, and truly becomes the unhistorical. And it is this that is God's judgment, announcing itself in the tribunal of the times. History is theodicy.

The Common Origin of Humanity

The men of the Bible envisioned this way of history. The opening of the Bible is itself a sign and a witness. Humanity is one. It comes from *one* father and *one* mother, from human parents fashioned out of earthly forms like the animals and yet separate from them since God formed man "in His own image" (Gen. 1:27; cf. Gen. 5:1), since He formed man as a being of the spirit and of the commandment. Therefore humanity is terrestrial form and divine image, the two united. Covetousness approached the terrestrial; evil, the sin against God, entered man. Out of this, there constantly emerged a new malignity, that of sin against man. "And the earth was corrupt before God, and the earth was filled with violence" (Gen. 6:11).

Evil destroys; first within, and then openly before every eye. Humanity now lost its right to existence; destruction descended upon it. Only one man was saved, together with his family, Noah, of whom it had been determined: "This same shall comfort us in our work and in the toil of our hands, which cometh from the ground which He-Who-Is hath cursed" (Gen. 5:29). By this name, "comforter," a later time would also call the redeeming man for whom it hoped.

From Noah, from the first comforter, the new families of earth proceeded, and humanity again existed. The great list of the peoples is set down in the first book of the Bible (see Gen. 10). They differ by reason of land and manner and name; and yet they have grown out of one root, out of the one consolation on an earth which has become hard and stony. They are one in origin, one through God's will. They are to create unity by faithfulness to God's will. Where unity is only a means for "making a name" for oneself, for preparing a place for the selfish desire for might, it signifies rebellion against God. It is opposed to the true unity, and all too readily becomes the separation, the doing without one another, the striving against one another. The image of the tower of Babel, and of the scattering of humanity across the earth tells of this (Gen. 11 ff.).

The parting had come because men desired to become more than men, wanted to be, in a sense, supermen. This rebellion could only be overcome through separation, taking place for the sake of humanity, and through the humane. In order "to be a blessing" so that "in thee shall all the families of the earth be blessed" (Gen. 12:2–3), someone, upon hearing the word of God, went forth from his land, from his birthplace, from the house of his father—just as, called by God, his descendants later went from Egypt, out of the land in which they had lived.

God's Judgment in History

It is in this manner that the men of the Holy Scriptures view world history, the rise and descent, the winding ways and byways within it. Because they were certain of the beginning, they also remained certain of the end, the goal. Thus, when, as it so often happened, one people wanted to destroy another and ultimately, in its desire to break another, shattered itself, Israel heard their fall as the word of final judgment. Often, the judgment was pronounced only after generations. But Israel knew that beyond history and revealing itself within it, there dwells the great patience. World history has become patient justice.

When the world trembled, the belief in an established justice came to be all the more alive within the men of Scripture. They remembered the divine judgment which had come over Egypt when "the heart of Pharaoh had become hardened." They also remembered the prayer in which Abraham, viewing Sodom and Gomorrah, the habitations of sin, had once struggled with God for divine justice as if for his own existence: "Wilt Thou indeed sweep away the righteous with the wicked? . . . shall not the judge of all the earth do justly?" (Gen. 18:23,25) And the enduring answer, upon which everything is founded, the answer of each New Year, became the prophet's word: "He-Who-Is is our judge, He-Who-Is is our lawgiver, He-Who-Is is our king; He will save us" (Is. 33:22). They saw the light of the justice, which emanated from God, rising above the field of ruins.

It may also be understood, in this selfsame context, that punishment which is to be fulfilled on earth is at the same time uplifted and transformed. It remains a possession of that which is above human desire and selfishness. It belongs to the province of divine discretion. "He is come to judge the earth; He will judge the world with righteousness, and the peoples with equity" (Ps. 98:9). Only there where His light shines can justice endure. Man may judge his fellow man; the instruments of punishment are in man's hands. But only from God, only in the ways of God, may they act as judges. "Judgment is God's" (Deut. 1:17)—so is it established in the beginning of the book of Deuteronomy in which prophecy and legislation become one. A later teacher explained Deuteronomy 1:17 in this way: it is an act against God when a man acts against another by perverting justice. This is again stated in the last book of the Bible: "Consider what ye do; for ye judge not for man, but for Him-Who-Is. And He is with you in giving judgment" (2 Chron. 19:6).

The right to be the avenger where justice fails, where it cannot be found, or where it is too weak (let alone to succumb to the passion of the moment) is denied to man. It is preserved for the most tragic moments of recorded time. It is significant that the Holy Scriptures use the word "revenge," "retaliation," almost solely in connection with God. Revenge is reserved for God. It is true that the rabbis use all terms depicting God's attributes to set man's religious task before him. It is also true that there is a constant formula: as He is loving, kind, and merciful, as He is forgiving, pardoning, and helpful, as He is just, upright, truthful, and faithful, so shall you be as well. It is true with one exception, that of revenge, retaliation. These are God's prerogatives. They are His mystery, closed to human understanding and to human action. "Is not this laid up in store with Me, sealed up in My treasuries? Vengeance is mine . . ." (Deut. 32:34 ff.) Vengeance is prohibited to man. Rather, this alone is valid for man: "Thou shalt not take vengeance, nor bear any grudge against the children of thy people, but thou shalt love thy neighbor as thyself: I am He-Who-Is" (Lev. 19:18).

The Way of Prayer and Song

Only the prayer of man may make its way to God to ask for judgment. Man may call upon God: "O Lord, Thou God to whom vengeance belongeth, Thou God to whom vengeance belongeth, shine forth. Lift up Thyself, Thou judge of the earth; render to the proud their recompense. Lord, how long shall the wicked, how long shall the wicked exult?" (Ps. 94:1–3)

Man may pray for revenge, but he must show patience for it, for prayer is also the expression of a will for patience, a patience which possesses its certainty of fulfillment. There were days, of course, only too often, in which the waiting became heavy for the soul and in which it cried out to the God of requitals: "How long, how long!" (Ps. 13) —or, "My God, my God, why hast Thou forsaken me?" (Ps. 22) But as the soul spoke thus to God, it heard the answer given already in the question. Already in the question there can be heard the sound of the certainty: "My times are in Thy hand" (Ps. 31:16). When the prayer rose to God, there was the patience of certitude. In it, waiting was fulfilled. He-Who-Is came, for "He is come to judge the earth" (Ps. 98:9).

The remembrance of the exodus from Egypt, of the divine judgment with which it had begun and in which it was completed, strengthened the will of expectation. The will of patience never became mere remembrance—a remembrance which preserves only itself easily becomes either sadness or pride. The will endured rather as an idea. The duty of enduring speaks in it. The exodus here becomes a drama of the world. This is how the psalm presents the picture (Ps. 114): The depths of the world had opened themselves. The voice of creation spoke in the hour of deliverance, as the voice of freedom had already been audible in creation. In the old prayer which sanctifies the Sabbath with the blessing over wine and bread, the creation of the world and the exodus from Egypt are juxtaposed in wondrous poetry. The Sabbath, this "sign of God" (Ex. 31:13; Ezek. 20:12) is to be a reminder [illegible]n, of the meaning of the world as well as of the meaning of [illegible]tory, of the cosmos as well as of freedom. When the day of rest comes, when the soul takes breath, it is to breathe in this confidence as it is given by God, as it dwells in freedom, so that its life may be enlarged.

Only poetry could set forth the exodus. Therefore this people not only recounted and listened, but also sang of it. It sang in prayer and it prayed in song. One can only understand this people when one knows that it became a singing people, in a different way and even more so than other peoples. Singing, too, was not just a talent, but was the strength of life. This people's history, its knowledge of itself, had begun with the song.

"Then sang Moses and the children of Israel this song unto Him-Who-Is, and spoke, saying: I will sing to Him-Who-Is, for He is highly exalted; the horse and his rider hath He thrown into the sea" (Ex. 15:1). Thus the song of the exodus commences, and it concludes:

"He-Who-Is shall reign for ever and ever" (Ex. 18). It is a song of the judgment of God. It is, therefore, also a song of the future, of the way of history to its fulfillment. As it sings of having become a people here, so it sings of that which endures forever and will in the end provide all answers. The people remained faithful to this song and to this belief and with it history itself became a song. History was not only an apprehension and a narration of that which had happened here; nor was it only a possession of those who pursued this knowledge and power. It lived within the people as its certainty. History was interwoven with that day which came and which was to come.

This people is in fact a singing people. The song resides in it as long as it is a pious people. In Israel particularly, men learned to sing of God and to send their songs to Him. The songs of no other people have streamed as widely and as deeply into humanity. They flow within Israel through all its centuries, even its arid centuries. Two words are united by the Scriptures: strength and song. "He-Who-Is is my strength and song, and He is become my salvation"—thus is it written in the Torah, in the Prophets, and in the Psalms (Ex. 15:2; Is. 12:2; Ps. 118:14). No other people has joined such words so that they re[illegible] is confidence and joy. Mere acceptance speaks, suffering laments o[illegible] still, but confidence begins to sing.

Noisiness was regarded by Israel as a heathenish trait, an attribute of idolatry. Israel sought to be near to God, not in noise and clangor, but in song. Singing is a clarion call in the Bible: "Sing praises to God, sing praises!" (Ps. 47:7) To believe in the Eternal One means, here, to sing to Him; to "Sing praises to Him" seems almost in itself a commandment of faith. New fulfillment, new event, new witness therefore mean new song. "Sing unto Him-Who-Is a new song!" (Is. 42:10) This, too, is a characteristic word in Israel: the new song.

Every day desires its song; even the darkness must have it. In the book in which the "Nevertheless!" of faith proclaims its hard-won affirmation, in Job, we hear, "Where is God, my Maker, who giveth songs in the night" (Job 35:10). "In the night His song shall be with me," is the phrase in the Psalms (Ps. 42:9; cf. Ps. 77:7).

Even the commandment has prepared its song; the legislation becomes song. The congregation of Israel surrounded itself with an abundance of legislation so that, in bright as in dark days, their own particular spiritual life might be protected. Only someone who did not know the "law" and its blessing could speak of the "burden of the law." That the law was no burden is proved by the law turning into song. Above the law stand those words of the psalm: "Thy statutes have been my songs in the house of my pilgrimage" (Ps. 119:54). Past and future gave certainty to one another; the people could sing a song to them, the old and the new song. The genius of historical patience and of historical vision remained alive.

The Affirmation of Freedom in History

All certainty rests upon what is moral and, therefore, involves a decision. But every decision is at the same time a rejection; in every moral "Yes" there is also a "No." And the "No" often has to be the beginning, for with it, with the "Thou shalt not," the boundary is drawn. In the "No" man comes to recognize that he should turn away from the path he must not enter. The moral task achieves its clarity in the "No"; something is set down which may not be circumvented.

The exodus from Egypt spoke with such a "No." The Eternal One led forth the people. Only by reason of having been led forth was Israel able to come to possess itself. It went forth to speak the great "Yes" and to cling to it. In order to be able to do this, it had to possess the strength for the "No." Not only an external parting took place here, but also an internal one; and it was to endure. Israel had been brought forth out of the house of bondage. It was now to live with the will to freedom: servant of the Eternal, but slave to no Egyptian. At Mt. Sinai, it was proclaimed: "For unto Me the children of Israel are servants; they are My servants whom I brought forth out of the land of Egypt: I am He-Who-Is your God" (Lev. 25:55). The legislation concerning the king contains the words: "Only he shall not . . . cause the people to return to Egypt" (Deut. 17:16). And the utmost in punishment and vengeance is presented as "He-Who-Is shall bring thee back into Egypt in ships" (Deut. 28:68).

Out of such verses there emerges an acceptance of the preconditions of history. A principle is established here, the principle that history begins where freedom begins, where freedom is demanded in the name of God and where it sets its task. Where there is no freedom, there is no history, only the simulation of history. Without freedom history conceals the unhistorical, the common senselessness of a people's life. History and the unhistorical oppose one another within humanity. True freedom, aware that its commanding idea is the One, that freedom can only be *one* freedom for all, has to hew out the path for itself in opposition to supposed freedom. In such supposed freedom, for the sake of the false freedom of a few and their deceitful tasks, the yoke is placed upon all others. History develops in this struggle. It was a call to history which the prophet had heard: "Hark! one calleth: 'Clear ye in the wilderness the way of Him-Who-Is; make plain in the desert a highway for our God'" (Is. 40:3).

As the first datum of its history, and as its first feast, this people celebrated the exodus to freedom. It became a symbol, and in every genuine symbol there speaks a recognition and a commandment. This people was to be a people for freedom, more than a free people, and the Passover is a symbol of this reality.

Rome, Greece, and Israel: A Comparison

A comparison may be drawn here which is compelling and immediate. Three peoples of antiquity have dated the beginning of their history. Three chosen peoples, the Roman, and before it the Greek, and before that the people of Israel.

Rome's history begins with the building and the fortification of a city. And this is what Rome wished to remain, the fortress and the capital of a power, of an ordered, penetrating system out of which a world is ruled and toward which a world is expected to turn its gaze.

The land of Greece counts its years from the first of the communal games for which the cities of its regions came together (Rome was "the city"; Greece had its cities). They assembled in order to see how their men might measure the strength of body and mind, and in order to become conscious of the individuality given to each of the cities and to all of them together. This was the life of Greece; this was Hellenic existence. They saw with a curiosity of genius. Out of their conceptions humanity received an everlasting profusion of riches. Such was the gift of this people, to be spectators and authors in a "theater for gods and men."

The people of Israel counted its time from the exodus from Egypt, from the redemption that set them free to walk the way of history. Israel was not a structure, like Rome, in which a power sets its foundation, and not a contest in which a people views its talent. Israel conceived of something completely different: the great freedom. It was admonished to conceive of a drama, with itself as the active and the suffering hero (one cannot act in truth without suffering). And in its own drama it came to learn of the drama in which all humanity finds its history. Israel's history was thus set upon its foundation when the reckoning of its time, though achieved after much wavering, extended itself to the farthest reaches of humanity. Finally, it counted the years from the creation of the world. This, too, arose out of the great decision and the great negation which the exodus from Egypt demanded.

The Rejection of Egypt

The house of bondage was the first object of the great denial. But the rejection went even further. In its time, Egypt stood as the incarnation of greatness. That which then counted as knowledge and as ability, that which was splendor and magnificence, was connected with the name of Egypt. Men traveled there to be students of masters, to view and to learn. But for Israel, that Egypt was to be merely a world out of which it had been lifted and from which it was now separated. To this people it was the sick land, the land of a sick king and of a sick people. The eye had penetrated to the background, had seen beyond the shimmering appearance. Behind the splendor it had seen the misery, behind the tall edifices the need, behind the temples and palaces the tortures and suffering. Amidst the pomp, it had become aware of the deceased, of the dead idols upon which Egypt's pride was established. It had become aware of the violence, of the pressure that burdened everyone, destroying and dissolving. A depth of meaning speaks from the biblical words about the "sickness" and the "diseases of Egypt" (Ex. 15:26; Deut. 7:15; 28:60). And it is just as significant that the chapter which declares the commandments of sexual purity commences with the sentence, "I am He-Who-Is your God. After the doings of the land of Egypt, wherein ye dwelt, shall ye not do" (Lev. 18:2–3); or that, where holiness raises its demand, the refrain is: "I am He-Who-Is your God who hallow you, that brought you out of the land of Egypt, to be your God: I am He-Who-Is" (Lev. 22:32–33; cf. Num. 15:41).

This negation became important for the growth and for the development of the individuality of this people. From Egypt, and just as much from those who were like it, the Babylons, the Ninevehs, and the Sidons, it learned not to let itself be dazzled and deceived. This people was always a little people. The few and the weak so easily suffer the fate of becoming vassals. They revolve as satellites about the great, who seem to be firmly established, and seek to receive their light and their way from them. It is true that this people had come into the possession of the law of the only Existing One from the very beginning, through the covenant of its origin. It could always take its stand in the midst of what was its own, since the One God is the one and only focal point for it. But the will to do so had continually to be renewed; it had constantly to prove itself in new conquests and in renewed readiness for an exodus or a rejection. The Egyptian kingdom had been a first and a long test; centuries after its departure from Egypt, Egypt remained fresh to the eye and to the mind. If this people, in ancient, in later, and in modern days, had the ability not only to stave off defeat under pressure, but, what is often far more difficult, actively to resist this pressure, never losing itself in the face of oppression or of enticement, it had to prove this ability first against Egypt. "From Egypt until now" it constantly had to show whether it was able to turn away from temptation, for temptation sought it out in ever-changing forms. In truth, the resistance demanded sacrifices. Many of its people were torn out of life by acts of violence and insanity. Not inconsiderable numbers of its members deserted, because they came to believe in success or because they dreamed themselves into a romanticism which thought that the fulfillment of days had arrived. Though leaves fell, though branches were struck down, the strength of the trunk endured and continued to strive upward. The people remained faithful to itself. That it was able to cleave to itself is also its history.

Individuality and Social Legislation

Existence, apart from the greatness of which it tells, is an achievement here, a moral and intellectual self-realization. This people, under every coercion that pressed its chains upon it, through every oppression that harried it, remained the subject of its own history. Despite everything, it never became a mere object. In its resistance, in its will to say "No," there rested something creative, something that forms history. As in the individual, moral strength rises out of moral resistance, so, too, a people ascends by the way of negation. Achievement is predicated upon a refusal. Only someone who can turn away from delusive stars and deceptive gods can penetrate to where the existing dwells.

This people strove for and achieved this. An historical commandment developed that it should unceasingly differentiate itself from its neighbors, that it should differ from the rulers, the mighty ones, and from those who have received recognition. Existence therefore became its task, its mission through this life. Out of the very fact that this people existed, a sermon spoke to the nations, to all those who could hear: "Lo, it is a people that shall dwell alone, and shall not be reckoned among the nations" (Num. 23:9). This people stood and stands so often as the other people, the different one.

There is, of course, a danger in being different. When there is a "being different" that desires to exist solely for itself, it becomes a limited constraint and an eccentricity, a stubbornness; perhaps, even, a selfishness. Only when there arises, at the same time and just as strongly, the passion for a great interrelatedness and for the obligation which follows upon it, does being different enter a moral domain, a domain of dignity. The right to individuality and the right to its antithesis therefore predicates the reason for the humane idea and for the social commandment. One could say that the right to be different legitimates itself in the sensitivity to the right of everyone else who differs.

This sensitivity is put to its hardest test when it is to be extended to peoples whose position seems to rest upon weaker foundations, or whose attitude seems to contain a lesser reserve. Above all, it proves itself in relation to someone who is not in a position of independence but of servitude, and in relation to someone who has not grown upon the soil on which he now stands, but has just implanted himself and, moreover, may be disguised with unnatural features and forms of being. These two, the serf and the stranger, seem to belong to another sphere; they seem to be distant or separated. They are what has no life of its own, what is "other." In both of them, therefore, the *Mitmensch*, the fellow man, makes the clearest demands, he who is the other one and is yet inseparably connected with me.

In its Egyptian youth, Israel experienced both states. It was a slave and a stranger, and this became decisive for its manner of thinking. The social and humane idea did not only speak in Israel as a mere admonition. It could justify itself on the basis of historical experience. The personal possession of the past, the personal "Remember thou," could likewise speak.

In this people, the concept of the fellow man and therefore of human right, of the right of the other, was discovered. This right extends to the servant and the stranger above all. Israel wishes to be their spokesman to guarantee their rightful claim. This sense of the fellow man and of his rights became all the more vivid since it could draw upon all the teachings of religion for its strength. The Sabbath is commanded particularly for the sake of he who serves, for it comes "that thy man-servant and thy maid-servant may rest as well as thou" (Deut. 5:14). Thus a boundary is set for servitude: recognition is demanded for the servant's efforts and acts of loving-kindness are to be done for him as for all men. And there is the constant call: "And thou shalt remember that thou wast a servant in the land of Egypt, and He-Who-Is thy God brought thee out thence by a mighty hand and by an outstretched arm; therefore He-Who-Is thy God commanded thee to keep the sabbath day" (Deut. 5:15; cf. 15:15; 16:14, etc.).

The Sabbath also exists for the sake of the stranger; and he, too, is covered by all protective law and social assistance (Lev. 25:35; Deut. 14:29, etc.). Something humanitarian enters even the great and solemn rejection of Egypt: it is said, "Thou shalt not abhor an Egyptian, because thou wast a stranger in his land" (Deut. 23:8). Rabbi Solomon Isaac of Troyes, named Rashi, the medieval master of Worms, who was for centuries Israel's teacher of the Bible, gave the following explanation of this law: "Whatever the Egyptians had done to you, though they enslaved you and cast your children into the river, yet there was a time when they took you in."

Finally, the word cuts to the core: "for ye know the heart [Heb.: *nephesh* = heart, soul, life] of the stranger, seeing ye were strangers in the land of Egypt" (Ex. 23:9). This expression, "to know the heart [*nephesh*]," is found twice in Holy Scriptures: first, in this verse concerning the stranger; and a second in a verse concerning the animal: "A righteous man regardeth [knows] the life [*nephesh*] of his beast" (Prov. 12:10). Stranger and animal—they are as the mute; their voices are not heard and their words are not understood. Therefore, their souls must be understood; the living breath of their questions must be felt. They are those who are different, other. But, above that which separates, there dwells, directing, connecting, the knowing, the understanding.

This is not just one trait within Israel's religion. It is its essence. For Israel, there is no piety without the social, the sense of duty toward the community. Neither is there piety without the humane, the reverence for all of life. Or, to be more exact, there is no piety without the unity of these two. The humane enjoys its social dimension here, and the social has its humane aspect; the humane and the commanding speak as one. The social is therefore preserved from becoming merely commanded legislation; it receives its inwardness in the humane. The humane is guarded against becoming a hollow concept or an empty feeling: it receives a directing specificity from the social. The memory and the will of this people, its historical and its ethical traits, unite to reveal the way of man. Because of the social and the humane, piety can show itself every day in the commonplace. In piety, constricted man can possess an abundance of the substance of life.

God as the One Source of Right and Justice

Again, the fact became the task. The fact is that the other man is something other than myself, that he is created by God as much as I and, because of this, is my fellow man. Not only must I recognize him as another, who has the same right to be different that I possess, but I must also recognize him as my equal. He is God's man just as I. We belong together—that which separates and that which unites us supports us both. In the so-called accident of birth the many voices of the covenant all sound together; all the special and, because of that, connecting tasks established by God's commandment are sounded here. Only through this unity does difference receive its value; only through differences does unity receive its content.

There are clear commandments which confront man here. Without such definiteness, confronting the incontrovertible fact of diversity, unity is but a word. The commandment alone creates reality here. It brings those who are the *others*—the needy, the poor, the oppressed, the lonely, the widow, the orphan, the stranger—and sets them immediately before us. They have been sent to us as messengers and placed next to us through the word of God. With them stands the foundation of all being, admonishing: "I am He-Who-Is thy God." They have been sent by God, and they wait for us. They wish to be recognized by us; they wait for our understanding in order to affirm justice. Such is the sermon of this faith which demanded the great rejection. There was much that it had to contradict to be able to extend to everyone. Out of the rejecting, the negation of being different, there emerges the ready affirmation of the social and the humane. They belong together; by itself either would remain a fragment. There is no piety without the will both to turn away from and to turn toward one's neighbor. The two, the contradiction and the fellow man, are demanded by God. Only the two together give man his own place before God.

Perspective is decisive. Everything is seen from the standpoint of God, that is, from within faith. That history which chooses success as its measure and inflates itself to the status of "world history," views almost everything from the tribunal of power. Even right becomes for it the expression of might. Whoever controls power constructs the law for the sake of his power. Right then proceeds from might.

Among this people, for the first time, the law was seen completely from the standpoint of God. Only the right that will endure before divine justice and truth is the truthful right of humanity. It speaks for everyone created by God, especially for him who, above all, has to lodge his appeal with God because men have not heard him. It speaks for the oppressed, for the weak, the small, the insignificant. In order to aid him, it sets limits to power. Right is to be proclaimed, in the name of God who is "A father of the fatherless, and a judge of the widows" (Ps. 68:6), and "who regardeth not persons, nor taketh reward. He doth execute justice for the fatherless and widow, and loveth the stranger, in giving him food and raiment" (Deut. 10:17–18).

This is the basis upon which, for the first time, the right can be established in history. The Book of this people continually indicates it. Victories do not count before one who stands on such a place of judgment; on the contrary, it is often the one who was defeated who is called forth with gratitude. The one dividing line endures: that between genuine and false right, that between genuine and false history. History exists only where true right rules.

With that stand Israel overcame the evasions and ruled out subterfuges which eagerly strive to help that which men presume to be right and presume to be history. For there exists a philosophy of excuses, that submissive wisdom which arrives after the fact. It bypasses justice, evading its demand by representing the injustice that has come to be—as long as it already exists, as long as it has already conquered—to be something truly historical, an order that has achieved reality. That which was carried out and completed by men it declares to be something determined by God, a law of nature. It does not judge from God's perspective; instead, it tries to replace God by itself. Justice becomes justification, prepared for any action. Israel has always battled against such a view, starting with the fact that it never submitted easily to any situation, but looked toward the future, toward the great hope: "For right shall return unto justice, and all the upright in heart shall follow it" (Ps. 94:15). Hope is here a commandment.

Justice and Love

There also exists a piety of excuses which teaches and encourages a concealing or veiling of that which is injustice. It does not want to establish the right, but it wants to soothe and to appease by surrounding those who suffer under injustice with the *pallium caritatis*, the soft garment of love. It appeases justice through charity. It fulfills the one commandment of God in order to be excused from the other. Within this people charity was practiced more, and with greater patience than elsewhere, to their own and to others. But it was never a substitute for the right. The right way kept its definite signs. This people neither permitted the definite demand of the right to escape, nor did it make peace with injustice through acts of charity.

At times, it therefore became a disturbance to the nations. But it continued on its way, on the way of its history. The social and the humane preserved the definiteness of just legislation, and the memory of the house of bondage guarded against forgetfulness. The right was reality, was history. We cannot know if the manifold social and humane legislation found in the Books of Moses indicates ancient practices or gives evidence of the particular state possessed by this people. But history does show that the government of this people, this theocracy, was a communal form without an absolute power, without a despotism, without the rule of a nobility, without slavery, without the exploitation of the land and of the peasants, without a double law, and without a double morality. Later on, in the same way, the one right, the commandment which is the same for all, found clear and fearless expression from the days of the prophets in men who wanted to serve God rather than men. They cried into the ears of the great ones, the property owners, and those who wanted to enlarge their possessions, that God is the master over all the land, that He is the judge of all the land, the guardian of human rights.

Justice and the Future

The concept of the social right had all the more living power here, since it not only took hold of the present but always penetrated beyond it. It demanded the good for that day and at the same time the better for the days to come. The present was to be a step to a higher future. This gave the idea its strength. For the longing directed toward today is strongest and most fertile when it is filled with the confident expectation that today will give birth to a greater day. The great commandment needs the great hope. The human spirit proves itself in that which it places before itself as hope. In this people the social idea was always filled with strength because the enthusiastic, the visionary confidence lived in it. In Israel the word was spoken: "Where there is no vision, a people perishes" (Prov. 29:18).

Thus Israel's longing for the future was always filled with the social and the humane, it was directed to the ascent of all humanity. Its exodus "out of the house of bondage" had been its beginning. But all nations were to be granted the same. A new beginning, a rebirth was to be granted to everyone. To the oppressed, to the enslaved everywhere—such was the hope—there would come the day of their exodus. "They shall cry unto Him-Who-Is because of the oppressors, and He will send them a saviour, and a defender, who will deliver them" (Is. 19:20). "Freedom will be proclaimed:" such is the ancient and often repeated prophetic sermon.

Within Israel's own experience and own task, the life and goal of everyone is understood; the history of humanity is comprehended within its history. God speaks to one, but in that He speaks to all. Because the commandment of God is valid to this people and to its day, it is therefore valid to all peoples and their days. Only the one history exists, the one direction toward that which endures. It is not the windings of what came to be, not the crooked bends of what endures, not the interweavings of what is created and justified by force—but it is the straight paths of righteousness that show where the future lies. God calls the peoples upon these paths, so that they may begin anew from generation to generation, ever fulfilling and yet ever waiting. The image in which the future is seen is not the cycle, but the straight path. The longed-for time is that in which God's commandment and history have become one in the lives of the peoples. The peoples then remain peoples, those who are different remaining different; but they have found the way, the way of the one commandment, of the one covenant. It is the time which shall be, because it is to be.

And Israel is confident that when it comes, the commandment of being different and the commandment of the exodus will then have been fulfilled. Its foundation and its right will then have revealed themselves. The great contradiction will then have achieved the goal, the proof of the way will have been brought. No longer will this people, in order to exist, be different from those surrounding it. Its being different, which became its history, may cease, for all have become different, for unity before God has become a human reality.

History as World History

The prophet Isaiah spoke in moving words of this unity. When he spoke, he looked back upon centuries during which this people had been placed, almost forced, between the power lusts and the cultural enticements of the great and shining empires of Egypt and Assyria. Confronting them, Israel had to preserve and to prove that which was its own, its self, for generation after generation. And as the prophet now spoke of the future, the future of these enemies and enticers as well, his final word was nevertheless a word of the unity which ultimately will connect them all. Often the soul had to turn away from these peoples; and the warning word had spoken of the sicknesses, of the diseases of Egypt. But now he says: "[He] will heal them." And he continues: "In that day shall there be a highway out of Egypt to Assyria, and the Assyrian shall come into Egypt, and the Egyptian into Assyria; and the Egyptians shall worship with the Assyrians. In that day shall Israel be the third with Egypt and with Assyria, a blessing in the midst of the earth; for that the Lord of hosts hath blessed him, saying: 'Blessed be Egypt My people and Assyria the work of My hands, and Israel Mine inheritance'" (Is. 19:22–25). That is the final word. Despite all that had been and would yet be, that is the end of the words of the exodus from Egypt.

History is always world history for this people. Through its exodus from Egypt it became a people of history, a people of humanity. That which was, therefore, speaks of that which will come. Israel is a people of history; and therefore it is a messianic people. It is the one because it is the other, because it recognizes no history which is not world history. It breathes in the atmosphere of this history. That which was once in the past becomes for it that which will once be in the future. Once, as it was led out of Egypt, this people sang its first song, the song of the deliverance through God and of the kingdom of God. Once, such is the saying of one of the rabbis, they sang this song; and once again they will come to sing this song.

III

The Revelation

The Legend of the Exodus

Throughout its days, this people has been mindful that the Eternal One brought it out of Egypt. It thus kept re-experiencing a threefold knowledge: concerning its origin—it is rooted in a world of the covenant; concerning its beginnings—it has been set into a world of history; concerning its mission—it has a way to go in the world, the way demanded from it by the Eternal One.

The exodus from Egypt thus had its meaning and its goal. Israel had gone forth for the sake of the Eternal One, the Eternal One going forth before it. The ancient statement of Exodus says:

And He-Who-Is went before them by day in a pillar of cloud, to lead them the way; and by night in a pillar of fire, to give them light; that they might go by day and by night: the pillar of cloud by day, and the pillar of fire by night, departed not from before the people.

Exodus 13:21–22

God leads and God lights the way. This remained the confidence of piety.

Event here became experience, and experience became poetic imagery,* becoming that which is more than any likeness and different from any concept, that which ever anew seeks to lead toward the incomparable, into that realm where an ultimate humanness points toward the unending and the eternal. This symbolic presentation seeks to say the utmost that man can say, to show the most distant view permitted to the soul. "What seest thou?" This was the question heard by the prophets. During the beginning, middle, and end of the time of the prophets it was recorded in the Book (Amos 7:8 and 8:2; Jer. 1:11 and 13; Jer. 24:3; Zech. 4:5 and 5:2). And the answer which these men received was poetic imagery. It led up to that border which is the outer limit of human sense and feeling. This people had learned to live in both the visible and the invisible realms. Since it comprehended the two as one, it had to have an expression for that wherein the two touch and merge into one another. This expression is poetry.

The final and almost unique form of religious representation, the final and almost unique manner of speaking religious truth, is therefore poetry: not philosophy, not dogma, but the eternal legend. Only thus can the soul speak of the regions which it has attained. When a man senses something invisible and infinite in that which exists or happens within his visible and finite sphere, when he then begins to

* The German word *Gleichnis* ("likeness," "image," or "allegory") is used by Baeck to indicate that quality of any word or group of words—whether metaphorical, allegorical, or descriptive—whereby language itself is nothing but a tool for describing something basically nonlinguistic. Throughout the book, therefore, *Gleichnis* has been variously translated, in context, as: image, imagery, poetry, poetic imagery, metaphor, representation, allegory, legend, etc. [Translator]

comprehend something lasting, enduring—a covenant—then, to the extent that he possesses the gift of expression, he lifts up his voice in poetry. Even if it is just the existing or the approaching which seems to mean something to him, so that he assumes he sees or hears something special behind it or beyond it, he can only testify of this in poetry. How much the more so, then, when the Eternal, the All-embracing, reveals itself to him, when the One God calls him to revelation, when that which cannot be spoken enters into his soul and forces him to speak. The human being who experiences this and has to testify of it can only compose poetry; or, what is basically the same, he can only pray. Poetry such as this, according to Aristotle, is more philosophic and more serious than research. This prayer brought the Book of this people to the proud assertion that heaven and earth belonged to it.

The Bible as Poetry and Legend

The Book of this people, in every individual sound and in the harmony of its parts, is the great prayer, the great poem, the greatest created by humanity. Even the poetry of the Greeks did not rise to such heights. Teaching and commandment, narration and proclamation, remembrance and promise, warning and comfort, all became poetry and thus achieved a profound impressiveness. For it was drawn out of the first and the last. It was led toward the first and the last, from and to the One God, the Eternal, the Unending One. There is nothing higher and greater beyond Him, no one like Him beside Him. He cannot be compared to ought but Himself. In Him, meaning and existence are identical, for He is "the first and the last" (Is. 44:6; 48:12). Israel made the attempt, once and for all time, in a way never to be surpassed, to render into words that which cannot be spoken. Ever since, the far reaches of humanity draw life from this attempt.

Often, the word found here reaches beyond itself; often, it itself turns into a symbol. It therefore demands its organ of expression so that it can be received. He into whose soul poetry cannot enter will be confronted here by mere sentences. The truth that was spoken will find no entrance in him. He may touch words and turn phrases, but they will not move him, they will not transform him. He will not be gripped by that which once took hold of these men when the query went out to them: "What seest thou?" He will have no idea what someone heard who answers, "Here am I" (Gen. 22:2; Ex. 3:4), who could say, "Speak, Thou-Who-Art; for Thy servant heareth" (1 Sam. 3:9–10). Only the awe of holiness that trembles before the Eternal can approach this book. The way that leads to Him is walked by reverent love. The task is to approach the souls of men to whom God has spoken and whom He has bidden to speak. Even the silence behind the word must be heard if this book is to open itself. Mere scholarship, with all its ingenuity, only concerns itself with the outer shell; that which lives in the book is not yet revealed to it.

The Bible and Mysticism

Within this people there came times and there arose movements in which the meaning of this book was felt so strongly that almost every one of its words was expected to reveal a special significance. Men began to interpret. The language seemed to hide great meanings. This manner of thinking became prevalent for the first time when the old world itself sank back into its buried centuries. The boundaries of geography and of thought shifted at that time and were lost; and this living people, ever permanent, kept gazing into the future, and saw itself transplanted into new and different regions of the present. Changed questions and needs presented themselves. The forces of resistance and of assimilation, both strong within this people, now wrestled with one another. Finally, much that was of earlier origin was lost in the process of development, and much that was new was accepted. Yet the certainty of what was its own always remained. It was so strong, so definite, that everything new, all these further developments, were simply assumed as already part and parcel of Israel's heritage. The new was not considered an addition, but an outgrowth of that which was one's own. In the first generations, since there was a hesitation in placing anything new into writing, it came to be designated as the "Oral Law." What it said, they thought, was already contained in the "Written Law," the Bible. It did not exist apart from it but within it, growing out of it. So the words of the Book began to speak anew; the written word became the speaking word. A peculiar form and logic of such reasoning, the so-called Talmud or Midrash, developed. And the interpretation of the Book proceeded along these lines for a long time.

Already at that time (and later, with a broader and deeper total impact, during the Middle Ages, when doors were opened wide) the Greeks' gift to humanity, philosophy, came to this people. The apparent meaning of the verse in Noah's blessing realized itself: "Japhet [the ancestor of the Greeks] will dwell in the tents of Shem [the ancestor of the Israelites]" (Gen. 9:27). One individuality here joined another, one uniqueness reached out to another. Because Israel carried greatness within it, it was enabled to recognize greatness and to open itself to it. But the old conviction was alive; the newness, the philosophy, was thought of as comprehended within the Book, waiting, as it were, to be brought forth from its pages. The Book was expected to expound the best teachings of the Greek thinkers. Again both became one, inheritance and acquisition. Again the reading of the Bible was given a special direction, this time toward philosophy. Again it appeared as though the old Book had become a new one.

In those centuries and later, many a heavy day burdened this people, pressing the very breath from its soul. All experience contradicted hope and knowledge; earth confronted heaven. An ever-new longing then went forth, away from earth-bound hours, away from terrestrial barriers. The soul sought to wander upward, through far worlds, through cosmic spheres, to attain the immediacy of God. It wanted to view the rise and fall of terrestrial happenings from above, where the eternal light shines. No longer did it want to look from the here to the beyond. It wanted to see from the beyond to the here, through all the husks, all the shells, all the darknesses which hide reality and truth from this lowly world. Viewed from there, it was firmly believed that the riddle into which the history of this world so often turns would also find its solution.

Century after century mysticism thus gripped the hearts of the people. At times it led them to the heights, at times into depressions. Here, too, the new thinking and speculating wanted to walk in the ways of the Bible or to lead to it, so that the old and the new should join into one. The Bible became a mystical book, and mysticism became the expression of the Bible. At times, the spheres seemed to come down to the parchment; at times, the parchment rose toward the spheres. Verse after verse within the Bible entered that higher realm that shoots its rays downward and its summons upward. Each word of the text, its everyday expressions as well, now spoke from the other world where truth lives and where reality originates. A distant melody, a distant tune, announcing, comforting, sang forth from the Book clutched by man's hand. Once again the old book became a new one, a new testimony of the way to the future.

The pathways on which this trend toward the wonders of mysticism moved were twisted at times; were often tortuous. The new that was glimpsed showed the goal; and interpretation and allegory then guided the way in that direction. It also led to many illusions. Not infrequently they came up with that multicoloredness which seeks to usurp clarity; not infrequently they found that which robs the simile of its power to symbolize; or they found that artificiality which shatters the content of words into chips tossed in a game.

But the basic concept from which all of this emanated, in earlier and in later days, was sound. It showed true perception. The new day spoke, and the ancient wisdom was called upon to supply its answer. The new question led to new expression. It was discovered again and again that the words of this Book said more than they appeared to say, that they went beyond the mere sound of the words and beyond the first hearing or reading. The word of this Book won a new power of expression; once again, it rose above the accustomed and the ordinary. This also held true where pure interpretation sought to point the way.

The Boundary of Mysticism: The Commandment

One thing is characteristic and essential here: a limit was always set to all of this manifold searching and interpreting. It was the boundary delineated by the commandment. Here was the straight, immovable line. Where the commandment began to speak, nothing legendary remained. The categorical remained categorical. Since the commandment and the certainty resulting from it were absolute, the ruminations of midrash, of philosophy, of mysticism—even when they strayed onto side paths—never lost the road markers. Those always remained clearly visible, and every age found its way by them at the decisive stage. The wrong way, in the end, became a simple detour, and like many a detour added vistas and the surmise of distant reaches.

It is also significant that neither the ways nor the detours led to dogma. Philosophy and mysticism are usually eager to help construct the dogmatic statement in order to then base themselves on it. Yet neither desired it here. The sense of that which cannot and may not be imprisoned in any concept, the sense of the ultimate, remained alive; this first principle stood firm against all later temptations. Commandment and poetry here were the two forces which together prepared human expression for revelation. They cannot exist without each other: the commandment never without poetry, poetry never without commandment. The Book of this people is as much the Book of poetry as of the law.

In its Book, this people constantly rediscovered itself. In it, Israel could learn how the history into which it was sent was also like a great poem: the commandment of the One Eternal God to one people on earth and, at the same time, the poetry of the One Eternal God through one people on earth. Within itself Israel experienced this life under the commandment. At its greatest depth, is the expression of a poetic power, a quality of genius derived from God. In the sublimity of the "Thou shalt" laid upon it, this people in a sense experienced itself as a poem. Striving for self also became the striving for the poetry of its existence.

All existence on earth, individual or group, contains the conflict between poetry and prose. The very days of this people know of it, just as it is known to each of its members. They tell how sometimes the broad "philistinism" of the world sought to absorb it, how even the commonplace strove to deprive the historical of its power. The prose of the happenings and successes everywhere, the sheer might of trivial opinions and teachings spreading abroad, tried to achieve dominion. And then the poetry of Israel's history, the consecration of its great life, threatened to disappear. But this Book, and sometimes only this Book, was able to show this people the way to itself, to the allegory of its life. In it, it has been able to find itself again and again.

This Book is life and being of the being and life of this people. The people is this Book, and the Book is this people. This Book can never mean only history to Israel. It can never become mere literature, never just the material for knowledge and research. This can only happen where there is no inner intimacy with it. As long as the two of them, Book and people, are not lost, the Book will always again become strength and actuality, a summons for decision, and prophecy and promise as well. Without its Book, this people would no longer be alive. Without its people, this Book, or at least much that is essential in it, would no longer be alive. They cannot exist without one another.

As long as this people possesses its Holy Scriptures it will remain a people of commandment and of poetry. This people is therefore seldom understood by those who are ruled by prose, including those in its own midst. But as long as it clings to its Book it will always understand itself. Ever anew, it will then be certain of the great allegory and the great task of its history. It will live in the strength of revelation.

The People's Role

The history of this people is a history of revelation. The exodus from Egypt, as event and miracle, is the introduction to it. The Book says:

In the third month after the children of Israel were gone forth out of the land of Egypt, the same day came they into the wilderness of Sinai. And . . . there Israel encamped before the mount. And Moses went up unto God, and He-Who-Is called unto him out of the mountain, saying: "Thus shalt thou say to the house of Jacob, and tell the children of Israel [the old Aramaic translation reads: "say thus to the women of Jacob and tell the men in Israel"]: Ye have seen what I did unto the Egyptians, and how I bore you on eagles' wings, and brought you unto Myself. Now therefore, if ye will hearken unto My voice indeed, and keep My covenant, then ye shall be Mine own treasure from among all peoples; for all the earth is Mine; and ye shall be unto Me a kingdom of priests, and a holy nation. These are the words which thou shalt speak unto the children of Israel." And Moses came and called for the elders of the people, and set before them all these words which He-Who-Is commanded him. And all the people answered together, and said: "All that He-Who-Is hath spoken we will do." And Moses reported the words of the people unto Him-Who-Is.

Exodus 19:1–8

One word is spoken emphatically here. Ever since, in contemplation and in will, it has had special emphasis: "the people," "all the people." That is the fundamental principle. The people received this revelation here. Not just chosen ones within it, but the people as a whole, as one individuality, was placed into obligation, into responsibility, into unified existence. The people, as the prophet then said, is designated to be "the servant of Him-Who-Is." Before God no narrow circle exists, but all. There are no representatives here, no one who could assume the task for others. This people's appearance was immediate and complete, then and always. It itself was to be a priest, a consecrated people, in all of its parts righteous, holy. In the allegories of the Bible, therefore, the image of the ideal man that the experience of a generation or its hope visualized, and the image of the people as indicated by the ideal merge into one. The same word names the two: the people and its prophet, it and its anointed one, its messiah, are both "the servant of Him-Who-Is, the helper of the Eternal One." Everything is demanded of the people, from each one within it.

The Pharisaic movement, so often misunderstood or misinterpreted, often only judged by the hypocrites that existed within it, took this idea literally. It strove for the actualization of the people into the holy community, a kingdom of priests; the people was to become a *communio sanctorum.* No one within it should see religion as merely one thing among others, nor should one person find it less meaningful than another. Religion was to live in every individual, every day. This Pharisaic movement originated and grew at a time when the people once again had to fight for its spiritual and intellectual existence. At that time, Pharisaism determined the way, marking an epoch. But that which was its characteristic, that it directed the same great demand to all, had been required since the beginning and remained as a principle.

Only the great demand can be the line of history. History exists for Israel as long as the revelation of the Eternal One speaks, and it has, in fact, totally permeated this people, its men, and its days, as no other people has so lastingly come to know. The total view was taken "from generation to generation," that is, in that which unites the generations; religion became will and will became religion. This volition of accepting the command of religion became the foundation of the community. It reaches down to the depths and carries the whole. This foundation was strong enough to support even those whose existence had been weakened or who seemed to be only a shadow of something else. Indeed, it carried a multitude, days and natures completely different, and many a one, too, who had turned away from this religion or set himself against it. But even there, in the essence of being, out of the depths of the earth, something of this religion always endured.

The Soul of the People

That which is so rare, a people's soul, had grown up here. Whenever a people came to be, a corporate body also formed itself, substantial or tenuous. In many peoples, too, the features of the spirit emerged, lively in one, weaker in the other. But often soullessness dwells underneath it all. So very rarely does a relationship with revelation live within people: a common deep-rootedness of feeling and thinking and striving, an innermost quality, a soul which is present throughout all change, and in the end still answers the call of God's command. It became the gift of this people on earth. Certainly, and it must be emphasized, there have been men and times within this people that were singular and strove to say something singular. But he who hearkens to the whole hears the voice of one soul, the soul of Israel.

Much of the speculation concerning the soul of Israel has discovered in it a special talent of this people, a talent for revelation. One of the early disciples of that school of thought which strove to have the biblical word reach out beyond itself, a man of the so-called *aggadah*, told how God had approached many peoples with His revelation, how He had offered it to them, but how only this one people had been prepared and able to receive it, and to retain it as its own. This thought was later adopted by a poet of the Middle Ages, Judah Halevi of Toledo. In his philosophical dialogue *The Kuzari* (the Khazar nation in the south of Russia, during the early Middle Ages had, following its royal family, accepted the Jewish religion), he pursues the uniqueness of his people's soul. All people, according to him, have been granted a grace, a disposition for the perception of God, but only in this people does there also exist a prophetical power—the marked ability always to see, to hear, and to understand, the quick receptivity for that which stirs and strives in the depths and on the heights of humanity—the receptivity which so often must result in pain and suffering. For where the soul opens to all that is human, all that is agonizing will also address itself to it. Whatever there is harsh and heavy, whatever there is low and mean, asks its question.

This problem was grasped quickly. The earliest, most deeply moving answer was given by a prophet who lived with the problem in Babylonian exile. His word endures, his answer stands. In his vision, his people stood as "servants of Him-Who-Is." To him, to this people, God's commission was revealed, the path of all life was shown. His soul therefore experiences and feels all which on earth is oppressing, tormenting, sinful, hopeless, and godless. As servant of Him-Who-Is, he suffers from the people and for the people, and is understood by few. But one day humanity will understand this. Then they will say of him:

Surely our diseases he did bear, and our pains he carried;

. . . .

All we like sheep did go astray,
We turned every one to his own way;
And He-Who-Is hath made to light on him
The iniquity of us all.

. . . .

Yet it pleased Him-Who-Is to crush him by disease;
To see if his soul would offer itself in restitution,
That he might see his seed, prolong his days,
And that the purpose of Him-Who-Is might prosper by his hand.
Isaiah 53:4,6,10

What the allegory shows here is the way of the man called by God; it is also the way of the people when it becomes a personality, when it is a people of genuine gifts or, in the Bible's word, a "chosen people." Every people with such powers moves part way down this road. But this people had been designated to walk the whole road. The gift granted in its soul is not just to occupy a part of the world into which the human soul can march and out of which it can peacefully return. Its gift is for the one and the whole, for that toward which all strives, in which everything finds permanence. Whoever has been granted a talent is taken out of daily contentment, out of self-satisfaction, and is placed into a circle of awareness. Questions and mysteries, needs and tasks hold him there. And he must grapple with them if he wishes to remain true to himself, must suffer from them and with them. This people experienced this completely—their talent gave them no rest. For the revelation that came to them also presented the great mystery to all of life, to all mankind. It therefore gave all of humanity a struggle without rest. So the poetic word was fashioned that he who would walk the way to holiness must go from "strength to strength" (Ps. 84:8). From earliest days, the poetic image had spoken of this people's personality: "thou hast striven with God and with men, and hast prevailed" (Gen. 32:28).

The Congregation and the Individual

The expression "the people" could thus never become a mere concept, one that simply outlines an idea. In Israel it also meant the commandment and it therefore referred to all without exception, to every single one. Everyone is placed into the vanguard of the call, everyone is confronted with the fullness of the obligation. There is no separation here between the sanctified and the secular, between those who stand forward or behind, just as there is no sorting out of castes and classes, of nobles and commoners, of those constituting the people and those who merely have a place among them. No one is excluded, no one is disenfranchised. The totality and the individual unite here. Each shares with all the complete responsibility for the totality. These words "all" and "total," so often repeated, always possess the full religious tone.

Therefore, no one is merely a name, one in the group, one among the many. The image and concept of the one who is just a number to be counted among the rest, of the proletarian, who only exists to produce children, are far from this people, and are almost impossible for it to understand. Innermost feeling and thinking speak against the concept of the mass. Before God there is no mass, let alone a *massa perditionis*. Wherever someone exists, he is, as the old saying has it, a soul of Israel; he is, according to another saying, as important as the whole world.

In this certainty something different from Greek individualism is heard. There, man discovered how all things break against him, reflect him, and thus find their measure in him. This individualism is derived from rationalism; it derives its *raison d'être* from intellectual experience. Here, on the other hand, man experiences how, amidst all that throngs upon him, the One, the eternal, unending God calls upon him as the single one; then he, man, by the answer which he gives, creates his own life. Out of the ethical certainty and the personal right imbedded therein, individualism grows. The foundation and validity of man's life arises out of the fact that human existence, as it were, personifies itself.

Out of this religious individualism a particular form and structure of the community evolved: the congregation. It in turn led on to further growth. In the congregation, the will to individuality, to community, and to God find themselves united. This can be compared with the Greek *polis*, but remains completely different. The congregation can be designated the existence-form of religious democracy. It is the frame in which theocracy seeks to express itself, which it prepares as its organ. Like everything created by this people, it, too, achieved a history reaching far beyond the congregation's boundaries. The principle of the congregation became a fertile seed, its form a fashioning force in the world of men. The origin and development of national forms in the old and the new world go back to it.

The Congregation and the Church

The congregation is characterized by its giving a special meaning and dignity and power to the separate individual. In turn, it receives its meaning, dignity, and power from the separate individual. It awakens his conscience, and then in turn becomes the instrument of his conscience. Where public opinion becomes public conscience—and ethical progress depends on this—this has generally been achieved through the union of individuality and community, through the congregation. It could be said that the individual who would unite himself with other individuals achieves a focal point and a center of gravity in the congregation, and the congregation has its focal point and its center of gravity in each of its individuals. A peculiar tension continually develops, the tension between individual and society. In it, both can always achieve new form.

The congregation is therefore something different than the church which, after all, grew out of a different soil, that of the community of the sacrament. The church exists per se, has its own validity and its own demands. It existed before the separate individuals, before them both in form and in principle. The congregation comes to exist only through the individuals. It follows them—comes to exist through them and in the wake of their existence as substance and as form. The church gives man new strength and dignity, but does not itself receive these through him. The congregation gives and receives everything, and it can therefore give and receive that which changes. In the church, there is none of this tension which exists in the congregation, the confrontation between individuality and community. The church has given much and has taught belief and obedience. Many a wondrous human trait has responded to it. The congregation has given much and has taught belief and personal responsibility. Often, wondrous human expressions have responded to it. From the congregation comes the best of a free state: its religious, its moral, and its social dynamism, the strong, self-renewing drive of the conscience.

This people accepted as an axiom that whenever ten men meet, each joining as an individual in his own right in order to confront God, there a congregation is created, for the hour or forever. There, as the ancient metaphor states, is the place of the immediacy of God; there, to use the ancient Hebrew word again, is the Shekinah: God lives there. A separate people of God exists amidst God's people. In the congregation, this people has for centuries created its form of existence.

The individual of the family, the individual of the people, the individual of the state, the individual of humanity: all stand in the congregation at one and the same time. All want to be assured there of the commandment and the consolation of God, of freedom and responsibility; they want to learn to proclaim their allegiance, to prove themselves. All the drives of the individual soul, its prayer, its striving and its longing, its call to God and its readiness for God's call lose nothing of the personal, of the immediate; rather, they receive again and again the personal, immediate impulse. In the context of the congregation the word was spoken—the word of a master among the rabbis, Hillel—"If I am not for myself, who will be for me? And if I am for myself alone, what am I? And if not now, when?" * These are not three sentences, but one. None of the parts can be omitted without the collapse of the whole. It is the thesis of the congregation, and tells what religious democracy is. Out of it speaks more, and even something quite different from what the citizen of Athens or the Roman ever experienced when he became aware of his city and of his place in it.

The One Morality Against the Double Standard

In the idea of the congregation, an intrinsic principle of revelation within this religion is expressed. It is that of the unity of morality, or it could be called the unity of moral democracy. Many hours of human history, whether limited or wide in scope (history records so many descents), is a history of double morality, the real danger of all community life. Upon its conquest depends true morality and human progress. Double morality achieved its progress in two directions which quickly united. One let a half morality be valid for a certain group, while it demanded a whole morality from all others. A special law was established for the small, the weak, the poor, and a special one was permitted for the great, the strong, the rich. In the other direction, the moral demand is directed to the individual man, while the collective wholes, particularly the nation, the state, and the party, are excluded. Morality passes them by. It is the basic strength of the belief in the One God that the law is one for all individuals and communities. Monotheism means, in its very essence, the oneness of morality. Just as the multiplicity of gods is rejected, so is the multiplicity of morality rejected.

The congregation is founded on such oneness of demand. Through

* *Pirke Abot*, I, 14.

this oneness it helped mold the features of this people, and later, going beyond its borders, it etched its lines into the nature of other peoples. In this demand of unity and then through it, the relationship between the individual and the whole received its freedom and scope. In it, an order formed itself for the first time in which there could neither exist a commanding supraorder, coercive or oppressive, nor a corresponding subordinate order leading to subjection and self-renunciation. The congregation could thus become a school to peoples, the school of a vital and—the same thing—a free community. Here the life of the community and that of the individual, each in its own right and merit, could exist without displacing the other or even limiting it. In the congregation men learned that where God's law is the common foundation, individuality and community live with one another, yes, through one another.

Historical experience shows this. Where the one law speaks to all, where the monotheism of morality rules, there a strong, at times obstinate individualism and a definite, never desisting claim of the community both have their place. They flourish together because of each other; they have their free and common development. Just so does history show examples of the reverse. Where the one divine legislation has been rejected or has lost its determining validity, human legislation becomes all the more burdensome. Layer upon layer of human legislation is piled up. It becomes a law in the rise and fall of freedom, since the more alive the tie to the One God and the more surely morality thus remains the one and only morality, the less does human coercion forge its lasting chains. But where, on the other hand, men lack this obligating knowledge of the One God, or are repelled by it, they all too easily fall prey to slavery. All too easily they come to be just followers of men, ready to be mere subjects and slaves of anyone, and "bend their knees before every Baal." Very quickly the coercive and oppressing authority might seem to be a presupposition of communal human life, the despot finally becoming the worshiped idol. One of the strongest roots of the free community rests in the divine law, out of which grows a power that can weather the storms of history. The history of nations is witness to this.

In this people, the will to individuality and the will for the totality, the lively sense of independence and the firm community spirit are equally and sharply expressed. Everyone has been addressed by God, all as a whole, and therefore, once again, every individual in its midst anew. Thus the individual cannot exist without the totality, which in turn needs each individual. Revelation is revelation in the individual and his personality and at the same time revelation in the community and its personality. Every marriage, the closest of all unions, is revelation through the individuality of two humans, and revelation through their union, so that, as the ancient allegory says, "Man truly is not without the woman and the woman truly not without the man, and both of them not without the epiphany, without the Shekinah." This is so in every community, no matter how far reaching, in the congregation, in the people, and, finally, in humanity.

Wherever there is something of revelation in a union, in which the one covenant of God, the one mystery and law of God reveals itself, there the relationship is one of human independence and living freedom, with the ability of tension and movement, steady freedom, as it grows out of enduring certainty. An ancient allegorical exegesis makes a poetic statement through the untranslatable consonance of two Hebrew words: the word *harut*, engraved (used to describe the ten commandments on the two tablets of the covenant in Exodus 32:16), and the word *herut*, freedom. It says that though *harut* (engraved) is written, *herut* (freedom) is meant. Where God's covenant forms the personality of a man and the union of men, there, in truth, is freedom, freedom filled with the power of forming and of growing.

At the Periphery: The Deserters

The inheritance of God's revelation lives, despite all, in the generations of this people. The inheritance always demands from this source existence, representation, and form. Through its beginning, its history, and its idea, religion became the focal point for this people, the content of its life. In the name of God it had once been liberated and made a people, in the name of God it went its way, from generation to generation. In its religion and through its religion it preserved its personality through all times of pressure and oppression. The fight for existence which its people had to wage ever again and in ever-new directions was also, and primarily, a fight for religious existence.

Israel formed souls. It also effected a selection, since it only permitted those to remain within the people who had the inner strength and inner ability to cope with every change. The fight for religious existence became the great test. For a member of this people can scarcely exist without this religion. With its loss he would also lose a component of his being, a decisive aspect of his reality, of his particularity. The best part of his foundation, of his heritage, the genuine meaning of his self would be lost to him.

In days of transition, in days when something old seemed to have been proved wrong and when something new challenged the whole soul, this people experienced losses. It always had its special type of deserter. At times it was strength that revealed itself in him, yet more often it was weakness. At times he finds himself in tragedy, and, not seldom, in comedy. This people knows the many types who searched for their identity here or there and did not find it, who entered or thought to enter here and there and believed some particular environment or imagined position to be the basis of their identity. This product of transition presents himself in different ways. Sometimes he is the individualist (in the negative sense of the word), the man who has artificially created his self, willfully or forcefully. As soon as he begins to feel and think, he has to spur himself anew, has to exaggerate himself. And sometimes he is the communal man (again in the negative sense of the word), the man who is to be given his self through the group and the party. His feeling and thinking, constantly, restlessly, must move about in this one area. Despite that, on the deepest level, the real self remains in all of them; when the time comes, this may yet answer.

Throughout these manifold forms one line is discernible. It reveals how much the man of this people, once estranged from the revelation, somehow becomes estranged from himself; how he does not know his own essence and his definitiveness, no matter how great and far-reaching his knowledge may be; how he walks past himself and does not reach himself, no matter how many important pathways his existence may lead him across. When a man has grown out of a weaker, a more one-sided, or a less cultivated people's endowment, he may be indifferent to such an inheritance, and it need not attack his innermost individuality, his self. But a man of this people is touched in a different way. He only achieves his inner unity and certainty out of the soul of his people, in which the "I" and the "We," the "I" with its offering and the "We" with its circles, enter into a living relationship.

Perhaps, for many individuals, religion is otherwise only a question of disposition? For the men of this people, religion is a problem of inner existence. For that reason, the religion has its unconfessional and unorthodox aspects. The all-creative force had fashioned this people to take on this form. Revelation may here be heard in many tones. It always had its breadth and its variety. It may often leave room for question and answer if only something is captured from what the prophets heard when they could say, when they had to say: "Thus speaks He-Who-Is."

The Ten Commandments

The revelation was first documented in the Ten Commandments written on the two tablets, "the tables of the testimony" (Ex. 32:15), the "tables of the covenant" (Deut. 9:9). They are words of law and freedom, the constitution of this people and manifesto to all humanity in one. The introduction points to the foundation which alone can carry all of this. It says: (Ex. 20:1) "God spoke all these words" ("these whole words"). These words have meaning only in their oneness, in their totality. They have not been brought together and counted, but each one is an essential part of the whole, and this whole proves itself in each of them. The whole comes before the parts, it is the life which lives in all. "God spoke all these words" ("these whole words"); it is life from God which lives in them.

After this introduction, but only as its continuation so that the two could not exist without each other, the first of the sentences speaks. It is not just first in order, but first in meaning and in power; this sentence is of the One God who is God for every man, of the eternal "I," the origin and principle of every human "I." In this people's beginning this eternal "I," this eternal beginning, revealed itself and pointed out redemption, covenant, and meaning to this people. This "I" called it forth through the law and for the law so that it now knew what concerned its self, the particularity of its "I," and the uniqueness of its way. The eternal "I" speaks to it, and in that all is given: "I am He-Who-Is thy God, who brought thee out of the land of Egypt, out of the house of bondage" (Ex. 20:2).

This sentence is the first of the commandments, not just the first of the words. For when the eternal "I" directs its world to men, there speaks at the same time the enduring commandment, this foundation and meaning of all freedom. Essentially and primarily, revelation is the revelation of the commandment, of man's freedom. Only when man has heard the "I am He-Who-Is" is he aware of the commandment of his self, is he conscious of the origin of his freedom. The beginning of the commandments, therefore, is this first sentence. It would be misunderstood, and its loftiness and power would be impaired, were one to assume (as has often happened) that it became a commandment through the connection with the following sentence: "Thou shalt have no other gods before Me."

This new sentence heads the row of sentences which now point the way for man who has been called by the Eternal, his God. This new sentence is the second commandment. It turns against the evasion which leads to the many gods, and turns against the many compromises, and against the dual morality. The first commandment, as statute and as commandment, gave the aspect of greatness to the character of this people and to its history. The second commandment, and with it the third, that of truthfulness, imprinted the deep seriousness of this knowledge of the zealous God. Together they fashioned the belief which formed here for the first time: the determination for the one and complete life, the acknowledgment of the great demand which man is to fulfill in all of his days and in all his ways.

The final expression in the commandments is, "thy neighbor"—perhaps not an accident but intended creatively. Three times it appears in the final sentence, after already having been mentioned in the previous one. The expression is "thy neighbor," or, more exactly in this context and intent, in the great paradox of religion, "thy other one." He is another, but still your other one; he is yours, no matter how much he is another one. He differs from you, perhaps more from day to day, and yet remains related to you. He is set into another place, perhaps opposed to you, but belongs to you nevertheless. He is he, and you are you, but in the same sense the two of you are "I" by the grace of the same God, both alike addressed by God with the "Thou shalt," "Thou shalt not"; he is like you. Thus also did the later commandment of the Torah, the chapter of holiness, frame its words: "Love thy neighbor [thy other one]; he is as you" (Lev. 19:18). The fullness of the task, the great extension of the one way and its paths, is designated everywhere by the expression, "the other one." Just as "I am He-Who-Is" is the beginning of "all these words," its ending is "thy neighbor."

The totality of these words is like a work of art; the sum is more than its parts. Certainly each of them speaks its own message and speaks with a fresh urgency. At times the sentences speak with a fullness, at times with stringency. But that which lives in them is the same in all of them. The aura of majesty resides in them: man is called to great reverence before God and His law. He has been called to reverence before the One who is the origin of all being and whose like does therefore not exist, beyond whom is nothing, and who therefore cannot be described, whom alone the oneness of the heart, this truthfulness, can approach. He has been called to the reverence of that which is Sabbath, through which man becomes aware of his dignity and of all human dignity; to reverence toward the mother and father who gave him his earthly existence; to reverence of that which belongs to his fellow man, to the blood of his life, to the mystery of his home, to the right of his property, to the reverence of his person, and to reverence, finally, of what is hidden in one's self, that this intangibility may become the purity of life.

Divine Law and Natural Law

In the words of revelation, this inseparable whole, this people received something unchangeable, indestructible. As the old daring image says of these words, "they are written by the finger of God" (Ex. 31:18). Later imagery added, if the stone into which they were engraved should be shattered into bits, the words would not be shattered, "they would hover in the air"; they surround man, he cannot escape them. For the eternal "to be" and the eternal "should" reveal themselves in these words. Men do not speak in them, but the Eternal speaks in them. To this people they signify the constitution that cannot be changed, they determine the path on which man reaches life and the people reaches history. Only the spirit of man can answer them, the spirit which constantly creates new existence.

When the church, having achieved dominion, wanted to determine what belonged to the legal domain it had entered, many of its thinkers identified the Ten Commandments with the law of nature, in order to distinguish it from the law of grace. The essence of the law and of the freedom embedded in it was thus misunderstood. Law and freedom do not grow out of what nature has already given, out of something "natural," but they grow into it. They come out of a sphere which is a different one from the natural one. The realm of law is the realm of revelation and is as such the realm of grace. Through God's law, this higher, this completely different realm of revelation enters the world of nature. The eternal enters the finite, to fashion it, to form it, to complete it in such a way that it may be within the kingdom of God.

Later, in the time of the Reformation, when a new justification was to be required for the state, a "loyal-subject theology" placed the Ten Commandments into the domain of the state and its organizing task. The state was declared the "guardian of the two tablets." The meaning of the Ten Commandments was thus robbed of its content and power; it was disfigured. The head of the state was given what should be God's place on earth; his word was to be the authority and security for the law of God. But the quintessence of the Ten Commandments, as of all God's commandments, is precisely their immediacy; no authority can be the mediator between God and man. Political authority dispenses no revelation. It was always fatal to nations when they thought to use it in this way.

The One Revelation of the Absolute

Another characteristic evident in the Ten Commandments is the unity of the revelation. The revelation derives from God, the One, and thus includes all. The one spirit from which all spirit emanates, the eternal "I am," to which all belongs, speaks. Dualism, just as the worship of many gods, is rejected here and with it its tearing apart of worlds, its separating of the creative from the created, which caused so many cultures, particularly in antiquity, to die. Rather there is a oneness and a wholeness to the cosmos, and therefore the world of goodness and light cannot be finally separated from the world of evil and darkness. As part of the cosmos it is entitled to receive possibility, sense, and a vocation. For everything is created by God, one revelation is in all—as the old story of creation says: "God saw that it was good"; or, as a later, mystic imagery poetically states, some spark of the Divine is in all that lives. Creation means the great possibility.

The one absolute here gives meaning to everything relative. The emphasis is not on a separation of worlds, but on the comprehension of the revelation of the higher world in this world. Creation and revelation are thus basically the same. The "word" of creation is in the first page of the Book, and the "word" of revelation has its later place in the sequence of the story, but they belong together. Psychologically, the revelation is probably the earlier experience. As creation means possibility, so revelation means task. But possibility always simultaneously aims at the task, and the task, again, presupposes the possibility. The task enters possibility. Both mean the beginning, upon which the path can and should follow. Religion here is the belief in the never-ending possibility and task; the two cannot be separated.

There is thus no division between what is here and what is beyond, between what is immanent and what is transcendent, between commandment and grace, the ethical and the mystical, the personal and the cosmic. The same mystery, commandment, and principle rules in the one and in the other; the same reality reveals itself in both. The Eternal, Unending, Unconditional, the One, the Being, the Creating, works and speaks. That which is bound by space and time, the becoming, the manifold opening itself to the gazing and searching of men, is His creation and revelation. Everything created has its relations with the beyond as well as its connections within the present. Life presents itself in all. Everything testifies to the origin of life as well as of the way which life should take.

In this, the soul of this people takes its character: an attraction for endless reaches and for the near and tangible are woven together—sometimes incomprehensibly so to the distant observer. Idealism and realism become one. Therefore, the dynamic is much more characteristic of this people than the static, the flexible conception more than the exact organization, the vision more than the system. Its characteristic, and to an extent predetermined talent is just this sense for the creation and revelation of the One, this eye for the origin and for the final goal. That is why the tension between the here and the beyond is so alive in Israel. It appears in the being as well as in the thinking of this people. It is the contradiction within its life, and, at the same time, is decisive for it. It is the dialectic and the logic of Israel's history. In this confrontation, its prophets and poets, its thinkers, judges, and teachers, its personalities arose.

Moses

The origin and development of this characteristic is connected with the life of one man above all, the one with the Egyptian name and the Israelite soul. As a rule, in this people, the personality of a man who achieved something is hidden behind the outlines of his work. In becoming history, he becomes the work which he had completed. All the hero worship, so easily intruding itself between man and God and turning into idolatry, was to be far from this people. But this "man Moses" always remained himself. He himself spoke, not just his work; he always stood next to his work as a guardian, a spokesman.

After him there was another who fought his way into the soul of his people, who also stood at Sinai and fought for God and in God's cause, in whom Moses' holy zeal for the holy God again became personified—Elijah the "Tishbite." Perhaps the first in the history of man to do so, he called the few into decisive battle against the many and the strong. He appeared as prosecutor of the powerful, and as defender of him whose right had been taken away. He had walked the way for the sake of God, and accepted his life as his martyrdom, just as Jeremiah did after him, and later so many others who were willing to follow.

The contours of Moses' days lie in the shadow of the past. But the features which the might of his personality wrote into his life, and his strong effect upon his people stand in light.

We see him before us, this man who had fled from men and from himself into the desert, and who found himself and his people there. True life began for him there on the day when he heard the messenger of the Eternal One, the voice out of the flames of the *seneh* which burned and was not consumed. When he heard the call "Moses, Moses" and answered it "Here am I," great awe took hold of him, the knowledge of the mystery. Now he could receive the mission to appear before Pharaoh and to lead his people out of Egypt. He was the man who afterward ascended Sinai and descended, the two "tables of the covenant" in his hand, who then had shattered them because the people had become untrue to them. Afterward, he achieved God's pardon for it, brought back the people to itself, and again gave the people the two tablets of the covenant. Throughout the many years, with the strength of patience and the drive of impatience, he supported his people and carried them through. He led, taught, and conquered. With an unconscious ability not to be misled, and with a conscious, straightforward definiteness, he marched before them from the Sea of Reeds, where the people had begun to believe in him, up to Mt. Nebo, where his days were to end. The light of revelation shone out of him ("his face sent forth beams" [Ex. 34:29]), and his life became testimony and proof of the fact that, "He-Who-Is knew [him] face to face" (Deut. 34:10). Deeper than into others, eternity, infinity, origin, the "I" had entered into him.

Moses and This People

This man and this people belong together. The Five Books named after him close with the words "Moses" and "Israel": "Moses wrought in the sight of all Israel." He was the great educator of the people. His soul entered into the soul of this people. That which still existed side by side or fought with each other in the soul of the people had found union in his soul. He comprehended himself in this people, and this people learned to understand itself in him. Thus did he form this people for the mission. To him, this people was his people; he would not have been able to comprehend his life without this people. And it was his people, because it was to be God's people. The word of prayer which he directs to God for this people is the word by which, despite everything, he knows himself and the people to be one before God. Therefore he calls them in his prayers "Thy people, O God":

> . . . show me now Thy ways, that I may know Thee, to the end that I may find grace in Thy sight; and consider that this nation is Thy people.
>
> Exodus 33:13

Yet they are Thy people and Thine inheritance, that Thou didst bring out by Thy great power and by Thy oustretched arm.

Deuteronomy 9:29

When his anger is aroused against the people, it is always an anger of love. This anger was the inheritance he gave to the prophets who followed him.

That which he impressed upon this people is in all its variety basically one. He gave this people the will for the unconditional, the courage to accept the invisibly commanded. From it comes this people's spirit of decision and readiness, the will to begin and then to follow through to the end, defiant even of a world. From it comes the courage of the soul which, before the One God, renounces all that is mediating, all representation, all sacrament, all magic. From it comes the will to find nothing in God save Himself. Through it piety becomes a decision for the immediate.

Moses the Prophet

Moses stands as the first in the line of this people's prophets. Without him they would scarcely have come into being. But they are, each, that which he was himself: a servant of Him-Who-Is. They struggled with themselves in order to come to God, and they struggled with God in order to come to themselves—each in his own life and within his own destiny. They fought against their people because they fought in terms of their people. Their last word, therefore, was a prayer for their people and with it the certainty of the people's future. They plowed this people and drew furrows across its soul in order to implant into its being the seed of the one and the whole, the categorical. They also gave it their soul, and took from the soul of its history. Like Moses, they are men of God, successors, yet masters, not mere heirs or descendants. But in their greatness and in their own individuality they are still the prophets who followed him. They are prophets because he was a prophet. They had a people as their own because he had begun to form this people. The people clung to the sentence with which the history of his life closes: "And there hath not arisen a prophet since in Israel like unto Moses" (Deut. 34:10). The knowledge of the heights he reached remained strong through this people's history. Moses ben Maimon, of Cordova, probably the strongest and most independent Jewish thinker of the Middle Ages, gives special testimony in this regard. Maimonides views prophecy in his philosophical system as something generally human, a power of reason, a public domain, which could become effective and valid everywhere. Yet he too recognizes the unique position of Moses in relation to the other prophets. Moses remains for him within the sphere of the extraordinary, of the unique.

Moses the Teacher

Something entirely characteristic, if paradoxical, happened. Moses, exalted in his individuality, brought, as no other prophet could, the thinking and feeling of the people into closeness and confidence. Everyone in this people considers Moses his own teacher. The popular expression is not "Moses the Prophet," as, for example, Elijah the Prophet, but he is called "Moshe rabbenu," Moses our teacher. He comes to everyone at all times, not to address him only, but to converse, with answers and questions, statement and response. He belongs to all and wants to be with all when they choose to enter the Book named after him, the Torah, the commanding teaching of Moses.

The revelation which was granted to Moses, in particular, is to be everyone's possession. All are his students, brought to the same inheritance and the same task. The blessing with which "Moses the man of God blessed the children of Israel before his death" is introduced with the sentence: "Moses commanded us a Torah, an inheritance in the congregation of Jacob" (Deut. 33:4). The heritage is commanded, and the commandment is the heritage. The door of the commandment is open to all, and only he who enters gains the inheritance. Because this was the way, later prophecy, continuing this sentence, could comfort the people in the days of its suffering: "All thy children shall be disciples of Him-Who-Is; and great shall be the peace of thy children" (Is. 54:13). Again, this word "all," perhaps the most humane of all words, speaks eloquently. For this word does not lead downward but upward. To be a democracy of aristocrats—again the paradox of this people emerges here—remained the unshakable ideal. And it stood firm through the people's faith in the Torah of Moses.

The Mystery of the Divine Name

The Bible speaks of the first act, as it were, in the revelation which Moses received. Moses asked who God is or, as the ancient language expresses it, what is the name of God. Revelation's answer says that God is the Being One, the "I" as being and the being as "I," that God is the eternal I AM, the eternal unity of I and being. "And Moses said unto God: 'Behold, when I come unto the children of Israel, and shall say unto them: The God of your fathers hath sent me unto you; and they shall say to me: What is His name? what shall I say to them?' And God said unto Moses: 'I AM THAT I AM' [*ehye asher ehye*, or "I am always"]; and He said: 'Thus shalt thou say unto the children of Israel: I AM hath sent me unto you' " (Ex. 3:13–14).

This sentence sustains the Bible, indeed, through it is it comprehended. Its force grips him who ponders it. It, too, speaks out of the mystery. The wrestling for expression, the struggle to make the inexpressible nevertheless expressible can be perceived here. What shall I say? This one phrase, constantly, doubtingly, almost despairingly, keeps breaking through in speech. Yet something final is spoken which human speech can still receive, to which human speech can still reach. It is spoken in a finality of definiteness and clarity reaching almost beyond the metaphor: "I AM THAT I AM," "I AM hath sent me unto you"—the "I" and the being, the being and the "I" in one, the origin of all being and the origin of every "I," origin and being and "I" in one.

After that has been said, the sentence can continue; the "name" can be spoken, this nameless name, this naming of the unutterable, this "name" which alone can mention the One through human lips: the Being One, He-Who-Is, I am being, I am He-Who-Is. Thus, the Bible continues: "And God said moreover unto Moses: 'Thus shalt thou say unto the children of Israel: He-Who-Is, God of your fathers, the God of Abraham, the God of Isaac, and the God of Jacob hath sent me unto you; this is My name for ever, and this is my memorial unto all generations'" (Ex. 3:15). "For ever, unto all generations," a phrase used so frequently in the Bible, is spoken here for the first time and enters the holy language with its full tone. Men come to exist; their generations come and go, but when the Existing One, the Eternal One has been revealed to them, they have comprehended something enduring and something enduring has comprehended them.

Whether this new word, the ineffable name, has been hewn from older rocks, older word forms, can scarcely be stated, despite how much fantasy and shortsightedness have striven to find some such antecedents. Rather, doubtlessly, in this term something completely new has entered human thought and knowledge, and thus human speech. A new principle speaks in it that has not spoken before, which henceforth cannot be bypassed by human spirit and human feeling. All language, up to now and from now, in which fatalism, magic, and idolatry tried and try to portray themselves, is conquered by it.

God's Name in the Septuagint and Targum

This word and its sentences are extraordinary even in this Book. Previously, whenever the mystery commenced, it was rejected so that it might later be compressed into a definite word that would endure. Instinctively, the men of the Bible avoided everything that could lead to such an inclusion of the hidden within a definite word, to its dogmatization. Here there was a close approach to that boundary beyond which poetic representation may enter conceptuality. But it was not crossed. The original power of the biblical, the "holy" language, opposed to all that is abstract, preserving the word's power of metaphor, guarded against disregard of the barrier. The poetry of the word, which alone gives the right to speak of God, remained alive here. When the old Greek Bible, the Septuagint, with its language that in its widest extension had already become a language of concepts, then translated our sentences in what is undoubtedly a correct translation: "I am the Being One," "The Being One has sent me to you," it was most certainly only a philosophical-conceptual sentence which spoke to many a Greek reader. The metaphor which only points to the mystery, could not be expressed in the Greek. From this time on, the exclusively conceptual way could be taken.

Against this, as testimony of a sure feeling for the boundary of the word, the second old translation, the Aramaic, the Targum (which so often did not merely translate but transmit, seeking to clarify, to amplify), did not dare even to translate this short sentence of God's being. It lets it remain within its Hebrew sounds, in the sounds of the kindred language, as within a sanctuary; veneration is to approach it. This living reverence had already spoken, long ago (as proved in the Greek Bible) in that this one final word which was to designate the "name," the so-called Tetragrammaton (to preserve all of its dignity), was not pronounced according to its sound. Instead, the simpler word "Adonai," "The Master," "Kyrios" was used. In the true sense of the term, the word of the "name" was "circumscribed," a circle of unapproachableness was drawn round about it. Only once a year, while the temple stood, did the high priest, there, on the Day of Atonement, in an hour filled with mystery, when he confessed his sins, the sins of priests, and the people's sins, when he pleaded for divine forgiveness, cross this boundary. He pronounced the name according to the sound of its letters, pronounced it, according to the tradition ". . . in holiness and purity, and the priests and the people who stood in the sanctuary knelt when they heard it and bowed down and confessed and said: Praised be His name to whom the glory of the kingdom is forever due."* Later, to let the mystery extend its domain even further, the

* *Musaf* Service of Yom Kippur. See *High Holiday Prayer Book*, ed. M. Silverman (Hartford, Conn.: Prayer Book Press, 1951), p. 370. All quotations from the

people often just said: "The Name." The nameless name had its consecration preserved.

The word thus attained true freedom: It did not have to be forced into becoming a concept. Not only being spoke in it, but also the self. God is the one, the only true being and therefore the one, only, true self. Only He Himself can also name Himself, no one else can give Him the name or can be His name. No name other than "I AM" can reveal the name. Only through His "I AM" can He be designated. All commandment, therefore, which comes from Him, the basis of all commandment, is a commandment of the I AM. The true "Thou shalt," that in which man, as man, is addressed, commences and closes: "I am He-Who-Is thy God." That is what is meant by the helpful term personal God: being and self in one, monotheism and not pantheism nor monism, God of faith but not God of systems nor the mere idea of God.

This people clung to this one, personal God. To Him it turned with the most personal faith, even when it only said: "The Name." Always, amidst this people, a wide range and freedom of thought have been granted. Nothing previously ordained had set barriers around searching thought and the longing for the right expression. A philosophy, rational as well as mystic, with an intensity and a variety rare since the days of the Greeks, shaped itself here. One thing remained steadfast: the one personal God, the "I AM THAT I AM," "I am He-Who-Is thy God; thou shalt."

Moses at Sinai: The New Revelation

The ancient story tells that yet another experience of revelation came to Moses. The first came upon him when he heard the voice of

daily and special prayer books are Baeck's own and have been retranslated into English directly from the German. However, where the same passages appear in readily available editions of the prayer books, editions and page numbers have been noted for the reader's convenience. [Translator]

God for the first time. It made him conscious of his God and of the way on which he had been sent. Now he was certain of his God. Now when he had to struggle with his certainty, he had to engage his God. Only he who is certain of his God is able to engage Him. Once Abraham did so and now Moses grappled with Him out of his new experience, for the new revelation. His people, the people of God, the whole people had committed the sin while he had been on Mt. Sinai forty days and forty nights. They had fallen away from the Eternal God, who had led them out of Egypt. They had set up a god of gold and said: "This is thy god, O Israel, which brought thee out of the land of Egypt" (Ex. 32:4). Moses shattered the tablets of the covenant as he beheld this; and something within him threatened to break. Which was God's way now, God, who had given him his way?

In the telling of this struggle of a man for himself, of Moses seeking to gain insight, there enters sentence after sentence, the struggle of word with thought, of language with the unexpressible. Moses wants to be able to speak. Yet here again is the struggle of the metaphor against its boundary:

"For wherein now shall it be known that I have found grace in Thy sight, I and Thy people? is it not in that Thou goest with us, so that we are distinguished, I and Thy people, from all the people that are upon the face of the earth?"

And He-Who-Is said unto Moses: "I will do this thing also that thou hast spoken, for thou hast found grace in My sight, and I know thee by name." And he said: "Show me, I pray Thee, Thy glory." And He said: "I will make all My goodness pass before thee, and will proclaim the name of Him-Who-Is before thee; and I will be gracious to whom I will be gracious, and will show mercy on him whom I will show mercy." And He said: "Thou canst not see My face, for man shall not see Me and live." And He-Who-Is said: "Behold, there is a place by Me, and thou shalt stand upon the rock. And it shall come to pass, while My glory passeth by, that I will put thee in a cleft of the rock, and will cover thee with My hand until I have passed by. And I will take away My hand, and thou shalt see My back; but My face shall not be seen."

Exodus 33:16–23

The utmost of that which even metaphor may dare is reached here. Moses wishes to know God's way. "Show me now Thy ways, that I may know Thee" (Ex. 33:13), begins his struggle and prayer. To learn God's name—such was his demand when the first experience drew upon him—now he is struggling to understand God's entrance into the human world, into the world of his people. He seeks insight into God's "way." "To know"; "to know"; "to know"; this is the sequence of the next few sentences. Then, in the past, he wanted to hear; now he wants to see. "Show me, I pray Thee, Thy glory." This word "glory" appears here as a new word. It too was given new content by this Book. And it means the unending, eternal sublimity of which man becomes aware in a great hour. A later time termed it God's grandeur. It still meant the nearness of the eternal, unending greatness that seizes man.

Again Moses is granted an answer. "I AM THAT I AM"—I am always—thus had he learned the name of God earlier; now he is addressed in a similar manner and hears the name of God: "I am always gracious, . . . and I always show mercy. . . ." This is the categorical grace and the categorical mercy together. Now it is revealed to Moses that the Eternal, the "I AM," is the eternal "I am gracious," "I am merciful." The "Name" of "I AM" is now revealed to him in the fullness of its grace and of its meaning. The unity of being and self and mercy advances before his soul.

The Theophany

With all the wealth of words of which the language is capable, and once again with the ultimate which metaphor can achieve, it is repeated:

And He-Who-Is descended in the cloud, and stood with him there, and proclaimed the name of the Lord. And He-Who-Is passed before him, and proclaimed: "He-Who-Is is He-Who-Is, God, merciful and gracious, long-suffering, and abundant in goodness and truth; keeping mercy unto the thousandth generation, forgiving iniquity and transgression and sin; and that will by no means clear the guilty; visiting the iniquity of the fathers upon the children, and upon the children's children, unto the third and unto the fourth generation."

Exodus 34:5–8

The last sentence, translated in the Aramaic Bible once read at divine services in Palestine, reads:

He lets those who return be cleansed again, and those who do not return, He does not permit to be cleansed, but visits the iniquity of fathers upon children and children's children to the third and fourth generation, if children and children's children of the third and fourth generation remain faithless.

The one Being—thus it won its expression in this wondrous poetry—is one love. The eternal "I AM" is the eternal "I am gracious." The eternal Being is the eternal Mercy; the eternal Patience, the eternal Justice. One of the old teachers expressed it in this epigrammatic sentence: "Wherever in the Bible this name 'He-Who-Is' stands, there speaks the eternal, the unending love." As the eternal, unending love, the eternal, unending Being enters into man. That is the way of God. When the people had sinned, Moses wrestled in prayer to see the way. Now it has been revealed to him. The words which his self, praying to God, the eternal Self, spoke and then spoke again, "I and Thy people," these words won him the whole truth. "Thy people"—the ancient tale never lets him say, "my people."

These sentences of God's way became a confession of faith, or, more accurately, a prayer of faith, to be said on the Days of Repentance and the Festivals. When man thus acknowledges God, it is his God whom he acknowledges. He does not speak about God, but he speaks to God. The confession turns into a prayer. And everyone in the congregation prays the confession and becomes the carrier of the faith. Praying, a man experiences that he is, and as the personification of his belief and of his congregation he is fully aware of his belief and of his congregation. It is a prayer that he speaks, silently or aloud. It is not a philosophically confined confession that has been laid down by an authority. The poetry of faith, not a system of faith, speaks here. In poetry, he who opens himself to it becomes a creator, or at least follows in the path of creation. An unpoetic systematization may appear to be religious, but only praying and creating, can man attain faith.

Perhaps only in this people could the words spoken by one of the old teachers, Rabbi Eleazar, become the communal festival prayer, the response of the congregation on the New Year and the Day of Atonement. "Returning to faith, prayer, and good deeds nullifies the severe decree." In returning to faith, prayer, and good deeds man becomes a creator. He becomes aware of this creativity, this upward rising, when the statements of the way of God, as Moses heard them, can turn into pious devotion. Fate is vanquished. Again there stands revealed what is unique to this people, that which has determined its existence. There the creative within man, within each individual, is addressed. In his belief, too, everyone must be a creator.

The Mystery and Its Dangers

The mystery itself is forever real. The hidden too can be grasped with certainty, the certainty of intuitive knowledge. What is conceptually established easily leads man to think that through his concepts he can fully possess and understand all things. But in poetry, in prayer, the mystery always dwells. Genuine prayer, true poetry cannot be without it. What was poetically suggested, that God Himself cannot be seen, is experienced in genuine prayer. This is also true of the philosophy and the mysticism which developed within this religion. Such philosophy, which strove to prove the entrance of the Eternal into the world of the temporary and finite, such mysticism, which strove to prove the entrance of temporary and finite man into the world of the eternal and infinite, intrinsically form the philosophy of the mystery, the mysticism of the mystery. For this reason alone their ultimate end was always prayer, the prayer of philosophy, the prayer of mysticism.

To be sure, when brooding contemplation united with creative poetry, or when this poetry united with such thinking, the danger arose that much which is offered to man appeared merely as the token or husk of something, as something philosophical or mystical alone. There is a dangerous threat in image and metaphor, that in the end they visualize only pictures, not reality; and finally, they approach idolatry. In such ways, this people's naïveté and sense for the natural were threatened at times. The first man who strove to make a philosophy the expression of his religion, whose thoughts nourished the West for a long time afterward, Philo of Alexandria, initiated this tendency. Others followed. Colorful, often charming thought images appear in his work. But that which may have been presented to the intellect was taken away from life. It constituted at times almost a flight from existence.

An example can show how far such spiritualization can lead one astray. It is a pious custom of this people, in which dignity unites with charm, that a man who has a wife and therefore a home (an old expression says: "his home, that is his wife") will each week, when the Sabbath enters, proclaim from the poem of the Book of Proverbs (31:10 ff.) the praises of "A woman of valour." With the coming of Sabbath, he is to affirm his relationship to his wife, to give testimony before her, himself, and his family. One or another of the later commentators, in his striving after higher spheres, allowed himself to interpret this song as referring not to woman, but to the Torah, the teaching. Not only poetry, but one of the best things of life itself was here abandoned to enter the area of arid, moody contemplation.

Men sometimes breathed rarefied air and thought themselves close to something mysterious. But such days were few. After all, this people's way was such that it did not become subservient to the self-assertive factuality of life, but remained bound to it. The invisible was never renounced, neither was the visible. The impulse toward the commandment which directs man to the forming and shaping of existence already tended this way. God's ways are the ways which man is to walk; to know God means above all "to walk with God." Thus, the idea has no life all its own, existing merely in a beyond. It becomes the human task. Out of the realm of contemplation it is guided into that of action. The abstract wins its right only when it results in something concrete. It exists for the sake of the concrete. The metaphysical thus becomes the imperative. The beyond and the eternal speak in that which is now to be achieved. The men of this people became men of practical will, but seldom were only that; they have often been theoreticians, but hardly that alone.

Even the idea which most often seeks to be a pure idea and most quickly becomes an abstraction, the idea of the unity, enters the domain of the commandment. Man understands the unity of God and gives recognition, the Torah says, when he himself inwardly becomes one, becomes whole, no longer just a man of the occasional hours, of the fragmented soul. The Psalm, which echoes the pleading of Moses for the revelation, says: "Teach me, O Thou-That-Art, Thy way, that I may walk in Thy truth; make one my heart to fear Thy name" (Ps. 86:11).

These phrases became the prayer of our history as a motto of human life. It draws strength from the reality that truth is not limited to the domain of thought and speech, nor righteousness to that of action. Truth is found in striving and acting, righteousness in contemplating and thinking—this is testimony of a oneness of heart. Characteristically, the same word designates the intention of the deed, uprightness in thought, and devotion in prayer. Each is *kavvanah* ("direction"), in which the one turns to God. Direction is decisive; it determines one's relationship to the environment. One could add that revelation means task, for it demands the answer of man, the answer at Sinai: "All that He-Who-Is hath spoken we will do" (Ex. 19:8).

In few other ways did the uniqueness of this people express itself so clearly. Its members, so long as something of the voice of revelation sounds for them, cannot be brutal. They cannot be without feeling, without thought, without will. They cannot stand apart from the world. Everywhere and always they know themselves to be addressed and touched; everywhere an answer is demanded from them; everywhere the commandment reveals itself. Hasidism, the mysticism of the eighteenth century, has taught that there is nothing in the world which is empty and unsanctified, nothing profane. It says that something holy hides in everything and waits for its redemption. Therefore it is a commandment for man to seek this holy in the profane in order to free it, so that all the beings of earth may be unified with the one being, the Eternal, the Holy One. This mysticism found new, strange, and wondrous words for all this, but this people had been addressed this way long ago. Therefore, wherever its members were to be found, they had to approach the world and the world's rise and fall with questions that did not tire. They had to approach earthly fate with demands and hopes that could not be set aside nor assuaged. This people was often lonely amidst all the peoples, but it was never a hermit wanting only to be by himself, thinking then to be together with God. Everywhere in the world it sought the One God, "sought Him where He may be found." Everywhere it strove to witness to Him, and with that it brought something into the world which was bound to appear as unrest and disturbance to the comfortable and the settled. It could not be its endeavor to be accounted among the comfortable and the beloved on earth. No people that wishes to listen to the voice of revelation, to God's voice which demands an answer, can be otherwise.

Wisdom: *Hokhmah* and *Sophia*

In his words of farewell to the people, contained in the fifth book of the Torah, Moses speaks once again of the meaning of the revelation that has come to him: "The secret things belong unto Him-Who-Is our God; but the things that are revealed belong unto us and to our children for ever, that we may do all the words of this law [Torah]" (Deut. 29:28).

In this Torah, this commandment which is teaching, this teaching which is commandment, the hidden reveals an incontrovertible clarity. It wins thereby that definite expression which humanity is always able to absorb. It becomes, as the old expression says, the "wisdom" of man. Thus the first of the farewell speeches says: what this people has received, that by which it testifies before the world, its closeness to God, its greatness, is that it can become "a wise and understanding people" (Deut. 4:6–7). And in the last chapter of this book, which tells of the death of Moses, the chapter in which the most exalted became simplicity itself, it is said of the man who is to continue to lead the way, of Joshua, that "[he] was full of the spirit of wisdom" (Deut. 34:9). Revelation continues its influence through "wisdom."

The Hebrew word *hokhmah* is basically untranslatable; it was a word that received a completely new content from the spirit of this people. The first of the translations, the Greek, could only convey it through its word *sophia*, wisdom. But our word *hokhmah* reaches further and deeper. It speaks of that which is the power in the world and of that which human power shall be. As it bears upon the world, *hokhmah* is the great creative, artistic principle of the fashioning spirit which comes from God, the generating word, the logos. As it bears upon man, *hokhmah* is the creative, artistic principle of the personal which has entered into him to give him the ability to see himself, which forms and fashions him so that he may become what he should be. *Hokhmah* expresses the final connection between that which continues its enduring influence in a world of constant flux and that which is constantly to influence onward-moving man. World and man as well as idea and reality, metaphysical and ethical, are united here. In the world, *hokhmah* is therefore that which gives it totality, which makes it the cosmos. In man, it is that which makes him a personality, that in which his creative traits find themselves united. Thus his drive for knowledge which turns toward everything, his breadth of feeling opening itself to all, and his moral readiness which accepts every task become one. Knowledge, feeling and desire, understanding, experience and action, in a sense, spirit and soul, are a totality in *hokhmah.* Man, coming into his own, the actualization of the total man, the fulfillment of God's likeness is represented in it.

Job and Koheleth

The men who arranged traditional writings in the canon of Holy Scriptures included two books between which a contrast extends almost to extremes. The whole breadth—one almost wants to say the infinity of the Bible—is manifested in the fact that these two have a place in it. The power of tension which is contained in the one existing volume presenting itself in its many and diverse books can be experienced in the contrast of these two. Mutually opposed, they stand together in the Holy Scriptures. Yet both are books of *hokhmah.*

One, the Book of Job, is a volcanic book. Out of the depths the fiery glows, the lamentations, break forth with elemental force. The other, the Book of Koheleth, Ecclesiastes, is a book of coolness. It does not become excited. A playful muse spins, weaves, and unravels. Both are books of inquiry. But in the one the questions boil and burn, all the questions in which the torment of human need, inward and outward, seeks its way and outlet. The other one sorts and stacks questions, both those which the times in its changes brings near and those which the rise and descent of men or fate uncover. In one, a man struggles to the very last with God, and battles with the men who would be God's advocates, but who come to be the advocates of Satan the accuser. The words of his pain and his suffering urge and force themselves and rise before us. In the other, a man philosophizes about the world and God, dispassionately moving first to one, then to another curiosity existing on earth, ready to send them all away again, and he speaks no superfluous or insufficient word. One book forces its way down to the deepest human pain and agony and does not give way; it is a book of

Either/Or. The other sets up mirrors and moves them here and there. It bids us examine at times from this, at times from that angle, the concerns, the worries which, after all, exist. It is a book of the "as well" or "also." In the one book man speaks; in the other, a man does. Man speaks in the Book of Job, and that is why many of the old teachers could say: "A man Job never existed, was never born; rather, Job is the representation of the human being."* In the book of Koheleth a man speaks, and therefore some of the old teachers could assume: "They thought him to be King Solomon, and he was one who traveled from place to place and did not show his actual features"—a man.

In the Book of Job, the old friends, his contemporaries, spoke to the man who had encountered all the suffering that a human being can. They thought to find shadows in his life, reasons for his affliction. They demanded of Job, who had been called "whole-hearted and upright, and one that feared God, and shunned evil" (Job 1:1), that he confess dark ways, that he accuse himself so that honor would go to God, who had punished him. He replies to them; before God, he engages these men for his justification, trying to illumine the path of his life. He is always ready to confess that God is God, and that man is man, but he will never deny the way of his life. Every hour will he humble himself before God, but he rejects casting himself to the ground before men and their reproaches. After he has spoken concerning himself, concerning that which his life needs and expresses, he then speaks of that which the world eternally needs, and which yet remains within God's mystery. And in all the mystery, in all the concealment which surrounds him in the world and which surrounds the world about him, he nevertheless hears an answer. It speaks of *hokhmah.* It is the answer which God gives the world and to the man who asks, which this people in all its suffering ultimately always knew.

With the fullness of poetry the answer which Job heard speaks:

For there is a mine for silver,
And a place for gold which they refine.

* *Baba Batra,* 15a.

Iron is taken out of the dust,
And brass is molten out of the stone.

. . . .

He putteth forth his hand upon the flinty rock;
He overturneth the mountains by the roots.
He cutteth out channels among the rocks;
And his eye seeth every precious thing.
He bindeth the streams that they trickle not;
And the thing that is hid bringeth he forth to light.

But wisdom, where shall it be found?
And where is the place of understanding?
No mortal knoweth the pathway to it;
Neither is it found in the land of the living.
The deep saith: "It is not in me";
And the sea saith: "It is not with me."
It cannot be gotten for gold,
Neither shall silver be weighed for the price thereof.

. . . .

The topaz of Ethiopia shall not equal it,
Neither shall it be valued with pure gold.

Whence then cometh wisdom?

And where is the place of understanding?
Seeing it is hid from the eyes of all living,
And kept close from the fowls of the air.
Destruction and Death say:
"We have heard a rumour thereof with our ears."
God understandeth the way thereof,
And He knoweth the place thereof.
For He looketh to the ends of the earth,

And seeth under the whole heaven;
When He maketh a weight for the wind,
And meteth out the waters by measure.
When He made a decree for the rain,
And a way for the storm of thunders;
Then did He see it, and declare it;
He established it, yea, and searched it out.

And unto man He said:
"Behold, the fear of the Lord, that is wisdom;
And to depart from evil is understanding."

Job 28

That is the answer which the mystery gives. It stands in the center of the Book of Job. In it the life of Job finds its self-justification.

Koheleth, the "man of the assembly," heard the same answer. Koheleth always spoke only to men, unlike Job who speaks to God even when he addresses his word to men. Koheleth observes only what he is able to see. Everything is therefore in motion for him, in flux, rotating, coming and going. Only the world, this earthly foundation, abides, but nothing on it is certain. Measurement is impossible. Nothing is affirmed, nowhere is there a straight way. "Who knows?" the universal question, is Koheleth's question. Only the hour counts, the giving and taking hour, the wondering hour—the hour rules. Everything therefore has its time. Basically, each hour is as every other hour. What is, was; what was will be, "And there is nothing new under the sun" (Eccl. 1:9). Everything passes along, and everything returns. End and beginning, beginning and end find one another. The cycle completes itself to begin anew and come to the end again. Nothing endures and remains established. "Vanity of vanities, saith Koheleth; vanity of vanities, all is vanity" (Eccl. 1:2).

Yet for this man too one thing is certain: even he recognized the great "nevertheless," the other sphere out of which this people lives. First, he let the experiences speak, the days and the movements, the colors and the excitements, with all the variety of words which man can have for them. But then, in the end, he has the "And nonetheless" speak, the truth of this other, enduring domain. The experiences showed the many contrasts; they required the iridescent sentences. This truth has the one sentence, its oneness which exists despite everything. And so he too concludes, even through a final irony—mystery too has its irony, and the real irony lives by reason of the mystery—yet he concludes with the certainty that remains: "And furthermore, my son, be admonished: To make many books is not a goal, And much study is a weariness of the flesh. The conclusion, in which we will hear everything, is: fear God and keep His commandments; For this is the whole man" (Eccl. 12:12–13).

That is his final word, the word of *hokhmah*. It is not just that this man philosophizes and believes, head and heart, a precursor of that romanticism which is derived from skepticism; for he remained, with all his rationality, one of this people, which is unable to understand itself or the world without the law of God, indeed, cannot live without it. This people can have its members who, like Koheleth, can cast doubt on all else, because they never doubt the law of God.

Therefore the Book of Koheleth found its place in the Book; the old teachers were able to say that in it too is "holy spirit."

These two books are books of man. "And unto man He said," thus ends, in one of the books, the chapter concerning the search for wisdom, for the meaning of the world and life. And the phrase "this is the whole man" is in the second book the final answer to all questioning about that which endures. Already the prophet had spoken: "It hath been told thee, O man, what is good" (Micah 6:8). All of these books of the revelation are the words of man, and therefore the words unto man.

What the word *hokhmah* means actually embraces what the contemplation of another people called humaneness, humanity. But the idea and the law of *hokhmah* contain more. They signify what man is, and what he should be out of the basic fabric of his humanness, which unites man with man, and signify also what unites man with the whole cosmos into which he has been placed. *Hokhmah* is that in which the revelation and therefore the creation prove true, that which speaks out of everything, out of the world and its laws, out of human life, and its laws too. It is that which testifies to the permanence of the creation, to the permanence of the revelation.

In *hokhmah*, as in very few other words, this people came to recognize itself. This was so true that at times even a meditative humor (which can be a form of self-understanding) could enter into this world. Because it succeeded in getting to know itself in what this word meant, it consequently learned to understand nearby peoples. This understanding, too, was at times imbued with that humor behind which love may hide, behind which deep seriousness may hide as well. Thus, Israel has an old expression of gratitude to God, that "He has given unto mortal men of His *hokhmah*." A loving and serious knowledge of the universality of the revelation also sounds in this untranslatable word. It is as untranslatable as is this people itself.

Man and Infinity

Revelation formed this people and remained alive within it; the people lived in itself, secure in what was its own. When it withdrew or extricated itself from revelation, the people threatened to lose itself or even to degenerate. When the word was then rediscovered the morning hour dawned again, the hour of rebirth. God, as the old metaphor says, "returned" to His people; the Shekinah was once again among this people. And it always returned, here and there, having penetrated too deeply, from Sinai's day, generation after generation, for it to disappear completely. Revelation had become the essence of this people's existence.

Therefore no rigid confessional tenets were established by this people. God is to be in its midst; the Shekinah will have its place in it. God is not the revealed God here, but the revealing God. This religion therefore did not create a confession; that was to be its readiness for God. Not a formula, but the commanding mystery would speak and ever anew demand the answer. This belief, this decision for the One God, for His concealment and His law, was to prove itself.

Infinity embraces man, enters into him both as the universe whose boundary he cannot see, and as the law whose ultimate meaning he cannot behold. Within the universe he searches and meditates and marvels roundabout, in this room of rooms in which, as one of the ancient teachers says, "worlds are built and destroyed and built." Man projects his lines and fits them together, but they do not become the way, the path appointed for him. Created, he belongs to creation and has no idea where he is led. Within the infinite commandment he listens and waits and actively hopes, though the commandment lays the foundation of its world upon the world of the cosmos. He goes forth to seek his future, striving, taking to task, perhaps being defeated. Yet in this world of the commandment he always sees his way. Called forth, he belongs to the law, and thus knows where he must go. Into both, into the universe and the law, man has been fitted, into both infinities. It has been granted him to hear the one word hovering above the infinities: "I AM THAT I AM!"—this word in which creation speaks as revelation and revelation speaks as creation. And at the same time he hears, out of the hidden and yet with the utmost clarity, the word of the way: "I AM THAT I AM; thou shalt!"

The way shown by the revelation, indicated by God, the never revealed and always revealing, was to be recognized and taken by this people, clearing the way to God. Thus time and again a voice cried out of the mystery. When the people heard it, it knew in days of confusion where clarity was, and in days of darkness where light will shine.

IV

The Wilderness and the Land of the Fathers

The Way to the Promised Land

When the Book speaks of the deliverance and of the revelation, it names the land which has been promised to this people. In the land, just as in the deliverance and in the revelation, history and idea come together. The exodus from Egypt which led to Sinai also led to the land, to Canaan. The outward events at the same time proclaimed the inner meaning.

In the introductory chapter, which tells of the word God gave Moses to bring to the children of Israel, it is expressed thus:

> . . . and I have remembered My covenant. Wherefore say unto the children of Israel: I am He-Who-Is, and I will bring you out from under the burdens of the Egyptians, and I will deliver you from their bondage, and I will redeem you with an outstretched arm, and with great judgments; and I will take you to Me for a people, and I will be to you a God, and ye shall know that I am He-Who-Is your God, who brought you out from under the burdens of the Egyptians. And I will bring you in unto the land, concerning which I lifted up My hand to give it to Abraham, to Isaac, and to Jacob; and I will give it you for a heritage: I am He-Who-Is.
>
> Exodus 6:5–8

Covenant, deliverance, and land stand together.

The way toward the land led into the wilderness and afterward around in it. For "forty years" this "stiff-necked people" roved about there, wandering succeeding wandering, wandering for the sake of wandering. They roamed until the end of the generation of which God said: ". . . those men that have seen My glory, and My signs, which I wrought in Egypt and in the wilderness, yet have put Me to proof these ten times, and have not hearkened to My voice; surely they shall not see the land which I swore unto their fathers, neither shall any of them that despised Me see it" (Num. 14:22–23).

Thus did this people, year after year, recount its history. With an impressive monotony that itself created symbolism particularly through the traditional cantillation of the recitation, the stations of this wandering are listed, sentence after sentence, forty times, from station to station, always in the same words: "And they journeyed . . . and pitched." At the end, when their time was fulfilled, we find: "And they journeyed from the mountains of Abarim, and pitched in the plains of Moab by the Jordan at Jericho. And they pitched by the Jordan, from Beth-jeshimoth even unto Abel-shittim in the plains of Moab" (Num. 33:48–49). No longer is it, "And they journeyed . . . and pitched," but, "and [they] pitched. . . . And they pitched."

The Wilderness

The wilderness belongs to this land; it forms a part of its characteristics. The land can extend only to it. To the North, the broad mountains lie like a crossbeam, locking Canaan in. Its West is a seacoast set in a rigid, almost harborless line which nowhere reaches out, into which nothing enters; it seems to represent a rejection. Only the desert, embracing the land from the South and the East, delineates its outer form. The desert does not merely mark a boundary like the snow mountains and the great sea, but it also merges with the land and offers itself to it. The Greek looked out on the ocean, to the approach and retreat of the waves, and saw at times a closeness, at times a remoteness. So the man of this land looked out upon the wilderness, its approach and its retreat, its familiarity and its awesomeness. He could see it press close to the land and move away, for land and wilderness seem to seek each other.

The wilderness captivated the very soul of men. It spoke to the people of its time of youth, of the springtime of its freedom, of those days when they went forth from Egypt in "the month of spring." As one of the ancient teachers put it, the wilderness received this people as does a host. Here, after the bondage years of "panting breath," they could, within their breasts, inhale the air of freedom for the first time. Here they experienced distance and vista. Here they learned to win a way for themselves through battle, to "select the men" to fight against the enemy, from generation to generation, against Amalek. Here they discovered the drama of the way and the byways which were to lead to the goal. In the desert stood the mountain of revelation, Sinai, before which the people committed itself to the One God. Here strength entered its soul, the strength to return to God from error, the strength in which the stubbornness that was within this people became a stubbornness for the One God. Here in the desert this people constantly re-experienced the unexpected, the signs and wonders of the Eternal One, how water and manna were given to them, how the pillar of fire and the pillar of cloud went before them and led them "from Egypt even until now" (Num. 14:19) toward this land. Thus did this people see the wilderness; it remained in its memory.

Prophets of the Wilderness: Hosea and Jeremiah

This was particularly true of the two great lyricists among the prophets, Hosea and Jeremiah. The wilderness spoke to them of the people's great readiness for God which, when God demands, must also be a readiness for the wilderness.

One day Hosea heard God speaking to His people in words that begin like the Decalogue: "I am He-Who-Is, thy God, from the land of Egypt; and thou knowest no God but Me, and beside Me there is no saviour. I did know thee in the wilderness, in the land of great drought" (Hosea 13:4–5). Now he understood everything. God *knew* this people in the wilderness that it might *know* God, and in this language the verb "to know" always denotes closeness and love. Here, in the wilderness, where the far and the near are one, where heaven and earth seem to touch one another, where both become witnesses for man or against him, here was the great searching and finding, here history began.

Jeremiah heard something similarly wondrous.

And the word of Him-Who-Is came to me, saying: Go, and cry in the ears of Jerusalem, saying: Thus saith He-Who-Is:

I remember for thee the affection of thy youth,
The love of thine espousals;
How thou wentest after Me in the wilderness,
In a land that was not sown.
Israel is the hallowed portion of Him-Who-Is;
His first-fruits of the harvest;
All that touch him sin,

Evil shall come upon them,
Saith He-Who-Is.

Jeremiah 2:1–3

All this was not merely a song of the past, but was a song of hope, too. Days will come that lead from a land that has become stained into the cleanness of the wilderness. In the wilderness the people again will become pure and young and free. Hosea sang of this. He saw his people in the image of his wife who went astray, wronging him. He heard how the Eternal spoke:

Therefore, behold, I will allure her
And bring her into the wilderness,
And will speak to her heart.
From thence will I give her something precious,
So that the vale of troubling becomes a
door to hope;
And she shall respond there as in the days
of her youth,
And as in the day when she came up out of
the land of Egypt.

Hosea 2:16–17

And thus, too, did Jeremiah hear the hope:

The people that were left of the sword
Have found grace in the wilderness,
Israel comes here that it might have rest.
"From afar He-Who-Is appeared unto me."
"Yea, I have loved thee with an everlasting love;
Therefore with affection have I drawn thee. . . ."

Jeremiah 31:2–3

It is not a mere romantic longing after the bygone, the free days of youth, which speaks here. A poetry previously unknown has blossomed, the poetry of free self-denial, of negation and renunciation for the sake of God. The song is sung of the life that, for the sake of the way, moves from its fixed place, turning solemnly yet gladly from where the many desire to find their pleasure and fulfillment. It is the song of men who follow God through the wastes and desolations and through the dark valleys of existence, of those who, as Hosea said, "respond" in the wilderness, as Jeremiah said, "go after" God in the wilderness.

This poetry is different from the melody of life formed on Indian soil in Yoga, or on Greek soil in the Cynic way of life. There men strove for a constant independence and insensibility to the outer world in order to achieve inner independence, to gain the ultimate, inaccessible domain of their being. A noble desire of the self sought and found a fulfillment there. Here, however, a faithfulness to God's commandment spoke, ready for the sake of God to renounce that which the self might desire for itself alone, outer and inner calmness and contentment. Faith spoke, for only so might God's commandment march onward. Men thought here of the "Thou shalt." They did not want a place to stay; rather, they wanted to walk the way and to prepare the way which God pointed out.

Because of this, they did not merely resist the outward and inward profusion which affects each man's ability to see. Their experience was too deep. They discovered that such a diversity always seeks to preempt the space and the right belonging to the love for God, this love "with all thy heart, and with all thy soul, and with all thy might." They discovered how man's life can be entwined and entangled, his integrity and wholeness diffused, his single road confused by byways, his innerness usurped by the superficial, his values fooled by façades, his originality and creativeness impaired by much that is artificial and manufactured, and the communal undermined by the merely social. When they discovered this, they came to ask where a place might yet remain for God. Perhaps then they saw the wilderness before their eyes. There, in the wilderness, in its vast monotony, its pure light and its pure darkness, there lay no allurement. There Sinai stood. There room had been provided for the revelation of the Eternal, and there it had been echoed.

The Festivals of the Wilderness

Year after year the image of the wilderness was brought before this people in a special festival in a week that concluded the yearly festival of the fields. After the Passover Festival in spring had recalled the exodus from Egypt, and Pentecost, just before summer, recalled the revelation at Mt. Sinai, now, at the beginning of autumn, a third festival recalled the years in the wilderness. It was celebrated in a land that they now possessed, and when that land was lost, it was celebrated everywhere, from generation to generation. When new wanderings began, the people carried its land along with it in its festivals. Thus it took along the wilderness, its wilderness. This feast was named the Festival of Booths:

> Ye shall dwell in booths seven days; all that are home-born in Israel shall dwell in booths: that your generations may know that I made the children of Israel to dwell in booths, when I brought them out of the land of Egypt: I am He-Who-Is your God.
>
> Leviticus 23:42–43

The Puritan Message of the Wilderness

The history of Israel's prophets also tells of the wilderness. At the edge of the wilderness, in Tishbi in the land of Gilead, Elijah, the great prophet of the second commandment, the zealot for the decision of the One God, had grown up. When he tired, he gained new strength in the wilderness. At Sinai, before the cave of Horeb (where Moses had once been called by God), he heard in the "voice of the gentle silence" this silence in the wilderness, the word of the Eternal God which came to him again (1 Kings 19:8–13).

In Tekoa, in the mountains of Judah that look unto the wilderness, the herdsman Amos discovered his mission. He went forth from there to preach in the profaned sanctuaries against violence and slavery, against idolatry and ostentation, to demand the great penitence, the return to the right, to the customs of the fathers, to the worship of the One God.

Jeremiah, who had so often looked unto the wilderness, praised the "sons of Rechab" who lived there in keeping with the injunction of Jonadab, the patriarch of their clan: "Ye shall drink no wine, neither ye nor your sons, for ever; neither shall ye build house, nor sow seed, nor plant vineyard, nor have any; but all your days ye shall dwell in tents" (Jer. 35:6–7). From them a road leads through the centuries to the "pious ones," the "Essenes," who dwelled in the wilderness, in order to live in purity, contemplation, and community. Out of their midst came Johanan, the son of Zechariah, later named John the Baptist. In the wilderness of Judah the vehement spirit of Elijah and the call for decision had once again wakened and sounded in him, so that he began to preach the return. In the wilderness, the teachers in those days said, the same right applies to all, for it belongs to no one. Here, therefore, is the place for the clear "Yes" and "No" in the decision for or against God.

Where nothing distracts nor entices, where nothing external intrudes itself between man and God, the sense for the intrinsic, for the simple and straightforward trait, became much stronger than elsewhere in humanity. A kind of puritanism was born. The will for the determined attitude arose, for which clarity of line means more than ornament, and which does not dwell on the incidental or immaterial, lest they detract in the end from the necessary. This style of life, with its asceticism, without which it cannot exist, became characteristic of this people; a peculiar independence takes root in it. Wherever later, in other peoples or groups, the same or similar puritanical traits developed, there this people was also most readily understood.

This puritanism helped make it possible for the religion of this people to create for itself (and therefore for the religions which emanated from it) a religious service that was without sacrificial service and priesthood. Externally, an historical event, the twice repeated destruction of the temple, had cleared the way for this; but inwardly the men of this puritanical inclination had already prepared it. They understood how the sacrifice that was brought to God on the temple altar might also intervene between man and his real task and therefore between man and God.

Amos and Jeremiah, those independents among the prophets, saw the sacrificial rite in the light of the ancient wanderings in the wilderness. Amos spoke of it: "But let justice well up as waters, and righteousness as a mighty stream. Did ye bring unto Me sacrifices and offerings in the wilderness forty years, O house of Israel?" (Amos 5:24–25) Jeremiah continues:

> For I spoke not unto your fathers, nor commanded them in the day that I brought them out of the land of Egypt, concerning burnt-offerings or sacrifices; but this thing I commanded them, saying: "Hearken unto My voice, and I will be your God, and ye shall be My people; and walk ye in all the way that I command you, that it may be well with you."
> Jeremiah 7:22–23

The years of the wilderness had become an enduring idea in the heart of the centuries. It spoke of the oneness, the totality of man, and spoke against that which would divide man. A desire sounded in it, one that probably stirred here for the first time: Back to nature—all the way back to the One God and with that a return to the genuine, the straightforward, the simple.

Thus a worship of ultimate simplicity developed in this people. The character of the people brought it forth, and it then influenced the character. Something unique stood here before the gaze of the world, something seldom understood except at those rare moments when it left a strong impression. An ultrasimple festivity here won its form, a worship service without adornments. To the observer it might appear formless, for its form seldom presented itself in the external. It revealed itself rather from within. The devotion was determined by an invisible focal point, and toward it the service was guided; every individual was to experience this for himself. Nothing external or sacramental could be added or permitted to intervene when the congregation prayed to its God.

The plastic arts had already been essentially prohibited through the second commandment. Therefore, music developed more strongly, and the congregation could take part in its creation more directly. The congregation sensed the analogy of a heavenly choir, a harmony of the spheres in its *sanctus*, its *kedushah*, in which the song of the divine service came to a climax. Priests had been rejected as a focal point with the rejection of the sacraments; all the more vigorously, therefore, could the individual's voice enter the prayer of the congregation. For the sake of order, one man led the sequence of prayers, but he was only the "representative of the congregation." With the congregation, in its midst, he stood before God. But he did not lead it to God.

This unfestive, puritanical celebration, because it was not forced or directed, could represent the truest celebration, and also enter into everyday life. It gave the commonplace a degree of poetry for prose. A fullness of laws and customs, all of them with their "Thou shalt" and their "Thou shalt not," surrounds that which existence requires and brings, and ever again draws it closer to the moral. Everywhere the signs are erected which would point beyond the common and the prosaic. Asceticism has therefore been turned into something that orders existence. But something different from the commonly accepted meaning of the word is here embodied. Something affectionate moves within it, a spiritual happiness and brightness. It is a desired, a cheerful exercise. It is rich in song. It includes a world of symbols. Much as it means to educate for suffering and renunciation, it does not intend to narrow life. On the contrary, it would expand it. It wants to unite splintered and torn hours with spheres of harmony. All of this, this "law" as a later time named it (often in a wrong sense), could, in its ascetic forms, most readily be called poetry. The commonplace, the unfestive, has gained its festiveness. Its line, its tradition has been given it.

This peculiar puritanism, too, became an aspect of this people's style of life.

The People of Paradox and Tension

Once again a creative paradox, an ever-new vitality-producing contrast, presents itself; for this is a people of paradoxes. Countless are the apparent antitheses that reveal themselves in the character of this people!

Within this people there is a connection between the soil and the people it supports. In all the years in which farming and tree-planting were denied it, it clung to these arts with its soul and celebrated, year after year, their festivals. There remained also within it a peasantlike relationship with task and yield, with landowning and production. It never lost the desire to plow and to sow for the sake of a harvest. But at the same time something unpleasantlike exists in this people: an ability to give gifts and to make presents, an almost untiring love of sacrifice. Beyond that it has the power of mobility. This people is indifferent to its terrestrial home, to goods and chattel, as soon as the One God, His commandment, and His law are at stake. It was ready for every onward move, every wandering, for the way into the unknown and into the far distance when the task that extends beyond the day points to such a way.

The paradox goes further. At this point the soul opens itself in the direction of all that is bright and cheerful in existence. This tendency could become the law: "Thou shalt rejoice." It could be said: "Serve Him-Who-Is in joy!" This is the people of an innocent cheerfulness. It remains cheerful because it never goes beyond itself, never loses itself or becomes boundless in its joy. It knew from ancient times that that without bounds was a sure sign of paganism. A greatness of spirit creates the Sabbath and the festivals; a culture of mood sets hours and places. Yet this soul possesses another trait. It can turn away. Inside all enjoyments stand the boundary marks. On the meadows of life, signs of "Thou shalt not" are erected almost untiringly. Barriers are drawn around food and drink; there are stringent days of fasting. An asceticism is demanded, so that nothing can place itself consistently between the soul and its God.

A contradiction appears to emerge out of something else as well. On the one side there is a lively drive that leads to men, to their circles, their thoughts and speeches, to all the variety of their arts and discoveries. An ability to come along to listen and learn has always been present in this people, a receptivity to cultures and civilizations, an immediate readiness for every beginning that seeks the light of day, for everything progressive that follows the light. And on the other hand, strong, never relaxing, never yielding, lives the feeling for the tradition, the relationship with the ways of the fathers, with what they taught and how they taught it, the affirmation of the pathway leading from former times to today and tomorrow, of history as it came to be, and the rejection of that which is the manner of "all these nations" (Deut. 11:23).

Thus, this people is no character in a smoothly written book. It is a people with its paradoxes and its tensions: the most related and the most lonely people, surely the most conservative and perhaps the most radical, the patient and impatient, the believing and the critical, the people of the fathers and the people of the children, rejoicing in life yet ascetic, the people of receptive humor and of rejecting irony, the people of the way yet the people of "the fence," the people that more than others looks and listens outward, yet much more than others looks and listens inward; one could almost say that this people is of the land yet of the wilderness. It lives with tension because it lives in two streams at once. It cannot draw its true strength out of the one without gaining it at the same time in the other.

Such is this people: it can encompass such opposites in itself because it lives in the belief—as long as it lives in the belief—of the One and of the whole. Here (though ultimately this is true of all humanity) there is no true progress without a relationship to the past, no true interweaving with the earlier without courage for the future, no certainty without question and no question without a certainty, no confidence without search and no search without confidence, no joy without seriousness and no seriousness without joy, no seclusion without openness and no strength to open itself without the ability to reject. Such a law of the soul is entirely universal, but it is uniquely expressed in this people.

Part of the embracing significance of this stubborn people resides in its unique personality within the characteristics it shares with mankind. The creative tension that is within it enabled it to enrich many other peoples. Something of it acts and creates everywhere where the spirit and the Book of this people has been admitted.

The Transition From the Wilderness to the Land

The final chapter of the Pentateuch, telling its exalted tale of Moses' death, is the cadence to the decades spent in the wilderness:

> And Moses went up from the plains of Moab unto mount Nebo, to the top of Pisgah, that is over against Jericho. And He-Who-Is showed him all the land. . . . And He-Who-Is said unto him: "This is the land which I swore unto Abraham, unto Isaac, and unto Jacob, saying: I will give it unto thy seed: I have caused thee to see it with thine eyes, but thou shalt not go over thither." So Moses the servant of Him-Who-Is died there in the land of Moab, according to the word of Him-Who-Is.
>
> Deuteronomy 34:1–5

With the first chapter of the first books of Prophets, another time commences, the time of the land:

> Now it came to pass after the death of Moses the servant of Him-Who-Is, that He-Who-Is spoke unto Joshua the son of Nun, Moses' minister, saying: "Moses My servant is dead; now therefore

arise, go over this Jordan, thou, and all this people, unto the land which I do give to them, to the children of Israel. . . ."

Joshua 1:1–2

A history now begins with its battles, its byways and its detours, a history in this land.

Even this land has its contradictions. By itself it could well engender inner tensions. This people came into the land in the time of youth, of promise, in formative years, gripped by what the revelation had uncovered and by what the wilderness had then demanded. The land appeared to it as an inheritance, as the land of its fathers, but the people was not yet united with the land and its particular character. Now it was to begin to receive from the land, to struggle with it, to fulfill itself within it. Henceforth, they were to belong together: the people of this land and the land of this people.

The Land of Canaan

The ancient biblical name for this land is Canaan. Originally it denoted the plain which descends to the sea from the mountains, particularly the Phoenician area. In the Bible, Canaanite, as well as indicating a man of another people, means merchant. (This occupation appeared alien to this people then, though later on, when it lived in other lands, it turned or was often forced into it.) The Greeks named the land Philistine-land, Palestine, since here lay the harbor which gave access to their seafarers. The Greeks learned the particulars of the land beyond, and the people there, the Israelites, only at a late date, only when Alexander had opened wide the portals of the East, only when Aristotle told the world of this land and his student Theophrastus told them of this people, this "philosophic race," as he named it.

It is a little land, Canaan, small and slender as scarcely no other historical land. It stretches down from the mountains to the sea and from the mountains to the river. Not the river, which is more boundary than internal influence, but the mountains give the land its determining line. It is a land with a spine, similar to Italy. From the South to the North stretch mountains. In the South, the outposts lie between the Sea of Salt (into which runs the downward-flowing Jordan) and the Great Sea, the Mediterranean; while in the North, the white mountains of Lebanon form a terminus. Occasionally, in the course of the centuries, the boundaries advanced; but the land always remained small. Everything that occurred in it had an intimacy; only that which was outside seemed distant.

Nature divided this little land. It is, as Moses calls it in the Book, "a land of hills and valleys" (Deut. 11:11). It could thus become a land of regions similar to that in which the Greeks lived; separate districts are etched into its topography. The "twelve tribes" took their place in the land, sometimes next to each other, or against one another, or together, as in an earlier day, according to ancient tradition, "seven nations" had done (Deut. 7:1). The tribal names endured for a long time and surely the distinctions of the tribes as well: "their father [Jacob] spoke unto them and blessed them; every one according to his blessing he blessed them" (Gen. 49:28). Solidarity, unity, is not axiomatic here as it is on the vast plains. Here, as in Hellas, it becomes a task, a way of history. In observing how this task was understood in a given place or situation, one can grasp a characteristic trait of the people involved.

Despite these regions the land remains a totality. Natural boundaries circumscribe the whole to make it so. It is a land for itself, and because it exists as a whole between mountains and river and ocean and desert, it could bring the tribes together and essentially keep them together. Consciousness of a common history could assert itself successfully. When the tribes of this people of chosen talent came, they found a land chosen for the task of unity for which they were chosen—here, in this stubborn land.

The Interweaving of Land and People

Again paradox took hold of this people. The land, divided yet enclosed, nursed a will, often obstinate, for discriminating and sorting out, and a will even more obstinate for unison and unity. This contradiction, too, the people's personality assimilated and transformed into a source of strength, into an inner treasure.

After the death of the third of its kings, following the sequence of the judges, the people—in whom there had already been cleavages—set itself apart for centuries into two domains: that of the South, and that of the North. But the prophets of the North also addressed the South, and the prophets of the South also served the North. Here as there, the message of the fathers was told and transmitted. When Elijah reconstructed the altar on Mt. Carmel and summoned the people against Baal and Astarte and for the One God, he "took twelve stones, according to the number of the tribes of the sons of Jacob" (1 Kings 18:31). When after the decades of the Exile a land for this people was again prepared on the ancient soil, the regions again created their special districts: Judaea in the South, Galilee in the North, and Peraea beyond the river. But the prayer was the same, the "Book" the same, the commandment and the hope the same. They were one people, even when their descendants lived in other lands, in Babylon and in Egypt.

The greater test of this fusion of the strength for separation and the strength for solidarity had to be passed later on. It was first demanded in the centuries in which this people became one of the great colonizing people and founded its settlements along distant seas and rivers. But it was the same in other centuries, in which trying fate made this people a wandering people, when pressure and power forced it to move from one land to another, and when the ancient melody of the wilderness received the new, the mourning tone: "And they journeyed . . . and pitched. . . . And they journeyed . . ."

Something extraordinary came into existence in those times, something which is so difficult for the man without depth of soul to perceive.

To interweave themselves with the lands into which the road of fate had led, to adopt the new land inwardly as a homeland, to breathe its air, to think in its language, to win new expression and new form for it and therefore for itself—this the men of this people attempted and achieved wherever and whenever a land truly accepted them. More faithful, more grateful beings have scarcely been borne by a soil, more faithful, more grateful citizens have scarcely been possessed by a community, wherever and whenever there was a readiness to understand them and to grant justice to that genius with which God had formed them. For peoples and cultures this could turn into a gift, indeed into a blessing.

But in these same men there was also the strong will, capable of sacrifice, to stand together and to hold together with those who had descended from the same fathers and had passed through the same centuries, who had lived through their faith and therefore also had suffered for it, who had fought for the hope, who had wandered for the sake of God, as once they had. There always existed in them, though sometimes one became weak and turned away, the undeviating determination to remain for the sake of God until the day upon which He decides, to remain this people that He has made them to be. They dared not and dare not renounce this, not for the sake of a land, not even for the sake of their own, the old land of their fathers. To renounce this commitment meant to renounce the commandment and the expectation for which they had been chosen. It means the inner renunciation of the One God and His covenant and therefore, basically, also of this land. In such a denial of itself this people would put an end to its own history.

The Great Faithfulness

The history of this people, the only one which it can possess, is a history of a great faithfulness to God, and therefore to itself, to the world and to every people among whom there is room for men of faithfulness. It is also a history of loyalty to the ancient home. In this land this history gained strength, and it will be able to be the land of this people's strength if again it becomes a land of this people's unique history. In Rome, the great historian had spoken angrily of these men as having an "obstinate faithfulness," a "fides obstinata." He could not forgive them for wanting to be left to themselves, for not wanting to be one of the moons circling Rome, for seeing their light in God, not in Rome. As Balaam the seer had come to curse in the days when this people camped at the door of the land, and had to bless this people, so Tacitus had wanted to grumble, and had praised. He saw without realizing that he saw. In its "obstinate faithfulness" dwells the mystery and the strength of this people, the people of this land.

The land lies alone, but it had many neighbors. The people that lived here and matured in its endowment could never conceive of being alone. Time and again it learned that other peoples were there too. They were on all sides. Whether the free desert that brought them near, or river and mountain marked their borders, or whether they had their cities northward and southward along the great sea, they were as neighbors. It is characteristic that an expression in the Bible occurs relatively often which other literatures scarcely possess: "all the peoples round about you." It was a foregone conclusion that the prophets would direct their word to the others as well.

As one knew of them, had to know of them, so one might know of those who were beyond them. Since ancient times, the great commercial roads, leading from the Euphrates to the Nile, from the Phoenician to the Arabian harbors, passed through the land. Thus the world at large constantly approached it in quiet times as in the eventful ones, when the great powers or conqueror nations fought for this land, this bridgehead of Asia, opposite Africa. Voices from afar were heard, wonders from the distance were surmised. One learned of the abundance of humanity, of the many peoples and their languages, the "seventy" as a later time said. The Bible is filled with the names of foreign nations. Much entered the land; and from it, that which stirs in man's soul could go forth. It is not surprising that this people early became and remained a people of wandering thoughts and dreams.

This people could recognize itself, clearly marked off and yet in a land among lands. Sharply determined as it was, it became a people among peoples. Its way evolved: to stand firm in itself and to hold fast to itself, indeed to cling to itself to the point of seclusion, whenever the day demanded it; but also to look into the distance, into all the surrounding peoples, to their questions and their problems, thus to live in the world to the point of cosmopolitanism, wherever the day permits it. Often it appears that this balance is its recurrent task.

The One Silence and the Many Voices

When the tribes of the people came into the land, this was the first step toward this task. They came from the wilderness. There they had heard the word of God through Moses, and had experienced that other mode in which God speaks to man: the great silence. The Book often speaks of silence as an experience of the exalted and as an answer to the exalted. When Elijah had gone into the wilderness, a longing for death in his heart, he had gone to Mt. Horeb, where Moses had once found his most exalted experience. Elijah had tried to find himself again. God approached him in the silence:

> . . . and a great and strong wind rent the mountains, and broke in pieces the rocks before Him-Who-Is; but He-Who-Is was not in the wind; and after the wind an earthquake; but He-Who-Is was not in the earthquake; and after the earthquake a fire; but He-Who-Is was not in the fire; and after the fire a voice of gentle silence. And it was so, when Elijah heard it, that he wrapped his face in his mantle, and went out, and stood in the entrance of the cave. And, behold, there came a voice unto him, and said: "What doest thou here, Elijah?"
>
> 1 Kings 19:11–14

When the men of Alexandria, during the century after Alexander, translated the Book for the Greek-speaking world, they did not think it could understand the world of silence. They evaded it and wrote "a soft breeze," thus transforming an exaltation into an idyl. Almost all the later translations follow. Only the old Aramaic translation remained true to what the expression tries to say. In its style, which, while translating, explains, it returned our phrase thus: "a silence, that praised Him-Who-Is." This is surely the way in which the medieval Jewish martyr, who composed a prelude for the *sanctus* of the New Year's celebration on the theme of God's judgment, understood it. "The great trumpet is blown, and the voice of the gentle silence is then heard."*

Such silence this people experienced in the wilderness and could take to their land. Afterward, the Book of Psalms, which brings man before God, also taught the great answer of silence: "Be silent before Him-Who-Is, and wait for Him" (37:7); "My soul is silent before God, from Him cometh my salvation" (62:2); "Unto Thee silence is praise, O God, in Zion" (65:1). Knowledge of the great silence was one of the gifts of this people, though it was not always understood.

In the land the voices swept down upon this people. After the years of the divine word and the exalted silence, there came the voices of the peoples, resounding, various voices. The voices of those who had been in the land, of those who were still in it, and those who lived nearby, all demanded to be heard.

They were other peoples in a more definite sense than when one people hears foreign peoples or is confronted by them. They were others in an especially challenging way. They were the people of Baal and Astarte, of idol images and idol places, of indecency and immorality. They were those in whose way this people must never go, by whose statutes this people must never live. At times there was war between them and this people, and after the war peace was made. But with Baal and Astarte there could be no peace, no covenant could exist. Here, the constant battle had to be fought, the battle for their essential of existence, for the soul of this people, and the actual battle for the land as well.

It had to be won against a constant temptation within the land. The temptation grew out of the land's past. It approached from the

* See *High Holiday Prayer Book*, ed. M. Silverman, p. 147.

very fields and streets. One could not overlook it; one could not avoid hearing it. For many generations a battle had to be waged so that this people would not become a Canaanite people, on Canaanite soil. The images of old Canaan were everywhere; everywhere their voices remained audible; they enticed the senses, aroused lusts.

A great terror, too, could gain hold of many a frightened and moody soul. In the neighboring countries, and perhaps still here and there in the land, stood the statue of Moloch the god-king, who demanded the sacrifice of the first-born son, his arms outstretched. The people had been in the land for centuries when Micah the prophet raised God's accusation against "His people" and heard the people answer: "Wherewith shall I come before Him-Who-Is, and bow myself before God on high? . . . Shall I give my first-born for my transgression, the fruit of my body for the sin of my soul?" (Micah 6:6–8) Even a century later Jeremiah has to say:

> For the children of Judah have done that which is evil in My sight, saith He-Who-Is; they have set their detestable things in the house whereon My name is called, to defile it. And they have built the high places of the furnace-idol, which is in the valley of Hinnom, to burn their sons and their daughters in the fire; which I commanded not, neither came it into my mind.
>
> Jeremiah 7:30–31

Even more significant (it is a testimony of that time) is the ancient tale, so affecting in its simplicity, which commences:

> And it came to pass after these things [the many days in the land of the Philistines], that God did prove Abraham, and said unto him: "Abraham"; and he said: "Here am I." And He said: "Take now thy son, thine only son, whom thou lovest, even Isaac, and get thee into the land of Moriah; and offer him there for a burnt-offering upon one of the mountains which I will tell thee of."
>
> Genesis 22:1–3

What happened then in souls that became frightened or began to brood? The exploitation of the idea of sacrifice, this horror of child sacrifice, could appear as the ultimate fulfillment.

But this people was not made prisoner by the land into which it had come. The end which determined all, which led to freedom, was the call of the messenger of God, which Abraham now heard in the deep distress of his soul: " 'Abraham, Abraham.' And he said: 'Here am I.' And he said: 'Lay not thy hand upon the lad, neither do thou any thing unto him. . . .' " (Gen. 22:11–12) The answer that Micah gave to his people's fearful query was equally a setting free: "And it hath been told thee, O man, what is good, and what He-Who-Is doth require of thee: Only to do justly, and to love faithfulness, and to walk humbly with thy God" (Micah 6:8). When this became a possession of the soul, the people had won its battle for the land, had made Canaan its land, the land of Israel. Horror was not to conquer, neither then nor later.

The Purification of the Land

To commit oneself to the One God, to resist for His sake, was the people's task everywhere. This people was to be different from the surrounding peoples, and so the land was to be different too. The prophet saw the land of Canaan as a land which had been rendered unclean through its people, and which wanted to embrace the new inhabitants with unclean arms. But now it was to become a soil of purity, of holiness, the soil where the Shekinah could be, where God could dwell. In the third book of Moses, in the Priestly Code, as it was called in ancient times, chapter follows chapter in which the commandments of purity, holiness, freedom, and of the community are revealed. These commandments are also the great sermon of the land. Its first section begins:

And He-Who-Is spoke unto Moses, saying: Speak unto the children of Israel, and say unto them: I am He-Who-Is your God. After the doings of the land of Egypt, wherein ye dwelt, shall ye not do;

and after the doings of the land of Canaan, whither I bring you, shall ye not do; neither shall ye walk in their statutes.

Leviticus 18:1–3

All that was done and is being done in Canaan is then listed, and in conclusion it is said:

And the land was defiled, therefore I did visit the iniquity thereof upon it, and the land vomited out her inhabitants. Ye therefore shall keep My statutes and Mine ordinances, and shall not do any of these abominations; neither the home-born, nor the stranger that sojourneth among you—for all these abominations have the men of the land done, that were before you, and the land is defiled—that the land vomit not you out also, when ye defile it, as it vomited out the nation that was before you.

Leviticus 18:25–28

This chapter is read during the service on the Day of Atonement. The congregation is told on this day of that which profanes the soil on which men live, and that which alone keeps it pure.

Purity, in this people, primarily means that of the sexual life, that of the home. The Talmud names three cardinal sins: idolatry, unchastity, murder; It continues: The sons and daughters of this people can be recognized by three things, they are merciful, chaste, and charitable. Purity stands in the middle; it is a vital question for this people.

The battle which this people's soul, in its covenant with God, waged against the people of Canaan and the peoples nearby was above all a battle for this purity. It continued for centuries, and must certainly have had its changing days. But victory was finally achieved; only in morality did the people attain a lasting strength of life. It needed this strength, for the old danger threatened continually. This was particularly true when times and cultures declined and changed forms of life presented themselves. All guideposts then were down, and new ones had not yet been erected. There was always the threat, the danger of that unhealthy assimilation which adopts more of the vulgar and evil from the environs than of the noble and the vital. The soul of this people was then attacked; the old Canaan seemed to raise its head again. There is a real, a healthy assimilation. Certainly, many elements can enter into this people; in earlier and in later days ideas and movements from almost everywhere found a place in it, though they had their various, often controversial ways. Rarely was the essence of this people injured by this. Most of the time its soul was enriched. But when one let oneself be embraced by the arms of Canaan, the core of life, the marrow of the soul, the covenant with God lost its strength.

Purity of Family Life

In those days, in the old and changing times in the land, a victory was won and the strength which it gave proved itself. In the world of antiquity, the cult of the phallus was widespread; and then in the Middle Ages, in a world in which drunkenness, unchastity, and brutality ranged widely, this people, as a whole, remained unapproachable despite its surroundings. It remained a world for itself, a people on a pure soil. The healthy instincts through which life propagates itself were affirmed; the natural drives of the body were recognized; they were kept in a domain of purity. The house, the family, was the place for the fulfillment of life, its joy, and its security. The woman did not then have many rights, but the fundamental right of womanhood had been given to her. The verses of the psalm which speak of wife and children close with: "Behold, surely thus shall the man be blessed that feareth Him-Who-Is" (Ps. 128:4). And the word of the ancient teachers—it bears repetition—says of the woman, who said, "I have gotten a man with the help of Him-Who-Is" (Gen. 4:1), that man is not without the woman and the woman not without the man and both of them not without the presence of God, the Shekinah. That is the truth of existence.

Two poetic works that tell of the love of man and woman have been incorporated into the Bible. The one is the Song of Solomon, the Song of Songs, which sings of love awakening in the young soul and in the young body; and the other is the Book of Ruth, the book of the woman who hearkened to the voice of faithfulness, and for whom faithfulness then prepares marriage and a home.

The Song of Songs achieved its place in the Bible because of teachers like Akiba ben Joseph, the man whose thoughts were always searching, but whose readiness for the way never hesitated nor doubted, even in the face of martyrdom. These teachers saw in the Song of Songs an allegory of the love with which the "congregation of Israel" unites itself with its God, so that it also may say: "I sleep, but my heart waketh" (S. of Sol. 5:2); "I am my beloved's, and my beloved is mine" (S. of Sol. 6:3); "For love is strong as death, its jealousy is mightier than the depths" (S. of Sol. 8:6). As allegory, these sacred songs were included in the Bible, and were then added to the divine services. They are read at the springtime festival, the festival of freedom. Thus they entered into the life of this people, living in it as the great songs of love.

The Book of Ruth, that wondrous idyl, stands in the Bible as history, as the book about the maternal ancestor of David, God's anointed. It tells the story of the Moabitess, Ruth, and of Naomi, who had come to be like a mother to her. It tells how Ruth accompanied Naomi to Bethlehem in Judah, "to take refuge under the wings of Him-Who-Is, the God of Israel" (Ruth 2:12). It also has its place in the worship service, in the feast of the first harvest, the Festival of Pentecost. Year after year it is read to stir the soul, to tell how a man and a woman once became aware of one another and then found and possessed one another.

These two little books were part of the Holy Scriptures, not merely literary works. Thus they could never become commonplace or ordinary. An atmosphere of the Sabbath, of the festive, pervades them. The complete naturalness as well as the complete chastity that is within them could speak forth; no profane sound from baser strata could rise up. "A holy spirit," as the ancient expression says, wished to reveal itself in these books as protection against Canaan.

The Land of Freedom

Soil of shared purity, this land could become soil of mutual freedom, of free human association. Often the rigorous truth is forgotten: only a land of cleanliness can endure as a land of freedom. The land itself, as the place of men, became a focus of duty. While everywhere else the soil seemed to say to its possessor: "Thou hast," here it spoke to him: "Thou shalt." It spoke to him of God's law that makes the land into the land of God. "Ye shall . . . proclaim liberty throughout the land unto all the inhabitants thereof" (Lev. 25:10), is God's command for this land. The land may not be the goal of power, nor the means of rulers. Neither man nor the soil may be enslaved, so that the lust of possession or unrestrained abuse takes hold of the land, or the want of consideration seizes it and sucks it dry. It was not man who fashioned the land, but God. God gave it that men might dwell together on it. The claim of the community is always invested in it. Justly, the soil does not belong in the category of possessions, but to human rights. The motto here is "that thy brother may live with thee" (Lev. 25:36).

This chapter of brotherhood begins with the sentence: "He-Who-Is spoke unto Moses in mount Sinai, saying," and it ends with an expression of equal solemnity: "I am He-Who-Is your God." This chapter contains the basic principles of a constitution; a true constitution has to speak of the soil. When the people of this land later had to leave it, they took along the basic concepts of this constitution. It created the earth for a human community everywhere. Their congregations, in which they prepared a home for themselves, were often closed off from the world, and the walls of confinement were often drawn tight round about them. But inside, men lived together in freedom, in that human freedom without which political and civil freedom cannot fulfill themselves. Within they lived in movement and the breadth of social thinking. No barrier could block the way shown by the ancient constitution. One looked within and without, inwardly and outside, and knew that misery and poverty are the great reproach to human society, that they show the community the task that has yet to be fulfilled. When the old lanes were eventually past, and the great streets of the world were once again entered, when one no longer lived and thought together just with one's own, the old spirit worked under all the new conditions and the new relationships to give new form and new content to the communal task.

Certainly there were within this people, always and everywhere, rapacious, avaricious, envious individuals, people with "the evil eye," as the Talmud calls them. (Like the virtues, the faults often found their characteristic expression here too.) But on the whole, a greater willingness for social duty came to fuller expression than anywhere else in the world, and it did so in accordance with different principles and in a different manner. Seldom, much more seldom than elsewhere, did one become enchained by one's personal possessions. To possess meant to help. An example taken from the old religious law reveals this characteristic trait. This law received its final codification through the great jurist and mystic, Joseph Karo, about the time the Catholic church newly determined its area of teaching at Trent. Karo had been born in Toledo four years before the expulsion of the Jews from Spain, and had experienced the distress of wandering through foreign lands, until he found a home in Safed in the Galilee. There he summarized religious law, striving to order daily life and living, even its smallest particulars. The law assumes, as a matter of course, that everyone in this people would apportion a tenth of the year's income for the needy. It feels only the need to set a limit for the other extreme; no one should give away more than two tenths, so that the justified demands of the family would not be injured. What this people liked to say of itself in olden times probably held true, here and forever, that its sons and daughters are "compassionate, children of the compassionate." The power of moral propagation remained. The old constitution kept its creative stimulation.

Man and Soil: *Adam* and *Adamah*

This shows again how the spirit permeates life and its relationships. Even the soil, it could almost be said, has been spiritualized. Language, the instrument of the spirit, could lead the way; language can yield a reality that is the basis for subsequent action. Thus it embodies something particular, something scarcely translatable: the word "man" and the word "soil" are forms of one and the same word. *Adamah* signifies soil, *adam* signifies man. In the word "soil," the essence of man echoes, and in the word "man" the earth resounds.

At the same time something else is heard. Man came into being out of the material from which everything came, but he is not what everything else is. He was fashioned out of the soil, the *adamah*, so runs the ancient allegory, and unto the soil he returns. But God set a "soul of life" in him, and "man became a living self" (Gen. 2:7). Soul and soil become one, a twofold creation within a single entity, man. He is a body, something terrestrial, but he is also a self, the consciousness of an ego. In a special sense he has his life through God: he has received it that it may be a life before God and with God, related to God and responsible to God, directed and with a will to the One. In *adam*, *adamah* has its fulfillment; in a sense, it obtains its language in him.

Man on his soil; this human and historical problem speaks here. In so far as a problem can be solved within the human and the historical sphere it is achieved here. And does not the problem renew itself with every new day of human history? The point of departure is indicated and the direction is shown. Only thus does a problem become solvable, or, what is the same thing, fruitful. Faith in society, this faith which calls upon everyone and trusts everyone, this confidence becomes the way here; on it alone can this people proceed in justice. Wherever this road is taken, individuality and community are united. Possession, whether terrestrial or spiritual, then means justification and responsibility in one, means an inward, essential unity and not just an interweaving of the two. The meaning of freedom in possession was discovered here. One could also say that the unity of the ground was recognized which makes the one man the possessor and which established the other man as the fellow man of possession. The earth's surface, on which they all dwell, belongs to the Eternal God. From Him comes the right of this one and the right of that one.

Only in the Book of this people could the statement exist, spoken in the name of God: "the right of the poor of My people" (Is. 10:2). This became a kind of religious concept. Here the great "Woe" was cried out over the sin against the earth:

> Woe unto them that join house to house, that lay field to field till there be no room, and ye be made to dwell alone in the midst of the land.
>
> Isaiah 5:8

Of how this sentence continued to live and to speak we hear from the popular interpreter of the Bible, Rashi:

> The word "woe" means misfortune: misfortune that will break forth one day; "you are left to dwell alone in the midst of the land" means: you plan that no share in the land be left unto the Holy One, Praised Be He, and unto the poor. You commit robbery against God and robbery against the poor.

The Joy of Charitableness

In this style of life the joy of possession and the joy of doing good were interwoven. A special poetry of charitableness developed, the poetry of the contemplative, quiet, everyday generosity, an idyl of the work of love. It has its workday tones, and, when the special days come, it has its Sabbath and holiday sounds. The idyl found its place by the side of the great pathos which had announced the God-given, enduring claim of the fellow man. Here as there the moral fantasy has its reign, in which the simplicity becomes artistic (perhaps the most distinguishing of the talents given this people). It moves with its pathos to distant messianic regions, or it visits daily familiar lanes and quiet nooks. A composing power of imagination weaves in both spheres a moral, a commanding fantasy. Therefore it never became self-centered. The way was taken, through meditative thought and warm feeling, to determined action, at whose beginning so many people halt. The messianic did not become Utopia, since it must commence within the hour; and the idyl did not become comfortable self-satisfaction, since it opened the gate for the other man, and to the other man. The "religion of law" proved its merit. It prevented man from thinking that he had done his moral duty sufficiently when he asked to be told about it or when he rhapsodized about it. Within the fantasy the "Thou shalt" lived, just as the "Thou shalt" itself guarded the broad vision of the power of imagination. The soul was preserved from egotism.

Through all this sounded the exalted word of the One God who had created all, and who gives all. That which the Book of Chronicles lets King David say in prayer: "for all things come of Thee, and of Thine own have we given Thee" (1 Chron. 29:14), which one of the ancient teachers then formed into the admonition: "Give God from that which is His; for you and what is yours are still His," is a theme constantly repeated in prayer and in morality. The poetry of charitableness is part of the life's poetry of this people. Here its existence has one of its roots; this people would perish in prose. From the statutes of the soil, the nourishing substance of poetry flowed forth to vitalize the lyricism and the power of life.

Labor and Freedom

Through such poetry the land might be spiritually acquired, but it had to be earned by the laboring hand. Gain and acquisition were made difficult in this land; there would be no hasteful robbing of man and the soil. The old story lets the fearful people say that it "is a land that eateth up the inhabitants thereof" (Num. 13:32). But surely one should expect to apply to it, as to other lands, the expression which opens the history of the *adamah*: "Thorns also and thistles shall it bring forth to thee. . . . In the sweat of thy face shalt thou eat bread" (Gen. 3:18–19).

The very contrasts of climate that exist, crowding each other in the small area between wilderness, snow mountains, and ocean, harshly bared their teeth at the man who would make his dwelling here. Daily bread is here daily battle. It is a battle for the soil frequently sealed in between mountains and stone, which the downpourings of rain early and late in the year now threaten to wash away, now threaten to turn into swamp; battle with the wild growth, the briers and nettles; battle against the violent creatures, against the vermin and the mice, against the marauders and the locusts. It is a land that does not make a present of itself to its people.

A people in whom moral powers had been awakened could here become a people of labor done in freedom. It is rare that history has seen such an accomplishment. One might mention the Romans, before slavery and feudalism spoiled them. The covenant between labor and freedom is established in this land so that labor does not erect barriers but tears them down, does not divide men but brings them together, does not create a ruling group and serfdom, but sets both in a common task upon the same soil. Work is a service in God's creation, which has been assigned to everyone; as Joshua ben Sirach designated it, "that, apportioned by God" (Ecclus. 7:15). The ancient story of the first man already told of it: "God planted a garden" that man is "to dress and to keep" (Gen. 2:8,15). In the language of this people it could be expressed thus: work is the covenant of man with the forces of creation. Every blessing on earth comes from a covenant.

Physical Rebirth

The work of free men, for which this people was raised in this land, gave it a healthy body, and with it a strength for physical rebirth. History tells of peoples who suffered oblivion, of those who died spiritually, of peoples who degenerated. It tells as well of those who died physically. Enticement and might, in differing ways, at times tried to assign such a fate to this people. But this people outlasted everything. What is more, it vanquished everything. It was able to do this primarily because of the health of its soul, the covenant with the Creator. But it was also able to achieve this by the health of its body, the covenant with the creation. Its men were barred from the soil, from the light, and from the air. It seems a miracle that they remained healthy, healthier, more tenacious, more enduring than their oppressors. It seems miraculous, too, that when they could once again breathe in light, they shook off every trace of their isolation in a rebirth of the body too. And it is almost a miracle of our own time that these men could live for long in areas which quickly sap the bodily strength of the immigrant, that they could see their children and children's children.

This people learned another thing, another kind of health, in this land. It learned to preserve a great confidence. Confidence is always the soul of work, most particularly that of agriculture. The farmer experiences time. He knows that which the Greek poet called "works and days." He knows the yearly rhythm of duty which leads from the sowing to the harvest. But he knows, as well, what is beyond that, what is gift and grace, what comes without man's action. In this land of contrasts the two could be experienced strongly: the blessing of toil and the blessing of loving-kindness; that which waits for the work of man, and that which no labor can force. The call to great industry and to great hopefulness could be heard here.

Dew and rain became symbols, in which the great hope found something akin to a law of the justified hope.

> And the remnant of Jacob shall be in the midst of many peoples, as dew from Him-Who-Is, as showers upon the grass, that are not looked for from man, nor awaited at the hands of the sons of men.
>
> Micah 5:6

Throughout the history of this people, this history of a longing, there is perpetuated the belief that nothing is final, that life can have its rebirth, its resurrection. A fresh dew will again moisten it: "For Thy dew is as the dew of light, and the earth shall bring to life the shades" (Is. 26:19).

The Rejection of Nature Cults

To all peoples who had become tillers of the field, the field began to speak. The depths seemed to contain magical powers, out of which the seed corn receives its power of growth. Gods of the dark world below, striving up unto light, so it was thought, made that which the dark soil guards rise up to the sun. They would also take the man who surrendered to them, who made a pact with them, who was sowing himself into them; they would ripen him in the blackness of the depths and let him grow up to a light, so that he would have his life. All mystery cults originate from this. Often and differently did fantasy and reasoning unite in them. A characteristic mark of this people is its continued, desired poverty of such imagery of life after death. Before the One God, there was no place for these images. Barely a word stands in the twenty-four books of the Bible which could give food for speculation in the beyond or for a mystery cult; and this is also valid for the literature that followed it.

Some might find this a deficiency. But it would then be a deficiency lost in fearlessness toward the coming world. Out of the great "I am He-Who-Is; thou shalt" grows the great fearlessness; for the refrain of the commandments is: "Fear not, for I your God am with thee," "Who art thou that art afraid?" Just as the commandment is categorical, so is this fearlessness categorical. It involves the great recognition of the One. Both rise out of this great recognition: the will to the commandment, guided toward this life and this earth; and the will to the mystery, which draws toward the hidden and reveres it as the hidden. The mystery, the one, is to remain the one mystery, not to be crowded out by idolatry or through images of a beyond, images of coming punishment and reward. The sense of the mystery may not be turned into fantasy. Many chapters of the history of religion could be titled: the mystery rejected.

A chastity speaks out of this will for the mystery, and all unchastity begins with a lack of respect toward it. Only where chastity rules could an adage such as Simon ben Azzai's be spoken, the last part of which Spinoza wrote into the ending of his *Ethics*: "Hasten to the commandment, though it be little, and keep far from sin"—a commandment can be great or little, but sin is always sin—"for one commandment draws another toward it, and one sin engenders another; thus the reward of the commandment is the commandment, and the punishment for sin is sin."

This people thus became the people of the one mystery and the many commandments. "The Holy One, praised be He, wanted to guide Israel to what is right, therefore He let it have the law and many commandments." This is easily spoken here and it becomes the refrain of all "learning." Perhaps something of the "busybody's" nature came into religion here, but, on the other hand, it was preserved from many a danger, preserved also from the fantasy that fancies itself to be pious when it has knowledge of heaven and of hell.

Experience and reflection lost none of their wide vistas in this "this-worldliness." Rather, the harmony of the worlds opened itself. The great poetry of nature came alive. The poetry of antiquity concentrated on the individual in nature; here, the totality, the cosmic, and then everything individual emanating from it, was comprehended. A universal spirit like Alexander von Humboldt first pointed this out. Everything speaks here of the One, lets its revelation be heard, the revelation of the one mystery. There are no separated realms in this world, no separate communions. The melody of the All to which everything belongs is heard: "The heavens declare the glory of God, and the firmament shows His handiwork; day pours forth speech unto day, and night reveals knowledge unto night" (Ps. 19:2). In the "this-worldliness," the work of man has in a sense become cosmic. Into the six days allotted to it something of the symbolism of the work of creation enters. Man's life and the world's existence join together.

This theme runs through two conjoined psalms, both of them beginning and ending with the words that seek to impart everything, "Praise, my soul, Him-Who-Is." As in one endless sentence they sing of how God reveals Himself in infinite pity, how all unites in the one love that is "from eternity to eternity." Verse after verse is strung together, each interlocked into the other, singing of how world after world, province after province became one in the creation; they sing of how the water was gathered and the soil was established, and how one law again unites them, so that all which lives may have its place and sustenance; they sing of how in the sun and moon, day and night are governed; how a way and an order rule in all; how a beginning and growing and ending, a perishing and new birth creates the fullness—"How manifold are Thy works, O Thou-Who-Art!" And in the midst of these strophes stands the verse: "Man goeth forth unto his work and to his labour until the evening comes." The labor of man is part of the order of the universe. (Pss. 103,104).

The Sabbath: Rest for this Land and this People

Rest is also an element and expression of this law. The day of rest became the holy time in the week for this people, the day through which the human soul raises itself to the sphere of true being. It marks completion; it creates harmony. It is the day sent down from God, the day raising man up to God. "Six days shalt thou labour and do all thy work; but the seventh day is a sabbath unto Him-Who-Is thy God" (Ex. 20:9–10). Man offers one day unto God, consecrates unto God something of that which he has received through God, and with that comes to consecrate himself. Gift and commandment, grace and demand are one here.

Consecration thus found its basis in this; the eminence of the pause, the loftiness of silence was experienced, was discovered in this day. Nobility became a commandment and therefore communal, a nobility for everyone. There is no Sabbath which only belongs to an individual or to a few. As it is a people freely joined in labor, so this people is to become a people freely joined in rest, united in its rest. There is—taking the two words in their true sense—scarcely anything which is as aristocratic and as democratic at the same time as the Sabbath.

One could also say that the genius, the power to receive revelation which exists in everything, seeks to open itself in the day of rest. It points and reaches toward a world of harmony, toward a great peace, toward that which is about the terrestrial. The Sabbath is a guidepost from man to God: "It is a sign between Me and the children of Israel for ever" (Ex. 31:17). In it is protection from bare being-in-the-world, salvation from the monotony of everyday which presses upon man, a guard against the profanity, whether of haste or whether of idleness.

The Sabbath does not mean a mere not working, nor an empty idleness. It connotes something positive. It has guided the soul unto its mystery, so that it is not a day that just interrupts, but a day that renews, a day that has its own world. It is not just something pedestrian that speaks through it, but something eternal. It is the expression of a direction for life and not just an instituted day of rest. If it were only that, or if it became that, its essence would be taken from it. It would then be only a hollow shell. The question of whether religion dwells in life is clearly outlined in it.

In ancient days it spoke to the land as well. Just as it seeks to embrace all in their different stations in life—man and wife, old and young, master and servant, maid and beast—so too it embraced the very soil. The soil in its turn, the soil with its slower existence, its stiller creation, is also to pause. Every seventh year it is to belong to itself alone. True enough, ancient experience speaks here, that the field, the vineyard cannot be permanently asked to give strength without becoming exhausted. But the uniqueness of this people is that in everything which it experienced the one idea was revealed unto it, the idea with its extension and its symbol, with its commandment and its promise. Deriving from the people's experience with the soil, the idea spoke to man of that which should be and which will be. This people would not content itself with prose, would not surrender to utility. To them, and probably to no others, it could be said: "When ye come into the land which I give you, then shall the land keep a sabbath unto Him-Who-

Is" (Lev. 25:2). All mystery-fantasy is vanquished with this sentence. As man is the man of God, so is the land the land of God, of He-Who-Is.

When the people left the land, it took its Sabbath day along. Week after week, in distress and under unsettled conditions, the Sabbath made a noble way of life possible for this people, one that was divorced from everything common. This day was, so to speak, embraced in gratitude by this people's spirit, which readily thinks and wills to the ultimate. Rest was to reign on this day down to the last and smallest instant, from evening to evening, in order to banish all that draws downward, to provide the soul with a broad and lofty space. An old poetic image says that this people and the Sabbath belong together. A later poet out of the mystic circle of Safed sang that week after week they experience one another anew and enter into their union. Without the Sabbath this people would not have been able to live. Without it this people would have to cease being what it is, and what it should be. When the Sabbath flees or loses itself, this people is under the threat of becoming commonplace or ordinary. If it parted from it, this people would dispossess itself. With good reason, the sentence stands at the beginning of its history: "Behold, He-Who-Is hath given you the sabbath" (Ex. 16:29).

From this people the Sabbath made its way through many lands and times. As this people was blessed by it and is to remain blessed, so did it bless the peoples to whom it came. It has its history in them as well. It often appears as if the difference between nations is how much of its spirit and commandment they accepted. And it seems also as though the Sabbath opened a portal for this people. Where the Sabbath is understood, so is this people understood.

The Land as an Enduring Possession

The land promised to this people also entered world history. It came to belong to the memories, the wishes, and the hopes of many peoples; and, as they tried to deny this people the heritage of its truth, so did they want to deny it the heritage of this land. But it remained its possession, for its soul clung to it. This people never ceased inwardly to live in it. They prayed for it, edified themselves about it, celebrated the harvest season of its plants and fruits year after year. In its longing for that which had been promised to it, this people sensed the harvest of the hope which it had sown in history. A difference of tones and accents can be heard in the course of the centuries but seldom did the land become mere tradition, seldom did it become just a dream of the future. Almost always, it had a spiritual presence, an immediacy for the soul. Reverence and will embraced it in a similar way. Two strong concepts, that of history and that of freedom, came together in this faithfulness.

There is scarcely a second example of such constant and steadfast faithfulness of a people toward the soil on which its youth and its character developed; scarcely another example of a people, physically separated from its ancient land, remaining spiritually connected with it and drawing spiritual power from it. It was a faithfulness that is not afraid, that does not hesitate to see also a reality in its symbolic demands, and it could therefore recognize something symbolic in every reality, something which reached beyond it.

Perhaps faithfulness is the decisive characteristic of this people, and in all humanity as well. One could say that just as faithfulness is the great reconciliation of I and thou, of the I and thou of two human beings, so is it the great reconciliation of the I and thou of groups, of peoples, of entities, of differences and opposites. So, too, is it the great reconciliation, finally, of the I and thou in which idea and reality address each other. Faithfulness is not based upon likeness. It must be proved true by that which is different. And this difference exists in man himself, so that faithfulness to himself is demanded of him; or this difference confronts us in men and communities close to us or against us, and faithfulness is to be shown to them; or this difference is above us, a holiness to which we must remain faithful in all our ways. It is only necessary that this difference be a real one, one which can stand the test before God. Therefore, the ultimate goal of all humanity is not a sameness of everyone, but a faithfulness of each to each, a faithfulness before God.

The Trait of Faithfulness

Faithfulness creates unity, the only unity which can exist in the human sphere. It is the living human contribution to the covenant, which, according to the wondrous, inexhaustible metaphor, God has made with man. In its enduring and eternal quality the covenant is called law. In its human, time, and spacebound quality, it is called faithfulness. Faithfulness is the likeness of the law. Through it man carries the enduring, the lasting, into earthly transitoriness. Through it he reconciles the singularities and individualities.

One could say that three levels of existence come to develop in man. First, there is the knowledge concerning his specialness, his uniqueness, his singularity, concerning this personal grace, that through the personal he exists in God's image—and this is after all the limit, the ultimate of all experience. Next is the consciousness of being able to give an answer every day, an answer out of this individuality, a personal answer to God—and this is after all the limit, the ultimate of all freedom. Finally there is the certainty that something eternal exists beyond all antitheses, so that man may expect from God His divine word, God's answer, just as Abraham and Job, as Moses and Elijah and Jeremiah and the pious of all time awaited it praying—and this is after all the limit, the ultimate of all hope. And this threefold existence is one in its root. It is the great faithfulness toward the ground of our life, toward the commandment that speaks to us daily, toward that which emanates from us and must find its way.

In the language of this people faithfulness, truth, and belief are one and the same word. For these three are in essence and in expression one and the same. They are inseparable. Man can neither have one without the other, nor be one without the other. They generate one another: truth and belief rise out of faithfulness, and all faithfulness again becomes truth and belief. A vital strength rises in them when they grow out of faithfulness to God.

The existence of this people, as it was, as it remained, and as it is to be, speaks of this. The covenant of God is the principle here, the connection between beginning and goal. The inner freedom, that of the exodus for the sake of God, that His commandment might endure, this is the great possibility here; it gives the choice and the way. The revelation of God, the unnamable, is here the continual rebirth in which that which was, that which is, and that which should be, become one. The framework for the revelation is the earthly sphere, the wilderness and the soil, the one with the other, the circling with its poles between which there flows an enduring meaning. Only what connects itself with God remains here.

One of the ancient teachers of this people, in a time of new questions, dared to say that the creation of man is in a sense God's great experiment, undertaken so that the great confidence might come to be. This is daring, but it leads to the depths of all existence. Only a strong belief could dare such language. Only a man of this people could speak this way, for this was a people that constantly had to relive its election, God's test of His commandment. For this is after all the sense of the election, to be God's experiment.

For this people a question is asked by God. It itself, and therefore the humanity into which it has been placed, are to give the answer, an answer to God.

The question confronts them in this way because they are permitted to hear the answer that has come from God, speaking of the ultimate purification, reconciliation, redemption. Concerning him upon whom "God has put His spirit," it is said: "a bruised reed shall he not break, and the dimly burning wick shall he not quench" (Is. 42:1,3). So is it promised. Therefore, the separated will be united, the segregated will know that it belongs, those who searched and those who tried will learn of their reward, their blessing: "Love and truth find each other, righteousness and peace have embraced" (Ps. 85:11).

On that day the covenant will enclose all men and will renew them; freedom will call to all and will let them awaken; the revelation will then open its heaven and will lift them up. "And [He] doth make expiation for the land of His people" (Deut. 32:43). Such is God's answer to the answer of man, and the faithfulness of God reaching toward the mind of man. It is the revelation of the hidden God. The promise speaks here.

The Final Comfort

Man is a cosmic being. He too. Since he thinks, and because he thinks, he meditates upon that. His habitation, his wilderness too, have been placed into eternity. He cannot escape from it. His boundaries are set into this boundlessness; boundary and boundlessness at once are his existence. A birth and a death, a beginning and an end designate his span here, and they are still only part of an extension stretching to the beyond of all distances. They are inside an all. And man's spirit, as if rising to his own beyond, moves outward, into this all. He penetrates to an ever-new distance and nearness. But no goal shows itself to him, far or near. Wondrous things are told him by the all, and thus his exploring and meditating are likewise wondrous. But he never hears the answer to his life here; and never is he questioned on this level.

Only the world of commandment and grace calls him forward and proclaims his vocation. It directs the question to him and bids him answer, lets him ask and gives him the answer. It is injunction and promise in one, always showing the way and revealing the goal. Here question is answer, and every answer also asks the question. The grace of God proclaims the commandment, and the commandment of God enfolds His grace at the same time. Purification, reconciliation, and redemption are always the way and the goal.

At the turning point of an era, the prophet named this the "comfort," the comfort that comes from God. He knew that there is no finality to the historical. Stronger than all of history is this comfort, this messianic hope. He had heard the word of God: "I, even I, am He that comforteth you; who art thou, that thou art afraid of man that shall die, and of the son of man that shall be made as grass" (Is. 51:12). The prophet knew that ruins and dust and ashes are nothing final, that life remains to the living. He announced to this people the law of its existence: "For the mountains may depart, and the hills be removed; but My kindness shall not depart from thee, neither shall My covenant of peace be removed, saith He-Who-Is that hath compassion on thee" (Is. 54:10).

That is the commandment and the grace, for this people, and for all.

BOOK Two

Till Thy people pass over, O Thou-Who-Art,
Till the people pass over, that Thou hast gotten.
Exodus 15:16

PREFACE TO BOOK TWO

When the book *This People Israel: The Meaning of Jewish Existence* began to take its way to its readers, it also confronted the author again. This encounter awakened reflections. The book wished to speak of the development of a history, and there is no end to historical questioning; also, the man to whom history has spoken never finishes. A book, too, can scarcely be finished if it is a part of him.

This book tried to investigate the basic forces underlying an historic existence. All original power existing in man, whether in the individual or in the totality, will seek out its way. Men will prepare this way—or their inaction will let it come to nought. Thus, ever anew, the questions concerning this way arose: Did its men see it, and did they seek to further its direction? Or did they look past it and lose it in the end? Did they give it to each era of the present, to every epoch, and thus set up guideposts for the future? These are all questions demanding an answer for the sake of this people, but also for the sake of all who are prepared to look.

Thus did this second volume come to be, in days different from those of the first volume and yet in the same spirit. It is a book for itself, yet it belongs to the other. It, too, speaks of "this people," and speaks of "Jewish existence."

Leo Baeck

I

Growth and Rebirth

The Movement of History and the Sense of History

In the course of a millennium, in the coming and going of its generations, there gradually developed the growth of that which ever since has been within history as "Jewish existence." A form of human life entered humanity—form to create form.

A millennium is an extended span which takes a circuitous route. For many a people it encloses the totality of its historical existence. But the history of this people is shaped uniquely. It has its slow movement, and with it a direction toward the distant, the coming. Thus its growth acquired the rings of centuries. It is not the events, with their rise and fall, their conflicts and their destruction, that announce what history is. It is the generations that declare it. Every new generation needs its span of time, for it must begin anew. It signifies a new possibility that has opened itself. More depends on it than on the events. *Toldot* ("generations") is the old biblical word for history, and "from generation to generation" describes the movement of history.

This people had the sense of history. It had a gift uniting the artistic and the moral, a receptivity through which some of eternity enters the human essence. This ability so rare in human beings came to be the possession of this people through its gradual growth: it was able to have time. This people's Sabbath and festivals are not just ancient institutions, but they are evidences of a fundamental power, an ability which is as artistic as it is moral. This power was both the commandment and the ability of this people to take a step backward, as an artist does, to view the totality of his work. This people stepped back from the work of days in order to see the path of the weeks, from the events of the months, to see the journey of the years, and from the customs of the era in order to comprehend the enduring task. From this it gained the knowledge and the ability to possess time, to own time for its own life. In the same way, it acquired the ability to think in generations and to live in generations. It was now able to look backward into the far reaches and to look forward into the great distances. Through history, this people came to be what it is: the people of the great memory and the great expectation.

Patience and Vision

Within this people, two forces were able to unite which are seldom found together: patience and vision. Only where they are found together and permeate one another do they become an historical force. Patience alone could bring man to the point where his soul surrenders, where he yields to everything existing, where every pressure finds him giving way inwardly. Vision alone could lead to the point where man's conscience deserts him, where he abandons his daily duties, where he refuses to give himself to the task that approaches him. Only when patience and vision have found one another, when they grow together, are the forces born which master time. Only time can hold fast to the past to establish the conception of today, and simultaneously grasp the future in order to provide the present with courage.

Individuals among this people often were and are predisposed to an inconstancy toward every impulse, every restlessness; on the other hand, they are inclined to empty dreams and imaginings approaching futility. But the people as a whole, ever since its growth, always preserved vast vision and patience, the combined facility of both in one, in visionary patience and patient vision. Because it gazed into distant vistas, it could endure and persevere in each day as it came; and because it persevered each day, its visions remained to guide it through reality. A permanency was promised here, this life from "generation to generation."

The Dialectic of History and the Breakthrough of Genius

Ever again human thought and poetry have been approached by the query—often raised out of anxiety over the future—whether and for how long there is an enduring existence for a certain people, for its historical form and its intellectual achievements within the world of man. Does that which had reality and was creative of life truly remain in its reality? Does it endure in an historical existence?

The rhythm of history, the constantly returning sequence of blooming, ripening, and withering, of rise and decline, would give a very "natural" answer. This rule applies in history as in nature. At times it fulfills its sequence slowly, at other times quickly, but it reveals the one and only law, fitting and encompassing all that exists into this one nature and its order.

But one fact is overlooked here, that of the intrusive individual genius. With the birth of every human being, humanity enters life in a particular, individual form. And when genius appears, once, any place, something completely unique, completely personal, breaks through. Something completely different, something outside the old order has its beginning. A new order begins. A birth has fulfilled itself in history. A new blooming and ripening, perhaps after long days of decay, has commenced.

Another answer states that nothing is enduring except the process of becoming. An inner logic, an immanent dialectic of that which once came into being, maintains control since the beginning. That which is, is followed by its opposite, and both are dissolved in something higher, which then again commences on the same road. *Natura non facit saltum,* "nature makes no leap," used to be the saying. It now became "history makes no leap."

But here too an actuality was ignored which showed in fact what genius revealed in the personal: the actuality of intellectual upheaval, the historical revolution. Sometime, someplace, a new basic concept is established which renders the previous one invalid. A new position is taken which sweeps aside the former one. The previous manner of thinking no longer has substance. The old process which, for perhaps a long time, fulfilled itself and seemed to have proven durability, was stopped, again and again. Something completely different shows its actuality, its truth, its logic. The completely different way commences.

The Revolution of the Rebirth

The history and the existence of this people, this history of a spirit and this existence through the spirit, can only be understood completely when one recognizes how the force of genius realized itself and achieved a breakthrough here. A revolution was at work and it remained at work. Genius, in the form of a revolutionary spirit, began its work here; that which already existed was not continued and improved, not completed, not simplified. Instead, that which had been established until then was completely disputed in all its conclusions. Nothing of it was to be valid any more. A new position, a new point of departure was demanded; a completely different principle was established, a completely different manner of willing and thinking was required. A new existence was to begin.

An act of creation in the realm of the spirit occurred. It was the dawn of a different world which cleared its way in and through the men of this people. No might, whether of yesterday or of today or for tomorrow, could therefore be its guarantor. Those who were powerless and wished to remain powerless were the spirit's spokesmen. They did not seek or need a philosophy to be certain, or to substantiate their position. They themselves, in their genius, were the proof. They presented themselves. In themselves, in what they had grasped, the logic was given. Through themselves, through the power that had entered them, they stood firm. These thinkers had experienced the revelation of the Eternal and Infinite One, this greatest of all revolutions, this deepest essence of genius. They were "full of power by the spirit of Him-Who-Is" (Micah 3:8).

A people formed and determined by so radical a beginning carries its own law within it, the law "according to which it stepped forth." It does not have to be subject to those apparently natural laws of coming into being, blooming, and withering. The revolutionary force of genius from which it came to be can continue to live. In hidden recesses of the soul, in the depths of the generations, it can continue to exert its influence. It is a force born of tensions, the force of all possibilities born in the world of creation. In it fate itself always finds an effective counterclaim to challenge it. Thus this people always carries its future within it; it possesses the full sweep of its possibilities in greatness. The centuries of coming to be can break through in a time of growth. Out of the genius, out of the revolutionary nature of its beginnings, something—a spirit, a will, a hope—is reborn; something returns.

The rebirth arises only out of that which is its own, out of what are its characteristic beginnings—out of nothing else, whether from within or without. Only the self is reborn. Only that which dwells in the foundations of the particular returns. This individuality one day arises again. The beginning, and with it the great belief, commences anew, this belief that is always revolutionary, always born out of genius. It never seeks to possess, but it always searches, always struggles. It knows itself to be a beginning. And therefore it never settles in precepts, but moves ever again toward new striving, new expression, new commandments, new hope. In this it lives; rigid dogmatism and empty need of ownership would cause it to die.

It is not often directly experienced in this way, and almost never on a broad scale. But one day, out of soil, perhaps even desert, the forces of the beginning break forth. They may have been pushed back for a long time, and to a great distance; shells of selfishness, layers of thoughtlessness may have covered them for generations. But then, in a man, sometime, somewhere, the roots of the beginning stretch forth. The return commences, and the days create other days, roads join roads, men find men. The man of the return lets other men come to him. The strength of the centuries of growth finds new existence, becomes history again.

The Meaning of Rebirth and its Special Nature

A dichotomy is revived through the rebirth. The rebirth can reestablish the spiritual connection with the origin and the original powers, thus giving the community the knowledge of itself, of that which forms it in reality. At the same time, new pathways of formation and development open. New forms, new expressions can present themselves. In such a return, the coming forth out of the depths, out of the beginning, and the striving upward to new heights become one. This upward moving is a shooting forth out of the primal beginning. Each conditions and carries the other. Each causes the other to develop.

This union of primal spiritual powers and the creation of new pathways distinguishes the rebirth both from nationalism and from cultural humanism. The first retards and finally prevents the rebirth;

no matter how much it assumes it is strengthening group feeling. The other only simulates it, no matter how rich it may be intellectually. The first lacks the upward striving; it cannot rise to moral freedom. The other lacks the inner connection with the deepest roots and is without the strength which comes from them. In rebirth, it is not just mind and not just will that is called forth, but the complete soul, with all it grasps and fills; it has been awakened and led to new life. It is best expressed with the simile of the poet of the return: it "shall again take root downward, and bear fruit upward" (Is. 37:31).

Such is the way of the return. Because this people found its way in days meant for decision, it endured; and it will only endure if it is always able to find access to this way. It is not just a natural rhythm and not alone a logical process that make the path of history and make it the fate of peoples. When individuality, a gift from above, has been set into a people by the Creator, it can become renewed and live anew. This may even happen in days that seem to be arid. History is also the history of possibility, and is therefore the history of the generations. The generations decide upon history, because they must decide upon themselves. The existence of this people gives testimony of this. It was able to live on and on because the old strength of revelation always broke through again.

As such, this people is the great "comfort," the great hope in the history of humanity—perhaps, in its rebirths, the only hope reveals itself. Yet even if it is the only one, is would be worthwhile for its sake alone for history to exist.

There are scenes in history to which skepticism draws attention in order to disprove the theory of rebirth. Many a people, following its leaders, has attempted and striven, in a driving, pressing effort, to bring a new morning, a morning full of the future out of its yesterday. But their only light was twilight. The darkness came and with it descent, perhaps even downfall. The ruins are extensive on earth. Imbedded in them is the debris of a will which had presumptuously dared to assume it meant rebirth, of a spirit which believed itself to have been renewed. And out of the crevices there arises here the mist of exhaustion, there the miasma of presumptuousness, for the people to breathe.

But above the ruins, descending to earth and ascending from it, coming as if from the Infinite and Eternal, stretches the "bow of the covenant," a symbol of the law of the rebirth. The return will draw near. For wherever the strength of the revelation still lives, perhaps only in concealment, and where, one day, early or late, souls are open to it, there rebirth occurs. This people has never abandoned this confidence. In it, this people possesses its right of existence.

The Dynamic and the Messianic: Problem and Task

Rebirth appears as a dichotomy that is nevertheless essentially one: as a problem that has awakened in us and that never loses itself in the present, for it has become part of our self, and as a task which began to speak in us and is now no longer silent, for it also has become part of our self. If the two are genuine, they cannot be separated. From the beginning they became one, since the I, the self, is one. The problem is at the same time the task; the task is the problem. Together they are the great certainty which is filled with questions, the great belief which is filled with tensions. The problem as task is the dynamic in the individual; the task as problem becomes the messianic in the generations. Together they become the sign of the genuine, the testimony that the revelation, the covenant, the commandment of God lives in them. Only that which is united with God's law possesses genuineness, this human and historic consistency; and only that which remains united with God's law is reborn.

The dynamic here is the force in which the revealing breaks through, the force which thus through itself becomes force again and again. The messianic is the way into which revelation guides that force, the path that renews itself again and again. Force which prepares the path and path which directs the force are one, a unity in which the times of men and the generations of history are joined. The dynamic is the messianic in the individual, the messianic is the dynamic in history. Individual existence thus becomes part of human history, and the latter becomes the realm of existence of each personal life. Rebirth is characterized by the way in which the personal and the general realms of human life enfold one another and, without losing their individual definitions, press their forms into one another. Or it might be expressed in this fashion: the dynamic, the personally spiritual, and the messianic, the historical aspect of individual man and of humanity, give each other meaning and content so that life can become history and history can become life.

On one occasion, in a time of deep emotional excitement, this experience took on historical meaning: men who experienced this became conscious that life from a higher world had entered into them to become their strength, to determine their way. Ever again, therefore, this force and this way had to encounter or confront every strata of existence comprising man's days. Almost step by step new questions with their stimuli, new commandments with their demands could arise. The goal remained, but the beginning ever anew was to become the beginning. The force from God, this strength of the way endured, though new pathways opened, since new generations were born. Something from a higher world, the world of the completed, had poured into the reborn human being. But this world, into which he had been born, had arrayed the temporary, the fragmentary against him through the very day of his birth. Precisely because strength from above was in him, problem after problem (this glance from afar) had to make him contemplate, commandment after commandment (this call from afar) had to make him pause and listen.

It is understandable that men whose souls had been wakened—and just they—were appalled in their innermost being and retreated from that which always promised the end and yet never let it come to be. They wanted immediate fulfillment in the realization. They did not merely want to hope, did not desire to be reborn just for the expectation. There were, in fact, directions here that took their own way, particularly in this people, where they reached further than anywhere else. Belief separated itself from belief. At that time, the men of this people marched forth to encounter new history.

A decision had to be made. What did the unfolding revelation mean? What did it mean to be reborn? That which had been achieved, this experience of the rebirth—was it not in all truth the fulfillment of their days, the completion of the prophecies? Had not God, the Concealed One, revealed Himself to us human beings? Did this not signify the answer without any new questions: the complete, the ultimate answer, the goal without the new way, the ultimate goal? There were men who wanted to affirm this, and this affirmation became their faith. With it, a certain peace entered their hearts; in fact, they felt their task and the promise vouchsafed to them to consist in their rejection of the call from afar. The enduring life had commenced for them; its call spoke to them from nearby. No longer were they able to see the glance from afar upon them. Immediacy had entered into their lives, had gazed upon them, and had blessed them.

Vision and Patience

The totality of this people, nevertheless, carried within itself the certainty of the mystery which renewed itself in every new experience of the soul. In days of rebirth, this certainty always gushed forth life, emanating from God, like a light of confidence, a light shining forth from God. The mystery of the expectation with its question and its commandment took hold of the inmost soul of such men, ever constant, ever new. The old decision, the decision of Sinai, renewed itself. It, too, had been reborn.

Vision and patience had once more become one. The distant had again become the near, and the near had become the distant. The future began in the present, and the present achieved its future. The souls had received their portions from that which was at hand as well as that which was yet to be. They experienced the grace of the way and the grace of the expectation, both from the one source of grace. Once again the decision had been made. This people had remained within its possession. It expected God, the One who reveals. This people remained certain of this possession; it rejoiced in it.

It is strange to say—but true—that this people, more than all other peoples, always carried within itself a feeling of joy and of happiness. This people never ceased writing poetry, not only for others, but also for itself. It wrote in the old language which it alone possessed. It sang of its suffering and sorrow; and it was no sentimental hurt that poured itself into words, but it was the pain of the days, the year, of total existence. Silence was not permitted them; they had to fit together their often awkward sentences. More than others, this people poured forth its blood and "sowed in tears." It had to speak of this to itself and to its God. Yet in the darkest, most oppressing days, in its first and last word its soul breathed deeply and enlarged itself: despite all and everything, it had fallen into pleasant places, into what was good.

The reason is clear: this people always knew what sustained it in life; it knew where it lived and why it lived. It always heard the great "If" of being chosen, sounding above the abysses and the valleys of night: He-Who-Is has chosen thee *if* thou choose Him—this great "if" of being chosen that lets the essential, the decisive aspect of life become man's free decision. This great "if," with its question and its commandment for these men, remained the possession of their life, the joy of their soul. It had become part of their faith. Within their faith, the eternal, infinite mystery, never completely revealed, spoke to them as revelation. In all the days of their years, they therefore commenced the morning hour with the prayer: "Joy is ours; how good is our portion, how lovely is our heritage!" This became involved in this people's spiritual existence; it was a special gift not found in the history of other peoples. And it always caused this people, as a totality and as a people, to think of itself as set before God. It had the right—more than that, it had the obligation—to speak to God. A special sentence was formed here, one which gave a special introduction to this people's thinking: "The congregation of Israel speaks before the Holy One, praised be He"; and this is followed by words of self-examination, words of knowledge, but also by words of search that had proved fruitless. It was followed by words of confidence, but also by words of mourning expressing the pain of the times. This people stood before God, in order to hear and to ask questions, in order to hear and to answer commandment. "The congregation of Israel has spoken."

The people stood before God; but within it there were always diverse types of beings. One could almost say that it often suffered because of its men, that its men often stood in its way. There were always those who were only here and there, and who never knew where they were and who they were. Sometimes they were harmless, sometimes harmful. At all times there were also those who "walked in the counsel of the wicked," who "stood in the way of sinners," who "sat in the seat of the scornful." But they were only in the passing parade of time. They rushed by that which endured. The Psalmist speaks of them with a certain calm deliberateness: "But they are like the chaff which the wind driveth away. . . . [Their] way . . . shall lose itself" (Ps. 1:4–6). The word here, commonly translated "shall perish," actually means "shall lose itself," shall go astray. Their way lost itself, and the way of this people endured. Much could be told of the men of this lost way.

The Great Way and the Great Hope

The history of this people is the history of a way, of the way. The way becomes history only for those in whom the constant, the dynamic, the messianic hope lives. There is something called hope which men fashion for themselves in their fears and their hesitations, attractive images which seem to call to them. Yet that is only an appeasement of weakness. It lulls them to sleep; but it does not arouse them for the day. At times it is good for man to dream and to fashion in this manner; it carries him over many heavy hours. But the true hope is something else. It always has the imprint of greatness upon it, that of the demand and of the expectation. It is the expression of a strength that has its origin in the certainty of the way. Hope and strength therefore became practically one word in the Bible. When the strength within man becomes aware of itself, when it draws in new breath, it becomes hope and it gives man the certainty of that which will endure. Hope is a reconciliation of the finite with that which remains.

In those men who saw the way and through it became capable of the great hope, only in them, but also ever anew in them, this people envisioned itself. Because this people had them, it had the permission and the ability to "speak before the Holy One, praised be He." Its books are the books of this hope, its history is the history of these men. Much speaks in this history, much speaks in these books: teaching and wisdom, demand and question, prophetic speech and prophetic allegory, law and counsel, mystery and recognition, decision and action, faith and faithfulness, love and sacrifice. And out of all, rising from the depths to the heights, this one voice gives forth its sound: the voice of the great hope. Hope was always reborn.

There is a poetry in which the unconscious, residing in a people, creates an expression of itself, a poetry of customs and practices. There are many other things that can present themselves in this way: that which is low and common, something twisted and tangled, all that does not possess the spiritual quality and uplifting ability of poetry. But in this people a holiness of customs and practices developed. Within it, poetry became a religious service, as the people's soul spoke before God. In manifold ways, this people gave a special sound to the day, a rhythm to the year.

This became a practice of this people. Year after year, when end and beginning meet one another, when that which has come to be and that which is to be interpenetrate one another, in those days before and after the New Year's Festival, at the end of every religious service, the congregation utters the psalm of the great, the hopeful certainty. It commences with the words: "He-Who-Is is my light and my salvation" and closes: "Wait for Him-Who-Is; be strong, and let thy heart take courage; yea, wait thou for Him-Who-Is" (Ps. 27). It is as though these words are to fashion a bridge leading from the passing year to the coming year. The years change, and the way endures; for the strong expectant hope builds the bridges.

History that is to become the history of humanity cannot contain any hope without the way and no way without the hope. Without that strong expectant hope, the way would disappear as day is set against day, time battles time: the way would "lose itself." And without the way which always points out the direction, hope would shatter when that which it confronts opposes it; it would become lost. The history of this people is thus the history of one way and of one hope; and it could not have been the one without the other. This can be stated even more clearly: the history of this people is the history of an always reborn faithfulness to the covenant and to the expectation. The covenant itself guarantees what is expected; and the expectation draws its strength out of the knowledge that the covenant exists. For that reason, the history of this people is a history of many a return, many a rebirth. A one-time renaissance would be no more than a final flickering, a tragic shining forth of the flame as it sputters into darkness, a "death in beauty." In such a renaissance, the strength consumes itself. And history tells of many an individual and many a people who came to such a moving end, just as it also reports the base end, in which baseness destroys itself. To be reborn, and then, when the day comes, to be reborn once again, testifies to the strength emanating from the knowledge of the covenant and from the expectation. One day, the great creative strength reappears in all its power of creation. The periodic reappearance of that which returns is the great proof in history of this people's special strength.

The Inner Inclination: The *Yetzer*

From early times, the reflections of this people concerned themselves with a special question: does a creative and a destructive element exist in the cosmos of nature and in the cosmos of man's world? And, since all reflection is struggling for expression, new meaning had to be given to old words. In the Bible, and, even more, in post-biblical literature, both question and search can be easily traced. As we survey this field, it becomes a changing panorama in which rise and fall, deep insight and shallow insipidity alternate.

One word was used to name both the creative as well as the destructive elemental force (indicative of a time of plasticity of speech), the word *yetzer.* What it indicated or ultimately stated cannot be reproduced completely by using a word from another language. Generally it has been translated by using the word "drive." Since post-biblical literature customarily connected this word with the adjectives "good" and "bad," one therefore spoke of the "good drive" and the "bad drive." But this translation is insufficient, and it often leads astray. It is not a "drive" that is meant here, not a pressing and pushing within the will, although this enters into the larger meaning of the word *yetzer.* The root of the word means "to form" and "to fashion," and it relates to the inclination of man. For there is an inclination in every man, constantly developing, an ability that drives him to participate in a special manner, to penetrate into other things, those that exist around him or those that are represented to him, in order to form them or deform them, shape or misshape them, fashion or destroy them.

What is meant, then, is the ferment in the soul of man—that yet uncertain, brewing strength which then becomes a certainty, either for good or for bad. What is meant is that which is active within man, which leads and guides the subject to the object in order to define and clarify itself with this object and through this object. What is meant by our word, then, is the inclination which must first establish itself. It has to reveal itself. For it can turn either toward the way or to what is no way; either toward hope or to that in which there is no hope. It is therefore no "good drive" or "bad drive" which is under discussion here. We are concerned with the human "ability to form what is good," to be a *yetzer tov* (a creator of good), or with the human "ability to form what is bad," to be a *yetzer hara* (a creator of evil). "To form the good," is what is spoken of, for the good has a multitude of shapes and a wealth of forms; and "to form the bad," for the bad is always alike in its formlessness and distortion. Men and peoples differ more in terms of the direction they pursue than in anything else. They are different from one another because the direction of their lives differs.

The Word *Kavvanah*

The contemplation of this people was always fascinated by this question and task of the proper guidance of life, of the direction that life is to pursue. This question absorbed them particularly in the time following the era of growth. The idea that spoke out of that concern fashioned a word that soon became classic: the word *kavvanah.* It meant the totality of human striving for direction: the intention in the action, the piety in prayer, the direction of the *yetzer*, the behavior in daily life. This word speaks to man of the oneness which man's being is to attain, this oneness which is the fulfillment of his faith. It is also the great directional sign that points to the meaning of his life. The ability of man to form, his *yetzer*, is to be incorporated into God's law, into the eternal covenant, through the *kavvanah.*

A biblical work of the final period of the millennium of growth, the two books of Chronicles, contains a prayer in which the directing of life to God is entreated for as the great blessing for the people. This work is not read often, but it has its significance within the Bible. Its purpose is to show all history as the succession of generations; and it wants to show the history of this people as rising out of the history of man. In the beginning, name merely follows name in the line of generations, the sequence of eras. But when one listens to these names, one hears much more. One hears the tidings of the many possibilities which are given to humanity and which endure for it; and one hears of the special possibility which is revealed to it in this people. There is the story of world history and of the history of this people, the two joined together as one; there is the tale of the beginning of days, from the time when men journeyed across the earth, to the beginning of this people when its patriarchs went forth and when it itself, having become a people, entered the Promised Land. The story continues throughout all times, in which one generation walked the way of God and another generation strayed from God's way, continues and leads to the days when Assyria and Babylonia took the people away from its land, continues and culminates on that day when Cyrus, the King of Persia, opened the door for the return to the land, to the new possibility.

Such is the fashion in which Chronicles is written. It begins with the three first names of the first men, the first possibilities: Adam, Seth, Enosh, joined together as blocks of a foundation stone into one sentence. And it concludes with the sentence which opens the door for new possibility for this people: "Thus saith Cyrus, king of Persia: . . . Whosoever there is among you of all His people—He-Who-Is his God be with him—let him go up." The great line of history reveals itself here. The discussion deals not only with men and with events, but with that which unites the men and the events. The tale is not only of what exists in space, and of what moved in yesterday and in the time that is past, of what moves in the present; the tale is also of that upon which everything depends and rests. The attempt is made to show that which turns an event into history. Such a task could only have been undertaken within the horizon that outlined the area in which the author of Chronicles lived. What is characteristic within those boundaries is the touch of greatness, the wide scope of vision which views the one history amidst the history of humanity.

The Book of Chronicles and Greek Historiography

We gain in insight when we consider the two masters of history whose work was written a century later, on Greek soil: Herodotus and Thucydides. Herodotus, filled with inspired curiosity, wandered forth to the lands of the East and the South in order to see the wonders of which he had heard; he wanted to learn of the gods' actions which had become men's fate in those faraway lands. Thucydides' explorations were along other lines. He had the genius of penetrating deeply the soul of mankind. There, in the depths, he searched for the foundation of fate, for the reasons of rise and fall, of success and loss, for the reasons underlying failure and confusion. The quality native to both of them, which made them masters, was not given to the author of Chronicles. But he had what they lacked: the vision of the way, the vision of the future, the vision that reached beyond the sequences of the generations, and an understanding of what is essential in world history. Out of the Chronicler speaks the great enthusiasm, that admonishing, warning, proclaiming spirit emanating from prophecy. Later on, the ancient land of Greece died because of the dissolution of that spirit.

In the center of Chronicles stands King David, the "anointed" by the grace of God, the man in whom a longing found fulfillment when it looked back to a splendor of former days. He was the man who had the ability to be brave and humble, who passed the test of days of trials and failures. He was the man whom God had called and who sang of God and of God's "sign," the man ready to listen to the word of God when it came through His prophet. He was the man from whom the bow of the covenant stretches toward the man of days to come, the messiah, the "son of David."

The description of the life of King David is brought to a climax: people and king have become one in their surrender to God. "Wherefore David blessed Him-Who-Is before all the congregation" (1 Chron. 29:10) in order to proclaim gratitude for everything to Him who has created all and who has given everything to them. Pleading to God, David concludes by placing all his dreams and hopes for his people into one all-important, all-inclusive sentence: "O Thou-Who-Art, the God of Abraham, of Isaac, and of Israel, our fathers, keep this for ever, even the forming strength [*yetzer*] of the thoughts of the heart of Thy people, and direct their heart unto Thee" (1 Chron. 29:18).

That is the verse of the *yetzer* and of the *kavvanah*, of the "forming strength of the thoughts of the heart" and of the "directing the heart unto God." This book presents it as the final testament of God's anointed to his people. It was set down at the beginning of a new epoch. It presents the task as it appeared in the last period of a millennium, the decisive task that the new generations would have to labor for, that they might live for it and for this people.

Education and Constitution

The problem of education and of the constitution now occupied all thought and required untiring labor. Through education individual life is to receive its constitution, is to be brought into relation with an ideal. Both intend a style of life. A genuine form of existence is to be received and is to be passed on as heritage. Century after century, through the revelation and the knowledge of the covenant entering the soul, through the never silent memories of the exodus, through that which the desert had given and which the land then gave, a characteristic quality had developed, a relationship to the infinite and to the eternal which became a spiritual strength. This relationship was now to be guarded so that it might stay alive; it was to be protected now so that it would continue in its direction in the midst of the world. As an aspect of a constancy it was to permeate the days, so that it might be reborn in days to come.

That was the task which those men set for themselves in whose souls the memory of centuries remained alive. The responsibility for this inheritance confronted them, an inheritance destined to be the possession of later generations and to give them the power of rebirth. They were responsible for the existence of this people. The demand was all the more pressing since they knew or surmised that the realm of civil and political independence would keep narrowing for their people. That which would be lost by the diminution of outer independence was to be restored through inner independence. The type of striving permitted to other peoples might be denied to them. But its place would be taken by the great decision which has far more meaning than all the contrivances of the powers of earth; in this people this inner independence would become its vital strength and the guarantee of its future. The strong will for the "direction," this direction of the whole life to God, would supply the means by which greatness would find its task and glory would find its fulfillment. The way and the hope, this choice that could never be denied them, would always open itself. This would be achieved by the constitution and by education. From earliest times, Moses and the prophets and the men of wisdom and prayer had enjoined study and teaching; and these became the key words. This people was to be a people of masters and disciples, of teachers and students. The word "Torah" is now sounded in a new way; Torah becomes the expression for the new way of thinking that has grown out of the old way. It appears as a force in which the creation of the world and revelation announce themselves.

The Denial of an Evil Force

There is an ancient question, rising out of the events of the world, that now could raise a doubt; more than that, it could invoke an opposing belief. Was there, after all, a force opposed to everything and working against the idea of the education of every individual life which the constitution of the community tried to proclaim as the goal of life? Was there not something inimical in the world, the opponent of all things, something revealing not only an element of evil, but the one principle of evil? Was there not a power in which something beyond man forces its way upon humanity, a power in which impossibility arrays itself against what is possible? In that case, was not all the striving for the sake of the "Torah" destined to be futile? And was it not fated for this way and this hope, as envisioned here, finally to shatter against this opposition and arrive only at disaster and fatality? Would these not come to mean the absence of a goal, and, even worse, the absence of God's grace? This belief in education—was it not, basically, a fundamental heresy?

Ever again, and from every place, such questions were voiced. Everything turned on the question of whether or not there existed in the world the principle of evil, the more-than-terrestrial force of sin. Was there something that was radically evil, that was stronger than all the decisions of man? Mysteries, rising out of ancient and out of more recent days, came forward. Each of them proclaimed that it alone possessed the miracle through which the force of evil could be conquered, through which man would be elevated to a new life by means of a rebirth into the true reality. A parting of ways took place here; belief confronted belief. Final questions of mankind, ultimate, cosmic questions seemed to arise here; and they demanded an answer. Again the existence of this people and the particularity of its soul were tested.

These questions could turn to historical investigation for thought, to what the Greeks called *historia.* But they could find even more in personal experience, in what the ancient literature of this people called "the days of the years of man." In its most basic form, life is the meeting of soul and hour. That which comes from within, this possibility, this *yetzer*, this basic possession of man, encounters that which comes from without: this opportunity, this form of appearance of fateful chance, this entrance into the state of becoming. Will and complication, the drive to determine and that which cause and effect present as a given fact—these confront each other. Nothing that is finished, no gift from above, is ever placed into man's hand. All that is granted him is the hour, the opportunity which always unfolds to his soul and to his strength for attaining the possibility which he possesses. It is also the "messenger" which God sends to him. Man is to recognize this opportunity, is to see what God shows mankind, is to hear what God has to say. A life fulfills itself when it understands and accepts that which is sent to it. A life goes astray when it does not find the possibilities which are innate in it, when it does not clarify them with the opportunities that approach it; it is lost when it lets itself be bypassed by the "messengers" who come to it. The way that "loses itself" of which the first Psalm speaks is the way of the possibilities and the opportunities which remained unused or were disregarded and thus "lost themselves." History's story, and life's story—more than anything else, before anything else—is the story of these lost ways.

The Concept of Satan

Out of these frustrations that make up life and history, a special thought could then arise: the thought that a radical hindrance dwells behind everything which exists and takes place. It is the work of that hindrance to confuse the possibilities and to frustrate the opportunities, so that soul and hour might not meet. The imagination then creates personal traits for all of this. The radical hindrance appeared as the radical evil; and the radical evil appeared as that radical maliciousness that does not only seek to ruin everything, but, full of spite, selects the hours and the souls it wishes to destroy. A principle of deception, a superhuman power, seemed to join the element of evil and to participate fully in its activities. It seemed to work almost industriously in a regular sequence that could be called the law of the penultimate hour. Men and peoples had searched for the right way and had even entered upon it, moving upward, toward the goal. Then, just before the final, decisive steps, they were overcome by the great delusion which forced them into destruction. In truth, a history of the penultimate hours could certainly be written. A "satanic" might, it was surmised, stood behind all. The belief in an anti-God gained strength. The thesis of the "devil" was established; and it was the antithesis to the existence of this people, against that which was its way and its hope.

It is true that the word "satan" is a Hebrew word, and that it is used at times in biblical poetry. But the meaning which it has there is completely different from the meaning given to it in other spheres of faith. Here, it belongs to the category of poetic expressions which want to give form and language to human characteristics and particularities. "Satan" is used as a tangible representation showing the nature of those who cannot or who refuse to see the light, the bright, and the good, of those who only have eyes for what is dark, for what is lacking, for what is hidden. In the beginning, the word meant setting oneself against something, stepping into the way. The men who translated the Bible into Greek did not find an identical word in that language; and so they used a word indicating a scattering about, a hidden accusation, a slandering, and ultimately a causing of ruin. Out of the soil of that translation the "diabolos," the "devil" arose, this "satan" as destructive force, as the power of malignity.

Nothing of that is contained in the biblical writings. In the Bible there is no trace of an anti-God power in Satan; he can only do what has been permitted to him. On his own, he can only interpret and misinterpret. In the last analysis, he only exists in order to be disproved, in order to show how he cannot maintain his existence before God, before truth and before reality. Thus does he appear in the prologue to the Book of Job: he would like to be God's procurator, he "goes to and fro" on the streets of earth, in order to discover weaknesses, insufficiencies, or possible impediments in anyone. He proceeds with his task on the person of Job. He appears in the book of the Prophet Zechariah, making an attempt on the person of the High Priest Joshua. But this is the answer which he has to hear: "He-Who-Is will reject thee, O Satan; yea, He-Who-Is that has chosen Jerusalem will reject thee; is not this man [Joshua] a brand plucked out of the fire?" (Zech. 3:2) That is Satan here: the poetic personification of spiritual insufficiency, the image of one who does not have the ability to see and to understand.

And yet it seems as though the genius of the faith and its language had surmised the danger that could come from "the satan." The definite article is taken away from him, and only the indefinite one is permitted him. No more is there talk of "the satan," but merely of "a satan," someone, anyone, who here or there falls upon a man or seeks to attack him. This is how an ancient prayer phrases it, one that has been the evening prayer and the night prayer of this people for many centuries. It begins with the words: "Let us lie down to peace, O Thou-Who-Art our God, and let us arise unto life, O Master, and spread over us the roof of Thy peace."* And it closes with the words: "Guard us in the shadow of Thy wings, for Thou art God Who guards us and saves us, for Thou art God and Master, gracious and merciful, and protect Thou our going out and our coming in, now and for all times." In between stands the sentence: "Keep far from us enemy, pest and sword and hunger and sorrow, and keep far a satan from before us and from behind us."

The ancient morning prayer speaks in the same manner:

> May it be a will emanating from Thou-Who-Art, Thou, my God and God of my fathers, that Thou wilt save me today and every day from those who are presumptuous and from presumption, from an evil man and from an evil companion and from an evil neighbor and from an evil encounter and from a satan who despoils, from harsh action and from a man harsh in action, be he a son of the covenant or be he not a son of the covenant.**

The multitude—without and within—of those who do evil or from whom evil threatens are named in this prayer, which appears so prosaic in its presentation. It is a morning prayer admonishing one to consider the day that lies ahead. It reminds one of all that awaits him after the peace of the night, of all that can become sober reality. Listening to this, one can discover something extremely moving. The fullness of sorrow descending upon one man from his fellow men has no pathetic tone here; the pathos is reality itself. Something of that desperation out of which the great doubt, the doubting of the good, the belief in radical evil, can be heard here. Desperation rarely grows out of doubt; but out of desperation there arises the most stubborn doubt. Alongside all those who are clearly named in the prayer, whose attribute is given as "evil," "hard," of whom one knows the identity and desires, there stands one other figure, from whom one may fearfully expect anything; as yet, he is not recognizable, and does not want anything recognizable.

* The evening prayer may be found in *The Authorized Daily Prayer Book*, ed. J. H. Hertz (New York: Bloch Publishing Co., 1948 [1952]), p. 312.

** For the morning prayer, see *ibid.*, p. 24.

He is, precisely, just "a satan," seeking everywhere for imperfections and weaknesses, trying to "dig an abyss" somewhere. But he who is able to do so prays to God, who will also deliver him from this.

The word "satan" means this and nothing else. It is used here to indicate a type of evil neighbor and the harsh enemy. A different meaning is only possible on a completely different ground. There is no room, let alone a special place, for a principle of evil which would explain all wickedness. The certainty of the soul that it originated in God, that it is pure and therefore able to be free, this certainty abdicated at no time and in no place. It clung to itself, in spite of the constant threat in hours or days or years. At the beginning of the morning prayer there stands a sentence that became a fundamental statement of belief. Only in prayer did this people formulate its statement of belief: "My God, the soul which Thou hast placed into me is pure. Thou hast fashioned it, Thou hast formed it, it is Thy breath within me."• This statement of the fundamental origin of good stood firm; all teachings of the fundamental origin of evil shattered against it.

The Danger of Fantasy

This people knew that events are intertwined with good and evil fortune. It often contemplated, either cheerfully or sorrowfully, the tendencies within the spheres of causes and effects, all that is called chance, with its partiality and spite. But it was never assumed that a force of antireason was at work. On certain occasions, in certain strains of this people, a number of superstitions had arisen which wove their varicolored webs between the worlds into which man had been placed. They became nets in which many a searching spirit could be trapped. There is that fear of emptiness which populates space inaccessible to man's vision with all kinds of swarming figures. It was active here as well, creating morbid speculation and fearfulness. And there were many naïve desires to spin fairy tales inside this vision. A certain dan-

• See *ibid.*, p. 18.

ger approached. Fantasy, a heritage of this people, could lose its piety and its reverence. There was danger of losing the vital feeling for the one great mystery, this eternal, infinite, deepest feeling of the soul which gives life its reverence and with that its piety. The piousness of man is established or falls in terms of this feeling, this ultimate affection of his soul, this monotheism of his senses; and it could become lost in such games and trembling excursions. The one great mystery, the sublimity on which life rests, could be crowded and finally displaced through those many mysteries that want to embrace all of life. The fantasy which entered those mysteries had to surrender what was best within itself, its uniqueness. And fantasy without reverence ceases to be a vital force. It becomes a weakness that wanders without a goal. Somewhere along the way it has lost its blessing.

Yet this danger was always conquered speedily. The certainty of the closeness, the immediacy of God, which kept alive the feeling for the purity and the freedom of the soul, was always strong. It prevented fanciful images from fatal interference between men and the One God. The existence of this people remained unimpaired. The rest of the figures created by superstition were ultimately driven away by humor, that basic spring of life which constantly gushed forth within this people. The direction to the One God, the *kavvanah*, endured. It could not be shaken or led astray by any teaching concerning original evil and its power; the fantasies of the little demons of evil and of their game with man could not confuse the *kavvanah*. David's final prayer had been answered.

The Encounter with Persia

Kavvanah had to pass a decisive test in the final period of the first millennium. At that time, this people confronted in Persian dualism the teaching that a force exists paralleling God. This people was deeply impressed because of the clearness of the teaching and, even more so, because of the clarity of the people for whom it had become religion.

The confrontation with the Persians and with their belief was one of the strongest experiences in the existence of this people. It could be called its first moral confrontation with another people. Rarely did this people again experience something similar.

In the young Persian people, in its King Cyrus, and in the belief through which and for which they entered history, something completely new faced this people Israel, an Israel which was centuries older. Up to then, Israel had seen tribes that became peoples, and peoples who vanished. It had come to know the inimical as well as the enticing. It had seen much that appeared grandiose in its manner. It had encountered the splendor and the knowledge of Memphis and Thebes, of Sidon and Tyre, of Nineveh and of Babylon. It had to learn of the grandiosity of fearfulness which had spread out its arms upon the soil of Canaan and its surroundings. But never had it had an internal encounter with a people. All of its history—for the sake of which this people lived, and which was the only one it could have—had been a solemn negation: it had said "No!" to all these encounters, "No!" for the sake of God. In order to preserve its own existence, it inwardly turned away from all of this. Something completely different, previously unexperienced, now confronted them in the Persian nation. A completely different voice could be heard. It seemed as though God's word spoke from there as well.

The fact of such an attraction is clearly established, even though it is impossible by now to see the actual features in which the impression expressed itself. But it is there in all clarity; and the reasons for it are self-evident. For the first time, this people Israel saw a clean people confronting it, a people with an ideal. What had separated Israel from the other peoples, and was still separating it, and would continue to separate it from them, was the uncleanness of those peoples. Ever again the prophets had proclaimed it as the great task of this people Israel: it was to be a people of cleanness, and it was to fashion the ground given to it by God into a ground of cleanness. Only the ground of the one cleanness would permit the belief in the One God to draw strength out of its depths. Their development had fulfilled itself in the battle of the one cleanness against the luxuriant growth of the uncleannesses. In this battle, the soul had become aware of what was intrinsically its own. Something of this intrinsic self now addressed them out of the manner of the Persian people; and this people Israel responded to it.

It was the first time that this happened, that such an impression was made upon this people; and that which was awakened by this new experience remained awake. This people always remained receptive to the moral event and to the moral encounter. It was always both able and willing to understand and to honor the clean idea, the clean hope, the clean strength in every people and every community in which these manifested themselves. This people often looked for such manifestations with deep longing, listened for them with high expectation. The centuries that followed this first experience testify to this. No disappointment, no ultimate discovery of an opposition could destroy this readiness of the soul nor overcome this will.

The prophet and the historian of those days speak of Cyrus in almost the same manner in which they spoke of King David. His name seems to gleam upon the bow of the covenant which, set against darkness, curves from David to the "son of David," from the promise of the reality to the reality of the promise. "An anointed of God," "a servant of the Lord"—this is the only nobility recognized by this people—one "to whom God speaks": that is what the prophet calls Cyrus. And the author of Chronicles, to whom a name has more significance than all the tumultuous noise round about, concludes his book of world history, this history of the generations from Adam to David and from David to the generation in which he himself lives with the sentence: "Thus saith Cyrus king of Persia. . . ." It was a word of deliverance which Cyrus now announced for this people; out of a ground of cleanliness the sense of freedom drew its sap and strength. Cyrus did not have to be shattered like Pharaoh for freedom to come into existence. He understood this people's way, and pointed it out. An exile was to end, an internal and external one.

All of this must be seen clearly for a full understanding of the strength that characterized this people at this time in its holding firm to the one direction that led to the One God, to Him alone, next to whom there is none else. New experience had entered these men, at that time, in the form of Cyrus and the Persian people. Before Israel stood something that resembled it. A people *of* a faith confronted it, not just a people *with* a faith, like others near and far. Moreover, the faith was spiritual, a faith with an ideal, and it rejected the many gods and their idols. It taught the battle between the two great original forces, between the god of light and his opponent, the god of darkness; and it called upon humanity to help the forces of light. For the first time, there approached that temptation which seeks to entice understanding by presenting similarities and shared traits.

But the temptation was overcome then, as in later days and in other realms. The faith of this people remained assured of itself. It neither capitulated before the victors and the greatness they possessed, nor walked the way leading to compromise. Compromises are all to the good and often indispensable in the problems of the peripheral and its conditions, but they are fatal in the problems of the central and the unconditional. The respect created by the new experience remained alive; but the fertile strength of the will for what was one's own endured. And the faith in the two forces was also rejected, despite the fact that behind it stood a deeply impressive spirit.

Deutero-Isaiah and His Teachings

The decisive word leading to certainty was spoken by that prophet whose life blessed the Babylonian Exile. At an early period, his speeches were added to the Book of Isaiah, and we do not know his name. It is possible that he was also named Isaiah. He is one of the great anonymous authors of the Bible. We also know nothing of the events and the encounters of his life. Yet this man stands before us, speaking out of the ultimate depths of the personal. There had been one prophet before him, Ezekiel, who, led forth from the land of Judah, had sustained and supported the exiles. Visionary ability and architectural talent had united in him. In a wondrous manner he guided the present to the ground of the past; and wondrous was the way in which he built the promise of the future on that ground. This great prophet who now arose, this genius without a name, wanted to plant the present into the ground of the future. The time into which he was placed appeared to him more than a time directed toward the future; it was also a time supported by the future, nourished by the future. He therefore felt that it was not he himself who was speaking, not he and his era; it was the future that was speaking, and he was only the "voice of one who calleth," the "voice of one who saith" (Is. 40:3,6). The task he set his people was this: the present grows out of the promised future, this unshakable, enduring future; and the future is thus in the process of achieving existence in the present; man must therefore fashion the present out of the future.

The prophet lived in the land of Babylon, amidst a people who spoke another language. He therefore became all the more aware of his own language. He was able to give new content and new sound to ancient words. This is a process duplicated in other places and other times. There was one word in particular to which this prophet added a new meaning: the word "comfort."

"Comfort ye, comfort ye My people, saith your God" (Is. 40:1) is the beginning of this prophecy. "Comfort" is the answer here in which the certainty that will always endure speaks to the uncertainties which come and go with the day. The future which endures receives the present into itself through the "comfort." Eternal love enters also into eternal justice and becomes forgiveness; both love and justice have fulfilled themselves.

For that reason, there is nothing sentimental, nothing appeasing or disguising in this word "comfort." Rather, it is the great demand, the dynamic messianic that speaks out of it. "To comfort" means at the same time to liberate, to open the way, to "take up the stumbling-block" (Is. 57:14). Therefore, the expression "Comfort ye My people" continues:

A voice of one who calleth:
"Clear ye in the wilderness the way of Him-Who-Is,

Make plain in the desert
A highway for our God.

. . . .

And the glory of Him-Who-Is shall be revealed,
And all flesh shall see it together;
For the mouth of Him-Who-Is hath spoken it."

Isaiah 40:3,5

Once Moses had prayed in the wilderness: "Show me now Thy ways," "show me, I pray Thee, Thy glory" (Ex. 33:13,18), and these words kept sounding through the centuries. Now they are sounded anew by the prophet of the Exile speaking to the people: 'Clear ye in the wilderness the way of Him-Who-Is. . . . And the glory of Him-Who-Is shall be revealed." And that is the comfort for this people, the comfort that never fails because it is at the same time the way. The way became the comfort, for it is the highway that is cleared for God. In this comfort this people lived; through this comfort it was able to endure. Much was denied this people, and much was taken away from it; but it never became a people without comfort.

The great task set for this people was to clear the way, this way leading from the enduring future to each of the changing presents. In the second millennium of this people, its teachers called this task the preparation of the kingdom of the Eternal, the kingdom of Heaven. "That we might order the world through the kingdom of the Almighty" was the hope and prayer promulgated by one of the teachers eight hundred years after the prophet, on the same Babylonian soil, within a new Persian empire. He set these words into a prayer for the New Year's Day; and this prayer became a confession of faith and a song of martyrs. It speaks of the One God and of His people, and of this people's waiting for its God, speaks in a two-line rhythm, commencing with the words: "It is incumbent upon us" (in Hebrew this is one word: *alenu*) and concluding with the words: "and all who live on earth will give honor to the glory of Thy name." In the third millennium of this people, the "pious in the land Ashkenaz," along the Danube and the Rhine, in their mystic language, named this task "working along with God in the work of coming into being." In that, they followed a significant sentence of the Talmud. Six centuries later, in the Eastern lands of Europe, the men of the new piety, of Hasidism, expressed this as "solving that which is unsolvable in God's creation." But it did not matter how the expectant soul, in which commandment and longing had united, formed its expression. That which it knew and tried to say was always one and the same. This people knew of the way and of the comfort; they knew the one grace of the One God.

The Certainty of the One Creator of the Universe

The prophet of the Exile had proclaimed the certainty of the comfort. It speaks all the stronger since another certainty, basically the same, also reveals itself in it: the certainty that everything enfolding the world is a creation of the One God. Within creation, comfort holds sway; for the One God is the One Creator, "He-Who-Is, who forms everything." The word "everything" and the word "all" receive new emphasis here. Nothing is outside of the one creation, nothing in the world is a world to itself, outside the totality of possibilities named "world." That which we call history also stands within the creation; nothing is a power by itself, "For He is the Creator of everything."

For that reason, the prophet calls to the people of Babylon who fashion idols and worship the stars as the gods who determine their fates:

Lift up your eyes on high,
And see: who hath created these?
He that bringeth out their host by number,
He calleth them all by name;
By the greatness of His might, and for that He is strong
in power,
Not one faileth.

Isaiah 40:26

The one great certainty, out of which all certainty comes, speaks here. It also assures the prophet of the words with which he can then turn to the king of the Persians:

Thus saith He-Who-Is to His anointed,
To Cyrus, whose right hand I have holden,
To subdue nations before him,
And to loose the loins of kings;
To open the doors before him,
And that the gates may not be shut:
I will go before thee,

. . . .

That thou mayest know that I am He-Who-Is,
Who call thee by thy name, even the God of Israel.
For the sake of Jacob My servant,
And Israel Mine elect,
I have called thee by thy name,
I have surnamed thee, though thou
hast not known Me.
I am He-Who-Is, and there is none else,
Beside Me there is no God;
I have girded thee, though thou hast not known Me;
That they may know from the rising of the sun,
and from the west,
That there is none beside Me;
I am He-Who-Is, and there is none else;
I form the light, and create darkness;
I make peace, and create evil;
I am He-Who-Is, that doeth all these things.

Isaiah 45:1–7

The words of the Bible, particularly those contained in the prophetical writings, and, in those, most particularly the words of this prophet, demand that we think along with them, think them through, and quite often also think beyond them, carrying the thought to its conclusion. Two sentences in this proclamation to Cyrus rise like signposts. They point beyond the immediate context of the word. The one sentence wants to show what history is; the other wants to teach how God's creation can reveal its meaning to the mind. Man is placed into creation and into history. His thought processes should extend to meet both.

The Prophet's Word on the Meaning of History

The first of the two sentences reads: "I have surnamed thee, though thou hast not known Me." The concern here is with preparation in history, or one can speak here of providence in history: men and peoples fulfill a task which leads to the great, to the essential task. They prepare an entry onto the pathway that is being cleared for God. They faithfully serve a purpose which in good days is visible to them in some fashion; and God helps them. God gives them the space in which to work. But they do not see what is beyond all this; they do not see the ultimate purpose. God "has surnamed them, and they did not know him." They are the men, the peoples of the preparation, they are those designated by providence. The encounter is granted to man, to people, and to a certain place—to man, to people, and to a certain time. According to the great teacher of the millennium of education, Akiba ben Joseph: "Everything is foreseen, and free will is given."

In the third millennium of this people, when its old knowledge again achieved new expression, its thinkers often approached the problem of providence, or, as the language of the conception expresses it, the problem of God's "seeing." They spoke of a universal, a cosmic providence which made itself known through the preparing and sustaining forces of nature and through the species and forms of all creatures. They also spoke of an individual providence which was imprinted in the lifeline of men and which was apparently guided by a higher force. Two of these philosophers, always viewed by later generations with the deepest gratitude, Judah Halevi and Moses ben Maimon, also pointed out this providence in history, these preparations, these arisings and developments in the life of humanity. In doing that, they gained the answer to an essential question: What is the historical meaning of all that which could not simply be rejected, of that to which they could not answer "No," and yet could not offer an unconditional "Yes"? At best, they could answer with *a* "Yes"—but not *the* "Yes." And this they expressed in terms of their contemporary concepts. But what they saw and heard was precisely what the prophet of the Exile had seen and heard when, in the name of the Eternal One, he directs his words to Cyrus: "Whose right hand I [He-Who-Is] have holden"; I have surnamed thee, though thou hast not known Me." The philosophers also knew of the preparations in history, of the ways for the sake of the one way, of the ways that led to the one way. With grateful readiness, they recognized everything that was great and clean and therefore alive, wherever it was encountered. It made them all the more certain of the way, and it gave them a deeper comprehension of the meaning of the expression: "For the sake of Jacob My servant, and Israel Mine elect."

The Prophet's Word on the Meaning of Creation

The second sentence striving to lead thought to the contemplation of final questions is the sentence dealing with creation. "I am He-Who-Is, and there is none else; I form the light, and create darkness, I make peace, and create evil." With these words, the prophet confronts the teaching of Zarathustra, the Persian, that two forces exist and have their effect, the god of light and the god of darkness, the principle of good and the principle of evil. An utmost in religious paradox seems to speak, to struggle for expression in language, when the prophet says that the One God, the One Creator, fashions all these. But he could hear the answer only in this paradox. He had to proclaim it, even if what had been revealed to him and what he now wanted to say had come from that domain which is beyond human words.

One thing always sustained the certainty of this people in days of need, enabled its soul to grow strong, and enabled it continually to re-create thought and contemplation, will and hope: the truth of the One God who reveals and who creates, next to whom there is none else; the recognition that the absolute exists only in Him, that everything remains relative without Him. Outside of Him, everything is His creation and the work of no one else. But it is certain, and it is therefore always in the realm of the relative. "God divided the light from the darkness" (Gen. 1:4), tells the story of the creation. God has "set before thee life and good, and death and evil" (Deut. 30:15), warns Moses before he dies. The absolute lives in Him-Who-Is, in the One alone. The worlds which He has created, the worlds of the universe and the worlds of man, are only worlds of possibilities. But they are worlds of an unlimited fullness of possibilities, because the One God has created them. They are the spheres of the relative with all their tensions between the relative and the absolute as well as between the relative and the relative. The possibilities have been set into creation, in all their reach and relation, in their rise and in their fall. The One God forms light and creates darkness, makes peace and creates evil. The worlds are the sum total of all tensions.

For that reason, the perfect, finished, completed man does not exist; only the man of possibilities, of courage and tensions, exists. Ever again and ever anew, he has to choose and has to decide. "For there is not a righteous man upon earth, that doeth good, and sinneth not" states the Book of Ecclesiastes (Eccl. 7:20). He can only be nearer or further from God. His way can "become lost"; and with that, his thinking and striving can become directionless, senseless. But God's creature cannot lose himself completely, cannot suffer a complete loss of meaning. The prophet who spoke to Cyrus also said this: "Seek ye Him-Who-Is while He may be found, call upon Him while He is near; let the wicked forsake his way, and the man of iniquity his thoughts; and let him return unto Him-Who-Is; and He will have compassion upon him, and to our God, for He will abundantly pardon" (Is. 55: 6–7).

The two expressions belong together, the final word of the proclamation to Cyrus and this word of return and of pardon. Together they give one another full strength and meaning. The Persian religion lacked the knowledge that Moses had discovered at Mt. Sinai when he had sought to see God's ways, that knowledge of God who is "merciful and gracious, long-suffering, and abundant in goodness and truth" (Ex. 34:6). What Moses received as a revelation of God lived on in his people; it was constantly reborn, it constantly gained new speech. Because of it, this people could reject the temptation that appeared in the great thought of Persian belief, even though this belief approached them as the faith of a clean victor, of a liberator.

This people Israel thus had to be able to cope with two tasks in a new epoch of its existence. It confronted two enticements. Each of the two, each in its way, was hallowed and ranged widely. Often, the two strove to interweave. The one rose out of that later mystery cult of the redeeming, which promised the goal without the way. The other rose out of the cosmic dualism of that time, which proclaimed the victory of light and of the good without the decisive struggle and suffering of the human soul. Here and there, the two seemed to come close to the belief of this people; it seemed possible to draw connecting lines between them. The vision of what was related could draw this people from what was intrinsically its own. If this people had walked on such a path it would have ceased guiding its present into its future. The future would have sunk backward, into the past. But the enticing idea, promising so much, was rejected; the labor within one's own, the work of the education and of the constitution, gained its millennium. The will to what was one's own proved itself; the strength of rebirth was preserved.

The Entrance into the Second Millennium

What had grown and come to develop in the first millennium fashioned for itself the most definite forms of its existence in the second millennium. The forming of a life after the time of growth, drawing from the strength that wakened during the time of growth, is almost a decision to live. Life fulfills itself in the complete form; it sickens in unformedness. And life only creates its forms in the correct tasks which it sets for itself. That which is clean and original in its essence can only express itself in the correct tasks. In them, the will to live becomes the moral will, the true will of a being unto itself.

When this people Israel entered into its new era, the hour of fate had been sounded for "the peoples round about." The two ancient great kingdoms of might and of culture, at the Euphrates and the Nile, ceased to determine Israel's fate, even in their own lands. They had been the two poles between which the destiny of this people moved; even Israel's concepts had moved between these poles. Moreover, the first had been "a house of servitude" from the beginning, from which the Eternal One had led Israel forth; and the other, at the end of the time span, had been the place of exile whose doors had been opened by the king of Persia. Now, the intrinsic form possessed by these countries began to fade away. They lost their faces, and the peoples between them lost their appearance as well. The time of the one great land commenced, the land of the "hundred and seven and twenty provinces," "from India even unto Ethiopia" (Esther 1:1) as Cyrus had founded it and Alexander tried to establish it. The peoples continued to possess their space within this new empire, and perhaps maintained their old names; but their world had been taken away from them. Only this people continued to possess it and gave it new form. The old forces of growth within this people became forces of new creativity. This people maintained its own space and its own history, even when it was set within the space of a world empire.

This took place because the forces out of the time of growth continued to live in this people and could be reborn to fashion new forms. It is not a sequence of centuries, not a succession of generations and their periods that reveals itself here; it is something completely different: the encounter of the origin and of the new tasks. Only in such an encounter is something creative again awakened. The renouncing of new tasks stunts creativity and causes it to waste away, just as a renunciation of the origin born of genius would scatter all tasks to the winds. Thus is the fate of men and nations decided. Originality renews itself only in the struggling with genuine tasks; and originality is the great possibility of the personal. The true tasks are those which life, and eternity in its tension and demand, place before the individual. History, too, confronts a people with those tasks. The insignificant contains the continuations; within the great, only rebirth exists. Within the great, there is a return of what lived within childhood, within youth, as genius. And anything of genius can only be something clean, something clear, something true, can only be that in which something human becomes a likeness of the divine. That is the spring constantly gushing forth. Men and peoples can be contrasted by the continuations and the rebirths.

That which is low, brutish, and common does not even have its continuations. It is only repeated. It cannot do anything else; always and everywhere it is the same, the same baseness pulling downward, always this commonness which extends its circles in mere constant repetition. That is the most decisive line of differentiation in life and in history. There are men, and peoples, and times of rebirth; and there are men, and peoples, and times of repetition. Or, there are those who keep attaining themselves, and there are those who always throw themselves away and lose themselves. Through their rebirths, the first groups live, live in their own life, ever new; originality creates new forms for them. The others dwindle away in the repetitions; when a different era comes, they are unable to give expression to it.

II

The Way and the Comfort

The Questioning People

It is the great accomplishment of this people in its second millennium that, in a sense, it rediscovered itself. To rediscover oneself is the sign of rebirth. After Cyrus and his people had entered history with an idea different from that previously held by great powers, conditions and relationships changed basically and in a far-reaching manner. What now disrupted others and made them reel only gave this people a new certainty. During these new days, and because of them, it gained a new view of its way, this way from the beginning to the end. It gained, as it were, a new insight into itself. The new demands showed new possibilities latent in this people and permitted old traits to reveal themselves more clearly. Patience and vision received new expression, and the words "from generation to generation" gained new content. The self-confidence that formed itself anew became such a vital power that this people was now able to confront itself, to stand before itself. It met itself in the new task, and recognized itself. On its own, it took its stand before God so that, before Him, it might render account to Him and answer to itself. The people could now become its own admonisher and prophet. This people was granted what can be the best gift of youth, the time in which growth reaches reality: the self, as itself, learns to hear the voice of the self as it is meant to be.

History asked its question, and with it pointed to the future. Out of every real question rises, sooner or later, the commandment. A question to a people is an historical one only when the moral summons is sounded in it. In this people, then and later, there were romantics whose dreams looked backward and who hoped to discover their selves in a real or in an imaginary past. But one who keeps the whole in perspective quickly becomes aware of how far from the thinking and feeling of this people such an approach remained and had to remain. The spirit of this people remains dynamic and messianic, because it always asks itself the question. In contrast, in a romantic approach the visionary, rambling quest crowds out the definite question.

This people, then, in completely characteristic manner, became a questioning people. In that, its particular features were impressed upon it. In the course of its centuries it renounced very much, as it had to; but this trait, this duty to ask, this right to question, could never be taken from it and never suffered itself to be changed. The Bible itself is a book full of questions. When the people in meditating upon itself discovered itself again, it discovered new questions. It has often been surmised that this people is characterized by a type of questioning that sprouts—and at times grows wildly—out of speculating and brooding. While many examples present themselves, it must be recognized that this people is characterized by a completely different kind of questioning. It is the question which life asks and in which eternity speaks. Again and again this people heard and received the voice. Through it, it learned how to question. Because eternity and infinity spoke to it in life, because it experienced the depths of this tension, therefore it had to ask. And it could ask the same question of others, having previously posed the question to itself.

It could be such a questioning people, because it possessed the one great, enduring, unshakable answer, the answer which its belief had given it. This answer was: the one, the only God, the revealing, creating, redeeming one; the one, the only God, who speaks to man in the mystery, in the commandment, in the promise, in the grace. Alongside this one answer and what it encompasses, other answers could not exist; alongside this one finality, nothing else could be accounted final; alongside the one, the absolute, only the relative could exist. Around this one answer the fullness of the questions could now circle. This people was permitted, and had the ability, to pursue its questions to the very end, because it knew of the one answer which it never permitted to be taken away.

In the knowledge of the one answer, self-confidence had its firm roots. A grand style of thinking developed for the search, and meditation progressed ever further; it could not rest halfway. Someone who can or wishes to see only a part, to consider that to be the whole, might convince himself that he had found expressions of the small and the petty in the searching and thinking of this epoch. He could present many examples as proof. Since this thinking plunged to ultimate ends, it could lead into the very minute last branchings and twistings, into the thin endings as well, in which the strength itself seems to be attenuated. But always and above all this thinking went in the other direction as well. It led toward the far goals and tasks, toward the messianic, in which eternity speaks to humanity.

Certainly this epoch is one of developing dialecticism, of untiring questioning with its tendency to point out even the tiniest thing. But it is equally the time of the happy tidings unfolding themselves, the budding and sprouting visions of the final fulfilling days, the time of untiring hope and expectancy that would penetrate the uttermost distances. Both ends bring thinking to its ultimate conclusion. Only one who grasps the totality grasps the essential; he alone becomes aware of the power of existence and recognizes the grand line, the great trait in thinking, whether it be the thinking plunged into research or the thinking confronting revelation. Then the two become one in the totality of time and in the particular of individual personalities.

They could be one because all searching and seeking was determined by the one great task, that of education and of realizing the constitution, this task of taking the individual and his days, the totality and its history, and setting them in a realm of holiness. Man and people were to be prepared inwardly against every change, against all that could threaten or entice. They were to be made strong so that they would be able to live for the promise and the commandment of the great realization, "the kingdom of God." The time had begun in which their existence, more than before, was an existence amidst others. The ancient expression born in the early history of this people, "the surrounding peoples," won a still stronger, more immediate meaning. To be a sphere amidst spheres, a province among provinces, a group alongside groups, and always a circle of the few among the many—such became the manner of this people's existence.

Syncretism and Provincialism

Existence, moreover, was understood as part of an extensive striving. A great fulfillment, a great peace was promised. Everywhere men endeavored to discover, in the name of an empire or a belief, a philosophy or a culture, a wonder or a mystery, the one universal sea of the spirit into which all streams poured. To be amidst the others and still to stand upon one's own ground, to belong to a world and yet belong to oneself, to walk one's own way amidst the fullness of that which flowed together from everywhere in order to form a totality, a oneness —that was the set task. It stands behind all that was thought and was said, not only behind the messianic but also behind the dialectic, behind that which may appear small or even petty, and thus gives even that a share of the great trait, of the grand style.

Something else, opposed to it, had to be faced too. Provincialism had developed around this people at the same time as syncretism. As the old kingdoms and states became provinces, one or two or three among the "hundred and twenty-seven," the people in them no longer knew who they were and what they were. Now they had only space, but no longer history. Now they saw only a district in which they existed, not a way upon which they walked. They searched for their selves and did not find them. Since they thus possessed no true self, they could have no respect for themselves. With the loss of outward independence all inner independence had ceased.

Where outer freedom has ended and inner freedom is lacking, two tendencies emerge. Either a maliciousness develops, an ability to hate but not to love, which only seeks to attack and never really knows what it should defend or turn to (the special enmity against this people is often a product of such a perplexed condition), or else all culture that once developed there becomes, to an extent, a stagnant pool: nothing flows into it, nor does anything flow out of it any longer. In either case, in place of respect for itself there is now boastfulness and egotism. The sense of the great becomes stunted; the exaggeration of the insignificant flourishes; sentimentality supplants honest sensibility.

The old cultures along the Nile and in the valleys of the Euphrates and Tigris lost themselves, and the magnificent Greek spirit narrowed. They all saw no true task before them. In tasklessness, when their time comes, peoples and cultures die of this lack of faith. This is what the biblical verse in Proverbs means: "Where there is no vision, the people perish" (Prov. 29:18). One could also translate: where a people has not attained to history or has suffered the loss of its history, it perishes from within.

In a time when peoples and cultures lost their history and therefore lost their existence, this people preserved its history and its existence; it enriched and fortified them by clinging to the task of its life and giving it new content. In a decisive move, too, it undertook the great experiment of placing the individual in its life's task, in history. On the whole, this was achieved. As scarcely elsewhere, an inclusive community, a *communio historiae*, was created in history.

For the individual, the task of life, primarily and peremptorily, means all of the tasks of the day, the many commandments, these manifold appearances of the one commandment of life as every new day brings them forward. Through the constant, faithful dedication to all these details, the days become a man's life, and reach a complete and integrated life that, after all, is more than the rise and fall of single days; and all the little tasks become the one, the complete task, which is more than a broad or narrow line of tasks. Through the task of life the messianic, the promise of fulfillment, enters shining and "comforting" with its continual renunciation into the finite earthly existences.

It is otherwise with peoples. For them the task of life indicates first something messianic, a conscious service to the idea, to the promise, a clear-eyed service to a vision, which must be performed by every generation. Through such service, the generations, many of whom perhaps experience disappointment to the point of despair, fit into an historical unity. In each generation history reveals itself, and into the messianic vision there enters, with its demands and its fulfillment, the determined work of every generation. In the great task of life the many tasks create a place for themselves and make their claim. They are imposed for the sake of the one great task. What is withheld from one generation, succeeding generations then achieve. For them and for their sake, and therefore for the sake of the goal, that generation worked, whose labor seemed to be in vain. That which seemed vain in the passing becomes fulfillment in the enduring; it was part of the way, this way of the great, the complete demand.

Ever again it is shown that the commandment of the day and the messianic promise, the "law" and the "good news," demand and authorize one another. They belong together, so that the totality may come to be, so that the one truth may appear. The task of life realizes itself in the tasks of the day, and the tasks of the day fulfill themselves in the task of life.

This living, inner unity of the two, this spiritual ability to possess the future and the beyond in the here and now, to accept the time to come with the immediacy of the hour, this unity of action and of vision always infused new strength into this people. Now the unique character of this people began its rebirths and thus ever again created its own forms. This uniqueness had grown through a millennium. Only what has grown is reborn, and only that which is reborn passes the test of time.

The Way of Torah

The verse in Proverbs which points in warning to the peoples who have no vision also shows the way: "But he that keepeth the law, happy is he" (Prov. 29:18). The first psalm, which introduces the major motif of the entire book, speaks of the Torah in similar apposition. To the man "whose way is lost," another is held in contrast: he who has "his delight in the Torah of Him-Who-Is; and in His Torah does he meditate day and night." The Torah was also praised as the great gift, which Moses had entrusted to his people. In one of the verses which leads to the "blessing, wherewith Moses the man of God blessed the children of Israel before his death," we read: "Moses commanded us a Torah, an inheritance of the congregation of Jacob" (Deut. 33:1,4). Thus was this idea of the Torah reborn in the second millennium.

Like *hokhmah* and *kavvanah*, "Torah" is an untranslatable word. It is untranslatable because no other people, no other cultural or language group has achieved an idea of its own like the one which found expression in the word "Torah." It has been translated in many ways, as "law," "teaching," or "instruction." None of these words communicates the complete and intrinsic content. The first of these, the word "law," to which the old Greek Bible translation gave preference, even led to many a misunderstanding. A harsh tone could sound with it, a tone of something dictated and imposed, of something statutory and oppressive. In its original sense, the word meant the choice of the right goal, just as, conversely, the biblical word for sin originally referred to missing the mark. The best way of doing justice to what the word contains would be the translation: the task of life, in essence, that which God has set before man to do.

The word reveals its significance in a twofold way. One is its inner connection with the messianic. There is no true messianic confidence without a realization of Torah, without the "ways of the Torah." In the tasks of life the messianic encounters man step by step, and keeps meeting him here and now. Torah is the fulfillment of the present in which, generation after generation, "the fulfillment of the future" commences anew in order to lead mankind forward. The other direction of the meaning of "Torah" is toward belief. Belief is the perspective chosen by man, and Torah the line which he has stretched from this vantage point. There can be no right way without the enduring, correct perspective. Torah cannot exist without belief. And the perspective is not the right, the real one, if no path leads forth from it. Belief is inauthentic without Torah.

Belief, Torah, and messianic certainty belong together inwardly. If one of them is lacking, or if one leaves the others, they are without their proper, full strength. The unity, the completeness is lacking. Belief is the strong bond with reality; the way which leads from it "does not become lost." Torah is the realization always to be renewed, always to be undertaken anew, always to be dared boldly; the belief that streams into it never dries up. The messianic is the completion and the fulfillment of the struggle for the realization, the completion which gives the day its justification. Whoever absorbs it into himself neither tires nor despairs. Belief without Torah would be stagnant, would be encapsuled—an unfruitful belief which also loses its messianic quality quickly. Torah without belief would be an external separation, a mere "busyness," an acting without content in the realm of that which is then called religion; in this, too, the messianic would disappear. The messianic without Torah would be an ecstatic raving, a dreaming for the sake of the dream. There is a wandering forth into the distance which is nothing else than a flight from the commandment; thus belief itself is abandoned. Spiritually, the three belong together. They must be one if they are to live and bear fruit. They form the threefold demand rising out of the one eternal ground, set before man for him to make a decision of his moment, his road, and his goal. Together they are the decision of man in the life which God has given him. Thus Moses said to his people: "Choose life" (Deut. 30:19).

Here the life of man is recognized as a commandment from God. Life, so it was understood, can and should open itself to the tasks of the day, because it is itself a task. As many as the days are the commandments; and life can and should open itself to all of them, because it is itself a commandment. The days of man change, and in them rest the changing fates. But the life of man can and should be more than just a sequence of days, more than a fate that has come to be and is coming to be. When man chooses his life, when he makes it the task which God sets for him, the commandment that God has given him, then even amidst the flux of the immediate his life will have its share in what is coming to be; amidst the coming and going, the rise and the descent, it will possess its individuality, its line, its style, its imprint, its "likeness of God." When he makes his life the decision for God, man grasps the great possibility. Men are born in various situations. There are the narrow and broad vistas, barren stretches, and gardens of existence. But whatever the nature of the place, a way can lead from it. Wherever a man is placed, he can build upon a foundation, and he can see a promise before him. Through his life he can decide upon God. That is the deepest and most essential meaning of "Torah," just as it is the deepest and most essential meaning of all belief and of every message granted mankind.

The Torah

As the second millennium commenced, the word "Torah" became the designation of the Holy Scriptures and, within it, that of the Pentateuch in particular. "Torah" now became the Torah.

The Holy Scriptures encompassed twenty-four individual books according to the arrangement which became final at approximately the middle of this second millennium. These individual books were named and counted, and became known in their specific form and character. But in the thinking and feeling of the people, in the spiritual and intellectual relationship which teaching and learning continuously created, they signified but parts of a whole, the parts of the one Book, of the one testimony of the One God, entrusted to the "one people on earth." As there are no other gods before the One God, so there were to be no other books before this one Book, no books that would be honored in like fashion. Since then, this people and this Book came to grow together, became one, as it were. In this Book this people possesses itself. This possession of itself, through this Book, ever again comes to challenge it, comes to set its task before this people. It discovers itself, and the great "if" of the selection by God can fulfill itself. An entrance into a higher domain is opened. The nearness of God begins to speak; world joins world.

This Book is a great opening-of-self. It grants the soul of man a seeing and hearing, a seeing and hearing of that which previously was not seen or heard, and is seen or heard nowhere. It is no mere accident of language that these two words "seeing" and "hearing" keep turning up in this Book. What it says shows something and at the same time, lets a voice out of the distance be heard. The present rises out of a past and raises itself to a future. What occurs in the finite, reaches back and outward into infinity. Never is anything to be seen and heard only for itself. A later thinker of this people, Spinoza, demanded contemplation *sub specie aeternitatis*, "under the aspect of eternity," so that thought might become knowledge. This is a part of that which is characteristic of the Holy Scriptures, and is therefore demanded from one who would enter it. But what Holy Scripture gives and demands is something more encompassing. It demands both seeing and hearing, so that one cannot remain without the other. Thinkers may after all be divided into seeing and hearing ones. Spinoza was one of the seeing thinkers, one of the great ones, but what the gift of hearing gives to genius was not granted to him. What man learns through the Bible, so that by its strength he may penetrate into it continually to derive something new, is the unity of hearing and seeing. Worlds join worlds in this respect.

The All-Embracing World of the Bible

On the whole, the Bible is a world extending in every direction. Everything toward which human contemplation and searching may tend is here brought to expression or to new meaning, is set into word, allegory, or symbol. Revelation and creation, mystery and commandment, promise and determination of life all are to be found in it. All phases of the soul, when it unfolds and when it retreats, sound forth: praying and calling, loving and longing, fearing and trembling, doubting and questioning, waiting and hoping, humility and reverence, the faith of inquiry and the certainty of understanding. Everything in which the will can gain speech, when it rises to the spirit, and the spirit, when it then lifts the will up unto itself, speaks here and reveals the near and the far: the tendency to the grand and the entry to the innermost, the prophecy and the teaching, the wisdom and the proclamation, the moral and the legal, the surmise and the experience, the vision and the law. Everything in which the community seeks the coherence and finds continuity, where parts join a whole, here finds its statement and its affirmation, has its direction and its forward thrust: the worlds and the totality, the forms and the cosmos, the creatures and the all-pervading life, the lands and the earth, the I and the we, the man and the fellow man, the places and the all-upholding soil, the peoples and humanity, the borders and what moves across them. Everything in which thesis and antithesis seek unity and where harmony sounds out of contradiction has here its form and its voice: the near and the far, the narrow and the wide, the suffering and the consolation, death and life, guilt and reconciliation, the enchaining and the liberating, the degrading and the redeeming, the lost and the promised, the discord and the peace, the past, the present, and the future.

As the second millennium commenced, this people felt and experienced the extraordinary quality of this Book to the extent that they considered it to be more than a book. It appeared to them as the great constructive principle of creation, the great ordering power, the logic, the *hokhmah* which fits and holds everything together. Previous to the Torah there had been chaos, and without it there would be chaos. Because of the Torah, or as another of the teachers said, for its sake, that it might exist, the world had come to be. One of the teachers used the Greek word "basis," in its Greek form, in order to indicate what Torah signifies for all that exists: it is the supporting foundation. A daring expression, one that might sound presumptuous to one who does not know this people, was attempted by a pious preacher. (Only one of the pious ones could dare venture this—on the lips of any other man it would indeed have been a blasphemy.) He said: "The Holy One, praised be He, said: when this people goes astray, they may also have left Me! If only they keep My Torah! In it there will be the driving force, it will effect the return to Me." This Book had given this man such a depth of comfort and confidence that he could hear such a voice from above. What he experienced in his generation, in a time of bypaths and blind alleys, is different from that which sounds forth in the joyously grateful outcry of the Psalmist: "Unless Thy Torah had been my delight, I should then have perished in mine affliction" (Ps. 119:92).

Centuries of history and experience lie between the one statement and the other, between psalmist and preacher. The preacher had experienced the complete dynamic which fills this Book. He did so in his days, when the certainty of this people's belief was threatened, when ideas and hopes wanted to lead them from the one way to the One God. The light and the dark days, in which this Book was to be not only possession but also strength, had begun.

When the great test is put to a man, his whole life, all which he has had and has been and which lies before him, enters this one hour. His whole life speaks to him. So, too, is it demanded of a people when it is put to the great test. Its whole history in its journey from the former to the now, from the now to the coming becomes its present. Past and future must pass the test of the now. The now is confronted, and past and future can become vital forces only as they stream into the present.

Only rarely, and then not always as a blessing, did this people have days without spiritual and intellectual strain. Then perhaps the Bible could appear as a book written and in a sense ready at hand, a book that told of what had been, that stated what had been commanded, that announced what the expectation then foresaw. But when the questions pressed and oppressed, when question crowded question, then this Book had to elevate itself and set out on its ceaseless way. As the Book of this people it could only be, to a degree, a book in movement. It had grown together with this people. When the people was reborn, the Book was also reborn, and the rebirth of the Book created the rebirth of the people. Its history runs from present to present.

The Oral Law and the Written Law

To designate this unique quality, this dynamic nearness and immediacy of the Book, a special, characteristic expression was coined in early rabbinic times. One said that the Book presented itself in a two-sided manner: as "Written Torah" and as "Oral Torah." It could also be rendered thus: It is a book composed and written down, and it is at the same time a movement, awakened and renewing itself from within. It has its word with which it begins and its word with which it ends. But in reality it never ceases and never ends; ever again it commences and continues. Its word seems to be a word that was spoken once, but it is in reality a task that starts itself again and again. He who believes that he carries it in his hand does not have it; but he who is driven by it, to him has it come. One of the teachers could say: "The men of this Book can never rest completely [and added with hyperbole], not in this world nor in the world to come." It is a book in movement, and therefore it belongs to no generation and to no epoch completely. It endures and remains because it takes its way from generation to generation. Therefore it is the "Written Torah" and the "Oral Torah."

In the spheres of the soul, every movement is a question and a demand. The men of this Book are, therefore, the ever-questioned and the ever-commanded, as this people then come to be too. Both question and demand derive from one and the same spiritual root. The real question is the one which grows out of a readiness to fulfill the commandment, and the real demand is the one which can also answer a question of the soul. Thus this people became what it is, a people of many commandments and of much inquiry and meditation. In the true commandment the question is always born again, and in the true question the commandment is always reborn. There are no static questions and no static commandments. As long as the hours change and the days of man turn, the final question will never be asked and the final demand never raised.

Midrash: Interpretation and Search

The concepts of interpretation, of exposition, are too narrow and too weak to characterize the Oral Torah. Certainly Oral Law explains and clarifies biblical words, points out connections and peculiarities, and has even developed special methods for these. But that is not its unique character. It itself terms its mode and manner "searching," or "midrash." What this searching seeks to find is, as the expression has it, that "which is written," something which "announces," which "teaches." The word is not to be closed off; its gates are to remain open, so that question and commandment can have entrance and exit in their ways. The many questions, born out of the commandments and creating commandments, circle around about the One God, the one great, firmly established answer which accompanies man in the great task of life set by belief and the fulfillment promised by the message. This is likewise true in miniature of midrash. Around each of the words which are written and stand firmly established as such, the many questions and what is contained in them move in and out, up and down. "When" and "why" here are the frequent beginnings of speech. A great "searching" takes place, so that what "has been taught," what is "announced" will be heard.

The supposition thus becomes the premise; the thesis is also the hypothesis. Nothing is therefore isolated, existing somewhere just for itself and to be observed by itself; everything enters in interrelationship. It is as though a power of attraction held sway here and brought everything into connection with everything else. Analogies can move along their paths and streets. The single word, as insignificant as it might appear, thus gains its meaning. In its relationship with other words it shows its special validity, it begins to say something particular. One word lets the other speak. That is the foundation as well as the method of the Oral Torah. One could call it an analysis for the sake of synthesis. Through the investigation of the individual, a reaffirmation of the system keeps taking place. This "searching" is therefore without end, for there is no end to individuality.

This determined the whole approach and manner of thought of this people, and again a paradox within its nature was created. On the one side there exists within it the reverence for the particular, the sense of the insignificant, the respect for the little: the little man, the little commandment, the little circle, the little hope—often to the point of exaggeration. On the other side there exists within it the living sense of the connected, or that which can mutually find itself, a striving and driving to a system in which all interlock, a drive for the world-embracing task, to the far reaches of the problem—here too at times to the point of exaggeration. Sometimes the two—inquiring after particulars and after system—went their separate ways, until they did not understand one another or turned against one another. This did not benefit this people's self-understanding, a necessary presupposition of its will to live in goodness. The two need one another.

The method used by the intellect has developed its particular differentiating form in the various cultural spheres. But everywhere and always one thing holds true: thinking becomes knowledge only when it is an orderly thinking; through this order judgment is distinguished from the sudden notion. And thinking can only be called orderly when the whole can justify itself through the detail and the detail learns to understand itself through the whole. In this people, the two required one another even more necessarily. Through its second millennium this fusion of the two became a manner of thinking, and a form of thought became a manner of life with this people, the logic of existence. The way is the one and only way. But the forms in which this people's thinking gradually developed its style have their peculiarities and occasionally their oddities. However, the line which is to determine everything and in the best days has determined everything anew, is that of orderly thinking and of orderly mentality, so that the particular does not ignore the general and the general does not look down on the particular. Only when they are fitted into each other again does the human intellect develop into a cosmos, into a creative order.

The Oral Law Becomes the Talmud

It had been the hope in early rabbinic days that the Oral Torah would remain what the name implied. It was to convey the living tradition from teacher to student, who in turn was made a teacher by passing this on with all the possibilities it gave to thought. It was not to become a final and conclusive possession. But the needs of the time spoke more strongly. Teachers in whom the tradition lived and created died as martyrs in days of persecution. Out of the depths of need the worry arose that "Torah would be forgotten in Israel." With doubts and pangs of conscience, much that was "oral" was then written down. Yet the dynamism of the spoken word which had developed and grown through the centuries was irresistible. The spoken word with its tradition continued in new forms. Much later, after about seven generations, under the pressure of an imperium of faith that had extended its rule to Palestine, when checks and restraints imposed themselves more and more upon the places of intellectual work, this old worry renewed itself. What teachers had spoken and students had received was again written down, first of all in Palestine and then, under the impact of such authoritative example, on the soil of Babylonia where congregations, from the time of the Exile, had established themselves and had founded schools. Thus, through the writing down, the Oral Torah, in two periods, became different books and yet a single book. Two books, the first called the Mishnah, the "teaching," and the second called the Gemara, the "continuing," were now in the hands of the people. Together they were one book: the Talmud, the "learning."

That which this millennium of teaching and continuing instruction had implanted into this people continued to grow. This book, written down but not really composed, remained a book which interpretation filled with ingenuity and loving industry kept studying. But above all there remained the driving strength through which it had originated. This strength was but the result of the never-ending movement which emanates from the Bible, grasps man, and then leads him back again to the Bible that he might strive to understand it. The searching, the untiring questioning, the expanding vision has not ceased since then.

The *Sefer Yetzirah* ("Book of Creation"), the first product of a mysticism that appeared at the end of the second millennium, was the work of an unknown author or perhaps a school of mystics, though it was certainly the conclusion of a long, esoteric oral transmission. In this "Book of Creation," the Holy Scriptures are the very essence of all creative building power, as the older teachers had already said. All comes from the One God, and in the Holy Scriptures the ways of this becoming are revealed to us. Using an image from Neoplatonic philosophy—the philosophy in which Eastern thinking conquered that of the West—an image which the author of *Sefer Yetzirah* tries to find in the theophany of the prophet Ezekiel, he says that out of the One God the many arise and press onward, thence to return to Him, the One. The mystic's image was Neoplatonic, but he may have looked and listened to the Holy Scriptures at the same time. Out of the Scriptures breaks forth strength which penetrates everywhere, and whoever is taken by it is drawn toward this one Book, drawn back to it ever anew.

The Holy Scriptures was and remained this force, even when the

Talmud came to exist. The Talmud never wanted nor could be that which the Holy Scriptures is; never was it said of it what was said of the Bible, that the Holy Spirit speaks out of it. But it nevertheless achieved something great, something unique for this people. The Talmud made this people come alive inwardly, so that it would always search again, so that it might never cease to live in its Bible, so that through its Book this people might always be reborn. To use a metaphor of Philo of Alexandria, Philo Judaeus, who also belongs in the history of the Oral Torah, an image used also by the ancient preachers in Palestine, the Talmud became a wonderful instrument of motion.

The Language of the Talmud

A completely individual style reveals itself in the Talmud as well. Like the plastic biblical style, the style of the Talmud was already determined by the nature of the Hebrew language as it developed in Bible times and then through the Bible. This language, in distinction to Greek and Latin, does not encourage a wealth of phrases, roundabout ways upon which a sentence first moves, saying many things before it comes to that which it should say. The Hebrew language is a language of immediate goals; it is the expression of immediate thinking. It speaks as if it too were directed by the idea of the one and the whole. The overtones of a language give it its absorbing qualities, but they may not detract from its directness, its intentionality. That which is only incidental sounds and resounds in this people's speech, audibly and clearly, but never interferes. A trend toward the sublime thus pervades it. When a Greek author who was able to compare languages wrote his book "On the Sublime," his example for sublimity in language was the sentence in the story of creation: "God said: 'Let there be light.' And there was light."

In the first draft of the Oral Torah, the six orders of the Mishnah, the old linguistic style, adapted to the new subject and the new task, appears in a new form. Precision dominated without ever causing monotony. However, in the second work, the Gemara, the manner seems to have changed. A dialectic, a tense movement, is characteristic of it. The "leading onward," the forward direction, seems to have become a leading in circles. One who approaches it from the outside may perhaps think that before him are twisted and serpentine roads that do not point forward. Then, as he moves along, he becomes aware of a central point, and he recognizes how everything strives toward it, indeed, how everything was guided toward it from the beginning. He sees the style and comprehends the order. It is the style of directions dominated by a focal point. From here and from there, sometimes from nearby and sometimes from afar, the lines go forth; but clearly unhindered, each one strives toward the goal, the focal point. Precision rules here as in the Mishnah. It shows its structure as soon as everything is seen from the focal point.

Architecture, music, and language, in process of becoming forms of thinking, reveal many similarities in patterns of development. An architectural style may thus serve as illustration: the manner of ordering, as fully developed by the Roman style in its first, its classical period, in its walls and portals, can be set against the style of the Gemara for comparison. In its buildings, too, it seems at first as though the whole loses itself in its parts, in the fullness of shapes, forms, and lines which seem to strive, now toward one another, now away from each other, now against one another. But when the focal point is understood, it becomes obvious how every individual thing has led to it: the plan, the order, the structure uniting the details.

Talmudic Logic

Through its style, the Talmud taught the people patient thinking; through the centuries it educated it to a patient learning. And, what is more, the logic of patience became the logic of life, and a philosophy of life thus penetrated this people. In the course of time, almost all of this people came close to the Talmud, to a greater or lesser extent. But to be close to it, to penetrate, meant walking the way of perseverance. For what mattered here was not only one's receptivity to particulars, but arriving at connections, constantly discovering something new. The word "learning" fused itself with the word "Talmud," and out of this word "learning" a twofoldness sounded: the quality of the will to endure, not to tire, always to be ready to begin anew; and the quality of confidence possessed by the searching investigator, the discoverer, who knows that he may come to exclaim, as once the master of the art of mathematics exclaimed: "Eureka, I have discovered it!" Such learning could never be peevish; it could afford to be patient. Later on, it gave birth to its own songs. It could itself be called a song of patience, assured of fulfillment.

This patience of learning was accompanied by a vision, a vision of learning in which heights revealed themselves and distances opened. Thus the Talmud encompassed not only the legal, but also the poetic—both aspects were included in its wide scope. Its task, according to the old expression, is not just the "halakah," the "direction of going," the right way, but also the "haggadah," the "direction of announcing," the right insight and outlook. Both are in the domain of Talmud, and they do not stand alongside each other, let alone opposed to each other, but they are inwardly and basically interconnected. Only together do they comprise the totality. "Learning" here means penetrating the demands of the day and its routine, penetrating into the fullness of its commandments, but also into that which stands behind the day and reaches beyond the single day with the fullness of wisdom, poetry, and promise, with a whole wealth of enduring meaning. Everything emanates from a unity, no matter how many spheres it travels through.

Talmudic Literature

The force which created the Talmud extended its effects beyond the second millennium. After a time which only desired the one Book, the Bible, and next to it only the Oral Torah, a time which only hesitantly decided that it would write down this other, there came the centuries which wanted to possess many books. But they too, these manifold books, had something of the old character of the spoken word as it is possessed by the Talmud. With all their differences, this yet gave them a certain unity of style. They have the line of tradition, the passing on of something received. They often show a personal strain, and a particular talent or a determined will is clearly evident in many of them. Still, generally, it seems as if no one speaks of his special searching and inquiring and finding, or at least not exclusively, but rather as if a man stood before us who wants to pass on to the next generation a tradition that has been entrusted to him. These books are also new forms of an Oral Torah. Perhaps all literature is the transmission of a cultural possession, but in these books something differs, and something is completely different. In them there lives not only the wish that the book will find the reader, but a stronger desire of one in search that he might attract other seekers, so that "Torah be not forgotten in Israel." In that sense one spoke afterward of an uninterrupted "chain of tradition" (*shalshelet ha-kabbalah*).

The two directions of talmudic thought also continued in themselves. Both created a literature which reaches into depths as well as into distances. It is characteristic of them that they generally preserved the unity of their relationship as derived from the Bible and Talmud. That which deals with law and its custom, on the one hand, and with the poetical, mystical, and philosophic on the other hand, are not closed to one another. They are considered part of a totality, and therefore they possess validity. It cannot simply be attributed to a wealth of talent that, in the third millennium, philosophers and mystics and poets all explored the law. Something more intrinsic and deeper is disclosed. The men of such universality strove after this totality—or at least preserved the sense of it—because they were aware that the part detached from the whole loses its true life. There were days among this people in which halakah and haggadah—taking these two concepts in their broadest meaning—wished to exist by themselves or thought that they could do without one another. Then halakah shriveled, and haggadah evaporated and lost its essence.

The inner relationship between the two, wherever it was understood, etched a special highlight on the richly formed paradox which gives the existence of this people its individual character. Halakah and haggadah met here; and in their connection, they left their imprint not only on the world of thought, but also on the personal realm. On one side the man who experienced such a union experienced a living and loving sense for the legal, for statutes and ordinances, for the ordered, established, statutory. He is not afraid of the many laws and prohibitions. On the other side such a man experiences a lively desire for the free and active, for the outgoing, for that which drives forward, as well as for individual expression and personal attempt. He is not afraid of many and daring thoughts. Such an attitude appeared always only where the two directions coalesced. Only when a man lives in both, in the "law" as well as in philosophy, mysticism, and poetry, only then does what is most personal in his existence unfold.

Paradox and Tension in Talmudic Thought

A general human problem is revealed here. With the harmony and reconciliation of the contradictions in which his life seems to move, man leaves the state of the primitive. The so-called savage knows only impulses and frustrations, satisfaction and failure, the friendly and the hostile. He leads his life within those circuits. As man began to think, he then entered upon a different stage. For contemplation means to rise above that which happens in oneself and around oneself, in order to be able to gaze down. He stands no longer merely in the domain of that which flows out of him and presses upon him, but is in still another sphere, the world of his thoughts concerning his condition. When man began to think in this fashion, he became a man of two worlds, with their differences and contrasts. The paradox took place within his life. All the development of intellectual, spiritual, artistic, and moral culture—the history which is not only the history of tools, but of ideas too—is determined by the manner and reach of such thinking. If thoughts are for themselves alone, this history becomes a vanity that must exhaust itself; and if human existence is denied entry into the world of ideas, existence becomes a repetitive baseness.

Both of these happened whenever men were not capable or tired of fulfilling the problem and the task of the paradox, when they thought to find their life exclusively in the domain of ideas, or when they were ready to retreat into a romantic, political, or nationalistic primitiveness. (Such sought-after primitiveness becomes more and more a barbarism of feeling and acting.) True history, and also true personal life, consists of a reconciliation in the human spheres, and is what is meant by the biblical word "peace." This peace is a creative achievement. Like everything creative, it reveals an entrance of the eternal, the divine, into the human domain. It is an act of piety, for piety means creating doorways through which the higher world enters into the finite, limited world.

Only the soul's power to encounter tension is able to encompass the paradox. This power is what the biblical word "spirit" connotes. Spirit is the ability to bind together, to unite, to reconcile, to bring peace. This people, therefore, if it wishes to exist, can never be primitive, can never become one-sided. If it is to live, the spirit must live in it. The Oral Torah has been the ever self-renewing power which, by means of the knowledge of the unity, held together the differences and the contrasts which a millennium of activity permitted to arise within this people. To note the extent to which conflict has its way and finds expression here, is a continual source of amazement. Every thought, every desire, and every hope were permitted to search and to investigate, to struggle and to push forward, as long as the one, all-determining focal point was firmly established: He-Who-Is, the One God, His mystery and His promise, His commandment and His grace—He, the One, and none beside Him. Because this was established, it was possible, in days when teachers contradicted other teachers, for the word to be heard like a voice from above: "These *and* these are the words of the living God."

The Oral Torah was such a voice from above. It created an epoch, because it was born of the spirit, of the power that brings together, that fits together, and that holds together, because it kept the spirit alive and transmitted it. Only where the spirit lives and where the spirit rules is a true tradition found. Only there something specific is transmitted, not just for its own sake, but that it might be reborn, created by the spirit and creating spirit. The spiritless, like the common, only knows repetition. In the genuine tradition rests the power of rebirth. The one spirit always re-creates form for itself. Of this the men of the Oral Torah were certain, and therefore they could say: "That which they taught goes back to Moses, our teacher."

The Men of the Great Assembly

When the "Torah, by word of mouth" was written down, those who carried the tradition indicated in the introductory sentence of the "Sayings of the Fathers" (*Pirke Abot*) the manner of transmission to them: "Moses received Torah on Mt. Sinai and transmitted it to Joshua, and Joshua to the elders and the elders to the prophets, and the prophets transmitted it to the men of the Great Assembly."

Torah is spoken of here, not *the* Torah. Something which again and again shall find expression has been placed into history, into the sequence of generations, to live in search and inquiry—something never finished, a task without end. As a talmudic expression puts it: "generation, generation, and its searchers." These men were not to be merely followers in a line of succession. Occasionally the times followed one another on the same level; occasionally they were deeply separated. But the task always built a bridge. The word "transmitted" stands twice in this sentence from the "Sayings of the Fathers." The repetition gives it emphasis, probably not without intent: "Moses transmitted it to Joshua . . . the prophets transmitted it to the men of the Great Assembly." It is not easy for a prophet to transmit, and it is not easy to receive from a prophet; personalities cannot be transmitted and cannot be taken over. But here also the task creates the connection, and the sequence of unlike generations becomes history, if only the task remains.

Our sentence continues: "They [these men of the Great Assembly, of the Senate at Jerusalem in the Persian period] said three things: Be deliberate in judgment, and raise up many disciples, and build a fence for the Torah." This was a threefold truth for them, ever to be passed on, ever again to be accepted: judgment, education, and preservation of Torah: judgment as task and not as instrument; education as commandment and not as privilege; and Torah which should be placed into the world and, at the same time, guarded and protected against the world. It is significant that the first two demands find clear and unequivocal expression, but a poetic image is sought for the third. The first two constitute relatively sure and simple ways in the visible, almost tangible relationship of man to man. The third can only be shown through an image. The worried glance that looked around saw the inheritance, the unique amidst the people and amidst the world, endangered by the one-sided, the halves that masqueraded as wholes. It saw the unique threatened by so much which was called holy and was in truth unholy: threatened also by mysteries, by philosophies, by proclamations, and by much which seemed to elevate and in the end only debased. These men saw or surmised all of this in its multiformity, in its fluctuation, its dispersion; and, indicating and comparing, they could only say: "Make a fence for the Torah," let nothing foreign force itself upon our possession.

The Great Assembly does not represent a mere historical reconstruction, as has sometimes been assumed. The news out of that time of Exile and Restoration, the first centuries of the second millennium, is pitifully meager. It was a quiet time, and it needed to speak little of itself. Community life could proceed in peace, for it took place within the Persian provincial system which assured peaceful borders. But if knowledge can be gained in retrospect and through retroactive conclusions, drawing upon later days which do give definite report of themselves, then what was achieved in those two centuries of the Great Assembly is reasonably clear. Upon old historical soil, but amidst completely changed claims and in the face of basically new demands, room was prepared for that which had grown and had proved its strength. New forms of the old moral and intellectual life began to unfold. Confronting cultures which were merely cultures, confronting religions which could only be religions, an old religious culture grew and flourished. That is to say that the two worlds into which thinking man sees himself placed, that of revelation and that of investigation, that of the one great answer and that of the many problems and doubts, that of decision and that of obligation, that of infinity and eternity and that of limitation and of transitoriness, that of grace and that of error, all these were led toward unity in new searching, toward the unity in which this people could ever again find its own individuality. That which had grown, this belief filled with the drive for knowledge, these searching statements filled with the power of the commandment, was reborn. Only where the two worlds have met one another, so that the unity encompasses them, only where areas of culture and religion do not merely exist side by side, can a religion filled with culture, a culture filled with religion, come into existence ever again—a growth without end and therefore a task without end.

The Fence Around the Torah

These three injunctions, judgment, education, and the preservation of individuality, all commandments put in a new form for this people, became a living possession of the people in this era. Yet here too the great demand had often met with weak men who sometimes avoided and sometimes evaded it; or it came upon little men who wanted to take the great for themselves through artful diminution. There were those who saw judgment as a tool to be manipulated. They did not see before them the sublime idea toward which they were to strive. There were those for whom the knowledge carried within, great or small, real or assumed, was only a possession which they had earned and of which they now wanted to dispose. They did not understand the duty resting in this possession. They did not have the modesty of the student, nor the humility of the teacher. There were those who, at times, forgot the Torah for the "fence," men of the fence without the Torah. They strove for security, and did not know what it was that they were to secure. But despite pettiness or insufficiencies, which can be and will continue to be man's earthly lot, despite many other lacks in which virtues became constricted or exaggerated, despite all of this, the greatness was accepted and transmitted.

In those years this inheritance became an ever-renewed possession, an ever-renewed task, a justice that remains conscious of itself and therefore also of its social task. Therefore, this inheritance does not serve expedience nor become subservient to might. It possesses a dedication to education alive with the piety which seeks to fulfill a commandment of God, a pedagogy which, as a talmudic expression says: "has concern for the children of the poor, for Torah will go forth from them." It possesses a strong sense of the individual and the personal which nonetheless opens itself to all that which moves the world outside, and thereby creates continually a characteristic manner of thinking, feeling, and striving, a life-style confronting the world, even opposing the world, yet remaining in the world and for its sake. Out of such a unity, true religious culture could arise.

The inner connection which binds these three injunctions together in the personal sphere exists above all in the historical sphere where it functions as a law of relationship, a law of mutual rise and fall. Where justice falls, there too education sinks, and one's own conscience declines. So does the lessening or the weakening of any one bring on the downfall of the other two. In the same way, they can only rise or come to life together. There is no isolated justice, no isolated education, no isolated feeling for self. Out of the same soil, out of the inner, moral freedom, out of this living knowledge of what God commands, they all in like manner draw their strength. The secret of all worthwhile efforts to guide life, individual or communal, is the understanding of this relationship. When one of the three seeks to displace the others or one of the others, it only displaces itself in the end. In the long run, there cannot exist, each for itself, a government of law, a government of education, or a national government, although in theory or even in fact, the attempt has been made to create such entities. Inner freedom cannot be partitioned.

The Pharisaic Movement

The historical achievement of the Pharisaic movement is that they kept this understanding alive. One can only speak of a Pharisaic movement, and not of a Pharisaic party, just as the Sadducean group and the Essenic circle, generally compared or contrasted with the Pharisees, should also not be designated as parties. Flavius Josephus, an historian of this people, spoke of them as parties. He wanted to recount the many aspects of his people to the Romans and the Greeks who had to think of parties whenever they thought of differences in a society that had its own internal development. A party wishes to win adherents, to unite them, to lead them to success; but a movement wants to awaken the conscience and effect a change in life. Actually this people was at that time seized by the Pharisaic movement which might even be called the Pharisaic awakening.

To accept in all seriousness the great demand of Sinai, "And ye shall be unto Me a kingdom of priests, and a holy nation" (Ex. 19:6), to take it seriously always and everywhere, this was the great idea which emanated from this movement. An idea is great and genuine only when it becomes an enduring task; and such a task can only be one which approaches everyone, each exalted and humble soul, in the same manner. The manifold contrasts of caste and divisions of rank basically can be traced to groups which originally or retroactively ascribe to themselves a higher ideal. Upon it they base the claim to set themselves apart from others or to look down upon them. The circle of the conqueror, the usurper, the oppressor, is to be considered the domain of the higher idea for whose sake it is to remain protected and secured. The Pharisaic movement, in a decisive manner and with decisive historical success, undertook to bring the higher, the determining ideal to everyone simultaneously, so that they all might come to possess it now, completely. The law of Sinai, with which the true history of this people begins, was rejuvenated, in order to meet changed times and to create for itself new expression and new form. Now each individual was addressed even more strongly; to him, responsibility and through it the right to his place was more firmly given.

This too is part of that paradox in which higher human life attains fulfillment: The community carries the individual and is his assurance; but, at the same time, the individual lifts up the community and holds it upright. The individual has his definite place of action only in the community; and only through its individuals does a group experience its special, great hours. Here too there can, indeed must be, tensions. The individual and the group may suffer because of one another: the individual, because his existence is completely bound up with the group; and the group, because of the struggle and effort of many individuals within it. Only a spiritual energy can make individuals welcome within the community. There is a long history of groups and individuals losing one another, and equally of their discovering or rediscovering one another. Tired and living, arid and creative periods find their distinction in this.

The Pharisaic Achievement

The Pharisaic movement and the Oral Torah, to which it gave great life, reveal, on the one hand, a strong concern for the group and its life, and on the other, an extraordinary number of personalities giving leadership while contradicting and opposing one another. This world suffered them all, and they suffered one another, knowing that all of them had their right and their place within the whole. Rabbinic literature, as well as other writings of the time known to us through recent fortunate discoveries, gives testimony of this. Such tolerance could exist because the great demand raised then appeared in the same manner before both the rabbinic world and every individual within it. This world was to be "holy," and everyone within it was to be "holy." No man could represent another in this cause, or substitute for him, nor could he assume himself to be represented or substituted for by the existence of the totality. The same commandment was valid for the totality and for all within it: there was no great commandment for some and a little one for others.

Two related things were achieved by this. Everything was to be permeated by the great unity of morality and its reason, and thus by the respect for moral thinking, the life-giving air of true community. The community became a community in the task, a community for the sake of God's commandment. The totality, the people, the state, or the ecclesia could not stand as structures alone, nor have any separate existence. The community could not claim a special holiness for itself nor a unique profanity appropriate to it; it could not hope to possess a mind, a morality, or standards for itself alone. The unity of existence could not be compromised. On the other hand, moral action and moral thought, which arise from it, were made a permanent, constant concern of this people. Both thought and action must continuously be present, and are not merely to remain an occasional, necessarily incomplete, concern. The Pharisaic movement and its Oral Torah sought to take seriously the injunction of Moses: "when thou sittest in thy house, and when thou walkest by the way, and when thou liest down, and when thou risest up" (Deut. 6:7). The little man was guarded from thinking that he might endure without the task, the insignificant man from assuming that his was not the place, his not the hour. He won that moral respect for himself out of which alone moral existence can arise. The unity of existence, this inner truth which must become reality, is his. Thus existence becomes one and the same for the community and for its members.

The Pharisaic Idea of Righteousness

Three great commandments united here, proclaimed by the Bible and required by every new day: the commandments of holiness, of purity, and of righteousness (and "righteousness" here encompasses, in the religious ideal as in the language, the love that proves itself through action). The inner relationship between holiness, purity, and righteousness has been expressed in countless ways, through the understanding that one leads to the other. It is significant that the word which first stood for purity, for cleanness, now also means true proof within the law. And it is just as characteristic that in the exhortation to holiness the demand to guard oneself internally, to keep far from all that is low and common, from all the defilements, always speaks. But the sense of righteousness in particular is enlarged and deepened. After reading a verse from Psalms (145:7)—"They shall utter the fame of Thy great goodness and shall sing of Thy righteousness"—one might say that righteousness is the piety of the way, just as love is the piety of action. Within the Pharisaic movement and the Oral Torah, even language is in flux. As the idea demands new form, it also demands new linguistic expression. Language exists because of living ideas. It has its history because of the idea, just as it can be or can become devoid of history where the idea is lacking or where it withers away.

Yet above all else it is the commandment that is enriched in Pharisaism. Out of the great commandment grow the many little ones, the commandments of every day and every way. They appear to be little, but they too are great, it is often emphasized, for they are commandments from God. Man is not to wait for the extraordinary hour and for the place that clearly points into the distances in order to fulfill the commandment. The commandment waits for him every place, even in the narrow confines, to which he can give dignity. Wherever he stands, there too a commandment stands which is meant for him; and he may say there: "Praised be Thou, Eternal our God, King of the universe, who hast sanctified us through Thy commandments." Such is the principle of the Pharisaic movement. One of its teachers made the pronouncement: "The Holy One, praised be He, desired that Israel be just and pure. Therefore did He give it much Torah and many commandments."*

* *Pirke Abot*, I, 19 (cf. *The Authorized Daily Prayer Book*, ed. J. H. Hertz, p. 626).

It need scarcely be said that this all-embracing idea was not to be realized always and everywhere. There were those who were not capable of it or who failed one day. There were also those who would be "zealous" for the ideal and in this zeal ultimately, often very quickly, lost the ideal. There were also those who sought to make the idea exist for their own sake. Self-righteousness arose, in which righteousness becomes merely egoism and unkindness. And there were those, living in hypocrisy, to whom the ideal became the means for their private purposes. The Talmud speaks of all this with harsh words. It tells how a ruler of the Maccabean dynasty warned his successor of the "painted ones." He had come to know those whose piety was only a play which they acted before the world. Then and later there were many such, the so-called "pharisees," and they could at times stand in the way of the dignity of this people.

But one who sees the totality cannot fail to observe this dignity. An instinctiveness of doing and permitting, acting and evading, lives here and gives distinction to external existence, to the rush and pressure into which need often forces men. Man can always remain in his world of distinction. A daily unity of the intellectual and moral was achieved. A religious culture permeates everything, so that everything becomes its expression, everything small and everything great.

During the second millennium, as the Pharisees stand in the forefront, the time of martyrdom begins for this people. The martyr's death was not only the affirmation of an hour which demanded a final decision, but the climax of a life, the self-evident, final response given by the life of a man. The commandment of sanctification had spoken, and in its call the group heard itself and became conscious and certain of itself. In this martyr's testimony for the One God and for the grace of His commandment, the individual and the community stood as witnesses for each other, and gave each other their dignity. This was but the same testimony of their common prayer when they recited that ancient sentence: "Praised be Thou, Eternal our God, who hast sanctified us through Thy commandments."

III

Prayer and Learning

The Life of Prayer

In this second millennium, prayer unfolded its soul. At that time, it became the life of this people's life, the expression of all which its life possessed, strove for, and longed for. Everything therefore speaks in it: Torah and message, admonition and comfort, question and confidence, insight and peace. Nothing of what the soul seeks to say when it confronts itself or the world could exist without prayer. Philosophy and mysticism prayed here. Thought and creativity also formed prayer. Prayer became this people's confession of life, a confession which this people and every individual—always—placed before God. In prayer they brought themselves before God, the "congregation of Israel" and everyone within it, this "one soul in Israel"; they met one another in the sight of God. They spoke to God of themselves and therefore for themselves and therefore to themselves. The people thus became a praying people, just as it was a searching and learning, an awaiting and fulfilling people. It could not have been the one without being at the same time the other. Only thus could it have its true, its complete existence.

The ancient book of prayers, to which nothing compares, the Psalter, had reached over into the second millennium. It connects the two early epochs of this people's history. Whatever changed, however deep the breaks had become, the Psalter remained with the people. It lived in the people, receiving life and giving life; like Torah, prophecy, wisdom, not merely a book, the Psalter was an element of existence. The people itself prayed when one of its men prayed; the I became the We, and in the We the I spoke once again. In prayer the people encountered every individual, and every individual encountered his people. It was as if life were to encounter itself. The people spoke to itself before God.

Perhaps such a meeting, which is more than that which is called self-recognition, is the deepest and most intrinsic sense of prayer. In duty, in the commandment that he is to actualize, the human being finds an entry to his life, to his tasks as to his sorrows, to his goals as to his obstacles. He begins, and learns to understand himself; he is enabled to cope with the pattern of his days. In prayer, he enters into the world of his life, he holds a dialogue with his life. He learns to understand his world, the world that is within and around him; he is enabled to cope with it. The man to whom duty does not come will scarcely be able to pray truly; and he who cannot pray, while he knows his duty and serves it, will gain no knowledge of the world of his duty, of the world of commandment.

Houses of Prayer and Learning

The world of its life moved with this people when it went into exile. There life fashioned new organic forms for itself to house its creative spirit. It brought into being the form of the community and the congregation, the form of the divine service and its abode, the house of prayer and the house of study of the Holy Scriptures. These belong together; the house of the divine service was the "house of congregation" (*bet keneset*), and the congregation was the abode of the men of the house of God. With the same twofold words, "eidesia" and "synagoge," the Greek language designated each of the two, both the congregation and its house of God. The temple, the sanctuary of the ancient sacrificial service, lay shattered, part now of the distant past. The people did not forget it; the heartfelt memory remained ever alive. But before the eye, wherever this people lived, there was a house of prayer, of scripture reading, and it too was a sanctuary. When the homeward-bound exiles at last reached Mt. Zion and rebuilt the Temple, turning past into present in the ancient land, the present they had possessed remained. Everywhere in the land congregations arose and in them there arose "houses of congregation," houses of prayer, study, inquiry, houses of Holy Scriptures.

In these synagogues a union was fashioned that remained a characteristic of this people, and which determined its intellectual being, and thus its historical character, in many ways. In the synagogue prayer and learning were understood as two parts of a whole. In prayer man is placed before the foundation of all; he becomes aware of that *through* which and *because* of which he lives. In study, as the Talmud says, he is "led to the deed, to the task"; he discovers that *for* which he lives. Through prayer he is led beyond the day; through learning he is led into the day. To be within the day always, yet never only within the day; to hear in the day's demand the voice of eternity, and to discover in that which sounds forth out of eternity the day's demand: to indicate this simultaneous life within two worlds, in which two worlds receive a unity through human life, is the deepest, is the fundamental sense of the Holy Scriptures. Therefore, what the Book proclaims, what it commands, what it promises is unity. In the houses of Holy Scriptures, the houses of learning and prayer, this unity addressed all who entered. Dedication had its contemplative aspect here, and learning partook of divine service.

The Teachers

In this setting, a singularly human phenomenon arose, analogous to one in Greek philosophy. It is that of the teacher who speaks for himself, yet continues a tradition whose guarantor he remains. He wins students, leading them his way, and yet is himself conscious of being a disciple. He is a judge, a maker of decisions; he is at the same time a preacher, an admonisher, almost a supplicant. He is a man of action to whom the needs of the total community have been entrusted and who will, if necessary, act as its messenger, its apostle. He is the man of the commandment who brings the suffering and the longing of the congregation before God, whose devotion creates new poems of supplication and confidence. A sober examination, doubting, questioning, measuring in its approach to daily affairs, is united with that furthest depth of self-dedication that hears voices and sees visions. A prudent thoughtfulness, able to negotiate and mediate, is united with a simplicity, even a childishness of disposition. An ever acute mind in the tension of dialectic is united with an unwavering readiness, even an enthusiasm for martyrdom. Only men whose souls could encompass all of this were able to lead through extraordinary times.

The people called such a man "Master," "Rabbi"; it spoke of them as "the wise." They themselves wished only to be called "students of the wise." They would have rejected the term "scribe," this generally erroneous rendering of the Greek term which designates them "men of Scriptures." In a sense they wished throughout their days to be only apprentices, to stand as men within the people, learning among the learners, listening among the listeners, so that they might not have to descend, nor condescend. They received no recompense for their pains. When in later centuries need forced them to receive payment, those who did suffered inwardly for a long time. Occupations, which they somehow exercised—handwork, farming, trade—preserved their outward independence; their knowledge, as well as their piety, preserved their inner independence. They were free men. The authority which they possessed was achieved, not inherited. The decisive word was spoken by the personality. They could stand alone, although many of them warned against this, and they could join with others. But they did not need partners or adherents, not to mention a party, that their voice might be heard among the people. Their place was their own; for they were always themselves. Nothing arose anywhere else at that time which was in any way comparable to the nature of these men. Wherever, later, something comparable may be found, it developed, in one way or another, from this source.

Rabbis cannot be equated with prophets. The "hand of the Eternal" had not grasped them and brought them forward. Their portion was not the revelation of the Eternal seizing them, some with an ultimate upheaval, this deepest revolution of the soul. Yet only because of this people and its prophets could this people, in its second millennium, bring forth men who had the power of fulfillment, who guaranteed that the prophets had not lived in vain. Because these men were here and possessed their millennium, the prophets remained the prophets, Torah ever anew became Torah, and prayer never ceased. These men shaped the flow of history. Ever again, with clear consciousness, they brought their people to rededicate itself to that which alone can be its history. Without them, the people could not have endured this period, in which catastrophe followed catastrophe, crisis joined crisis, and change pushed upon change. Without these men this epoch would have been unable to create a new epoch.

Certainly the ideal did not become reality for everyone. Many passages in the Talmud show how zealousness occasionally might become jealousy; and pedantry, scholarship without strength of character. A way of thinking which is great in trivialities and is petty when confronting the great also reveal itself occasionally. But these patterns were peripheral. Beyond the periphery may be seen the extraordinary truth that in generation after generation a great, an uncommon demand found men who would accept it. In these men, a vital intellectual power, an unshakable will, a dedication ready for any sacrifice unfolded in response to the challenge. Human history has few parallels to this story.

It must be emphasized that only that special expansive power of the soul, and the will for unity rising from it, were able to meet the tasks set by this epoch. These people had to prove themselves early in tensions between social destinies that had developed out of different fates and dissimilar hypotheses. The world about them, in which they lived and wanted to live, which made and enforced demands upon them and on which they themselves also made demands, had changed greatly. This people had become a people of two lands, and it soon became a people of three lands. It was now a people in the land and a people in the lands. Even when it only thought of itself, when it wanted to observe and understand itself, it had to be able to attain a wider, a "catholic" view.

Ezra and Nehemiah

The one polarity was that between Palestine and Babylonia. More and more the congregations in the Babylonian land had achieved a character of their own, and were well aware of it. Together they fashioned a separate community. Furthermore, three times they had been required to send almost decisive help to the old land.

The first two times this help came through Ezra and Nehemiah. A double danger threatened destruction to those men who had returned from the Exile to the old land. Their intellectual and moral powers did not seem sufficient to withstand the difficulties posed both by an advancing enemy and an enforced confederation. These two men, one after another, then together, stepped into the breach. Called by the voice that addressed them, they had appeared and brought the assistance which became the deliverance.

The two books in which these men give account of their beginnings and their labors have entered the sequence of the biblical books. They reveal how the first millennium passed over into the second. One could say that these books are themselves the bridge of that passage. They are books of the old and of the new, of a growth that fulfilled itself, and of a rebirth that consummated itself. The final, the concluding time of prophecy was still close, and the time of the Oral Torah and of the Pharisaic movement had already begun. The two men who speak in these books stand before us, their characters clearly defined Henceforth, only one who shares something of their nature could be of help to this people in difficult times. Their particular task, as brought about by time and circumstances, could scarcely occur again, but their personality can become an enduring admonition. Personality cannot be inherited, but it can be a constant admonition, an admonition that is more than a so-called example, whose demand is often deemed fulfilled when one admires it.

Common to both men is a courageous piety—the prophetic trait in them, the piety which never seeks to be pious but always is, which never seeks to serve as piety but at all hours serves God, and therefore fears no changing hours nor any new commandment—in contrast to the cowardice which calls itself piety. Common to both is the power of love for their people, which adds new strength to the old from every disappointment, which is therefore able to scorn, but cannot hate. Common to both is meekness, the simplicity and genuineness of self-recognition, and therefore also the deep humility of prayer, this reality of all dedication. Because of this, their prayer finds individual expression.

These two men stood alongside one another; they complemented one another, and they knew they did. Yet they were distinct individuals. It was not just that Ezra was a man of thought and Nehemiah was a man of the way and the action; nor that one understood how to awaken the people, and the other was able to lead and to direct. Rather their point of departure, the sphere of their origin differed, and they probably only met one another on the way and later at the goal. For Ezra, the Torah was the world in which he lived; it gave the answer to all questions. What counted was to open it, to search it. He wished to give to the old land, that had to be renewed, men and Torah: men, that the Torah might live there; and Torah, that men might truly live there. Nehemiah's environment had been what is called the great world. Though set into it, surrounded by it, he had lived in the world of the Holy Scriptures. This was his own world, his individual, his personal world. He had gone to his brothers in the ancient land that they might live in it too, secured against the enmity near and far, protected from the baseness of the self-seeking in their own midst. They too, within the surrounding world, were to possess and keep their particularity.

In these two leaders, Ezra and Nehemiah, a new character, a new expression of the life of this people, arose. With them, it becomes apparent that the new epoch began with new tasks.

Hillel

About four centuries later, a third leader came from the Babylonian reaches of this people to the ancient land, in order to fulfill a task and to become a helper. It was Hillel, whom the people believed to be descended from the House of David. A man who made his own place, he stood as an uncrowned prince amidst the people. He bequeathed a principality for centuries to come to his descendants. He had become a legend in his lifetime, and stories told about him show him as never appearing, but always present. When he spoke, this whole people spoke, not just a part of it. He stood above all that separated and divided, beyond all groups and parties. Like Ezra and Nehemiah, he was always himself. In him the Torah again began to speak anew, to affirm and to indicate the new. This was his "method": The whole precedes the parts and the unifying, therefore, takes precedence over the divisive; it is thus in the Torah, and should be thus in life. His words could be spoken, because his life spoke them. They were the commanding and therefore comforting words of peace, of love, of the near. They were words of joining, of standing together, and of beginning.

To the priests, who were state officials, to the descendants of Aaron, Hillel said: "Be one of the disciples of Aaron, one who loves peace and pursues peace, one who loves God's creatures and brings them nigh unto the Torah" (*Abot*, I, 2). It is not enough to be a descendant; one must also be a disciple. He told those who did not think of themselves as called to anything: "Where there is no man, strive thou to be a man!" (*Abot*, II, 5) and, "There is no man who does not have his hour" (*Abot*, IV, 3; Ben Azzai's saying). Many of the words which he thus spoke in an unstrained, artistic fashion, words in which life itself seemed to speak and in which everyone heard himself addressed by his own life, have become part of the life of this people. When it remembered them, it remembered itself. A new pattern, a new form of human nature and human wisdom entered the existence of this people with Hillel: A configuration stood within and before it as an admonition which it was to hear.

These three men, and others who followed them, in coming and going, in receiving and giving, preserved two domains of this people's existence—their inner history, and their existence as an enduring unity. They did this despite a growing difference in the fates of individual communities, despite new and separating boundaries drawn between states. The thinking of the people in both areas of its settlement was enlarged. They could not just think of one land, not just of the old home, nor solely of the new.

Western Influences: The Mediterranean

Thought, meditation, and poetry were set into a still stronger tension, a grasping for the distant, when a third domain, that of the West, opened itself: the Mediterranean Sea became a mediating sea for this people. During the first millennium it could be called the "hinder sea" (Deut. 34:2). The people had turned its back to it. Now, more and more, it turned its face to it. A new historical domain opened. A world stood before this people, attracting men and ideas, and also permitting new ideas and hopes to arise. Around the Mediterranean, settlements of this people grew. These congregations, these colonies, were named by the Greeks by the same word which they used for their own colonies, and were outfitted by the Romans with colonial legal titles. Through its colonies the motherland now stretched itself to the far ocean. Its world had become that of three areas. Man could, and indeed had, to think of all of them together when he became aware of his belief, his way, and his expectation. The times would not allow a pettiness of spirit but demanded that it stretch and expand itself. The time permitted few little souls.

This was all the more true since the line of sight became the line of thought, and of hope as well. The spirit of this people and the Greek spirit met one another; and spirit reached an understanding with spirit. When, later, Rome entered this people's sphere of existence, will confronted will. Each had included, though in completely different ways, a belief in itself and a belief within itself. They could only dwell next to one another. Within the Hellenistic world, at that time, ideas from here and there could meet. And while the attitude of this people, its belief, remained the same, the vision of its soul found new paths of exploration.

Something historically significant arose then. That is to say that a fertile present brought forth an idea as a creative seed of the future. (Is it not history, that though the field rich with fruit is destroyed, the seed waits for new fields; it endures?)

A dialogue between men of this people and others began; and men of different beliefs entered into the belief of this people and won hearth and home within it. All genuine, all honest mission is such a dialogue, a free dialogue between men. Out of it grows, in turning toward or in turning away, a new inner freedom, a new certainty. It is a community of search. The prophet of the Exile had already told of such an encounter. He speaks of "the aliens that join themselves to Him-Who-Is, to minister unto Him" (Is. 56:6). He had heard the word of promise that goes out to them:

Even them will I bring to My holy mountain,
And make them joyful in My house of prayer;
Their burnt-offerings and their sacrifices
Shall be acceptable upon Mine altar;
For My house shall be called
A house of prayer for all peoples.

Isaiah 56:7

In psalms of that time they are called "those who fear Him-Who-Is"; and in verses of acknowledgment and of gratitude they are placed next to the priests.

The time was ripe for the spirit and the poetry of this people to exert a strong force of attraction. The lands around the Mediterranean were full of mobile peoples, of a variety, a manifoldness of philosophies and mysteries, and the search for the unknown, for the unknown God, for the unknown messiah, the unknown savior, had taken hold of many dispositions. Men from far and near began to speak with one another. Men asked, and men answered. Amidst all the indecision and unrest, the thinking, the will, the hope of this people appeared as a firm pillar. Amidst all of the differences (which turned out to be alike in the end) it stood there as something incomparable, something that revealed, as nothing else did, that which is and that which should be. Philosophies which had sought for a foundation of their systems here appeared to find that which might support them. The spirit of this people gave answer. Yet it received as well; it gained new breadth as well as new problems. The existence of this people was enlarged, the viable strength of its spirit was tested to the full.

The Septuagint

Moreover, this people, almost without desiring to do so, sent a messenger to the nations. Men of its congregations in Egypt, which had become a Greek land, had translated the Holy Scriptures into the new, world language of Greek. With that, this Book became the greatest of apostles. It traveled road after road, and into whatever distances it reached, there this people had arrived, even without being present. The world of this people could open its portals in many lands. This people had often spoken, in exhortation, in hope, of "all peoples," those who are near and those who are far. Now it began to speak directly to all of them, and many answers came back. Something new was heard.

But to express the contents of the Bible in translation also meant to learn something new. The Bible now had to find appropriate form in a language based on a different manner of thinking, in a language which contained a neuter form, whereas the Hebrew possessed only male and female word forms. The possibility of abstraction with its enticement and its danger opened up. The personal could give way to the impersonal, the definite could surrender to the indefinite. Philosophies and mysticisms, in which the word was no longer the instrument in the hand of the master, but had made itself master, could prepare a sphere for themselves in the conflux of the two languages. This, too, is part of the history of the Greek Bible translation. Beside the fact that it was the first translation of a book of many styles, that it was a pioneer undertaking extraordinarily performed, it was also a great achievement in terms of substance. The Bible was not just translated; it was also reconsidered. New problems arose, old ones became new. The power of Oral Law operated here as well. He who looks attentively at what was accomplished must be filled with admiration. An almost fully creative process, rather than one which merely reproduces, is evident in this work. The spirit which lived in the Bible returned to this Bible, and that special blend of the here and the beyond manifested itself.

Yet that which proved decisive was what this people came to experience in its existence. Its strength became a will to the distances. The Greek Bible translation became the great apostle, the missionary of the Hebrew Bible. Men who spoke of this people and its belief had preceded the book and now they followed it. They found people who seemed to have waited for them. Torah, prophecy, and wisdom now began to speak, to show, and to lead. The existence of this people mingled with the existence of peoples from among the "seventy peoples." Its heritage became their heritage, its hope became theirs. The time of those who "join themselves to Him-Who-Is," the proselytes, as the Greek word terms them, had appeared. It is a great period within this people's second millennium. This give and take brought forth a literature that breathes confidence, poetry, philosophy, commandment. A catastrophe, a second war against Rome, ended it. But the task had now been set, the idea had been placed before this people's eyes. Task and idea would belong to this people as part of its way and its comfort. They had become a new source of strength for its hope, even though they could scarcely be active now for centuries, and indeed slumbered long.

The Congregation As Spiritual Colony

The humane, which evidenced itself everywhere in the Bible, in the Torah, in the Prophets, in the Wisdom literature and thus ever anew in the prayers, received a new tone at that time from men who discovered their way to God. A way of thinking about these men was introduced which has become part of the heritage of this people. These men were called "the pious of the nations of the world." One of the great teachers, Rabbi Joshua b. Hananiah, said: "The pious of the nations of the world have a share in the world to come." This became the classic, enduring statement on this subject. Respect toward those in search speaks out of it. This people has always been a searching people, and understood those who were in search. This statement reveals, too, the deference toward a piety which differs from one's own but comes out of the depths of the soul where there are no more differences. In the "world to come," in the great fulfillment, all the pious will find one another. This humanity of reverence was never lost within this people; in those, and in later, harder days it met the test. There has never been a humane reverence as steadfast as this.

The epoch of the proselytes, those who stood on the doorstep and those who entered, was abruptly broken off. A force from without, the decree of a Roman emperor, proscribed every type of approach. Within the people itself, disappointments which had been experienced here and there led to a desire to turn away. But existence had been enlarged, and the breadth remained. This people had become a colonizing people, in spirit as in space. A new form of colony, which appeared here for the first time in the life of humanity, and almost remained unimitated, had been created. It was a colony behind which there stood no power. It carried only the force from which it had come. It therefore oppressed no one, suppressed no one, dispossessed no one, but thus always prepared the way for new colonies. All of them came from a spiritual, an invisible focal point, which held them together. This unique form of colony, the congregation, has since then increasingly determined the history of this people. A people of congregations! It sounds like a contradiction, but it is one of those fertile contradictions out of which spirit and power are born.

The Role of the Homeland

Among the three geographical areas in which the people lived at that time, with many ideas crossing back and forth between them, the old land had its special place. It was situated geographically in the middle and, what meant far more, it was the center of the spirit and the power. It was able to exercise attraction. It was also the great historical battle place. Fates were decided here, thousands gave their lives there battling for their own. It was the land of martyrs and taught martyrdom. To stand in the van there meant becoming a martyr.

But it was just as much the battleground of the spirit. The fight was waged here for all of this people. It was repeated in later epochs, one area having to undertake spiritual battle for all the others, bearing wounds on their account. Every idea, every hope, every longing that was born at any time within this people or forced its way in from the outside, came to this ancient land to contend with one another. Here their battles were fought to the finish: the great decisions, which then were to become historical, approached the people here.

The colonies close by in the West stood within the perimeter of the earthquake area. One could hear the voices of storms clashing with one another in the ancient land. But on the other side, over the community in Mesopotamia, silence reigned most of the time. One generation followed another in quietness. There it was easier to remain certain of one's self. External thoughts did not pound commandingly or challengingly upon the portals. One could turn almost completely to halakah, to the way. Haggadah, this coming to terms with ideas, had to give ground. How comprehensive, how rich in content, how filled with problems is the haggadah which unfolded in Palestine compared with that of the Babylonian teachers! For there, between the two areas and their colonies, in the old land, the arduous battles were fought. There the soul of this people had to preserve all of its viable strength.

There too, a trial of history placed its heavy load upon the people. Its oppression lay heavily upon belief and hope. That which decisive days and years of heroism had achieved was destroyed. The heroism of Maccabean times had won the right of religious independence. Now the free state founded on that victory was first limited by Rome and then done away with. The imperial governors were in the land, at times administering, but mostly ruling as dictators. Then came the revolt against Rome; the Temple, rebuilt by those who had come home out of exile, was burned. Only a wall remained standing, and all this people's pain turned toward it.

The sacrificial service ceased with the Temple. But for centuries, everywhere in the land, as well as in both the East and the West, the synagogues existed with their divine services. This divine service had entered into the life of the people, had become part of it. That ancient metaphor of the ark of the covenant, the ark of the two tablets of the Ten Commandments, said: "It carried them who carried it." Now this became true of this divine service: the people carried it, and it carried them. Day after day the congregation formed it anew, and day after day it created the congregation. Everyone within the people participated in it, carried and was carried. The divine service, in its immediacy, had already won its life, its matter-of-fact existence, long before the indirect, the sacrificial service came to an end. Historical preparation, this providence, this "foresight of the Lord" had prevailed. The Temple had ceased, but the divine service endured, and this people endured. The congregations within the people, the near and the far, made that existence certain. The form of the state, in whose midst the Temple had stood, existed no more. But the people remained, and to them came the days, and before them was the way and the comfort.

The Destroyed Sanctuary and the Enduring Faith

To others in the land and outside of it, the burning of the Temple meant something else. The flames which consumed it spoke to them of a turning point in time, saying that the time of this people had ended, that the time of the nations had begun. Because this people had rejected the "son of David" born to it to be the "anointed of God." the deliverer and redeemer, it itself had now been rejected. The burning Temple stood before them as the flaming exclamation point of this end. The term "rejected people" now became a colloquialism for those who believed that the "anointed one" had appeared. (A belief which had begun in this people and for this people and had become a belief against this people.)

The question—Had God turned away from His people?—may already have been raised when the First Temple was destroyed. Songs of lamentations were composed then which were accepted into the Bible and which one tradition ascribed to the Prophet Jeremiah. Now the same songs became the songs of lamentation over the burning of the Second Temple. The last of these songs ends with a solemn "No" of an oath. This prophet had once heard the emphatic "Yes" of an oath, when he heard the word of God concerning the covenant with His people: "Yes, as true as My covenant is by day and by night, as true the ordinances of heaven and earth that I have appointed . . ." (Jer. 33:25). Now, when it could be said that this covenant was no longer valid, the great "No" of the oath spoke forth in the closing words of Lamentations: "No, truly, Thou hast not rejected us, even though Thou has been exceeding wroth against us" (Lam. 5:22).* This was the answer, and it remained the answer when, after the destruction of the Second Temple, rejection was mentioned and became a slogan to many. Much had ceased to be, but the belief endured, the way went forward, and the comfort spoke day after day.

The firm, continuing oath made it possible for thought to preserve its assurance and certainty against that confluence of events by which the spirit is so easily led astray. Men have the tendency to surrender to the impression of *post hoc, ergo propter hoc,* "after it, therefore from it." Events that follow one after the other seem to be determined one by the other. In individual existence, as in history, there are interweavings, linkings, entanglements. A man whose way was lost is surrounded by them. A man who departs from the way is threatened by them. But they are not the laws of life and history. Law is that which endures, that which lasts from generation to generation, that which appears anew before every generation, demanding a decision, promising grace.

Through catastrophe, the people became all the more conscious of this enduring element. At that time, variations to the verse of the Song of Songs (5:2) "I sleep, but my heart waketh" were composed, always with the introductory sentence: "The congregation of Israel speaks before the Holy One, praised be He; Lord of the worlds." They tell also of that which has disappeared, of the Sanctuary that has been destroyed, of the old, hallowed forms that have sunk into the ruins, of the rights torn away and cast to the ground, of all that which together lies in deep sleep. Verse after verse sounds forth in pensive melancholy.

*Baeck's strongly positive translation of the last verse of Lamentations is in accord with modern scholarship, and is in keeping with a key characteristic of the Bible: A biblical book ends on an optimistic note. [Translator]

But the end, the refrain, is always the same happy, almost joyful refrain of that which endured because it always endures, of the words of the commandments which man may always fulfill, of the good that he can always practice and realize, of the Torah and of prayer whose portals are open, of the promise that constantly leads from that which is to that which will come. These are the ever present, the ever awake, "my heart waketh." And the answer of all answers is sounded in conclusion: "God waketh"—the heart of my heart also wakes. "He will redeem me" is therefore the final phrase, the all-enclosing statement of all that can never be torn away. Thus did the "congregation of Israel" know the truth of endurance: "He will redeem me."

They could sing joyfully amidst all suffering with such complete certainty, because an experience rose out of the depths of the soul which took the sting out of all vicissitudes and changes—"O death, where is thy sting?" It was the experience of return and rebirth. In it arises the living certainty that man can always come again to God, can always be close to Him. All fatalities shatter against it, and so they cannot enter the soul of man. About two hundred years after the destruction of the Temple, one teacher expressed it in a phrase that this people has made its own, "Repentance and prayer and charity will cause the evil of fate to pass by." Fate remains fate, but its evil does not penetrate the soul.

The songs of Lamentations had already closed with that certainty. The great "No" was preceded by a sentence that forms a unity with it: "Turn us unto Thee, Thou-Who-Art, and we shall be turned; renew our days as of old" (Lam. 5:21). It is the verse of the rebirth, and the prayer for it. Malachi, the last in the sequence of prophets, also heard this answer (for all prayer is already its answer): "Return unto Me, and I will return unto you, saith the Lord of hosts" (Mal. 3:7). This prophet, like Ezra and Nehemiah, had experienced many disappointments from those who had returned to the old land. He suffered in the conflict between the ideal he carried within himself and the realities that confronted him. There are changing moods in his speeches. At times he proclaims the admonishing word of God: "Remember ye the

Torah of Moses My servant" (Mal. 3:22), at times the divine judgment. But the certainty of return endures. Without belief in it he could not have lived among his people. The conflict between the generations also oppressed him, this conflict into which history seemed to sink at times. But here too he envisioned a return, in which history will yet fulfill itself. He also heard the promise, and closes his prophetic speech with it:

Behold, I will send you
Elijah the prophet
Before the coming
Of the great and terrible day of Him-Who-Is.
And he shall turn the heart of the fathers
to the children,
And the heart of the children to their fathers;
Lest I come and smite the land with utter
destruction.

Malachi 3:23–24

In the return to God, the generations again find their way, and they walk it together.

The Idea of the Return

The idea of the return challenges that which is supposed to be final, the so-called results of history, which have often been cited against peoples, in particular against this people. Only this idea preserves the sense of history. It shows the possibility that always remains, the seed which creation has sowed in everything that it might flower. The strength of return resides in all the children of men, and thus the present is the ever self-renewing meeting with time. The past is not a fate which coerces, nor is the future a portal that can be permanently closed. The possibility, the return, the rebirth may always have its day. Again and again they will conquer the tensions of time, the conflict between the going and the coming. The return of the parents to the children and of the children to the parents is the encompassing testimony of the return to God. Elijah, such is the promise, will smooth the path. He will prepare the way which leads from belief to consolation. There, parents and children will discover themselves and one another, and will find the expression of its truth that has become an introduction to prayers as well as a justification of communal prayer: "Our God, and the God of our fathers."

The meeting of the generations is discussed in these closing words of the last of the ancient prophets. Only through the generations is history given structure; without them, happenings would remain without form and configuration. Every generation has its particularity, that which has been assigned to it and is to belong to it. With every human being born, humanity, the human problem, the human task, step into the world anew; and with every generation that matures, humanity, with its problem, becomes the task anew, the task through whose fulfillment history comes to be. It is always the same task; for it is the task which God has set for man. But it presents itself ever anew, sincc man follows man and generation follows generation. Therefore, it cannot merely be continued, let alone merely repeated; it must be constantly renewed. Every individual, with his talent and upon his place, and every generation in its time and upon its field, are to accept the enduring task as their own, as though it had been set for the first time for them.

In the field of moral fulfillment, as in artistic fulfillment, one cannot really see progress as in technology; rather, again and again there is a new understanding of that which is demanded. Whenever and wherever men sought, or seek, to fulfill the commandments of God with all their hearts and all their souls and all their mights, there something completely new and individual breaks through. A man born anew, a generation that entered history anew, has grasped the challenge as its own, has, in a sense, personified it. Only he who has met a task with this morality, or this creativeness, this artisticness, having accepted it into himself, into his ego, only he possesses his life's task.

No one sets a true, great task for himself; one can only accept and meet the demands of a day, for the noble task endures and remains.

The Meeting of Generations

In that task, parents and children find one another in the days of their lives, ancestors and descendants, in the days of their history, in order to recognize and to understand one another. In the task, there is room for them all; it belongs to everyone, and all own it together. For even though the world is always the same, it becomes a new world with every life it enters. In it the generations come together to look at one another from their own viewpoint. The more a generation comes to understand itself, the sooner is it able to understand those who precede it and those who follow it. The meeting of generations is facilitated. Just as the meeting of individuals makes genuine community possible, so does the meeting of generations open the way for history. There is one more way in which men and generations can meet, and that is through poetry. The history of this people had its poetry, without which it could not exist. Within this poetry, Elijah came to every generation and "turned the heart of the fathers to the children and the heart of the children to their fathers." The great zealot, in a daring development of poetry, here became the great conciliator.

This verse, in which one millennium stretches out its hand to the other, also points to the rebirth, a rebirth arising from growth. Every such rebirth is also a meeting. Earlier powers, of childhood and youth, rise out of the circumstances and possibilities of the present in order to be renewed. In the present they win new existence and, at the same time, new form. This happens in the life cycle of individuals and generations. One might almost say that, in a great experience of self-discovery and self-understanding, in individuality, a generation becomes aware of a great unity above and beyond the decades and centuries in which it lives and in which it seeks to create and work. Old powers, which yearn to be renewed, are discovered. That which came to be was predetermined to rise into becoming; and the becomings, which can never cease arising out of what came to be, meet one another.

Such an encounter of times presupposes the will to self, to individuality; and all will to self, including, in its essence, even the aesthetic, is a moral will. The so-called will to power is only an oppression and displacement of the individual, the true self that continues to have the ultimate connection with the commandment. It carries on its existence by substituting for the self artificial or purloined images that take possession of the will. The self is man's chosenness by God; it is therefore the chosenness of every man. It is man's predestination. It is his great ability to unfold through commandment and grace into an individual, a unique entity. It is his great possibility of being "God's image," this great possibility for which God created man. Life is a battle for self, for the sake of self. It is enjoined upon every man, upon every generation, upon every people. It is imparted in the unity of what is demanded and of what is given, a unity in which everything that comes from God proves itself. Man, generation, and people must each accept it for his own sake and for the sake of him who has come before, as for those who are to follow.

The second millennium of this people succeeded in letting the people's will to self, to its ego, to its election, to the decisive moment grow strong within it. It renewed the old forces, formed them for the present, and prepared them for the future so that now every generation could pray: "Our God, and the God of our fathers . . . Thou wilt bring a redeemer to the children of their children."* Here this people's particular gift, the genius to view the inner relationship between space and time, to experience totality in individuality and thus to know unity, proved itself. This is one of the deepest meanings of "Torah," that it endures and is one, because it always renews itself. He who prays, perhaps experiences this best. He sees the ancestors, contemporaries, and descendants together. He becomes aware of a great unity. He becomes aware of his self as a man, stepping before the Eternal, the Infinite, in order to be embraced by Him. He becomes assured of all

* See *The Authorized Daily Prayer Book*, ed. J. H. Hertz, p. 130.

the powers that live in his own self, the early-existing ones and the awaited ones; as the last book of the Bible, Chronicles ("The History of Days"), says: from Adam to the Messiah.

Thought and Prayer

Like Torah, prayer had its oral form in those years. In a sense, it was prayer in movement. Teachers composed "short prayers," and their students then transmitted them to their own students. The spoken tradition was, thus, also a tradition of prayer. At its foundation were the specially constructed, established, and universally accepted prayers, each meant for a definite time. To those, petition and confession added to each other, and that which the individual implores joined that which his longing urges for the group. All always flow together. They are great confessions of faith or hope. The certainty arising out of faith sustains man's confidence, and the confidence in turn gives warmth and new strength to the faith. One thing is characteristic of these prayers. Out of the depths, a contemplative mood arises. The world of man, which questions and which he questions, and all which he may have experienced and hoped for, speaks in prayer. Thought and prayer find one another, and henceforth cannot be without one another. Thought lets the longing within man turn into prayer, and prayer, raises the question that oppresses him into the world of thought. Thus philosophers could be poets of prayer.

A fixed prayer is accompanied by a thoughtfulness which it arouses. In this period such prayers were applied to everything that makes up the day. They were to enter that which seemed small at the moment; the minutiae were to be given a relationship to something higher. Thus this people created the sequence of *berakhot* ("blessings"), and brought into the march of hours and days a practice no other people has known. Man is to bless everything that enters his existence, all that is granted him, all that is fated for him, by thanking, by praising God. He is to be the priest of his own life. Every one of these short sentences begins, "Blessed be Thou-Who-Art our God, Ruler of the universe." With these words, the small is led into something great, indeed, the greatest, and becomes the expression of that which is exalted beyond all things. Nothing is to be small only; nothing is to be only a matter of course. Man is to hear and answer the voice of eternity first in minor things. Only if it has spoken to him out of minor things will he be able to hear it in what is great. The fight against forgetfulness, out of which thoughtlessness grows luxuriantly, begins here. A receptivity for revelation is kept open.

Gratitude and Prayer

The blessings permeated life with a sense of constant gratitude. Thankfulness becomes an element of existence. Few things give such a vital, inner independence, such a strength of resistance against the oppressing and the limiting of existence, as gratitude. Without it, a man, a people, cannot be morally free. Thanksgiving is never directed solely toward past good, but it opens itself to the future. It searches, it hopes for good, and it thus becomes a susceptibility for the good. It brings to life not only an ability to appreciate the good, but also a will to see it, to discover it, and to recognize it. And in this, too, inner freedom has one of its roots. Such gratitude and such readiness for gratitude is implanted in this people through its prayer. The people's ability to remain spiritually free, which it has proven so often, also derives from it. This people also became a grateful people in its deeds: As it was grateful to God, so was it grateful to the men who acted in goodness toward it.

Doubtless, this people has had men who were without prayer, who were ungrateful, and men, moreover, whose prayer and whose gratitude was not free, but only set in daily motion by a mechanism. But whoever is able to lend an ear here to the characteristic, to the determining, hears something else. He hears the pure voice. He hears it rising out of the many centuries in which this people, though threatened, afflicted, and oppressed, never forgot gratitude and, because of this, never forgot or lost the ability to cherish the inner freedom through which it could possess happiness. Prayer gave strength with which to cherish freedom. He who can still pray can never be completely unhappy, nor can he be completely captive. He always retains his faith in the strength of the good that dwells within him. He who prays and becomes grateful in prayer, sees before him, even when the hour is black and the day seems to show no way forward, lying open, the road which leads to consolation. Prayer also gives the will to the way. The ways men command can be barred, but he who prays knows that nowhere and never can it be denied him to "walk in God's paths," to be close to God.

A time of wanderings was to begin again for this people with the end of the second millennium. "And they journeyed, . . . and pitched. . . . And they journeyed . . ." But this people could say to itself that the "presence of God," the Shekinah, traveled with it. It knew itself to be sheltered within the deepest, the ultimate reality, as long as it remained faithful. Within it was the strength of rebirth emerging out of its past growth. Before it were the road and the promise. With it went Torah and prayer. As a "sign" of all this, it had the Sabbath.

These men knew that they could always live in a higher world, that they had their real life there, that no man could touch them there, that no one could drive them out of that world except they themselves. On the Sabbath, when the afternoon came, they prayed: "A diadem of greatness and a crown of salvation hast Thou, O God, given unto Thy people."* In days when they appeared rejected and lost in the eyes of the world they spoke thus before God. As long as this people in its truest self can speak this way, so long will it endure.

* See *Daily Prayer Book*, trans. S. Singer (New York: Bloch Publishing Co., n.d.), p. 175e.

IV

The Kingdom of God

The Book of Daniel and the Vision of the End of Days

In the second millennium of this people, one question had awakened much contemplation and stirred many minds. Here and there the people assumed it had arrived at a clear answer. But in its third millennium, the answer had fled into those distances in which the outlines of certainty are obscured. Only an ultimate confidence could still see the ultimate outcome.

This question concerned the extent both of space and of historical time apportioned to earthly powers. Or, to speak in the words of those days: Is there a sequence of "kingdoms"?

Kingdom upon kingdom, sooner or later, had followed one another. How long would it continue, one "kingdom" pushing aside another, in order to prepare or to force a place for itself? When would the end commence for these kingdoms, these enslavements? When would the true kingdom appear, "the kingdom of all times," "the kingdom of the Almighty," "the kingdom of Heaven," "the kingdom of God"? Such was the question that could raise itself again and again, indeed, had to raise itself; for it sprang from a confidence in the meaning of history, and the existence of this people was founded upon this confidence.

A book of the Holy Scriptures, the Book of Daniel, had spoken first of the kingdoms which come and go and of the kingdom which will endure. The continuing moral revolution, which entered the world with the Bible, also brought a special revolution for many personalities. It taught them of apocalypse, that capacity of the soul which turns surmise into a vision standing before one's eyes. In the Book of Daniel expectant patience is expressed: "Happy is he that waiteth. . . . But go thou thy way till the end be; and thou shalt rest, and shalt stand up to thy lot, at the ends of the days" (Dan. 12:12–13). Thus the book closes. Much impatience rested in it as well, and the teachers of this people had to warn against "computing the end" or even "forcing the end." More important than either was the comprehensive breadth of the book's historical-moral outlook in which longing for the future becomes certainty. The view emanating from this book took a deeper hold of this people than did impatience or the idea of the apocalypse. This people was suffused with a conscious longing for the fulfillment of right in a world of right, in which the many receive their right, not just the few who receive some manner of right, a world in which "a light shines about the thoughtful" (Dan. 12:3), not only around the powerful. This book plowed its furrows through many times and lands.

In the order of the Hebrew Bible, the Book of Daniel has its place in the third major section, the Hagiographa. It was not placed into the sequence of prophetic books. Chronological considerations already determined this. The book was created at the time of the Maccabean independence movement and thus was separated from the last of the prophets, Malachi, by three centuries. Yet there was also an internal reason. The Book of Daniel is not characterized by prophecy which addresses its words to the people, admonishing, warning, comforting, promising, proclaiming the commandment, and showing the way. Something different, though not completely new, precedes everything else: a vision in which a higher world opens itself, an apocalypse, which discloses what was seen. The gaze turns not from the present into the past, but from below to above.

There, in the upper world, Daniel sees a picture of history, period after period, kingdom after kingdom: one grasping, rapacious animal after another, with horns, claws, and teeth fights another in order to destroy it, to possess the land itself, to rule over countries. It is thus established in the upper world, in which everything is determined. Down here, in the lower world, it happened then and happens now and will continue to happen until that time comes which has been announced. Daniel sees that time also. God is enthroned,

And, behold, there came with the clouds of
heaven
One like unto a son of man,
And he came even to the Ancient of days,
And he was brought near before Him.
And there was given him dominion . . .
Daniel 7:13–14

The times of the wild animals are ended, the time of humanity has dawned. Those in this people who have remained "holy" will share in it. They are preserved for a future which is firmly established.

The Word *Olam*

In this context existence acquires an enlarged meaning and domain. It may be seen clearly in the variety of meanings of the word *olam*, another almost untranslatable word. Before the Book of Daniel, it designated time in its unmeasurable forward reach. Now it comprehended the totality of all spheres and worlds, the whole, in which everything below and above, terrestrial and eternal, in earth and in heaven, is drawn together and enclosed. It is as though time and space, period and kingdom now found their all-embracing unity. (The Greek word *aion* was used to give this new comprehensive meaning.) Man was to see himself as placed into all of this, into space and beyond space, into time and beyond time, in "this *olam*" (*olam hazeh*) and the one beyond, "the *olam* to come" (*olam haba*). All could and should be his *olam*, his time and his world. His future now meant a world, and his world signified a future. He could and should, in order to renew his life, constantly experience anew the totality and unity in which his day and his place belonged. Thus not only thought, but life, was henceforth determined by this view.

An epigrammatic sentence of those days, speaking of *olam*, can make this clear. It is told in the Talmud that, when teachers took leave of one another (and how easily then might every farewell become the last), they would say: "May you see your *olam* in your life, and may your future be for the life of *olam* to come, and may your hope be for generation upon generation." This sentence leads us into their belief, into the basis of their existence. They were certain of a world, a time, which stretched far beyond the spaces and enclosures of their own existence and which, nevertheless, everyone was able to possess, to turn into his personal life, to his *olam*. They were placed into circumscribed days, but an infinite and eternal *olam* could nevertheless be theirs. These men were certain not only of the change of hours, its mutations of fate, its beginnings and endings, but also of the future, of the "*olam* to come," that everyone may look to for the fulfillment of his life. They were certain that every life could continue in those that follow it, generation after generation, that there is a renewal of existence, a rebirth, which is the true history of men and peoples.

All of this was uttered at that time by these men who became the teachers of their people. They were teachers because they were always able to preach, and their teaching became a gospel. Their day might be mean, their space might be narrow, but around them was a fullness of power into which they entered. The kingdom of the Almighty had become a reality to them. The arrogant dominions, no matter how bitterly oppressive, enslaving, and surrounding, became a sign to them of that which will disappear, since it can have no place in that which endures.

In the third millennium of this people, this certainty was reborn in order to create new forms of understanding and of existence for itself.

Rome as "Edom"

The composer of the Book of Daniel thought, that in his days, the time of the kingdoms tended toward the turn that would signify the end. Thus he interpreted his visions. The continuing battles between the powers, brought on by the disintegration of the balance of power among the heirs to the Persian kingdom, seemed to indicate this. Many of this people had gazed upon Alexander the Macedonian (as he is called in the Talmud) with great respect. He seemed almost to belong to them, and so he became a legendary figure for them. After Alexander, they saw only little figures, engaged in petty quarrels. Then, through one of these figures something extreme took place: an idol, "a destroying abomination," as the Book of Daniel calls it, was placed in the sanctuary in Jerusalem and the daily sacrifices were brought to an end. These events seemed to indicate something decisive, something final was about to take place. The people was ready for the hoped-for day. A time of fought-for freedom, the time of the Maccabees, was then allotted. Martyrs, told of in the Hebrew and Greek books of the Maccabees, bear witness to it.

Then and later, this appeared to be an extraordinary, a wondrous time. The ancient prayer, filled with gratitude, praised God who had given

Strength to the hands of the weak, the many into the hands of the few, the unclean into the hands of the clean, the blasphemers into the hands of the righteous, the wicked into the hands of those who practice the Torah.*

To recall the miracle, the feast of the rededication of the Temple, Hanukkah, was celebrated. Year after year, throughout the eight days, one lit the candles in order to celebrate the miracle.

In the course of this people's history this time of freedom was but an interval. The author of the Book of Daniel did not yet know the power then in ascension, with which the epochs of the West were to begin. He did not yet know of Rome, of Edom, as this people later designated Rome. This word "Edom," the other name of Esau, Jacob's twin brother, arouses consideration. Again they faced each other: Jacob who was called Israel, and Esau who was named Edom.

The Midrash of Jacob's Dream

About five centuries after the Book of Daniel, a teacher of the school in Tiberias, at the Sea of Kineret, Rabbi Samuel ben Nachman, wove a wondrous poetic vision. The subject of this creation is Jacob's dream at the place which was later to be called Bethel, "House of God." In his dream Jacob saw "a ladder set up on the earth, and the top of it reached unto heaven; and . . . the angels of God ascending and descending on it" (Gen. 28:12). They did not descend and then ascend, but ascended and then descended. These messengers of God are the essences of the kingdoms. One after another, first in ascent and then in descent, Jacob saw them in his dream of future history. But finally, Rabbi Samuel continues, Jacob saw one who ascended and kept ascending ever further and higher, rung after rung. It was the spirit of Esau, Edom. And Jacob was frightened and called up to God: "How much longer will he rise, higher and yet higher? Is he to reach

* See *The Authorized Daily Prayer Book*, ed. J. H. Hertz, p. 152.

even unto heaven?" It was as if the proud motto of Rome, the motto of *Roma aeterna*, had become an outcry of fear in the mouth of Jacob. But now the poem concludes; Jacob heard the call of God. He heard a twofold answer of God. The first, spoken to Edom, which Obadiah, the prophet, was to proclaim later: "Though thou make thy nest as high as the eagle, and though thou set it among the stars, I will bring thee down from thence" (Obad. 1:4). And after that, God's word to Jacob, spoken by Jeremiah: "Therefore fear thou not, O Jacob My servant . . . neither be dismayed, O Israel" (Jer. 30:10). And Jacob was comforted.

Many of the people must have seen the situation as Rabbi Samuel pictured it in his poem. Rome itself was now a millennium old. It had overcome every danger threatening it from without and within. It had created its all-embracing law, and stood ready to accept everyone as a citizen who was not a slave, thus overcoming provincialism through the idea of the kingdom, the Imperium. Did it not seem fated to be that kingdom which its poet had promised would "direct the nations in an Imperium"? To face this might, this people needed a complete certainty of soul, a consummate internal stability that even now it might remain true to itself, comforted as Jacob in his vision.

But now it must appear noteworthy, almost bizarre, in the interconnecting lineage, almost as an attempt to unite attraction and repulsion, that Rome, the Imperium, was called Edom, and was presented to this people as its twin brother. There are certain linguistic interpretations that might be at the bottom of this; but the usage is, essentially and specifically, psychological. A poetry of history speaks here, comprehending in imagery something that is characteristic, but almost impossible to bring into the realm of formula. The inhabited, historical world of those days, the world ordered internally and externally, was unified in the East through Alexander, and in the West through Rome. Together it was a world for itself, an *orbis terrarum*. In this whole vast domain there were only two peoples left who stood for themselves, who had never renounced themselves. This people was one, and the Roman people was the other.

Rome and Israel

Most other peoples can be treated with complete silence. It must be said of the Greek people that with all the strength and abundance of its genius, with all its immortal gifts, it had morally abdicated as a people before its first millennium had ended. After military defeat, the people's will had lost the way. Only when a people renounces its soul, when it no longer clings to its right path, is it really conquered, whether or not arrogance or even pride remain.

Roman power fought down the Jewish people, defeating it in two wars, after heroic battles. The first time the conqueror celebrated a triumph; the second time he carried out an embittered revenge. Both times this people stood unconquered. One is tempted to say, if it is possible to use a higher scale of comparison, that it was less conquered than ever before. Then as before, the people saw its way. The voices of those days speak clearly. Despite different centuries, a comparison between a leader in the Greek war of independence, Polybius, and one in the Jewish war, Flavius Josephus, is instructive. The one became a Roman inwardly; the other, despite everything, retained his individuality. Living in Rome, he only wanted to tell the world of one thing, of the history and the task of his people.

Only two peoples stood thus in that continuing history, related to it by a determined will. Could it not, in fact, appear as though they were not merely two peoples, but *the* two peoples? They differed as much as peoples can differ, the one living within power, the other living through the spirit; and they were yet alike in the faith with which they clung to themselves, to their chosenness. Could it not seem likely that a common soil had given birth to them, yes, that a common root had brought them forth? As though they were brothers, the one, Esau-Edom, the man of weapons, and the other Jacob-Israel, the man of the spirit? They appeared as two worlds risen out of one world to oppose one another, two worlds that are sibling rivals. The words which Isaac, the father, spoke before he blessed the sons, "The voice is the voice of Jacob, but the hands are the hands of Esau" (Gen. 27:22), were often pondered at that time. They filled themselves with symbolism; they were to be a sign of history, pointing toward the future. These were to be the two portions of the world: "the hands," grasping, holding fast, and "the voice" in which the soul calls. To one, the Imperium, would belong the might, to the other would be granted the power, the kingdom of God. One would be granted his time, the other the time of fulfillment.

There was something completely unique at that time in the relationship of Rome to this people and in that of this people to Rome. Despite many an act of harshness and bitterness, Rome's dealings here are generally different than when it dealt with other peoples. Rome seemed to feel that this people constituted an exception among the peoples. And something similar speaks out of this people. Despite many a bitter, accusing word, it often testifies to itself that Rome had made an impression, an impression that was different from that made by the powers preceding it. The words "Edom" and "Israel" could thus become historical concepts, could rise almost to the metaphysical level. An antithesis which never should nor could become synthesis, but which could lead thought to a higher plateau, here stood before the spirit. For a long time it etched its lines into the meditations and the existence of this people.

The Imperium of Faith

The might of Rome, which appeared invincible, again confronted this people in its third millennium. But the word "Rome" had gained a different meaning now, had won another "sign," a new level of significance. The Imperium had become the imperium of belief. The acquisitive hands now aspired to be the hands of blessing. The congregation of those who believed in redemption in the present had become the Church. Two martyr apostles of this people fashioned the missionizing, then the competing, and then the conquering Church. The state,

Rome, established a covenant with it, and it afterward established a covenant with the state, with Rome. Rome took it into itself, and it took Rome into itself. It now was also Rome, *Roma aeterna*; it now was also the might. Ordering and commanding, it proclaimed its words *urbi et orbi*, "to the city and to the world." The Imperium had become the imperium of belief. The phrase *coge intrare*, "force them to enter," was spoken, an old Roman phrase. Then as before, they were set against one another and watched one another: Edom and Israel, Rome and this people, the one basic might and the one exception to earthly control. Just as before, if in a completely different way, indeed, with a strength that had to be even more alive, the existence of this people had to encompass this confrontation.

Relatively few communities of this people were outside the Imperium. Besides those in the Arabian peninsula, there were those who lived in the old Babylonian land of exile. They could look back upon the long history of their congregations, that by now had assumed a tradition of their own. Moreover, they possessed a certain autonomy within the new Persian Empire. They could appear to be the heirs of the state which had previously existed in the old land of Palestine, and, as such, had their own unique social structure. Most importantly, their schools had become the heirs of those of Palestine and had succeeded naturally to their authority. They stood as guardians of the tradition, as protectors of the Oral Torah. Their teachers were gratefully recognized as teachers of the whole people, wherever it lived. Thus this people, which had lost its old motherland and had become a people of colonies, possessed an enduring spiritual focal point. The loss of the land had been followed, in a vital sequence, by the establishment of a spiritual center. The totality as such had remained in its unity. In the domain of the spirit, boundaries could not become separations. Wherever there was a synagogue, a prayer for the leaders and the schools of the Babylonian congregations was recited: "May Heaven's salvation descend upon them." A fervent gratitude wells up from this. One was conscious of what it meant, particularly now, to possess a spiritual focal point, and thus to share the endurance which only the constantly self-renewing spirit can give.

The Clash with the Imperium

The focal point was needed. For within the Imperium which enclosed the greatest number of this people's settlements, the conditions of existence had changed decisively. The old Imperium had been a unity of government, of administration, and of law, a *regere imperio*, a "directing through the Imperium." Within this unity there was much room for diversity. But the new imperium wanted to assure a unity of belief, wanted to be an imperium through belief. A new concept, later much elaborated, entered history. Now only the ruling, prescribing Church gave the individual his right to a place in the land or within the civil law. Sooner or later every people in the empire bowed to this principle, except this people. This people was determined to remain what it had become through the power of millennia, and what it wished to be with all the certainty of its soul. Thus it became a people within the imperium and at the same time outside it, a people that knew its unshakable foundation and at the same time had almost no place in the land. The fight, silent or loud, for its right to a place and for the place of its rights became more and more a part of its history. Still new colonies were founded, often with sheer daring, in order to prepare new dwellings, and the horizon of its history expanded. By this too, the third millennium of this people brought new qualities into its existence.

This people's intellectual approach to the outer world changed. In its second millennium it had developed relationships to the surrounding world of thought, first to the Persian, then to Greek, and then to early Roman thought. Now there was scarcely such an inner relationship. The only way in which this would have been possible would have required self-renunciation. Even the Book, which might have become a source of unity, was forced to be a source of distinction. The Church had claimed the Bible for itself. It had to do that, in order to justify itself before itself. The Book, which was a book of this people, and a book for this people, now was to be a book against this people and was to belong to others. Thus the spiritual battle for its rights which this people carried on was also a battle for its patrimony, for its inheritance. It wanted to guard and to protect its most particular possession; for that reason too it withdrew into itself. It had turn to itself, had to seek to enter itself, when it was oppressed by questions that at times became threatening accusations. Only in the verses of its venerable Bible, in the words of its ancient teachers, could an answer to such questions unfold. Only in its own life could it see its world. Meditating on that which was its own became its existence.

In retrospect it seems tragic that the Church, with all the riches of its inner world, with all the depth and fullness of its piety, confronted this people most often only as the Imperium. It thus did not see the world of this people and could not see its own world. It is true that the Jewish philosophy, which developed in another imperium of that time, the Moslem, found its way into Christian philosophy. But only one philosophy had come to another one; it was not a religious encounter. They only confronted one another: the Imperium, mighty and growing in its might, which yet remained powerless against the certainty and the will of this people; and this people, continually threatened, constantly attacked, outwardly helpless, which yet knew itself to be independent, free, and unconquerable in the certainty and will of its existence. When the Church wanted to regain this people's ancient land (for it was considered the land of their holy thought), it developed and nourished a zealousness, which, despite individual examples of noble feeling and noble courage, this people experienced only as a destructive fanaticism. That age of zeal has lived on in this people's memory as a time of "evil destiny." Many destroyed congregations and the names of the numerous martyrs testify of it. Yet the will remained, and the certainty remained. Congregations were rebuilt, men moved on along the rivers and the roads, colonists preparing new homes. They knew that the kingdom of God would endure and that one day all would serve the One God. It was a peculiar historical apparition, this wandering universalism in withdrawn humanity, this effort to find the world through a renewed self-understanding.

The Inner Serenity of This People

It is therefore understandable, as strange as this might first sound to one who knows those times only from their savage events, that a harmony of inner serenity speaks out of the literature of this people, testifying to its thought in those days. It is true enough that touching prayers of mourning were composed then, that many lamenting calls rise from them to God, and that in the martyrologies, the memorial books, the names of those who had to give their lives are heartbreakingly present. But the characteristic quality of this literature remains, nevertheless, one of equanimity. Despite all that happened, despite all that was destroyed, the effort to think everything through makes steady progress. One generation of scholars follows the next. In the books which directed themselves to the masses, the so-called books of morals, a simple and lucid humanity is revealed, a determined lucidity of the moral demand everyone must fulfill. The demand seeks its word and maintains its word, despite everything endured and suffered. Even the mysticism of that time lives in the moral sphere, so that total inner deportment preserves its integrity. This quietness of disposition, this matter-of-factness in thought and action, gives the existence of this people its character within the lands of the imperium of belief. This lucidity represents something almost unique.

Life and thought directed to God, in *kavvanah*, had become one here. Upright life created upright thoughts, and the blasphemer was he whose crooked life brought about crooked thoughts. As confused as the days might be, one could always look toward the way which the commandment and the promise clearly indicated. Set against oneself was the might with its invincible commands; but towering over it, reaching beyond it, greater than it, one could see—perhaps distant in time, but close in faith—the great justice, the fulfillment of history.

In those days, too, in the reaches of the East and the broad South, another power was already in view, arising, having commenced on its path to victory; another imperium, in ever more definite outline, had become visible. It now appeared as though limits had been set for this imperium of belief. News had come from the congregations there. In the land itself, it was assumed often that one was helpless; there was no support. But then one thought of Obadiah's closing words, his speech to Edom, one of the bravest, most dramatic speeches in the prophetic books: "And saviours shall come up on mount Zion to judge the mount of Esau; and the kingdom shall be His-Who-Is" (Obad. 1:21).

The Coming of Mohammed

Not long after the beginnings of the third millennium of this people, a new power arose in the East, and it was now to have a deep influence upon the form of this people's existence. Though its rise was sudden, it won duration for itself, a rare historical achievement. Its quick march of victory had commenced in the desert and in the cities of Arabia. It conquered the provinces of the old Persian Empire and penetrated into territory before which armies of Alexander were halted. It then stretched its borders to the Atlantic Ocean.

The man whose creative genius unfolded these days and continued to influence the movement that was paving its way was Mohammed, the one "sent by Allah." As had the prophets, so had he heard the voice of solitude; and that which appeared empty to common view had found form in him. The visions he had seen entered him, and the images he had viewed took hold of him and carried him forward. He too needed no man when he wanted to hear and when he wanted to speak. He was capable of solitude which awaits its day. As Abraham, as Jacob, as Moses once did, he could go forth from his home, from the house of his father, because he heard a call. With this exodus, this breaking loose, this "Hegira," his life, which had grown strong within him, begins to become history. He could now create his congregation and proclaim to it that he is "the Prophet," "the one sent by the Highest," that he reveals the way of life, and opens the portals of paradise.

He knew about this people and its Book; and this people gained knowledge of him. In the city which received him and which was then called "the city of the Prophet," an ancient congregation had existed, and it encountered the Prophet. Out of this meeting a later rivalry was to emerge.

In these days, so meaningful to him, he heard many stories from the Oral Torah, from the *aggadah.* They found their place in that wondrous book, written so that the faithful from generation to generation might know of his life and might hear his words. It remained their holy possession. With it they acquired the fiery faith that fills it, the force of the admonition and of the promise with which it moves and rouses tempers, and his gift for language, which prepares the word for the road to the many. What the Prophet spoke of the ancient people descended from Abraham remained a true message to his own peoples, no matter what circumstances of history might bring.

Isaac and Ishmael

Something out of its own tradition seemed to speak anew to this people Israel when it heard more and more about the Arabian tribes and the victorious march of their religion. Familiar names took on another, a new sound. The Bible told of the tribal father of the Arabian people, of Ishmael, the half brother of Isaac, the son of Abraham and the Egyptian woman Hagar. There is a special, loving warmth in the account of the mother and the son. A messenger of God spoke to them, with words of encouragement and exaltation, and had proclaimed the divine promise to the son: "And God heard the voice of the lad where he is . . . I will make him a great nation" (Gen. 21:17–18). As with the other imperium, so here, too, brothers seemed to face each other: Ishmael and Isaac, just as Esau and Jacob. But a different tone sounds forth. These two also served to designate history: Ishmael and Isaac. They too became a symbol of the life of peoples who have the same beginning and leave one another, experiencing that which separates them, but sensing still that they hold something in common.

In this epoch, when the name Ishmael spoke of a new religion, all of this won a new and special expression. A religious closeness, a spiritual neighbor seemed to speak. A pure, serious, indeed, severe monotheism had now found its word and its commandment there, among the sons of Ishmael, and nothing could lead away from it. The spirit of puritanism also drew its determining lines there; every sacrament, every picture, everything mediating was rejected. A will for democracy, which set everyone alike, and with the same right, before God, also achieved its place and created the congregation. Every special realm of action was rejected. There, too, a living asceticism asserted itself, one which set the same demand to all, which placed the same "Thou shalt not" before all; weakness was to be prevented as well as excess. All of this had to have a lasting impression upon the thoughts and feelings of the children of Israel who lived within the imperium of the sons of Ishmael. Their own existence took on a new form.

Islam and Judaism: The Geometric and the Functional

Certainly, differences also had to appear, and they were of an essential nature. They arose from forces which had operated in the formative period of growth. (Original forces can be stronger than later impressions and experiences.) A comparison—though only a comparison, an indication of a direction—can be made: One faith, the desert permitted to be born; the other, the desert embraced at a decisive time, becoming a continually effective experience for it, though the experience of the desert was quickly followed by a deeper experience, that of the soil with its constant social commandment that had to be realized again and again. The faith of Mohammed was not granted the experience of the soil. The desert spoke to it in its most penetrating language and silence. But the soil, with the call of its social admonition and its tension with the desert, was not experienced there in its beginning. The problems of tension, of the way, of history, of all that the expression "from generation to generation" and the word *olam* indicate, do not enter into this faith.

This different historical path gives rise to marked characteristics in each people. One might dare this comparison: The faith which took hold of the Prophet from Ishmael's tribe and clung to him, so that he had to proclaim it to his people, has a geometric character. Line adds itself to line, to what is clear, definite, closed. The vision is then assured of seeing everything, in all its interconnections. The faith which seized the prophets of Israel, with which they had to struggle without end that they might give it expression, that they might be able to speak of it, has more a functional character. Every line reaches out toward the infinite, toward the eternal; every answer creates a new question, and no question can exist without the living certainty of the one, the final and enduring answer.

Simplicity—taking the word in its good and noble sense—which sharply defined its outline, is a force in the faith of Mohammed, this child of the desert. It brought fast and yet enduring victories both at the beginning and in the following century. The victories were won particularly among peoples who did not as yet know the depths of man's questions or who had wearied of the complicated. Mohammed's faith leads along simple, straightforward paths. Later, when it had become an imperium, it welcomed Greek philosophy with lavish hospitality. Arabic philosophers then presented the world with a wealth of new thoughts, old problems given new solution. Mystics too had their say. They sang wondrous songs in which the old questions may be heard. But those questions did not really come out of the faith itself; it did not contain them.

From this vantage point, the individual particularities and differences seem to take on a new aspect. The faith of Mohammed presented itself before the world as a great proclamation, as once the faith of Israel had done. It came almost as a cry of battle, yes, a cry of victory which conquers the humanity around it. But there is no outpouring here of speech upon speech, in which he who speaks, because he must speak, either struggles with the insufficiency of the word, or perhaps calls God Himself to account. The tragic aspect of the soul, its portals opened by God, which the speaker must now unlock to all humanity, is not heard. For this reason alone, the one Prophet could here be the one and only prophet. He did not come from those who had preceded him; he did not call forth those who would be after him. The book written as his testimony could thus remain the one book and not become a Book of books. Thus, the revealing word had directed itself to one man, to this Prophet, and not to all of his people called before their Sinai.

Islam: Constant and Nondynamic

The lines of this faith continually show themselves to be sharp and straight. The one fits into the other, without imposing itself upon it, for to do so it would have to accommodate itself to it, or, to put it in other words, it would have to think of the existence of man to make it once again a task. The faith of Mohammed knows the finiteness and the transitoriness of the terrestrial, and the power of the eternal and the infinite. But it does not see the penetration by that which is always in that which always becomes. And it does not hear the questions which are always asked in the same way and yet are ever renewed by this process. It speaks of that which, transcending man, is hidden and at the same time predetermining, of that which has been set into our world and has been commanded to us in order that we fulfill it. But it does not teach how this commandment grows forth out of that power and receives its strength ever again from it. It points toward days which will come, so that they may be. But it does not reveal how the promised future can enter the limited present, is supposed to enter it in order to become the enduring "consolation." It knows of human failure and of human frailty, and also of a rising and of a greatness of man. But it does not preach a constant striving for the nearness of God, of the reconciliation of the terrestrial with the eternal. It demands, often in touching words, "Islam," a deep surrender to faith in the One who has formed and orders everything, who determines and judges all, in whom all existence is secured. But it does not proclaim this One as the Self of all self, that speaks the "Thou" to man, making him an "I," a self. It does not proclaim the mystery of man's being in the image of God, this mystery out of which alone a clear understanding of life can emanate.

Thus the unique strength of the religion of "the Prophet" which called forth the people of his land, of tribes and of cities, and afterward won and held far-off men and nations, is the proclamation of a faith, but without the paradoxes and the problems of faith, without the tensions and shattering cataclysms in which the *mysterium* takes hold of the soul.

The Spacious Imperium of Islam

When the quick victories had created a vast imperium, the external spaciousness allowed room for an internal spaciousness to arise. There was a readiness to consider the thoughts of the others who dwelt in the land and to grant them their place. There was an openness to other directions of thought and teaching. A common culture, an education that could embrace all, was permitted to develop. In particular, Greek philosophy was again presented with an empire that could receive its seed. Greek-Arabian philosophy flourished once more, and its fruit contained new and rich seed. The winds of the mind carried it across geographical boundaries into the other imperium, and deposited it there in open furrows.

To the children of the Jewish people who lived in the lands of the descendants of the Prophet there was vouchsafed, in all these developments, something great, something historical. A world of education, a culture, a language opened before them, and they did not hesitate to enter. Since ancient times, their soul had lived in a breadth of intellect and of time and space. Now new vistas presented themselves to their evaluation, their analysis, their vision and their intuition of possible new directions. Something that was universal yet resident in all this people's particularity strove to express itself, and in the process, this people became all the more deeply conscious of its own uniqueness. Above all, these "born philosophers," as Aristotle's student and successor, Theophrastus, once termed them, came to possess philosophy again, as once it had in the days of Philo of Alexandria. It now was an historical, continually productive possession, which ever found new forms for itself. Philosopher now succeeds philosopher with regularity for about six centuries, as long a time as philosophy had been known on its ancient Greek soil, and there alone. This succession gave these philosophers one especially noteworthy characteristic. Unshakably true to what was their own, their heritage, they became men of philosophy. In this respect, during the third millennium of this people, they differed from their brothers in the other, the older imperium, who remained without philosophy, and who at times, in days of excitement, even turned against it.

The Jewish people incurred a debt of deep gratitude to Arabian culture. This people, for whom gratitude is a commandment from God, must never forget this. Then and there these people experienced, as once in the good days of Persia, of Hellas, and of Rome—and most certainly they felt it deeply—how portals were opened before them, through which they could enter and through which one came in to them. There is no better index of their attitude than the fact that the explorers and researchers, the scholars and thinkers of this people at that time, chose to use the language of this culture, Arabic. They wanted to give new expression to what they had to say on behalf of their heritage and their hope. This did not detract from the loyalty they had for their ancient, holy language. Yet, a classic literature of this people is composed in Arabic.

In this cultural encounter, the existence of this people, this constant, ancient existence, was newly determined. Powers from the days of its birth were reborn, and new forms of living were created. Among the men of this people in the other imperium, too, men who had turned more and more to themselves alone, this way into self also became a rebirth and their life achieved new forms. It was the same, single life of this people which proved its strength in both realms. Nevertheless, it showed itself in different forms, in other features. Again, as in each of the preceding millennia, and now, in more certain and manifest fashion, the existence of this people centered about two focuses. The great unity of its existence remained alive, in consciousness and in will, now as before. But there was in it, now as before, perhaps even stronger, the polarity, the tension, the movement of internal streams. Religious paradox, the tension that rises out of the task and leads to new tasks, also existed in the rebirth. The strength needed for the new task is always crucial.

Ashkenazim and Sephardim

The men of this one people were thus divided into two domains where their existence unfolded. They gave themselves the names Ashkenazim and Sephardim. "Ashkenaz" is an ancient designation for Germany, taken from the Bible; "Sepharad," also a biblical name, designates Spain. Germany was used because it was the origin and the focal point for the one renaissance; and Spain was named because there, in the Islamic epoch, the other renaissance had its rich elaboration. These terms, however, designate all in the one and the other imperia. As these names became customary, one was aware that they did not merely express a geographic and a political distinction. Religious differences were known. One spoke—to give the names and their usual attributes—of the *haside ashkenaz*, the "pious of Germany," and of the *hakhme sepharad*, the "wise, the philosophers of Spain."

Certainly, geography had its differentiating effect. There, vision was drawn to the oceans and their highways. Here, it went up and down the rivers and from river to river. Understandably enough, the wide differences in historical conditions and political strivings acted upon the ways the separate groups surveyed and envisaged life. Here, this people was witness of an enduring battle between historical powers and was often the victim of intrigues and national passions. There, it experienced the change of events, sometimes the favorable and sometimes the negative and the evil, the rise and decline of rulers or the rebellion of the desert against the city. This too exercised its influence to create divergence.

But one difference cut deeper into the form of its existence: ways opened before the one, ways of education and of culture which led out to everyone in the land and to a real relationship with them. And, in contrast, the others were only permitted to see the road that led into their own self. True enough, in history the exceptions always exist alongside the rules. But in general this difference existed; it evidenced itself and maintained itself for a long time: one group was open to its environment, and the other one lived within itself.

The Piety of Culture and the Culture of Piety

As long as the concepts are not forced too far, one could say that the Sephardim experienced and lived a piety of culture in an epoch of rebirth, and the Ashkenazim, a culture of piety. Both became the enduring possession of this people. Only together do they reveal its existence as a whole and its continuing power of self-renewal.

The totality proved itself in the face of this duality as it was to do later. In the two realms with their differences, basically one and the same religious experience spoke, that of the kingdom of God. In the hopeful knowledge concerning the kingdom of God, aspiration becomes commandment and what was commanded becomes aspiration. Sometimes one strikes the stronger chord, sometimes the other. Always, the deep longing for the true unity and totality that comes from God and journeys toward God reveals itself. The sounds and figures of pure harmony, in which all fulfills itself because all gains its meaning in it, enter and elevate the soul. An old word for the harmony, *tikkun*, "order," entered the language of prayer more and more. It found its way into that prayer which begins with the emphatic word *alenu*, "it is incumbent upon us." The prayer had been composed by one of the great teachers of Babylonia for the New Year's Day that the congregation might solemnly announce, before itself and before the world, its belief in the One God and its expectations of the one future. It says:

> Therefore let us hope speedily to see the glory of Thy might, O God; to remove abominations from the earth, so that the idols be destroyed; to give the world a harmony, an "order" through the kingdom of the Almighty, so that every creature may confess itself unto Thy name . . .*

It is found as well in that other, simple prayer, which one is to speak in the evening, and which begins with the words: "Grant Thou-Who-Art our God, that we may lie down to peace and rise to life, and spread over us the tabernacle of Thy peace . . . and 'order' us through good reason which comes from Thee."** In the emphatic as in the simple, there speaks the admonishing longing for the kingdom of God, for its order, its harmony. In such confidence and its commandments both the Ashkenazim and Sephardim lived and were one. Thus from the one certainty of faith there blossomed forth unique forms in a unity of being and existence.

The individual uniqueness resulted from the different answers given the question about the permanency of a culture. It was the question of whether, in the human world, there existed preconditions, yes, perhaps even providential preparations for the great order and harmony, for the kingdom of God, whether the many avenues that truly approach it revealed themselves there. When the religion of this people and the philosophy of the Greeks met for the first time, this question was answered in the affirmative. It was possible for this people to recognize much of its own wisdom in Greek thought, much of *hokhmah*;

* See *The Authorized Daily Prayer Book*, ed. J. H. Hertz, p. 208.

** *Ibid.*, p. 372.

and many teachers were ready to say that *hokhmah* and Torah, in the last analysis, were one. A similar affirmative answer was now enunciated by the Sephardim, when, thanks to the Arabs, Greek science and Greek philosophy again opened their portals. Ways leading to religion, areas of the "preparation," were found in culture. One would become even more conscious of one's own truth, so went the credo, when one saw the totality. The word "harmony," "order," *tikkun,* was now also used for culture. Religion, in a sense, was a religion of culture.

The Different Path of the Ashkenazim

The Ashkenazim had a different fate. They saw no way before them leading to areas of exploration and order, upon which, receiving and giving, they could find themselves united with others in the land. The difference is clearly shown in the fact that the Sephardic scholars and thinkers had written their classic works, in which they presented the fundamental propositions and hopes of their faith in Arabic. But there is scarcely anything remotely resembling it that came out of the Ashkenazic domain. The reason is not difficult to find. In this *imperium romanum*, the days of history were days of change, as has already been indicated. Two historical ideas wrestled with one another. At times the one idea seemed to obtain the upper hand, that the state could only be a state within the Church; at times, the other, that the Church should be a church within the state. But no matter what the day, neither idea made it possible for this people to join an integrated culture. Both ideas provided only for isolation or self-betrayal. Thus they could only find culture, education, and intellectual dialogue in what was their own and in their tradition; they had to keep discovering themselves. For the Ashkenazim, only where Torah is could there be *hokhmah*; piety engendered culture for them.

The problem of the culture of piety and of the piety of culture raised itself in this people continually, and continually drove toward new formulation. This question is rooted in its faith as a task without end. This faith wants to be both, and only where it is both can it live. It must be *torah*, the revealed, with its commandment that is ever anew to be fulfilled, with its teaching of what this people is; and *hokhmah*, the artistic power granted to man, constantly realizing, constantly vitalizing, with its moral demand of what this people is to be. They belong together, and together they give this faith its totality and its unity, so that man may love Him-Who-Is, his God, with all his heart, and with all his soul, and with all his might (Deut. 6:5). They stand together in the Bible, the books of *torah* and the books of *hokhmah*, and together they are the Bible, the Book. They search for one another, they permeate one another, as the halakah and as the haggadah in the millennium of the Oral Torah, the Torah in movement; only together do they form the Talmud. They now come upon one another and find one another in the third millennium, this millennium of Torah and *hokhmah* in movement. Both *hokhmah* and Torah are possessed by the Ashkenazim and the Sephardim, and only together do they represent the spirit and the existence of this people in its third epoch. The Bible had been one great epoch, the Talmud a second. Now, together, the Ashkenazim and the Sephardim, each in their special historical manner, interwoven with the other in one creative unity, created the third great movement and let the Bible and the Talmud be reborn in it. This achievement of the two, in its totality and unity, then became both heritage and task to a succeeding millennium.

Hasidism and Mysticism

There are different accents in the unity of this people's existence, brought about by the fact that philosophy could unfold in one area, and in the other it could find no room. *Hokhmah* had its rich life, developing a mysticism and an ethic; but only among the Sephardim did it also take on the philosophic form. An untiring and fruitful intellectual labor took place; the religious possession was constantly rethought, was brought before each new generation in a new way. But the characteristic accent could also become a characteristic method. The simple facts that in one place philosophy presented itself to the mind while in the other it remained at a distance permitted different ways to develop within the same great domain.

This difference is most evident in that the Sephardim became systematizers while the Ashkenazim were empiricists. They worked the same fields: the interpretation of Bible and Talmud, the mystic *hokhmah* and the *hokhmah* of mysticism, and also the constitution, the ordering of the community, this preservation of the elasticity of existence. But they differed in the ways which they approached the tasks which were set for them and in the forms which they used and developed to meet them. The Ashkenazim centered their gaze primarily upon the individual in all his uniqueness, the Sephardim upon the structure of all being. The two could thus meet and complement one another, in a sort of Leibnitzian "pre-established harmony."

The way in which these two differing qualities fit together to create a totality is already evident in the form in which each led the Bible and the Talmud into the new millennium. In the congregations of the Ashkenazim there arose masters of the sifting explanation, the commentators; in the congregations of the Sephardim were masters who planned rational assignments, the codifiers. One could say that the Ashkenazim took reverence for the individual as the point of departure, and that the experience of the whole took hold of them afterward; that for the Sephardim, the deep impression of the whole came first, and that respect for the individual then took hold of them of necessity. One is tempted to say that it was a predestined division of labor. The one found the way from the outside to the interior; the other attained the external from within. There were two different methods. Together they produced a single understanding. Together they brought the Bible and Talmud into the soul of this people, and in this way they created new life. Again, as always in the history of this people, it was proven that particular qualities unite here; more than that, they are the foundation and the assurance of unity. Indeed, they create the power of rebirth as well.

The same diversity leading to unity reveals itself within the larger domain of mysticism. In the world of the Ashkenazim, mysticism was the religious experience of the individual man. The pious ones, the *hasidim*, were the mystics. Mysticism, if the term of a later age may be used here, was Hasidism. In this personalized form, mysticism renewed itself among the grandchildren of the Ashkenazim who had traveled eastward, from river to river, and had founded their congregations, their Ashkenazic colonies, everywhere as new plantations of an ancient life. The mysticism of later Hasidism also retains the peculiarity of the early Ashkenazic mysticism. For it is a mysticism to which personalities lend their individual features.

Ashkenazic mysticism came to Galilee in the Holy Land at the time when this millennium passed into a fourth millennium. A man called Isaac the Ashkenazi had prepared a place for it there. Because it is born out of the experiences of life, this Ashkenazic mysticism has a definite moral tone. The basic book of this mysticism, the "Book of the Pious Ones" (*Sefer Hasidim*), is as much a book of ethics as of mysticism. Life cannot be experienced without morality. The heart begins to open itself and to speak. Answers to the questions of human need must be supplied.

In Sephardic mysticism, the head spoke first. It was not as much the longings of life as the longings of thought that moved within Sephardic mysticism, and, as a result, called forth the problems of the cosmos. As in every genuine mysticism, there was search for harmony, for true "order." But it was not primarily the harmony in which all creatures become reconciled that was sought. It was the harmony in which the worlds, the spheres, the upper and the lower, unite. The problem that had stirred the great prophet of the exile when he opposed the Persian religion—the problem of an elemental evil in the world, opposed to every harmony within it—this problem once again took hold of the spirit. The unifying answer which the Sephardim gave was that of the prophet; and, to establish it, they built their systems. Just as the author of this people's first mystical book, the *Sefer Yetzirah* ("Book of Creation"), they utilized many Neoplatonic ideas to help them. Philosophy, above all other disciplines, was of use to them since it too rejected the concept of a radical evil. So they created a mysticism which saw, rising from the lowliest sphere, that of evil, paths that led upward from sphere to sphere to higher forces, the forces of blessing; and from above, through the same paths, from sphere to sphere, the fullness of the forces streamed downward. All is set into the one cosmos; the great possibility is granted to all; the great encounters now are possible.

In the presentation of such ideas, Sephardic thinkers displayed a rare wealth of imagination. One of them finally undertook to bring together this mystical tradition, which, assimilated and filtered through his own particular understanding of it, he presented in the form of a mystical Talmud. He named his book *Zohar* ("shining"), and a strange glimmer and a wondrous sound does indeed effulge parts of it. As the Talmud of mysticism, it influenced, if not determined, the feeling and thought of this people, within a large area, in a critical stage of its existence, for centuries. As the Sephardim brought forth their classic philosophers, so they created their classic mystics.

Here too the Sephardim and Ashkenazim supplemented one another and created a totality. All mysticism grows out of the longing to attain the immediate presence of God, the origin of all life and blessing. This longing unites with the belief that forces from God constantly stream down into the domain of man only to stream back up to Him, and that, through them, man could rise upward to the nearness of God. Sephardic mysticism promised the spirit that it would lead it into such paths if it would immerse itself in ever deeper devotion to the mysteries of the worlds existing between what is above and what is below. Ashkenazic mysticism promised the same to man's will through ever more intense acts of purification (by such acts, will shows its devotion). Here man would find his way to God by immersing himself in the infinity and eternity of God's commandment through which what is above enters what is below. Again, only together may these two approaches be called the mysticism of this people; for the cosmic sense cannot live in this people without the moral sense, and without the knowledge of the cosmos, the *olam*, world and time, the human task cannot exist.

The same individual characteristics may also be seen in the way in which, on diverse soils, community structures developed from their ancient congregational beginnings. In the Ashkenazic area the community generally constituted itself within an independent, individual congregation. Every congregation was like a little republic; it carried on its own ways and customs and clung to its local traditions. Each congregation stood freely next to the other. It is thus all the more remarkable and admirable that in this freedom and out of this freedom they achieved the forms of a living relationship and an effective partnership of labor. Congregational conventions and synods met, with no other task than that which they had set for themselves: to confront common sorrows, to meet needs of individuals or the many, to fulfill common tasks properly, to reach decisions demanded by the day or by the changing times. No high authority gave orders. The only ruling authority was that created by good will and secured by the proofs given by reason. Personalities, in whom knowledge and understanding were joined, did their share. Order itself had been given and vouched for by freedom. Something original entered the existence of this people with this; it kept maintaining, kept fortifying its existence.

In the areas of the Sephardim, the development of community structure often showed a more regional trait. Individual areas of power within the imperium could easily become districts for the administration of congregations. In addition, a psychological reason played a role here. The more a state or a governmental structure limited the civil rights of this people, the more eagerly did it seek to secure independence for its congregations. In them, it possessed the place of its own right and the right of its own place. Thus had it been in Ashkenaz, and, as indicated, it is all the more significant that a voluntary association was created and maintained despite this. In the Sephardic lands, this people could generally live within the feeling of shared law. It was easy there, and almost automatic, that the individual governmental areas of power became the districts of the congregations. Men of this people, who had received recognition at the ruling court, became the leaders in the total congregational structure. They were called to this task by the grace of the ruling power. Nevertheless, it is important to note that they remained through all the centuries men of this people. They lived within it, not before it or above it. In addition, almost all of them were men of individual significance, and they could be respected. The unity of existence was preserved.

Nevertheless, the difference between the two great domains of this people with regard to community structure became historically significant. The knowledge of the Torah and mysticism and its *hokhmah* could complement each other and create a new fertility in this completion. But such a complement was scarcely possible in terms of the directions congregational organization had taken within the two empires. In one, the rule of authority obtained; in the other, an autonomous rule. This was to be seen, even in individual tragic events, at the beginning of the fourth millennium of this people. Then the Sephardim, driven from their homes, tried to establish new habitations on ancient Ashkenazic soil and the contrast between the divergent paths was clear indeed. Great personalities, in earlier and later days, had risen above the differences and the contrasts; they always had experienced the unity of existence. For little men, who are, after all, little because they cleave to themselves, there is much that leads to cleavage. But what is wondrous and meaningful in the history of this people is precisely the fact that within it the great men always prevailed. They gave the final, the determining answers. Their history, in spite of everything, became the history of this people.

Divided and Still United

The third millennium of this people thus became the epoch of the Ashkenazim and the Sephardim. They were separated by the borders of the two empires of faith which confronted one another. On different soil, in a different atmosphere, each experienced a development which differed in many ways. How they remained, nevertheless, within the unity of existence without ever doubting, without ever wavering, how they came together inwardly, how they joined themselves to that which is more than all organization, to a totality and its organic unity:

this is what gave the epoch its content and its fertility, its strength and its endurance, so that it could continue to exist, so that it could be reborn.

Spiritually and intellectually the Ashkenazim and Sephardim kept meeting one another in the course of time. Constantly, from olden times, this people had known such internal encounters. They too became its history. It is of course true that every people knows something similar. Each has a day in which the individual or group born to the same soil encounters the total frame of reference into which it is placed. Such a meeting, whether friendly or unfriendly, takes place within its feeling and thinking. Home meets the land, or the place of childhood immediacy meets the state that opens itself later; they accept one another, or they oppose one another. This people experienced such encounters more than others. It was almost a constant occurrence for this people, from its beginning, from those days in which Ephraim and Judah, the Northern and the Southern Kingdoms, confronted one another. Such meetings continued through the time in which motherland and colonies, the state and the many congregations of East and West, found the strength of life in these encounters, receiving seed from one another, and giving fruit as well. Now an encounter took place again, though the ancient motherland had lost its independent existence and the people had become a people of colonies, of congregations far from the old historic soil. This people, and the world, appeared to have been divided between two great imperia of faith. Its history now appeared to be the history of Sephardim and Ashkenazim.

Another people would not have endured this division, quite possibly could not have endured it. But, for this people, such a separation (out of which rose so significant a task) became a deep internal challenge. The fact that the ancient language never ceased to be a mutual possession is great in itself, and commands respect. Both could always pray, write poetry, and think in it. But just as significant is the fact that the two, though set apart, never wavered in feeling and in recognizing each other as part of a totality, a single entity. The unity, the totality, the oneness, was real not because of the past alone, but also because of the present and the will to the future. Thus the tasks, the necessities, had to keep meeting each other, had to keep complementing one another. Within the great miracle which the history of this people presents, this third millennium, this epoch of Ashkenazim and Sephardim, remains a special miracle, a "miracle within a miracle," *nes betokh nes*, as the old haggadah expressed the paradox. Unfortunately one is often tempted to consider what in the history of other peoples would be thought of as almost a miracle to be self-evident in this people's history. This epoch, as fact as well as achievement, presents itself as something extraordinary in historical reality and in historical fulfillment.

This people has so often and at times so lightly been accused of having lost the possibility, the will, and the ability for true historical existence with the end of its independent state. In this creative, internal dialogue, it also demonstrated the will and strength to create its own history, to remain a true historical personality, the subject of its history, and never to become a mere object. There is little that reveals historical independence in as vital a form as this ability to maintain the oneness of care and the oneness of hope, the great messianic oneness and to be able to renew it and transmit it as one's heritage. The prophets had taught this people to let the future enter the present, to give to the past the meaning of the future, the meaning of beginning, of a gateway to the future. The future, the care for it, the hope in it, remained unshakable, and it created in everyone that certainty, that inner unity of all, without which no true history exists. In the centuries which demanded a life in the two separated imperia, developing individual existence here and there, an extraordinary unit remained the great self-evident fact of life.

The Economic Influence

Something further must be noted in this regard. The different manner of the Ashkenazim and of the Sephardim also extended to a difference in economy, influencing and determining not so much the individual as the type.

The individual is the rejection of the typical, and the typical is a constant threat to the individual. Personalities always understand one another finally, at least in what is final and fundamental in them; types comprehend and endure one another only with difficulty. The more individuals, the more inner unity and effective mutuality, the more types and the more typical the types, the more there is inner and outer conflict. The individual gains his power from the spiritual, out of the fundamental realm in which will, feeling, and thinking are a unity or become one. The typical often lets the spiritual become stunted; it is a rigid crust that places itself around the human and personal and that can stifle it finally. The individual has many questions, and every answer once again becomes a question for it; the type only knows answers, its typical answers, and to it the doubting question signifies a kind of backwardness. The individual, the personality, has a sense of the special, that which rises above the commonplace, the question addressed to the customary. The man who only represents a type and wants only to represent a type, sees something inimical in the exception, a doubt of that upon which his full and sole security rests. Thus in societies where the type determines everything, this untypical people, appearing as a constant exception, is little understood. Its very presence awakens an uneasiness which is an incitement to enmity. In recompense, it was all the more understood and appreciated where individuality became the trait of life and of being.

Within this people, to be sure, there existed men and groups whose character was but a typical formulation. This is clearly evident in various places in later days, and must also have been so in earlier days. Economic conditions in different times and ways saw to this. They also revealed themselves in the distinctive characters of the Sephardim and Ashkenazim. The Sephardim, seen as a whole, had been fully accepted into the general economic life of the lands in which they lived, and a certain breadth of vision developed, which was already manifest in their looking out to the sea. The heritage of the colony of Alexandria, whose ships had sailed to the North, the West, and the South, continued here. In general, the others, the Ashkenazim, were increasingly separated from the economic life of the land. They had to form an economic unity by themselves, within the constrictions drawn about them. Revolutionary methods were eventually initiated within this constrictedness in order to gain, in some way, some breadth. Money developed from a means of economy into an object of economy; constrictions were burst. Economic differences between Ashkenazim and Sephardim led to particularities—and to divisions.

In all of this, and despite all of this, now as before, this people was one people, and it felt its oneness as the certainty of its life and as the guarantee of its future. The motherland no longer could give strength as a visible, tangible center. All the stronger, the more alive, therefore, did Zion become as the ideal center from which flowed to all souls the streams of the one admonition, which is also the one confidence. One was never silent about Zion and "for Zion's sake"; all prayed for Zion, all created poetry of Zion, in Ashkenaz and in Sepharad. Zion became the kind of poetry which Aristotle characterized as "something more effective and more philosophic than history." Just as individual life, history is also a constant battle between poetry and prose. In the poetry of Zion history recovered the horizon's distances which gave it space to breathe, and out of which come strength and poetry. The boundaries drawn by the imperia no longer could enclose.

In some measure, on the road to Zion, on the road from what it experienced to that for which it longed, this people, in its historical realm, contained men of great and universal personalities, personalities of spirit and character, though it also had its men of affairs. Against such individuals, everything separating, everything that was merely typical, broke and shattered. Whether they were born in the North or the South, they belonged to both North and South. A strength of unity emanated from them. In these men too, the borders drawn by the imperia did not exist. In these men the total spirit spoke, which alone gives every particularity its historical place and with it its right and its duty. This spirit made these men men of this people. The will to the kingdom of God, this will to order and to unity, revealed itself in these men, in each of them within their own domain. They wished to educate their people, always and everywhere to permit the *olam*, infinity and eternity, to enter the people's existence, no matter how constricted the area of its being. They wished, always and everywhere, to prepare a place for "truth, justice and peace," the moral infinity and eternity which one of the ancient sages had called the "foundation of the *olam*." The goal did not change for these men, in Ashkenaz or in Sepharad. These leaders therefore did not want to be rulers, but teachers like those who had formed the people in its first two millennia. This people may count it among its historical achievements that such men could emanate from it, and that sooner or later it understood and recognized these men, thus winning them inwardly for its own. The third millennium was able to achieve this, just as the two millennia had done before it. This too was work for "kingdom of the Almighty," and therefore work within His kingdom.

The Prayer Book

This people held yet another thing, absorbing and making it part of its existence: its book of prayers. These prayers had grown in the midst of the people in the preceding millennium. They had been folk prayers even as there are folk songs. Now, in the third millennium, they were ordered and arranged, set into the sequence of the workday and the Sabbath, the festival days, and special occasions. Collected in a book, they were a folk book, which everyone, small and great, scholar and simple man, carried within himself. The book could speak out of him, through him, to him.

Because of this, every hour of life could discover and rediscover itself in man, so that all that was customary could renew itself from day to day, and all that was new could penetrate the human element which endures from generation to generation. Individual life here speaks out of the frame of group life, and one who prays becomes aware of the life which is everyone's life. Therefore, everyone prays both for himself and for the congregation. He prays as the priests pray, when he prays for himself. The "I" becomes "We," and the "We" once again becomes the "I."

This book is a book of the "We" and of the "I," because this people and humanity are led toward one another—more—into one another. The people, too, prays in these prayers, whether the individual speaks them for himself or whether the assembled congregation utters them. The totality of the utmost depths of being opens itself when this people begins to pray, when standing before God, it seeks to understand itself in its supplications and hopes. It can only pray out of the framework of its humanity. It appears as its own priest before God, and at the same time as a priest for humanity.

This people does not know prayer for the self alone. One who thinks only of himself is unable truly to pray. This people's book of prayers has nothing to say to him. Its prayers seek to conquer selfishness, whether it be the selfishness of the individual or that selfishness which believes itself unselfish simply because it is shared by thousands. Egotism is the irreverence of life.

The prophetic word "all" (an emphatic word) attains its full, strong tone in these prayers. We hear it in the *maestoso* of the special prayers for the High Days, the Days of Awe, the day of the New Year and the Day of Atonement. Section after section of these prayers commences with the exclamation *uvekhen*—a concise word, difficult to interpret as concisely—"however it may be outside."

However it may be outside, we pray unto Thee: Thou-Who-Art our God, grant reverence for Thee to all whom Thou has fashioned, and devotion unto Thee to all whom Thou hast created; and all whom Thou hast fashioned will fear Thee, and all whom Thou hast created will bow before Thee, and they will all have been fashioned into one totality, to do Thy will with a perfect heart; for thus we shall know,

O Thou-Who-Art our God, that dominion is Thine, that might is in Thy hand, strength in Thy right, and that Thy name is great over all Thy creatures.*

Such is the opening verse; only afterward, as its continuation, does the limiting context come:

However it may be outside, we pray unto Thee: Thou-Who-Art, grant honor unto Thy people, recognition to those who fear Thee, hope to those who seek Thee, free speech to those who wait for Thee, joy unto Thy land, gladness to Thy city, a sprouting forth of the rays of David, Thy servant, and a shining forth of the light of the son of Jesse, Thine anointed—speedily, in our days!**

The word "all" is the first and the determining word. Every congregation which commences this majestic hymn, no matter how small it may be, becomes the whole people and acknowledges the one kingdom of God.

The same grand purpose is served in the simple prayer over the family table. The prayer after the meal, the "blessing of the sustenance," is perhaps the most intimate, most popular of all the prayers. Therefore, it is referred to by the comfortable word *benschen* (a colloquial term derived from the Latin *benedicere*). The family speaks it, sings it, and, no matter how constricted the world may be around the family, through this prayer the family becomes a congregation of God. This prayer also commences with this word "all," this constantly repeated word. Day after day, out of the mouth of the man of the house, the prayer speaks its "all":

Praised be Thou-Who-Art, ruler of the world, who nourishes all the world in Thy goodness, in kindness, love, and mercy. He gives bread unto all flesh, for His love is eternal. And through His great goodness sustenance has never failed us, and may it never fail us, never,

* See *High Holiday Prayer Book*, ed. M. Silverman, p. 11.

** *Ibid.*, pp. 11–12.

for the sake of His great name. He sustains all and cares for all, and He does good for all, and He prepares sustenance for all His creatures which He has fashioned. Praised art Thou-Who-Art, who sustaineth all.*

"All," "all" resounds here constantly, for only in such utterance does the special and the personal gain expression. The progression is clear. First the all, then thanks for that which God has given His people and for that which He has given him who is now praying. After the expression of thanks, only after it, comes a petition for that which He might give the family. In masterly composition, masterly in its simplicity, the one is always added to the other and set within the other. This people was to know itself to be within the kingdom of God, in every demanding instant. That is why they pray, that they may never forget this.

This book of prayers has to be known, has to be understood in the fullness of all its parts by anyone who would know this people, who would want to understand it in all its traits. This book is a book of confessions of faith; man, in prayer, here confesses his faith. All confession of faith is, at the same time—if not primarily—a confession to faith, to the task set by God, to the situation which He has apportioned man. This confession of faith is a confession of will. Deep feeling, seeking expression, speaks in the prayers of this book; and equally, a conceptual drive speaks, formulating the sentences. But in everything it is always the will that speaks, that seeks realization. Everywhere may be heard this will to the One God, to His mystery and to His commandment, to His promise in which that which is beyond and that which is commanded are one. Only in prayer does the soul grasp both in unity, the infinitely unknown and the manifestly given. This sense of unity becomes the ultimate knowledge, the great confession or—it means the same—the great gratitude. That is why the Bible has one and the same word for confession and for thanking. This book of prayers is a book of decision for God. Praying, man makes his decision—"whatever may be outside"—for the One God.

* See *The Authorized Daily Prayer Book*, ed. J. H. Hertz, pp. 966–68.

Confession is in the prayer, and readiness is in the confession. The innermost readiness is that for the kingdom of God.

The Third Millennium and the Rebirth

He who hears the voices of the third millennium, the voices of the South and of the North, hears all this. It is as a wondrous "Song of Songs." At times it is the soul that pours forth in it, at times it is the spirit that expresses itself in it. At times it has an abundance of words, song after song of experiences, and what has been learned. At times it is a song without words, a song which the existence of this people itself begins to sing. And everything finally becomes part of the song. The books of law and of philosophy also sound in it—somehow, somewhere. For their thoughts, no matter from where they emanate, finally flow into the harmony of the kingdom of God, into this Song of Songs. One is often tempted to say that even its logic becomes music. Before all of this the little and the petty, which after all have always existed here and everywhere, disappears.

This third millennium also, in that which it was and in that which it created, is truly an epoch in the existence of this people, as were both the millennia that preceded it. For true existence is the unity of that which we are and that which we create. That which first grew and was reborn in those two epochs, now was reborn again; that is to say, what this third millennium was and what it created was being of the old being and was yet something new. For rebirth stops, but moves forward. It is not a decreed administration; rather it is a power that proves itself. It is the power by means of which something that has come into being turns into something new in a process of becoming; that which is grown, begins to grow anew by blossoming once again, by sending forth new shoots, by gaining new expression. The meaning of rebirth is disclosed by a Talmudic legend. One day, during the second millennium, Moses came to earth again and entered the academy of Rabbi Akiba. He listened there and could not understand what was being taught, until he was told that it was the Torah of Moses. Only then did he understand and gratefully recognize that which was clearly his own. During the new millennium, Moses could have entered Worms on the Rhine, where Rabbi Solomon Isaac of Troyes, called Rashi, taught; or Fostat in Egypt, where Moses ben Maimon of Cordova, called Rambam, had his home; gratefully, he would have experienced the same, the testimony of rebirth.

The Wandering Recommences

Yet another strength of earlier days, the power of colonization, proved itself again, in this millennium. At times it was wakened by the drive of the will, at times, more frequently, under the pressure of need. It continued to live, this ability to bring the old to new ground, so that it remains what it was, proving the strength of what is one's own by showing, that under new conditions, in another part of the world, in another atmosphere, it can accept the new. Communities arose which were not merely communities which a different land permitted or endured; rather, these communities received the value, content, and merit of the land into themselves, without losing possession of their own value, content, and merit. True colonization must be from its beginning or become a readiness on both sides, a mutual receptivity.

Ashkenazim, from generation to generation, were drawn toward the East. At first, and also in later times, they were led by the desire to find new economic opportunity there. But primarily, the stream of refugees seemed to see hope shining to them from the East as they looked about for new soil to establish their congregations. Fanaticism had fallen upon the old congregations and had done its work. In one place it had been the fanaticism of belief, in another that of unbelief; rapacity had often been joined with both. But no congregation, such was the will of these people, was to perish. That which had been destroyed was to be rebuilt, if not in the old place, then in a new one.

None of the old congregations ever ceased existing in some fashion, inwardly, historically.

The chronicles of the Ashkenazim at this time are an almost endless report of afflicted or destroyed congregations. But their essential history is otherwise. It is the history of a strength of life which ever again gave witness to the force of beginning. One is tempted to say that it is the history of a spiritual and intellectual strength which ever anew brought forth powers of expression, of realization, of concretion, this ability to maintain a dialogue with oneself, even during the most difficult days. It was a fight for existence, a fight for the air and the food of each day that had to be carried out. But the fight for existence was also, and always, a fight for history. It was not just an instinctive struggling like that carried on for daily life; it was a conscious striving, one which in every day had a clear vision of its goal. One could be driven out of cities and countries, but one could never be driven out of history. Wherever these men traveled their history traveled with them. History was not merely tradition here, as faithfully as this was preserved; history was the future, the future which enters the present. It remained the way and the message. Every congregation was a special part of this history, carrying and carried by it, and therefore it did not cease existing.

Toward the end of the third millennium, the time of wandering also came to the Sephardim. It knitted itself together in the decisive events of a few years. A whole people had to emigrate that the imperium of faith might proclaim its victory. The Sephardim traveled to the East, just as the Ashkenazim had done, but they traveled southward and the Ashkenazim remained in the North. They took a language along with them, the language of the land which had ruled their congregations for so many generations. This language persisted in its own form, while that of the Ashkenazim, upon the new Eastern soil, developed a new and expressive form, almost a new language. The Sephardim of the land Sepharad went forth into exodus. The old land was submerged for them and sank into the past. It now belonged to the other imperium completely. But this great past still maintained a home within them. The Ashkenazim also went forth at that time. They left Ashkenaz, but this land remained a present reality for them. Upon the roads that led there and back, men traveled in both directions. Here, and there, they were in the same imperium.

Everywhere, and ever again, this people came to know how much of its destiny depended upon chance when it was wandering. Chance could exalt man, or could cast him down. In the third millennium, Purim, the day which is connected with the biblical book of Esther, a book concerning "chance," came into its own. It turned its hours into a cheerful joking that could make the outer world disappear. One laughs at the persecutors; the gallows become comedy. The dark clouds that had lowered are forgotten. The Book of Esther is remarkable in itself; it is a book without the word "God." Its chapters apparently dare not speak of God, since they let "chance" hold sway. It is also strange in that it emphasizes that the "villain" Haman is not a Persian. But it is particularly remarkable in that it is part of the Bible, this book of chance, with nothing of the sign, its wonder and its way.

But it is in the Bible; and it must be understood in a biblical way. It seeks to remind man of something twofold: first, that for a long time to come slander and vanity (both, after all, coming from the same root) will point a finger against this people and will open many mouths. In the awesome days of its New Year, this people commences the great litany of confessions and of petitions with the words: *Avinu malkenu* "Our Father, our King." Four sentences follow, one upon another: "Our Father, our King, destroy the thoughts of them that hate us"; "Our Father, our King, turn to nought the council of our enemies"; "Our Father, our King, take every oppressor and slanderer away from us"; "Our Father, our King, close the mouth of every slanderer and accuser."* The Book of Esther reveals all that takes place within these accusers and what goes on behind their slander. This could come as a justification of this people; it could almost be a comfort. Another point of which the Book of Esther serves as a reminder is expressed in the sentence: "And all the king's servants, that

* See *High Holiday Prayer Book*, ed. M. Silverman, p. 94.

were in the king's gate, bowed down, and prostrated themselves before Haman; for the king had so commanded concerning him. But Mordecai bowed not down, nor prostrated himself before him" (Esther 3:2). Everyone to whom this sentence spoke knew where to take his special stand, the one place from which the way could be seen clearly.

The Achievements of the Middle Ages

This people carried its place with it in its wanderings. Nowhere and never did it lose it, just as it never lost its way and its consolation. This third millennium tells of this time, which later was called the Middle Ages by an annalist of the imperium, writing from his own standpoint.

For this people, it was an epoch of creating and of suffering. Suffering, when it draws its strength from conviction, has something creative and fruitful in it. It generates ideas of the future, out of which the new reality can develop. Existence itself becomes creative in suffering. On the other hand, all creating also signifies suffering; it demands patience which enlarges and expands itself. Whoever is unable to suffer is unable to achieve. This third millennium proved this people capable of that great historical achievement in which suffering and creating relate, an achievement which characterizes this people.

Whoever tries to view this epoch in the totality of its intellectual achievements, is filled almost with awe. What a wealth of legal work, poetry, philosophy, mysticism, philology and recollection of the past! What works searching for the basis of the totality, what works of contemporary knowledge! It is as rich in its abundant sweep as in its special areas. And all of this is carried and nourished by a wondrous strength of existence, revealing itself as much in the will and the ability for unity as in the ability and will for variety. Through East and West, through North and South, this people had become manifoldly different, and it could cling to its differences because it lived in unity. In its daily prayers it prayed: "Praised art Thou-Who-Art Our

God of Jacob." Wherever and however they were, no matter how separated, they knew themselves to be within the House of Israel, within the one existence and in the one history. They prayed to the "God of Abraham, of Isaac, of Jacob." The proselyte also, according to a decision of Moses ben Maimon, was to pray, "our God and God of our Fathers." When he entered this religion, he also entered this existence and this history.

It was an existence and a history for the sake of the kingdom of God. Therefore, it was also within the kingdom of God at all times. The way that was a way to the kingdom of God was already a way within it. This is one of the paradoxes of this religion. But still the expectation, this patience which exalts, is already a realization; the way itself is already a consolation. Philosophy recognized this; mysticism came to live it; piety which tried to fulfill the commandment of the Eternal One came to experience it. Thus had the epoch of the prophets implanted it in many a soul. Thus had the epoch of the teachers brought it into the people. Thus did this, the third epoch, now present it to this people—again there was growth and rebirth, and rebirth.

V

The Hope

The Fourth Millennium Commences

From generation to generation, this people was pledged to the One God against all gods, to the one way as opposed to all ways, to the one kingdom above all kingdoms, to the one hope beyond all hopes. "Ye are My witnesses, saith Him-Who-Is" (Is. 43:10). Thus did the prophet of the Exile give Israel direction. To this end had Israel battled. In its striving, the soul had made and kept the spirit fertile. This striving had maintained its life, and its power had created new forms of living. For the sake of this "Yes" it had to speak so many a "No"; it dared not tire either in the "Yes" or in the "No." Through this affirmation of the One God it became what it became, and it dared not cease becoming, entering into ever-new worlds to attain new epochs.

History only lives and becomes fertile if it is able to achieve what may truly be called an epoch. If, within it, events only add themselves in sequence—victories and defeats, times of serfs and slaves—history finally exhausts itself. A duration without epochs can then come into existence, but viewed in terms of the final goal, the messianic, all great historical life is a struggle for epochs. Even individual, personal life, the striving of man for himself, receives its intrinsic character in breaking through to the ordered stages of its own existence, its epochs.

A new epoch can begin for a community, a people, or a group of peoples, just as for an individual, when a new question, a new task approaches, because somewhere a new principle has been established and a new position is being taken. The old forms of the answer now become insufficient; old formulations of relationships are no longer applicable or are unsatisfactory. Whether the established, the developed, can grow, can develop further, whether a new form of thinking can unfold itself, whether the old, the enduring faithfulness can give the new its expression, now become decisive. If this proves possible, a new epoch begins, or, what is the same, a power for rebirth proves itself. If this strength, this ability to enter a new epoch, fails, a time of paralysis sets in. Rebirth is the beginning, the breakthrough. The epoch is the extension into distances which the reborn then fashions for itself in all the areas open to it.

With its fourth millennium, a new epoch of this people commences. It is one that has not yet ended and which therefore cannot yet be surveyed in its ultimate aspects. The three millennia that preceded it are clearly recognizable as epochs, though they cannot be established through a meticulous arithmetic. True history always has its transitions, in which that which is in the process of becoming forms itself out of what came to be. Only events are sudden, in coming as well as in going. It is also true that there are times in history in which no determining thinking reveals itself. In a sense, those are days of unconsciousness paralleling the condition in individuals when a blow, a push, or a shock blocks all determined and determining thought within him for hours. But here as there, beneath unconsciousness, the forces of the will continue to exert themselves. There is no movement of the human will in which something of thought does not enter. Such days in which darkness descends upon body and soul, and in which the will works only with that thought resident within it, often precede the periods out of which the epochs are formed. For that reason, too, there are no rigid, carefully marked boundaries separating one epoch from another. But when the totality of the construction is viewed, the individual millennia clearly distinguish themselves. It is a wondrous thing in the history of this people that each of its millennia represents an epoch, that each of its epochs has its millennium, its "days" before Him-Who-Is, as the Prayer of Moses the man of God called them: "So teach us to number our days, that we may get us a heart of wisdom" (Ps. 90:12).

They are the epochs of the battle for the one, and with that the great epoch of faithfulness. Always the one; for he who confesses the One God, Him-Who-Is, at the same time confesses himself to the one way, to the one kingdom, to the one hope. In the course of time, one or another occasionally demanded a more decisive tone. In the first millennium, the oneness of God demanded the full strength of hearing and hearkening against the accepted multiplicity of gods. The second millennium demanded primarily the vision for the one way, from which the many ways deceitfully wished to stray. The third millennium presented as paramount the choice and the act of decision between the one kingdom and being one of the kingdoms. It can thus be said that the most important task of the fourth millennium became that of clinging to the one hope as against the many hopes that always appeared to be so close to fulfillment. The one and the same was and remained, from generation to generation, constant in its foundations and its goal of the One God, the one way, the one kingdom, the one great hope. But now the centuries brought something new, and its effect was to bring the problem of hope into the foreground.

Man's Hope and Man's Way

Attempts have often been made to find the decisive difference between man and beast. It has been found in that that man is a being who fashions tools, or in that that he is a creature who knows grandparents and grandchildren. It could also be said that man is a being of hope. By means of two distinct dimensions of soul, one of which creates the other and is then in turn awakened, man takes the wish which would bring the distant near, that which becomes the motive power of will, and makes it the motif of thought and fantasy. He seeks out the separating and perhaps restraining, even preventing gaps that lie before him, all dusk. And nevertheless he seeks to conquer them in contemplation, to make what was distant a tangible nearness. Particularly in a religious world, since nearness and distance seek to unite, hopes spring up everywhere. Paul, the great apostle who derived from this people, was right: where men believe and love, they hope. But the changing day permits the hopes to rise in changing ways. Within religion, above the hopes, there stands the one hope, the religious expectation, the unshakable and ineluctable certainty that the way, the one way, has a goal, the one goal, that it is not fruitless or useless to "walk with God." The motif of hope is the wish, clear or cloudy, which sustains itself with actual or imagined appearances. The spiritual foundation of the one, the religious hope, is the deep assurance, this deepest knowledge, in which the finite comes to experience something of the power of infinity, this certainty that the goal endures in which all fulfills itself and that, where the goal is firmly established, there is the one way that leads to it. That is the expectation which rises out of the strength of this people's belief. It is the hope above all hopes, the one which includes and unites all human beings within it.

Beside the One God there can be no "other gods." No compromise, no weakening, no diversion is possible. But next to the way, the one way, valid "from generation to generation," which is the only straight line that can connect the generations, serpentine paths stretch themselves. From them, time in its changes addresses us humans here on earth, and many are the hours that call us. The history of man is filled with serpentine paths. If only the soul of man stays alive, and it does stay alive, when it does not lose the one way, the way to the one goal!

Underneath the heaven of the one kingdom are the kingdoms of this earth. In them, man's work has its place. They want to command him as well, and at times also want to control his soul. The life of the religious man can become an honest and pure battle against the state, at times. Sooner or later, this battle becomes a giving and receiving of understanding with the state. If only men did not lose the knowledge of the one kingdom and the experiencing of its might while they live in the kingdoms!

We men wander through wishes. They begin in us and then gain their own existence in that which they reveal. But they still remain part of our existence, part of our self; in effect, they are our life as it projects itself in the distant reaches. Hopes, manifold as the days, always unite these two existences anew, so that they—distant and close life—always come to be one. Without the hopes, the self would split itself and life would finally break in two. Man is a being who hopes, and since there are many days, there are many hopes. If only the many hopes, rising and falling, apparently or tangibly near here, apparently or actually fulfilling themselves there, did not constrict the space within the soul given to the one hope! If only they did not wind up taking this space in the end! If only the strength of the great expectation, which seeks to bring the one world, the *olam*, into the life and self of man, would not seep away and finally disappear one day under the burden of all the hopes moving about in the world!

This people of the great expectation, the negation, the renunciation for the sake of the one greatness, always remained a people of many and changing hopes. This people and its congregations cherished the fulfillment of wishes that too often moves far into the distance; it thus could not be without the hopes that seek to conquer distance. Scarcely anything reveals its untiring nature as its hopes, those found in the emigrants to whom the new soil seems to promise something new, something better, or the expectation of the old settlers, those who persist, who hope to see a new day rise above the old soil. Therefore this people always understood both moving away to follow hopes, and remaining to wait for them. Above all, an expectation lived in them everywhere, for the children and the children's children. The spiritual history of many of these people, from generation to generation, is a history of suffering and renunciation, a giving up for the sake of children and grandchildren, that the hopes might fulfill themselves in them. One learned to live in what was coming; more than this, one became accustomed to live this way, to prepare in one's own narrow and short existence a breadth of space and an extension of days. Under all oppressions, patience preserved a viable strength. It even became active, indeed, gaining something of the messianic dynamism of the great expectation—"searching out with the soul" the land of the children.

The Expulsion From Spain

The fourth millennium aroused in this people hope after hope, in one century after another, now here, and now there. But it began with that darkness that had fallen upon the transition days of ending and beginning: the darkness of the expulsion of the Sephardim from Sepharad, out of the land in which their congregations lived from the days of the Roman Republic. Despots, in the hour of the edict of eviction, thought that they had pronounced judgment upon this people. In reality, they had uttered a verdict upon themselves.

The Sephardim took a rich heritage with them, a heritage of scholarship and of poetry, and the danger could arise that they might become mere heirs. A proud tradition went with them, a tradition of spirit and of responsibility, so it was possible in the course of time that they might exhaust themselves within that tradition. The language of the land from which they were driven went with them in their various ways. Fate could turn it into a language that would only be spoken and written, but would no longer be a language which struggled for living expression, which battled with thought in order to make it expressible. The Sephardim remained Sephardim wherever their way led, the majority who quickly headed toward the East, and the individuals who went northward and westward. Their name became almost an image of nobility. This might signify something great, but it could also signify a potential inner danger.

They remained Sephardim, but divorced themselves from the land of Sepharad. There is no doubt that their feelings and hopes were injured to the depths. It is told that these men pronounced a solemn ban on this land; never more was one of them to step upon its soil. Perhaps this is only a legend, but it is a legend which speaks the inner truth. It is also told that these men, when they left, dug up the gravestones out of the soil of the cemetery and took them along: no note of piety was to sound from this land to their new settlements. Again it is possible that this is just a legend, but in this, too, there dwells the truth of poetry. In these two stories we see the emotions which filled the people as they went forth from the land in which, for a millennium and a half (one half of all the time their people had known), their congregations had been places of honor and renown. They wanted future generations to know how these men, to whom gratitude was as natural as existence, departed from the land of ingratitude. All that they had been in the land, and what the land had been to them, no longer had any place. They wanted to begin anew, upon new soil.

Yet one bond continued to endure for succeeding generations, a bond that they could not, would not, dared not loosen. Some of their people had remained in the land at the time of the exodus. To do so they had openly deserted their faith in the sight of all; but in their own sight, in the inner vision of their soul, it yet remained and was to remain their true belief. They thought that fate's decree was not final, that they would experience the day in which they would be restored to their right, to their own identity. Perhaps they interpreted the prophet's word as applying to themselves: "Come, my people, enter thou into thy chambers, and shut thy doors about thee; hide thyself for a little moment, until the indignation be overpast" (Is. 26:20). They lived in their chamber, within their memories and hopes, waiting for the day in which they could once again reveal themselves before the eyes of the world. Perhaps they had heard tales of a similar situation from that time when in the land of Islam, a hot fanaticism—not a cool one such as this—had also given their people a choice of leaving their faith or the land. Then, too, there had been many, seeking to preserve home and hearth, who had hidden themselves from their real selves—for a little while, according to their reckoning. And indeed, when the darkness had lifted, they had been able to return to their identity. Should such a possibility not have been granted to those who stayed in the land of Sepharad? For their brothers, who had wandered forth, head high, they who now concealed their faces would preserve the old soil. But, no matter how much they longed for it, they waited in vain for such a day. It did not come; an age had ended.

The Marranos

The history of these *anusim*, the "coerced" ones, as their brothers outside the land named them, these "Marranos," as they were called within the land, is a soul-shaking chapter in the long and moving history of this people. It tells of a great longing for faithfulness, for it was not happiness, but faithfulness for which these *anusim* longed. Faithfulness was to be the fulfillment of life for them and their children. Many grew tired of waiting. That which surrounded them day after day, that which pressed upon them daily, finally conquered them. What had been an appearance became their existence; they lost themselves within the people in whose midst, until then, they had chosen their individual way. In those who endured, the longing only grew stronger with the passing days; it became inflexibility. Many revealed their faces, confessed and praised their God, the God of their fathers, and as Sephardim in Sepharad, ascended the funeral pyre. The longing for faithfulness fulfilled itself in the martyr's death; it had become that faithfulness which can be only all or nothing. As the old expression has it: "They gave their soul for the sanctification of the divine Name." Many others succeeded in fleeing to lands of freedom, so that they could be free. (Freedom, after all, is basically freedom from having to present a false appearance.) They founded their congregations in those free lands where men of longing attained the freedom of faithfulness.

We still possess pictures of these men, some of them painted by masters. Whoever immerses himself in these features, recognizes the character with which longing has marked them. Such character speaks in the features of a thinker, of Baruch Spinoza. In him the misunderstood longing became understanding, became philosophy. In many, the longing froze into rigidity, having been weakened for so long. They became fanatics—the zealot is always someone frozen into rigidity—and they pronounced the ban where their brothers in the East and West would not have invoked it. Many who have been oppressed would be oppressors. But he who can hear and see, and therefore sees the totality and hears the totality, finds these men speaking to him principally of the great, almost messianic longing for faithfulness, telling of men in whom longing became verification of self. This act in the drama of this people does not seek to rouse "fear and pity" as, according to Aristotle, the tragedy of the Hellenes does. Like the history of this people, it seeks to win allegiance to the One God, proclaiming the belief which signifies the great faithfulness.

"If ye will not have faith, surely ye shall not be established" (Is. 7:9), said the same prophet who spoke of hiding oneself. This people always believed in its "coerced" children, since the great faith was within them. It never cast them out or denied them, nor did it misunderstand them. A deep love filled this people. Out of it came the longing, the great style of its life, the grandeur of its suffering. This love always spoke to all of its people. An enduring splendor sent its rays to their days, brightening here, reconciling there.

The *Zohar* and the Men of Safed

Even in the transition from epoch to epoch, the Sephardim made a deep impression on the thought and feeling of their people.

It was primarily through their influence, during and despite the transition from the third to the fourth millennium, that the Jewish man became and remained for generations a mystic man, a *homo mysticus.* The tragedy of their fate, in which the prophetic expression "the setting of the sun at noontide" seemed to be portrayed, let mystic questions arise. The thought of the day was unable to give a satisfactory answer. An even greater impetus toward mysticism came from the *Book of Zohar*, composed by a man of Sepharad, in order to provide a mystic Oral Torah. Hebrew printing, a creation of the Sephardim before the exodus, was practiced in many lands and permitted the book to find many readers. The influence which it exercised for several centuries can scarcely be overestimated. The secret of its style, which created the secret of its contents, lent particular expression to the form of existence at that time. Everything in man and around man became an indication, a clue to another enduring world, in which the secret reveals its truth, its reality. Mystic man dwells in the world below in which all truth and all reality must be hidden, but he lives in the higher world, where his true existence takes place.

An effort was made in those days, in the Holy Land, in Safed, in Galilee, to turn a place of residence into a place of mystic life. The mystic ideas from Sepharad made it possible for these men to join together as a congregation of the higher world. From Sabbath to Sabbath, they drew strength from a higher world which enabled them to cope with the great expectation for which they lived, that through their life they might bring about its fulfillment. They sought to be strong enough for the final and decisive task of their people: to await the messiah and to be ready for his messengers.

From Safed messianic ripples spread forth and raised their waves. They are a consequence of inner tremors caused by the expulsion of the Sephardim. One assumed, and so much spoke for it, that one was standing at a turning in time. Eventually, a century later, a tidal wave did emanate from here. It overwhelmed the congregations in the Moslem domain and penetrated those within the imperium of the Church; for a long time, in both places, it held many minds. Like a final act, a postscript added to the drama of Sepharad, the messiah comes whom many thought they had lived to see: Sabbatai Zevi of Smyrna, who assumed the mantle of King of his people, and who then, without being coerced, became an apostate and completed his destiny in death. A mystic messianism and the Marrano consciousness united in a drama that had only one act. In this deception too, that great longing, at times joyful and at times fearful, had set the heart quivering. One who cannot respond to it cannot understand what these men thought they were experiencing. That great longing was within them which wants to bring nearer the end of the way, which wants to have the King before the kingdom comes into being.

The contemplating and the striving of the men of Safed was of another type. They waited for the kingdom and wanted to learn and to teach in order to come closer to it, to experience it more intimately, so that men of this people and the one kingdom might find one another. Indeed, this is what the prayer of the ancient teachers says, the prayer of the way from generation to generation. From ancient times, when the congregation is assembled it closes its worship:

> Exalted and sanctified be the name of God in the world which He has created. And may He let His kingdom come to rule in your life, and in your days, and in the life of the whole house of Israel, speedily and in an approaching time.*

No mere ecstatic imagining speaks in this, but the commandment of the way which is already consolation because it alone leads to conso-

* The *Kaddish*. Cf. *The Authorized Daily Prayer Book*, ed. J. H. Hertz, p. 106.

lation. It is the prayer of the one hope, the great expectation of the time when the name of God will be sanctified on earth.

Joseph Karo and the *Shulhan Arukh*

The man from whose work emanates a determining Sephardic influence, beside mysticism, found his home in Safed, after years of wandering. He was Joseph Karo of Toledo. His work is a new organization of valid law, Torah, and Oral Teaching.

The twofold nature of the Sephardim united in this man: the architectonic spirit and the mystic drive. With almost mystical industry, year after year, he achieved the far-reaching preliminary work. The mysticism of this people was almost always demanding, pressing, driving. The task became personified, seeming to appear before him and call him to it.

What was not granted to Joseph Karo was the genius of philosophy which had been given the three greatest sons of this people in Sepharad: Solomon ibn Gabirol and Judah Halevi, the two poets; and Moses Maimonides, in whom the Eros of healing and the Eros of learning united. As no one before him and as no one after him Maimonides fashioned the totality of the Torah into a wondrous edifice in which the whole never loses the parts and the part never leaves the totality. He was a great architect in a great time of architecture. The columns strove upward from a philosophical foundation, carrying or conveying, so that nothing can be without the totality, upward to the messianic idea toward which everything aims, to which everything joins, as in a dome, curving itself as a heaven above an earth, pointing toward a beyond, toward what is coming. When Maimonides built this edifice, he wanted to serve the law, which must constantly be searched for and comprehended anew, so that the law may enter life.

Joseph Karo also had a master builder's talent. But it was a different talent; a different motive unfolds in it. He wanted to structure that which had value, to present the valid law, simply and visibly, to build room next to room, floor upon floor, so that everyone, everyday, could find and possess what he needed—no more, but also no less. He fulfilled this task in a masterly manner. He discovered his own style for this task, a clear, terse, always appropriate style—not one word lacking, not one word too much, decision after decision in tight sentences. He wanted each of the people to find his answer at once, wanted to spare them the casting about and searching, whenever an hour or a place demanded an answer.

Karo kept in mind the many who could not or would not investigate, and who wanted always to have a definite answer to help them faithfully to fulfill the Torah. They were the ones he wanted to help. He named the four parts of his work the "Way," the "Help," the "Law," and the "Knowledge," for they were to be always near and accessible to the people. To the work as a whole he gave a prosaic title: *Shulhan Arukh* (the "Prepared Table"). Everything needed for everyone was presented here, but as much as this title seems to speak of utility, as prosaic as it sounds, it is possible still, for one who listens deeply, to hear the sound of poetry in it. When Joseph Karo chose his title, he almost certainly had in mind that psalm which begins, "He-Who-Is is my shepherd; I shall not want," and continues, "Thou preparest a table before me in the presence of mine enemies" (Ps. 23). No matter how prosaic the sequence of sentence after sentence, behind them all stands a great confidence in God and, therefore, an inner humility. This man wrote his book in humility, and humility was to fill everyone who wished to gather answers from it.

The Influence of the *Shulhan Arukh*

During the transition from epoch to epoch, the *Shulhan Arukh* entered the history of this people and molded its existence in its various settlements. It therefore must be spoken of if the creative forces and the restraining weaknesses of the epoch are to be discussed. Because it did not present problems, but answers, it influenced the manner of thinking and, with that, individual disposition. Moreover, thanks to the printing press, it could quickly achieve wide circulation, even among the Ashkenazim, particularly since one of their own teachers, Moses Isserles of Cracow, at once undertook the task of supplementing the book. In a congenial style, terse and direct, he added comments that pointed out Ashkenazic customs and judicial procedure wherever these differed from those of Sepharad, which Joseph Karo had followed. The *Shulhan Arukh* and the interpolated glosses became one book. Ashkenazim and Sephardim found one another in it.

The influence exercised by the *Shulhan Arukh* was considerable. Since it did not try to present the search, but the result, not that which was in the process of becoming, but what was valid, it could draw simple lines. The result of this was that it brought a deeper knowledge of the laws of the Torah than it had been possible to bring, at least of its functional parts, to the people. It helped make it possible for this people to remain a learning people. The widespread printing of books made the knowledge of the law available to many who had previously been unable to possess it, thus popularizing the law, showing that a book of laws could be popular in its own way.

But the influence exercised by the *Shulhan Arukh* was also, in different places, of dubious value. It is a book of answers, providing in a certain sense conclusive advice; and this people is a searching, a constantly questioning people. It is a people, to use a saying of Maimonides, before which the gates of searching and investigation are never closed. From the epoch of growth, through the epochs of rebirth, it had become such a people. Thus what was involved here touched something of its essential being. Intellectually, this people had to keep in constant motion. A book that could appear as a book of final decisions, as a canonical book, had something dangerous about it. The danger of an orthodox immobility, or, what is the same, an orthodox arrogance, could now enter in places. The feeling of intellectual saturation, or, even worse, of moral saturation, could at times creep in. It was possible to believe, within the religious or intellectual field, that one had arrived, that one had achieved perfection.

This threat became all the more real later when, in most lands, the congregations' civil rights came under the control of the states. An important part of the book, one which, at most, still stirred up questions, thereby moved out of real life and was almost lost. The *Shulhan Arukh* appeared to be a book of ritual law only. And, after all, nothing had been further from the mind of its author than the thought that it should, or could, serve such limited men or movements. A mystic had written it, one who lived in humility and who humbly wanted to help his people prepare for the great day to come.

Viewing the full extent of its path, this book fulfilled an important task. In a time in which much wavered or appeared to waver, many tired dispositions or weary minds could receive a blessing from it, could enter a book in which there was something firm and established apparently waiting, sentence after sentence. Here were men, oppressed in widespread need, who prayed in their workday worship service to the "Guardian of Israel": "Guard the remnant of Israel, that Israel might not be lost! Guard the remnant of the one people, that the one people might not be lost!"* These men, who trusted God, received strength when they were permitted to know that "a table had been prepared" for them, setting before them that in which their life could fulfill itself, so that "the remnant of Israel might not be lost."

In spite of everything, one should emphasize that questions also sounded from this book. This was true because, in the first instance, this became a book of two men, and Sepharad and Ashkenaz kept meeting one another here. Only together did they produce the totality. Every difference which is entitled to existence and inclusion quickly awakens questions.

Something else was added, something characteristic. This people, which long ago had become a searching, questioning people, now became, if the expression will be permitted, a "commentating" people, as it was a creative people. It knew itself to be constantly questioning, and, therefore, it kept questioning itself. The questions of the commentators joined those of the creators. Whenever a work appeared,

* See *The Authorized Daily Prayer Book*, ed. J. H. Hertz, p. 184.

out of which something personal, that is, a creative individual power spoke, an encounter with it commenced at once. The encounter did not become loud and verbose, as when someone, who feels inferior and afraid of his own weakness, desires to appear strong for once. The encounter, which enjoyed taking the form of commentary, sprang from a completely different base. It rose out of human depths, and was therefore, if this can be said, filled with purity. A deep respect and fervent love, a spiritual humility, an intellectual modesty, were revealed within it. The many commentaries permit the best in this people to be revealed. Throughout the centuries, such commentaries follow one another. And to them commentaries upon commentaries are added, all of them engaged in a search for understanding, born in respect and love, and with few exceptions, coming out of days of biased passion. The commentaries, too, are an Oral Torah, which was written down. The student here speaks of the teacher, and speaks to him. The commentaries are therefore an integral part of the intellectual history, more, of the spiritual existence of this people. Only someone who looks into the souls of their authors can understand this completely.

The *Shulhan Arukh* quickly won such commentators, and, typically, they give testimony both of it and of themselves. They brought searching and investigating with them and made them part of this book. The book of answers thus became a book of questions, after all. Where the one spoke, the other could be heard. To the men of this people, throughout all epochs, though expressed in different ways, came the proclamation of the human task: To receive the answer into oneself, and not to close oneself to the question. To remain true to the way and faithful to the goal; not to stand still because of the answer, as many thought necessary; not to reject the immediate way for its distant goal, as many thought to do: These make a God-fearing man. In the centuries in which the new epoch broke through, many who were frightened of the new kept to the way in order to stand still upon it, and they claimed the *Shulhan Arukh* as their authority. Others, the desire for the new within them, left the way in order to draw near the goal from another direction, and the *Shulhan Arukh* was used by them, too, as an authority or as a pretext. Both misunderstood the historical meaning of the book. It is both different and greater than any of them believed; it has its rightful place in the history of the existence of this people.

The *Zohar* and the *Shulhan Arukh* illustrate the final period in the influence, as deep as it was extensive, which the wondrous Sephardic world exercised for so long a time upon the total existence of this people, upon the intellectual cosmos in which it lived and in which it constantly renewed itself. Now, after a transition period in which history at times seemed to waver, at times to hesitate, the task was to be transferred to the Ashkenazim. They were to receive an inheritance rich in fruit as in seed, and were to unite it with their own. An ancient growth was to be reborn; a different, a new time was to begin. The lines of system and of individual were to meet.

Baruch Spinoza

Still, one Sephardi, Baruch Spinoza, one of the Marranos who were able to save themselves in the *arche des fugitifs*, "the ark of the fugitives," the new Holland, must be discussed here. He is the last of the great architects, the great Sephardi system builders. In much of his thinking, he still goes back into the old period. In fact, he cannot be understood completely except against this Sephardic background. Yet he reaches far beyond the boundaries of his people into a new epoch through one decisive quality of his mind. Without him, the philosophy of the new Europe cannot be understood completely.

Spinoza achieved a union of analysis with synthesis—the sign of the true philosopher—as few have ever done. As such, he often appears as a son of this people, to whom such power has belonged from ancient times. His analytic mind unerringly drove toward what, in the world of man, the world of two attributes of being, of *cogito et extensio*, "thought and extension," might be opened by the key of science. His method is that of mathematics. But in him the creative fantasy (from which all synthesis ultimately derives) simultaneously moved toward the hidden, the mystery, the unending, the eternal fullness of the attributes belonging to the unending eternal cosmos closed to the human mind. His genius surmised and viewed the unencompassable. As in many Sephardim before him, the mathematic sense and the mystic drive dwelt together. He wanted to survey all and everything from the aspect of infinity, of eternity, *sub specie aeternitatis,* that is, from the "one who is." As in the "faith" of his people one takes his position in relation to the One God, so, too, in Spinoza's faith.

Unity and totality are the great answer and, at the same time, the great longing. He hears the one and only everywhere and it constantly speaks out of him and to him. For the sake of the two, the answer and the longing, he built his system as a system both of the world and of the promise. In the unity and the totality everything completes itself and fulfills itself. The relative, the finite, the terrestrial, the transitory is placed into the absolute, the eternal, the unending, and enduring. In a sense, the transitory is reconciled with itself. The great longing is the great answer. A divine love, beyond everything terrestrial, the *amor Dei intellectualis*, emanating from God and returning to Him, embraces all and everything. In it all creatures attain to that which they are. Yet this is the ancient spiritual and intellectual situation of this people: the entrance of the eternal and unending into the transitory and limited, and the return of the transitory and limited, the multitudinous and differentiated, to the eternal and unending, the one and only. Some of this people were always seized anew by this problem. For the sake of what was most personal within them, they always struggled with it. In it they found the answer which is called creation, revelation, commandment, promise, reconciliation, comfort. In this problem too, Spinoza struggled with himself to find himself; from this he gained the inner answer which brought him peace.

He won an answer, but it could not be the answer for his people. An essential polarity, out of which this people still lives and for which it lives, the dynamism of the commandment and the dynamism of the social, did not attain its rightful place in the system of Spinoza. Great satisfaction dwells within this system, but driving force does not emanate from it. He knows and teaches an achieved present, but not the constant and demanding way to the future. He lacks the messianic thrust, for the great "I AM THAT I AM," and "Thou shalt . . ." are not heard. He is rich in fruit, but not in seed.

Yet behind the philosophy, towering above it, stands the man who has built it. Wondrously touching to the heart, wondrously conciliating, he stands there. He is greater than the system that he, the great thinker, has erected. Even where he is silent, he speaks. A peace born of understanding emanates from him, though he was not understood by his own. Characteristically, he named the book of his philosophy *Ethica.* For a man of this people there can be no philosophy that does not become ethics. Whoever reads this book from beginning to end and then thinks back from the end to the beginning, must see it as a great question on the theme of man, blessed, guarded, and enlightened, and who lives in peace. It is as if his name, Baruch, "blessed," sounds out of everything. What the Psalmist prayed for, "a pure heart" and "a steadfast spirit" (Ps. 24), was within him and blessed him.

When Spinoza started on his own way, his congregation expelled him through the great ban of the court, because his *Tractatus Theologico-Politicus* moved across dangerous boundaries. After so long a time of looking to the outside world with deep longing, after a life of danger that kept changing and yet remained the same, the men of his congregation had finally found a place of rest, an area of freedom and fulfillment. Here, after the first years of uncertainty, they had been able to found a congregation; here, they could freely confess what they, their parents, and their grandparents had been forced to conceal. Each day, every breath taken by their souls was one of grateful acceptance of the new era. Now Cromwell's England, too, held out the promise that it too would soon receive these refugees. But they still carried the scars of a century of suffering; the fear and trembling of those days still quivered within them. That for which they had suffered must now be firmly established; none of them was to interfere with it in any way. They knew, or thought they knew, that portals had opened for them because they had suffered for the old faith; and they hoped, that for the same reason the portal of a land close by would open itself to them. Should this peace be destroyed through one of them at this time? Should this hope be endangered? So, Spinoza was no longer to be one of them in the sight of the world.

His congregation cast him out of its midst; but his people never cast him off, nor did they deny him. To it, he remained one of the people. Those of this people, in their hours of truth, thought of him not as someone who is from another people or from another world, but as someone who is closely related. It looked to him as someone who is within the family circle, looked to this man who would rather be lonely, even among his own, than abandon himself. Such searchers recognized much that was of the best of his people in him. They found much which admonished them when superficiality attempted to enter their lives; much which pacified them when narrow-mindedness tried to exert its pressure upon them. He also has his place in the life of his people.

The Meaning of History

The lands in which the history of this people now took place in the beginning of its fourth millennium experienced a time of change and upheaval, as compressed as any mankind has ever known, anytime, anywhere.

Since the days when man began the first experiments, since he invented and fashioned the first tools and ended the rule of animals, since this first revolution on earth, the history of man is a history of experimentation. For that reason, the countenance of earth has continually acquired new features. But probably never before did these features set themselves next to each other and join together in such a deep and far-reaching manner.

In the distant past, men already began to send their thoughts out into the far reaches and into their inmost self. For the thought which journeys into the distance always returns to the heart of the man; he who questions heaven must then question himself. Thus, from the earliest time the mind of man strove to unite heaven and earth. Since those first astrologies and philosophies and religions, the world of humanity became a world of ascents and flights, moving ever higher and, simultaneously, sinking into itself, deepening itself. Ever again, new lines and new intersections were drawn to plot the spiritual cosmos. But never before this time had the forms and ways and extensions of almost every area of the senses become so completely different and new.

It is customary to designate this period as "modern times" and to separate it from the Middle Ages and antiquity. But, apart from the fact that the Middle Ages reach far beyond the borders normally set for them, neither this scheme nor any similar one grasps the realities of historical development. A survey of continents, lands, and their peoples nowhere shows a sequence of something old, something in the middle, and something new, whether or not new is used to designate some highest stage within easy attainment or a splendidly illumined decline into oblivion. Space and time disclose another pattern. Often the pattern discloses the lack of history, the lack of direction in a people's existence, in which sooner or later the people exhausts itself and falls upon the ground or into it. Or it is completely different. The history of a people, or a group of peoples into which it grows, attempts to maintain a constant direction in order to serve a true idea, with patient respect for time and space, for the time which is to belong to the children, and for the space which has been apportioned to other people. History, always and everywhere is the coming into being of a force, a moral, intellectual, or an artistic force. In the many areas, in the long reaches of the time of humanity, it sometimes rises here, sometimes there, as though a sun, following some mysterious law, would draw its path across the earth, bringing a force out of the soil, one day here, one day there. This force then grows, influencing, creating, sometimes extending itself, sometimes elevating itself. It then grows weak from what it has achieved, becomes more and more tired, and falls asleep. Sleep can be an end, leaving only creations behind it, but the force can experience rebirth after rebirth, so that all the working and creating endures. Here the force has renewed itself, for it can endure only as it renews itself. The sleep was a pause in which the force regained itself.

In this, the spheres of humanity differ. In some place the sun, surrounded by mystery, has not shone or has not shone yet; so far, no strength has been drawn out of the depths. There the time is still prehistoric; history is but a possibility which sleeps in the lap of the future, perhaps to open its eyes one day. In another place the waking rays descended, and a force arose; history began. Again, the spheres differ. Here, history lost its way and became the lack of history, self-destruction; only a force can destroy itself. There, history went its way, became tired and sank into a sleep of death, though a greatness had issued forth from it. But there again the slumber was a creative pause. The waters in the depths did not seep away, but combined to become a spring. The force was reborn to end in a dazzling cascade, or it was reborn into a constant and recurring rebirth.

All this reveals itself to one whose horizon seeks the widest, most embracing scope. He recognizes history, the possibility of history, and the absence of history, time after time, space after space. Is there an end to space, an end to time? Is this end perhaps the fulfillment? There is a statement in the Talmud, one whose poetry and meaning are almost inexhaustible. It is said: "The son of David will come only when the last of the souls within the vessel [the area of possibility] has traveled its way." Fulfillment, this comment wants to say, is the fulfillment of the possibilities with which the eternal God has graced men when He created them "in His image." This, it appears, is also the word of history.

Forces and Changes

When ancient forces again awoke in European lands, awakening new forces along with them, this people rested after the great achievements of the last epoch, as though it had to be prepared by a moment of inner silence. It needed this pause for its force to be reborn in it, for its force now would have to test itself against the surrounding forces and unite with their energies. This people rested, but with eyes wide open it lived for what was fulfilling itself around it. In its mysticism, it could catch a stirring of what lay behind the change going on about it, could sense a glimmer of its dawning. A historical task waited for the new generation, harder than that which had confronted any previous generation. A part of this people, primarily the Ashkenazim, was to endure it, this group for all the others.

One who could look around at the beginning of the epoch and see through the events, could see how everything began to shrink. The philosophy which had been deemed a highway through the cosmos, an expression of enduring, unfailing law, the revelation of an orderly and constant harmony, had now been proven an empty game in which reason had permitted itself to be deceived by the senses. A new center arose, the earth surrendering its place within the universe to the sun. The circle, the old image of completeness, was obscured by the ellipse. Mathematics, which until now had only desired to define limits, now journeyed toward infinity. Space expanded. What had been rigid became dynamic, and the energy that worked within all things was recognized. On the earth itself, the old concept of borders disappeared. That which had been, throughout time, earth's surface, the *orbis terrarum*, now became an example. A new world arose, new oceans stretched forth. The word "discovery" spoke of fulfillment and of promise, and these resounded equally in the word "invention." In dissecting, the material was liberated; in synthesis, it grew in breadth. Undreamed of means of power, helpful and destructive, were placed into the hand of man. The old philosophy no longer had concepts for such a world. A new one, that did not want to be a continuation but that commenced anew, started on its way. All that was new, that had been seen, experienced, and thought, could quickly and easily make its way to all who desired knowledge. The printing press became a helper to those who taught and to those who called, bringing the word speedily to all, overcoming old confines, bursting old limitations.

In every sphere of endeavor this time becomes a time of great and continuing change. In one area after another, man is grasped by the drive to desert the old ways, that he might seek reality and truth on completely different paths. Will and thought carried this into feeling, a feeling that became general. Men breathed a different air.

As well known, as familiar as all this may be, it must be realized anew whenever one wants to understand this force of change whose aftereffects continue through the centuries. The same applies if one would seek to know how different the world was that now surrounded this people (though it remained at rest), and how different the tasks awaiting it when the time of rest will have ceased. That for which time had been granted to all the peoples, men of this people wanted to learn and were to learn overnight. Head and heart together would be able to make up, to catch up, perhaps even to move ahead, while remaining within themselves and understanding themselves.

Changes in Islam and in Christianity

None of the changes taking place at that time had as immediate an effect upon as many people in the totality of their lives and their living together as did the transformation which had taken hold of the two imperia of belief, a transformation, going far deeper in the case of the Church. Nor was this people exempt from all the effects of this change and the questions it raised.

Within the younger imperium, that of Islam, the determining rule of the sons of Ishmael was displaced by that of the Turkish tribes. The place of the children of the desert was taken by the children of the steppes, and the climate of this world of faith changed with it. A new force of will infused the desire for conquest which had driven Islam forward from its beginning. In quick expeditions of conquest, it vanquished the Eastern domains of Christianity, the Eastern citadel of its imperium, Constantinople. Here then, doors could open for the Sephardim who had been driven away.

Western and Eastern Rome had formally separated a century earlier, but the will toward one another had endured in both. There was a cleavage but not a separation between them. Now, where

Caesaropapism had had its fortress, a "descendant of the Prophet" ruled. The focal point of the Eastern Church transferred itself from the South to the North of Europe, from the Greek-speaking world to the Slavic world. At that time, a Russian monk wrote the Czar that the time was now full, that the one Rome had forfeited its claim, that the other Rome had fallen, and that the great time, the time of the third Rome, which was to endure, would now commence. The new kingdom, and in it and with it the new time, would now come. This imperium also, to which the man of Russia summoned his ruler at that time, then became a part of this people's destiny, a part of its experience, a part of its suffering.

Protestantism and Calvinism

Two other movements arose which challenged the older imperium of belief and, indeed, touched its very depths of belief and structure. One, the Reformation, Protestantism, came from the middle of Europe; the other, Calvinism and Baptism, came from the West of the Continent. What they accomplished was more than a separation; it was a divorce. The two movements stand next to each other in time, but they differ in their natures and effects. One rose out of a need, out of the oppressing, frightening question: How, then, can man be saved? The other broke forth out of the innermost searchings of the soul, out of the question that is never silent: What sense, then, is there in human life and in human living together? One wanted to lead to a pure, unmixed faith through "reformation," to faith for the sake of faith. The other wanted to revolutionize the will, to turn the will into a God-given destiny, in order that this destiny become will. One, for the sake of the community, evoked the insurrection of local rulers against the imperium, removing the parts from the totality. The other confronted the principle of the Church with another principle, that of the congregation: Out of the community of the parts a totality was to come into being. The one, almost of necessity, led to regimentation under an absolute ruler, to a life under authority, whether under its protection or under its shadow. The other, as through an internal logic, led to constitutional life, to a parliamentary or republican form of communal life, responsible for itself and governing itself.

The New Concept of the State

A third factor, the new concept of the state, also arose to make possible essential changes in what had existed previously. Sometimes it advanced and established the other two movements, sometimes it retarded and held them back. A movement that affects men does not now come to the foreground, but a concept prepares room for itself and enters philosophy, in connection with a system, or it is brought forward by a political program, in connection with its plans. At times the philosophy is the original foundation, and then it seeks to realize itself in a political program. At times the politics are primary, and then it seeks to justify itself through a philosophy.

This new concept of the state designates and demands something radically different from what the state, the *polis*, had meant to the Greek, or what the state, the *civitas*, had meant to the Roman. The Greeks and Romans had made a considered analysis of the concept of the state. For them, it comprised the organic forms and limits of the communal life of men. Before them, the prophets had approached the foundations of the problem, at times admonishing, at times consoling. For the prophets the state was a place into which a higher world could descend, so that justice and faithfulness might be fulfilled on earth. "Thou shalt be called the city of righteousness, the faithful city" (Is. 1:26). In the imperium of belief, leading and troubled minds had also meditated upon this theme. The answer they gave themselves and the peoples was that the state existed so that the one kingdom of the one Church, this domain of the one Grace, might have the instruments for all its worldly needs; the state existed for the sake of the Church. Where the need arose, it was the handle, the sword, and the ax; it was to erect the fiery pyre.

The state, as it presented itself in the new concept, was completely different. It was to exist for its own sake. Its task and its function were not the good of the people whom it incorporated. The people existed for it, that it might have and strengthen its might. It did not demand its right from the imperium of belief, nor from the men from whom it took its existence; it carried its right within itself. It stood above morality, outside of conscience. It was a hard and cold concept, without conscience and without morality, the concept of a might whose virtue is might itself, whose form of being and whose goal of existence is egoism, which the new teaching now called *raison d'état.* This egoism all too easily formed a special type of law for itself, the law of lawlessness. That which was a binding obligation upon men and communities of men could not be a principle for this new state and its *raison.* As a concept, without belief and without commandment much could hide, and many could flee behind it. Something could arise here that even presented itself as a sense of duty to those who lacked all morality. Like the state, the "servant of the state" easily became something conceptual and mechanical—concepts can become machines. He ceased to be human as a "servant of the state." One is tempted to think of the legend of the "Golem," the untiring human shape without the essentials of a living human being.

All these changes influenced the congregations of this people in the lands of the old imperium. Outward conditions changed in many ways, but especially the inner attitude and relationship to surrounding peoples could be, had to be different. New possibilities existed of looking about, of creating; new forms of existence, similar to those of so many bright days in the second and third millennium, could develop. A wonderful fertility had prepared itself while this people rested.

The Many Churches and the Nonbelievers

The most important results of the two new religious movements were the changes effected in social conditions and human relationships.

No longer did the one ruling Church confront these people as solitary outsiders. At their side arrayed against the Church stood the other churches, possessing or demanding their own rights. Each denied the others or called them heretics. The men of this people were no longer the only unbelievers, the only *perfidi* in the lands of the old imperium; *perfidi* now applied to many others as well, men, peoples, and their rulers. Until now, the congregations of this people, these peculiar small republics in each land, had been the only institutions of their type. Now, out of the second of the religious movements, there arose many such congregations. They became a historical fact; they raised their claims, and demanded all the rights due them.

Viewing the totality of this development, one becomes aware that something new has come into being. A new figure, the man of another faith, a dissenter from the ruling faith, the dominant state creed, enters history. Opposition within the sphere of faith now wins its place and its right; it becomes legitimate. He who was formerly called heretic, whom the court had called before the bar to warn, to punish and, if he persisted in his heretic way, to deliver to his death, is no longer someone accused before God and men. Instead, he is now a man who has the right to walk another way of faith. He is no longer this reprehensible person, waiting to hear his sentence pronounced. Before God and before man, he can now say, in all freedom, what his faith is.

This development had its regressions. It was often hindered and set back; but its result is clearly visible. Unwittingly, it also caused fundamental changes in the position occupied by this people in the countries where it lived. He who until now had been the only man of another faith now stood as one such next to others. He had won comrades of the place, companions of the way. More than a century and a half after Crown and Parliament in England had decided upon the Toleration Act, a new law came into being. It was yet constricted in its complicated form; but, because there was a dynamism inherent in the Toleration Act, it now reached into distances far beyond the sight of its framers. Certainly, in its inception, neither there nor anywhere did anyone think about the children of this ancient people. But an idea lived in that law, and ideas, once they have stepped into the world, take their own way. The idea of this law, this gift of England to humanity, thus made its way to the sons of this ancient people. It placed itself before them, in order to demand a place for them.

Tolerance

These two words "tolerance" and "tolerate"—how strange, that the noun gained a different, nobler sound than the verb—now entered into everyday speech and thought. They carried a tension, almost an opposition within themselves. A demand and a rejection united here, a demand raised by life, and a rejection which based itself upon a concept of truth. Viewed from without, it is the antithesis between reality and the system; viewed from within, from the soul, it is the antithesis between practical tolerance and theoretical intolerance.

Men have always tried to live in close union with those who seemed to be like them, to be enclosed with them in the same area and the same form of life. The history of castes, classes, and ranks presents abundant examples of this effort. Those who were different or seemed to be different were excluded or segregated; one wanted to live together with one's own. The foundation for practical intolerance was always ready here, and it quickly creates its rationalizations that it may make rigid its stand. This is vulgar intolerance, and the inclination to save oneself the trouble of thinking could easily satisfy itself within it.

But there is also another intolerance, an intellectual one, one which rises out of thought. Men believe themselves to be standing before a truth, to have been graced by an insight; to them it is *the* truth, *the* insight, next to which there is room for nothing else. All else, whatever else might claim insight or truth, all of this, so they believe, must be rejected. To all such claims, they believe, they must deny both right and place in the world of belief, in the world of thought. They are theoretically intolerant. But if men preserve a sense of life within themselves, if they remain close to the broad, procreative waters of life, life brings tolerance to them. Around them, they see men, working and striving, struggling and hoping—just like them; they discover something of their own strivings and expectations in these others. In a sense, they find themselves in them. They become tolerant in their life, in their personal relationship to others; they live together with them inwardly; soul meets soul. They hold fast to their truth, without any wavering or compromise. They are, to use this expression again, theoretically intolerant. But this exclusiveness, which they maintain for the truth they possess, does not enter into life; it gains morality and is thereby deepened. Where life and living together begin, an upright, living tolerance grows that does not grant recognition to the other truth, but understands, with fervent thoughts and feelings, the humanity of other men; thereby it understands, indeed, honors its own steadfastness. Faithfulness is able to understand faithfulness.

At all times, in every cultural area, this has been the way in which an inner relationship between different types of men, who lived together in one land, could gradually break through, so that mere coexistence became community. Nations as well, with external and internal boundaries, have come together in this fashion. Men and peoples met one another, and life proved itself stronger than all intended or commanded intolerance. The practical intolerance was overcome, and the theoretical one was humanized. Men of different pasts, different presents, and different hopes discovered the humanity residing in the other; they began to understand the other, to recognize him. Through this other one, the thoughtful and the sensitive among them learned to understand themselves better. Behind the sufferance, acknowledgment arose; fact became right, and right became a new life. Everything thus depended upon honest confrontation in which life could hold sway. The men of this people sought it often, but did not find it, for every intolerance which possessed a land or ruled it feared such an encounter and strove to block it. Special systems of separating this people from others were invented. Only after the religious earthquakes had displaced all borders, and space was made for new thought, was a place provided for such confrontation.

The two new religious movements did not want universal tolerance, but it was made possible and effected through them. However, as we have already said, the way unrolled slowly. Humanity does not walk rapidly. An earlier philosophy said that nature does not jump—*natura non facit saltum.* It may be added that history also does not jump. Even a revolutionary force needs a long time, if it is not only to disturb but also to create; and the men, whom it chooses for the task from generation to generation, need enduring patience. They must unite the deliberate quietness of the one who is certain of his way and goal with that eagerness that drives forward.

This people knew early the concept of the stranger's rights. It knew through its commandments which gave definite expression to the demands of humanity. But in this regard this people soon assumed a more restful, at times even lazier pace; on some occasions perhaps it turned backward. Often, a long stretch of time must pass before a people can catch up to its own law as it applies to itself. Prejudice, injustice, and misunderstanding maintain themselves even when clear judgment, right, and insight have already started on their way. The new generation is born into intolerance; some, often only a few, overcome it. Others, often the majority, reconcile themselves to it; and some protect it in order to pass it on. Thus, this tolerance, which can affirm itself without rejecting the other or desiring to isolate him, this agreeing to differ, through which a new era was to prove itself truly new, had its arduous way. It was late before it was permitted to enter many lands.

Humanism

The way would have been even longer and more difficult had the new idea not had a confederate who seemed to wait for it: humanism, or, as it was called later, the spirit of the Enlightenment. It is the gift which the newly awakened spirits of Greece and Italy presented to the nations.

Probably the strongest force working within humanism, even more, the force that permitted it to develop, was the ferment of Stoicism. This teaching, for it is essentially more of a teaching, a Torah, than a philosophy, which developed in the neighborhood of the Promised Land and whose founder was probably a son of this people, created a new intellectual atmosphere in the old world. Out of a lack of religion, a piety developed; above a materialistic physics, a spirituality raised itself. A particular idea of right also developed here, that of natural right, the right which is born with man. The old Church had already attempted to accept it; but in humanism it became something new, something revolutionary.

Stoicism became the great boundary destroyer. Within its domain, it cast down dividing walls between classes and peoples; it permitted the citizen of the state to become the citizen of the world. It carried humanism beyond a certain narrowness in its beginnings, into a wide, unlimited horizon. It also prepared the way for the idea of tolerance. Bit by bit, it permitted humanism—which in its beginning had been only a new mode, a new manner of education—to become a movement, that is, that which the word humanism should rightfully represent.

Two forces, at times beside, at times within one another, operated within humanism and kept emerging from it: the new "classic" idea of education, and the renewed Stoic idea of life. In the idea of education there was an element of individualism; in the Stoic idea there was a social element. Both often united to become the idea of humanity, giving humanism its most vital force, a force rich in blessings. Depth and meaning were restored to the word "man" in its individual as in its social sense. The dissenter was not only a dissenter with certain rights, but a dissenting man with his rights.

As a new time commenced, this people, living in the South and North of Europe, in its many congregations, met humanism. This humanism had to speak to this people's spirit and being, in which the individual and the social, the drive for insight and education, and the sense of the breadth of humanity had long sought to unite with one another. Humanism threw down the barriers, and the congregations opened portals to it. A space for confrontations was prepared as this people, after the days of rest, began to experience the days of rebirth.

Humanism and Hebrew Study

Even before this became general, the men of humanism and men of this people had met one another upon a special field. The revival of classical studies had led to the scrutiny of the old texts of the sacred writings of the Church. The Greek New Testament again appeared in view, as did the old Hebrew Bible. The *Graeca veritas* and the *Hebraica veritas* were to indicate the genuine content of the writings. At an early stage humanists entered relationships with the scholars of this people, in order to become more familiar with the Hebrew language. They themselves then became teachers of this language in the circles of humanism. Almost through an inner dynamism, the domain of the relationship enlarged itself and grew stronger. Following science, life soon came to enter it as well. The question of the right of life, of "natural law," was sounded. Then, for the first time, Johann Reuchlin, whom this people will always lovingly recall, the humanist of Pforzheim, raised his voice. He raised his voice in the cause of returning to this people the rights which the Roman constitution had granted them. The moral encounter took place.

This man also exerted his influence and that of his friends in behalf of a strange book, or rather a book that must have appeared strange, since it is so difficult to understand from the outside. He spoke for the Talmud, when it was again threatened with fire. The attention of humanistic scholars was drawn to this remarkable book which, more than a book, is a literature. Almost in amazement, they found here a world of whose existence they had not known; they saw lines that led to the writings of the New Testament; they discovered ideas which, in similar or related form, had previously come to them from other sources. A confrontation of ideas followed and, characteristically, became a meaningful and richly creative encounter within cultural history.

When a new law of nations, the *jus gentium*, the first great legal concept after the Roman Law, was established again, the Stoic idea of natural law stood beside two legal ideas from the Talmud. These two ideas had grown out of biblical soil into the Talmud where they developed further. They are ideas in which law and morality interpenetrate. As the Psalmist saw it: "Mercy and truth are met together; righteousness and peace have kissed each other" (Ps. 85:11). Only when morality can become the law for all does it become the morality of life; only when law also realizes morality is it living law. The first idea is that of the "stranger," the *ger*, the man who has come from another land to live on a new soil. The Bible says that the same law must apply to him, and in one of its most wondrous and touching sentences (which the congregation, when the Day of Atonement commences, repeats), it says he shall have the same atonement as well: "The congregation of the children of Israel will be forgiven and the stranger who resides in its midst."*

The second legal idea derived from the Talmud is that of the "children of Noah." This idea determines the descent of all men from a man who had been saved because he "was in his generations a man righteous and whole-hearted; Noah walked with God" (Gen. 6:9). It is the idea of an indestructible imprint of moral obligation, the *character indelebilis*, on everyone who bears human features. When Hugo Grotius, the first author of the new law of nations, wrote his book *De jure belli et pacis*, these two legal ideas from the Talmud stood before him. The encounter in universality had taken place.

At the same time, besides the study of the Hebrew language, this people's mysticism found a way to the humanists, and encountered great recognition there. All mysticism is fundamentally the same, being born out of the universal human longing to travel the way to divinity, to be within its immediacy. Particularities and differences also exist, and variety can be glimpsed in the history of mysticism. The features of a single mystic longing have always been determined by the re-

* See *High Holiday Prayer Book*, ed. M. Silverman, p. 207. Cf. Lev. 16:29–30; 24:22.

ligion or the philosophy in which it originates, and the longings have been led into unique paths. But what is thus differentiated in historical appearances shows itself to be the same in its essence. The mystic from one place finds much of himself in the mystic from another.

The different formations of mysticism are all based on common ground. But in the mysticism of this people a still deeper internal property seemed to disclose itself. An ultimate mysteriousness, everything that could sound out of the word "Kabbalah" seemed to conceal itself in this people's mysticism, and one hoped to find the way to it. These confrontations within the domain of mysticism at times glowed with a special magic. Yet the confrontation of this people with mysticism belonged only to small circles and to limited times. A wider expansion would come later, in the new community that began to come into being then, within the commonwealth of the cultured. The history of gaining and passing on knowledge reveals changing periods. At times, insight was to be designated only for the few, the chosen ones; at times it was intended for all who longed for it.

Humanism also had its esoteric aspect in the beginning. But there was a dynamism within it which, on the one hand, enlarged the circles and, on the other, united ways which had been separated or which strove toward one another. Knowledge was to find a form in which it would achieve universality and become accessible to all. Knowledge was to become education, and this meant that it should be universal not only in its contents, but also in its reaching out to mankind. The many were to ennoble it and to unite through it. What had been an individual, personal striving gained a social trait and became the social task, the commandment of the Enlightenment. It was to loosen fetters, to lead out of the confines of the senses into the distances of the mind. The pathway was to be prepared for the spiritual forces within man, so that man might find man upon this way. Every darkness which covered men and nations, such was the great conviction then, would give way to enlightenment. To lead everyone toward it became the great commandment. Together with social feeling, the moral desire awoke here, and many encounters took place, including, finally, the encounter in which men of this people were discovered in the world of education and they themselves could discover others.

The *Rinascimento*

In the beginning stage of humanism, the first arena for such a confrontation was Italy, this essence of Europe within Europe, this middle land in the Mediterranean, to which many roads led and out of which roads went forth into the distances. Throughout a changing millennium, the consciousness of its ancient culture and a sense of duty emanating from it had neither been extinguished nor had it disappeared within the people of this land. Italy could thus experience its *rinascimento*, its rebirth in humanism. Men from North and South, from East and West, always met here; so, too, men of this people came here from eveywhere. Ashkenazim and Sephardim lived here; in many of the old congregations, the old culture and the old knowledge were nursed in a special form. Men from here had been first leaders and teachers of congregations in Ashkenaz, and Ashkenaz later had sent teachers out of its midst to this place. Men from Sepharad achieved a place here for their thought when the day came on which a people decided against itself and drove them away. For this people too, this was the area which led to all directions, the meeting place of roads and of ages: Men out of its midst, from everywhere; days out of its history, from manifold epochs—all found each other here. Thus a particular humanism tried to find expression for itself here in the men of the old congregations. This humanism could engage in dialogue with all that had discovered itself in the *rinascimento*. The two understood one another. There was something charming in this, but it was only something occasional, rising and then fading.

The many and the constant encounters on the many paths of the new education, in many lands and toward many goals, in the fullness of effect and possibility, could only manifest themselves at a later time. They came when this people, which had rested, roused itself in order to take a bright-eyed look at the world which had become different, and, following the law, the covenant which was within it, began to clear a pathway for its new epoch. Only then did a time of encounters commence.

The history of this people is a history of encounters. It was not permitted to stray from its way for a long time, nor to isolate itself for any duration. A determining trait of its being, toward which and in which it came to realize itself, was its universalism, in idea and in time. This always guided it, although at times it took hold of it sooner, at times later. Assent and acceptance always existed in the encounter. At times it was stronger, at times weaker. But as strong as the assent could be, a limit had been set. This people was not permitted to surrender and to lose its existence. In all assents it had to guard its existence and the feeling for it; for the sake of its millennia and for the sake of humanity, its existence had to endure. But every truthful encounter left deep imprints upon the form, upon the expression, upon the language of this one existence. The existence, old and steadfast, endured and could endure because of the strength which dwelt in the foundation, beneath all appearances, and which constantly broke forth. It endured and could endure for the sake of this great, perhaps greatest possibility, for the sake of the rebirth, its ever reawakening genius. In every encounter, just as in every rejection, this people could and should remain aware of its existence. That means that it was able once again to give an accounting of itself to itself. As long as it is able to do this —and until now it has always been able to do so anew—each genuine encounter becomes an enduring blessing for it. And not the least reason for that blessing will be the fact that this people, in order to speak to itself and to others, has to prepare a new language, a new expression, a new form for its existence. For such is the law of its existence.

The Discovery of America

The great encounters in its history show this: the encounter with the purity and strength of Persia, with the creativity and flexibility of the Greek spirit, with the greatness and the enduring quality of Rome, and then with the vastness and openness of Arabian culture. And all these encounters revealed something else as well—that every genuine encounter brings forth hopes. As long as these hopes are in movement, the one great, enduring hope threatens to disappear behind them. And then, when these hopes one day seem to be scattered into a nothingness, the one great hope also threatens to sink beneath the disappointment. Everyone of the encounters shows, somewhere, the battle between the one hope and the hopes. The commencement of this people's fourth millennium began with an abundance of encounters and shows the battle of the one hope with hopes more clearly than any age, except, perhaps, for the age of Greece. A battle commenced which, at times, reached into the inmost core of the people.

In all of these encounters and hopes this people experienced a world that had changed in its very foundations; but this changed world was the Old World, and entering its field of vision now was the world of America. The word "New" here took hold of the minds of men in a way that had not happened for a long time. One who allows himself to listen to the reports of the discovery of America hears the sounds of a great amazement. A New World, a New Atlantis shows its shores. Completely new areas of history open up spheres that also belong to the history of this people.

The New World is divided into two distinct spheres, that of the South and that of the North. Avidity for gold and power looked toward the South. For a long time, therefore, it remained without a future, without a future as well for the children of this people, who established their congregations there almost in hiding. The desires of the spirit led toward the other sphere, to find there a place of freedom for their life, their faith, and also for their industry, the industry of their soul. Here, a future arose, a sun of righteousness, and it sent forth its rays to waken new and ever-renewed days. There, in the Southern continent, an arrested past, which could only stand still, maintained its outposts. Here, in the North, a will to what would be could unfold itself. In the South, conquerors and their following brought with them the "Middle Age" in which they had lived and in which they still wanted to live. They wanted to set up the old soil on the newly discovered and conquered earth; and forms grown rigid at home only continued in their rigidity when transferred. Those who had landed on the Northern shores, hoping, searching, wanted to prepare a home for themselves, to cultivate for the sake of their future. They saw what they wanted to achieve before them, and they recognized what was past. It was, so to speak, a history without a "Middle Age" that began here; and a new world thus came into being. What they had brought along with them was not soil, but a seed, to be entrusted to the new, virginal soil. Whether they knew it or not, they carried with them the threefold, fertile seed which is the great and enduring gift from England to humanity: the seed of constitutional, organic state life; of common law, equal for all, in which right inheres in one's person; and tolerance, which creates true unity in diversity. Through the courageous belief in man and his vocation, they here drew the furrows for a new time and a new world. Into them, with the great confidence of the plowman, they placed the seeds.

The children of this ancient people as well, Sephardim and, later, Ashkenazim, who dared the way, in search and in longing, came into this land of many and diverse congregations together with the rights that God had given them. Founding their own congregations, they experienced this new time and this new world. It was the great encounter with America which, as few such events before it, became deep experience and created true history. In the year in which the Sephardim were expelled from Sepharad, at the turning point between two millennia in the life of this people, America was discovered. It does appear as something providential, preparing a way in history.

Hasidism: The Rebirth of the Eastern Ashkenazim

While this encounter fulfilled itself on the other side of the ocean, the ancient strength of this people had already reawakened in Europe.

The old mysticism of the *haside ashkenaz*, which did not wish to build up a mystic system but to create a life of piety as a teaching, was now reborn. This quickly sprouting teaching soon stood as something completely new in manner and utterance. It gave a new tone to the words of the Bible, as it gave new features to the *hasid*, the "pious one." As few others before it, it lifted up the oppressed masses; it enriched the many poor. The teaching of Hasidism appeared before mankind in its own individual pattern. Internally it is connected with the older Ashkenazic mysticism, and yet it is also an authentic, complete development of its own.

It is a strange meeting of the times, that just then, within Protestantism, a mysticism under the same name, the name "Pietism," a living of piety, found its expression. The founder of Pietism and the father of Hasidism, the Baal Shem, were born in the same year and died in the same year. But viewing the two teachings of life, one sees different worlds.

Hasidism and the Mysticism of Personality

Three things give Hasidism its historical and human particularity and permit life and fertility to issue from it. Hasidism is, first of all, a mysticism of personality and of the poetry of personality. Is not the strongest poetry man himself: A man who is selfless and through this, always and everywhere, is himself, who rises out of purity, out of a depth and an immediacy, in whom spiritual essence and the spring of God touch one another, who is always man, but who is one in whom, when the hour comes, the Shekinah, the Presence of God, enters? He speaks more than words; something out of the foundations of the word, out of the thoughts and feelings of this man penetrates into those who are near him—often without their knowing—and his word is therefore not to be repeated, but to be received and preserved. No poetry exists which is as strong, as arresting, as firm in its hold as this poetry of the spiritual personality. In a sense, it creates an atmosphere and purifies the atmosphere, so that souls may breathe more freely. From ancient days, at different times, such poetry has revealed itself in a special way in the men of this people, as well as among many in whom something of the best of this people lived. A purified personality is evidenced in it.

Such personalities and, along with it, such poetry was reborn in Hasidism. Its history can only be a history of personalities. It began in the Southeastern perimeter of the Ashkenazim, wandered to the North, there united with a philosophy, and, somewhat antithetical to its beginnings, undertook to construct a conceptual edifice. There too it possessed personalities and lived in them. Where personalities lacked, Hasidism became a rigid system of words and disciplines. Or, touching its marrow, the profane, the unholy, took hold of it. Men who had not achieved this kind of personality placed the mantle of personality upon themselves; much that had no true content and even much that was common could thus conceal itself. A bustling activity could then spread out, and spectacle replaced Shekinah. But the enduring strength and history of Hasidism is that, just as it was formed through the poetry of personality, so it continued to create personality.

Hasidism and *Kavvanah*

A second aspect of Hasidism which gives it life is the poetry of *kavvanah*, "devotion," direction to God; as in prayer, so in life. One might speak of poetry to illustrate this aspect, but one may speak of music as well. Actually no new prayers were created by the Hasidim; but the words of the old prayers, into which generation after generation had placed their knowledge, their sorrows, and their longings, now came to reveal new depths, new dimensions, and, with that, new poetry. The rhythms and verses in which the words united, in which every generation wanted to hear something of the harmony from "the heavens above," so that it might repeat it in human tones, in every land according to its manner, now gained in Hasidism tones never previously heard. It is true that the history of this people, even more than that of other peoples, is also a history of poetry and of music. Every epoch added its individual contribution, and poetry and music discovered one another in changing ways. But what makes Hasidism special is that men sang while creating poetry and created poetry while singing, in order to let the spring of prayer flow upward; and that presently the people created poems as they created their music and they composed music as they composed poetry. The congregations of these *hasidim*, these "pious ones," became congregations of song and of composition.

A livelier sense of the mystery, its poetry and its commandment, awakened in prayer. (In the faith of this people the mystery always commands, the poetry summons and promises, and all promise signifies commandment.) Where Hasidism sowed its fruitful seeds, the teachers who arose cultivated a new and special dialectic—that dialecticism which seeks the most subtle motive behind every relationship and seeks to understand through a dissecting analysis. In dialectic, the sensitive understanding of the mystery can easily become stunted or lost. The mystery does not allow itself to be split apart; it is the ultimate, perhaps the most intrinsic fact. Confronting it, the differences that have been erected cease. Confronting it, the man of intellectual strength and the simple man stand on the same level. Out of this people's power of rebirth, Hasidism rediscovered the mystery. The sense of the mystery opened portals of life, and with it Hasidism rediscovered the simple man and restored him to his ancient, rightful place. From the "devotion," the *kavvanah*, a way led to men, above all to the little men. And the old social trait of this religion came to life again, in a new manner, with a new melody. The presumably great and the presumably small all found themselves in a *kavvanah* of life. No doubt a mist raised itself at times, darkening the light. There is, after all, a mist of mysticism. Like the prayer from which it arose and in which it again ended, the mystery could become an undulating obscurity; and the obscurity could take on an elaborated or overly artificial manner—or could become arrogance. Wherever piety exists, hypocrisy can always find a place next to it; next to Hasidism, pseudo-

Hasidism presented itself with a ready supply of words and manners. But while the mist can conceal the light, the light remains and waits for the hour when the mist breaks.

Hasidism and Messianism

In yet a third way, the strength of rebirth within Hasidism proved itself. Or, one might say, it sought to prepare all the souls and to keep them in readiness for the decisive commandment. It wanted to let something messianic, something redeeming commence. It wanted to give it a now and a here.

The deep relationship between creation and redemption came to life again. An old Sephardic mystic legend had proclaimed that a creative ray dwells in everyone, hidden there since creation, like a spark waiting for that which will feed it, which will let it rise to a flame, to a light. The older Western Hasidism had brought new content and strength to the old idea of the Talmud that everyone has been chosen to be a helper, that is, a partner of God in the work of creation. This idea, in which the ethical and social become things cosmic, out of which something messianic emerges from the depths to enter upon its historic way, found new meaning in Hasidism. It became a new poetry, a new summons. It let experience blossom, it permitted the legend to flourish. By being open to the fact that redemption always and everywhere has its place and its day, and that something that strives to be redeemed waits for every man, messianism, the great expectation, the one great hope, won a constant actuality. That which had been viewed in the distance now confronted man in its immediacy. The touch of greatness entered narrow existence. It was as though men were meeting the great precursor and peacemaker, the Prophet Elijah, as though "days which will come"—the end of days—were speaking to them, as though the greatness of that which will be was already in existence.

Certainly, here, too, all days were not alike and all men were not alike. Following the generation of the creators came that of the imitators. What for one had been the experience taking hold of his soul, from which he would not, could not separate himself, became for the majority the substitute for experience, the amiable and humorously told legend. But as always with the poetry of the personality and with the inflaming of devotion, the rays of the messianic shone through.

Hasidism had its power in this threefoldness. It took on historical meaning in its own time. The soil had been prepared for it in consequence of a deep upheaval. The old Ashkenazic mysticism had evolved in an area in which hard affliction, the *gezerah* of the first Crusades, had destroyed congregations and had written page after page of martyrs' names into the Memorial Books of many congregations. Affliction had also broken upon the Eastern land through the suffering of a different crusade, through the revolt of the Cossacks; it tore apart the land that had seemed secure. It occurred in the life of the grandparents, and a new mysticism developed in the souls of the grandchildren.

In many ways, too Hasidism was related to the Eastern terrain. Over the far flat reaches, over field, over meadow, over steppe, through the forests' light and darkness, silence walks abroad. The flat land is a place sought out by meditation and dreams. Something of this great silence seems to stand within this mysticism where it is a singing, storytelling mysticism.

In this its time and in this its land, bound up with them, Hasidism already achieved something great. Many, many men—this bears repetition—were made inwardly happy by it. And this is not an inconsiderable achievement. It brought confined and oppressed men into a wide sphere, into a world of freedom. It let a light be seen, and this light penetrated far into the byways of the congregations. Thus, in remembrance of the age of the Maccabees, for which they had kindled the lights of the dedication, the Hanukkah, many of them sang, in the last stanza of the song "Rock of Ages," "Let the end of salvation approach . . . for long is the time, and there is no end to the days of suffering." They sang of their pain and of their longing. To them, Hasidism gave new certainty, and thus it became part of the existence of this people, not just a part of its history. The strength which grew out of it will endure as long as this people lives.

Hasidism Moves to the East

Soon after Hasidism had started upon its way, the newly awakened force of the rebirth broke a pathway for itself in the old Ashkenazic domain, and it later stretched forth to the East and to the South. It contained the stronger dynamism, and its results extended over many lands and in many directions. It carried men out of the byways of their congregations into the world, into the surrounding world, which itself was full of movement and excitement, in which all that was enduring threatened to crumble. This people now saw itself confronted with problems which forced themselves upon it, and problems which emanated from it, problems of whose existence they had not known. Many new questions began to encircle the old enduring certainty, which seemed at times to be seized by them, so that all that was enduring in the world threatened to disintegrate.

The rebirth in the East took place in a domain that remained enclosed. Little of the external world entered it. This confinement brought with it a feeling of being safely hedged in, of being secure. Conflicts existed within the congregations here which were severe enough to develop themselves into anthitheses. But all these differences and discords were within a world that essentially remained to itself, related to itself, existed within itself. The storms that roared outside moved past it. Perhaps they were heard, but one was not affected by them. One experienced one's own world, but not, at the same time, the world outside.

In the Western areas, doors had opened gradually and walls had fallen down; one could look out freely, one could enter the outside. The world within met the worlds outside, in all their flux. That which now awakened within had to reach an understanding with them, if an answer was to be found to the questions that now raised themselves.

One could no longer belong just to oneself. One had to—and wanted to—hold fast to one's own thinking and hoping and feeling, to preserve one's own existence. But if it was to be a living existence, if it was not to petrify, it had to move toward the worlds outside. One also had to struggle with these worlds if one wanted to achieve self-fulfillment, even if one wanted to continue to remain aware of the firm focal point within. The external change required an internal change; the great imperative was to let it be no more than a change around the enduring center. Outside the spheres shone with their many splendors; many hopes arose from both those that were genuine and those that were deceptive. So the battle between the hope and hopes had to be won. Such enticement and misleadings had not yet come close to the Eastern areas; there, this battle for spiritual and intellectual existence was not yet necessary. It was the task set for the Ashkenazim in the West.

They fulfilled this task, insofar as it is possible for terrestrial men to do so. They were able to do so by means of a strength of resistance of the soul and a tensile strength of intellect which has scarcely been surpassed, even in the history of this people. Against and amidst all that approached them with promise or attacked them with threats, all that promised them fulfillment if they would cease waiting, and that announced their doom if they continued to hesitate, they were able to do so. They lost men; the lines wavered at times. But they continued to march forward, upright and unafraid. They were able to do this, to achieve this not just for themselves but for this people which is to live for all people. Without this battle, which they accepted when the day came, and which they won, this people could not have remained within living existence, nor have been assured of rebirth in days yet to come. Whether they realized it or not, their particular history became a history for the sake of the great totality, just as this double function was born, proven, and experienced once, in earlier times of rebirth, in Judaea and Galilee and then in the lands of the Sephardim.

The battle carried on now by these people was primarily one for the meaning of a great universal community in the land and on earth. The endless query concerning the boundaries and the reaches of existence confronted them. Ever since the first boundary stone had been erected, and since men, families, tribes, nations, and communities thus decided to exist next to one another, this question has perpetually reappeared: What is it that unites despite boundaries? Is there a final unity beyond differences? To this the prophets gave an enduring answer that emanated from this people, that of the one unity which will be established, the unity in morality, in God's commandments. One of the great ideas of teachers in China, of Greek thinkers, and Roman statesmen, proceeded from that of union of common purposes and goals. As in the terrestrial domain, so did these two—the right and duty of the boundary, and the demand and value of extended space—confront one another in the world of intellect. Early and consistently, the questions were raised: How far does the area of the particular extend? How far the general?

For this people, which had not possessed land for a long time, the boundaries were engraved all the more definitely, filled with all the more meaning, in the intellectual and in the religious fields. But at the same time, since no visible boundaries constrained the view, the spirit was that much more unhindered in journeying toward that which would bring together all that was divided. It lived in the certainty of which a New Year's hymn sang (probably composed in the beginning of this epoch): "All the world shall serve Thee, O God." Boundaries fell before such a vision. But over all they had been entrenched even deeper. Separateness was the form of that existence. One thought and felt in terms of separation and one's recollection of the past took its structure in the making of distinctions.

It came as a great revolution when separating barriers fell and that which had seemed distant seemed to become near. It was a revolution in the history of this people whose belief had itself entered the history of humanity as another great revolution and remained such within it. It touched the life of every individual. Not just the outer condition of existence and the scope of every day changed, but the form of existence itself, the pattern in which the enduring seeks to express itself, had to be transformed. Only man himself, only the people itself, only the community itself can undertake the task of such a transformation. The favor of an hour may make it easier at one time or another; the disfavor of an hour may make it more difficult. But this work can be undertaken only by those, few or many, to whom history has tried to entrust it. History, too, is a great experimenter. The Ashkenazim in the Central and Western Europe had been called forth now. They could not escape the task; for history, proceeding on its way, conveyed it to them. And history is two things in one: that which cannot be rejected, and that which might be accomplished. One who understands the hour can turn necessity into freedom.

These men, in whom the ancient, the millennia lived, now were to enter into the newness of a threefold domain: a different view of the universe; a spreading, universalizing culture; and an increasing measure of citizenship rights. Their belief remained the same, the fundamental position upon which they first became fully aware of themselves, from which alone their most essential and particular thoughts and hopes could emanate. It had to, so that all their power would not go into the form of their existence, so that, in the changing of the form, their particular existence would not become weakened or ultimately lost. Indeed, it often happened in this period that in many of these people there was too much of form and too little of existence. Yet, as determining as the basic position in belief was to be, the directions, strivings, and desires which emanated from it could no longer be the same as formerly; they would have atrophied or disappeared. A position that is not a constant point of departure soon becomes meaningless and therefore dead.

That which sought to go forth from the one position, this ground of certainty and confidence, was now led—insofar as it wanted to move at all—toward the new, the three aspects of a changed world.

The Entrance Into New Ways of Thinking

The first aspect was that which viewed and investigated the cosmos in a new manner. The decisive qualification here was not the fact that science had conquered wide realms and claimed new ones. The willingness and desire for science were always alive within this people. Out of the same source—so this people taught—emanate the hidden and the revealed; recognition of the one is recognition of the other. The realm in which an adjustment of inner vision was required, so that it might find its way, was in the source of science. In the surrounding world, rationalism now determined all thought. It did not only reach to poetry and to religion, it entered into them. The broad, the rational, the logical covered over the depths of the psychological; experimentation meant forgetting the mystery, and optimism, which saw all things in straight lines, turned man's vision away from the problematic inherence of earthly existence. Into this world of rationalism, those men were now to enter who, through the generations, had become *homines mystici*, mystic souls. Those men, for whom thought, even when they were far from basic mysticism, remained at the beginning of the mystery, and for whom all law was rooted in the mystery, now were supposed to follow voluntarily after the evident, the calculable, which had been opened up in all of its new ways. They were not to attempt to set limits for it. Nevertheless, while on this new way they were never to lose the one certainty, that of the enduring which no rationalism can determine, the certainty of what is hidden, the foundation of everything.

It was the same problem that Spinoza had grasped when, a century before the rest, he had moved out into new spheres. He strove to solve the problem by placing the fullness of appearances into a complete framework of law which was set into an unencompassable, all-embracing oneness; he immersed the *intellectus* into the *amor.* For beyond his rationalism, the mystic element must not be forgotten. The generations in which the strength of the millennia now wakened and raised itself, had to prepare their own way. But their problem had previously been his and it had taken hold of him at the dawning of this era, even as it reached them in its ascendancy. Both Spinoza and this new generation could discover something of their own in the special demands of mathematics and ethics. Spinoza had intended to unite mathematics and ethics; the task of bringing the two together, broadly conceived, now became an essential part of the intellectual work of this people's new generations.

The achievement of the Ashkenazim in the attainment and then in the enlargement of the new science is great; one is tempted to say that it is prodigious. Seen in retrospect, one confronts it in astonishment. The century just concluded has seen four intellectual revolutions, beginnings emanating from a new basic position, together with new principles that demanded new directions. One after another, in the field of biology, of sociology, of psychology, and of physics, they commenced, and their influence reached deep and far. Three of them, the last three, go back to Ashkenazim of this people. Next to such works of genius there stand the works of talent in almost every area and in rare profusion. Achievement by men of this people in this one period cannot be talked away out of the history of science. It was as though deep streams, suppressed for a long time, now broke forth, sending their waters near and far in order to enrich the soil. The form of existence of this people, as well as its image in the sight of the nations, thus had new lines etched into it.

Yet more significant for its existence was that struggle for a new expression of the historically enduring possession, that it might remain possession. This new expression was the struggle to inherit and bequeath revelation. It was a struggle for the answer of the mystery to the question of the soul, so that in a world of new perceptions and discoveries, of opened vistas and reaches, the old certainty of the meaning of the world would endure. Existence itself was at stake in the effort of the newly awakened genius to win new self-consciousness, the task and the testimony of rebirth.

The Entrance Into European Culture

History, at that time, also demanded the entrance into general European education and culture. Compared to the renewed struggle for the enduring, this demand was much easier. Here, wide thoroughfares were traveled in all directions, all leading to the supranational republic of culture. In this republic, citizenship would be granted even to those who might be denied it by their state. Voluntarily—even with happy hearts—many of the children of the old congregations in Central and Western Europe turned to this new way and found rich satisfaction. They remained in their land and yet, in a sense, traveled far to another land, more distant and brighter. They dwelt in their old congregations, yet they dwelt together with many others in a spacious kingdom whose portals were open and which welcomed everyone who wished to enter. The congregations of this people thus often strove to be congregations of cultured people. History later followed them upon this way and the citizens of the republic of culture became the citizens of the states. They had granted themselves a right of citizenship before the state vouchsafed it to them.

This new culture, toward which the searchers, the visionaries within the congregation traveled, and which the whole congregations soon entered as well, often achieved something special and worthwhile in its connection with these people. Education that was in the process of becoming and in the process of enlarging, here encountered a deepened, completed education. A shrewd wisdom which gazed searchingly into a given day and also saw what rested behind and underneath the day, as well as a loving and also forgiving understanding for a talent that needed the light, here often gave men and women a special charm. The cultured of this people's congregations found a special place among the cultured in the land. It could also happen, and did happen—the longer the period of time, the more often—that the newfound culture, the new education, displaced the ancient one or allowed it to be forgotten. This old culture was rooted deep in inner existence, in the very form of being and its roots threatened to atrophy. It could then happen, and perhaps in accordance with some law of psychology had to happen, that the old culture, the old education, pressed to the surface. There it gleamed or glittered, but its depth was lost, and the background had grown wan and pale. It could occur—again as a psychological law—that for some, the spiritual lost its vital flow and strength, and that all striving streamed into the rational and the intellectual; or, for others, all feeling in life separated into a feeling of sentimentality. Both the heightened intellect and the thin sentimentality then could unite in one person. The appearances of these variants were manifold. In them stand revealed the gyrations that could not be avoided in a time of transition; with them was revealed the task which was to be solved as the renaissance gained its strength.

Entrance into the new culture simultaneously meant an entrance into the current languages of the lands. The century in which this integration commenced, the so-called Enlightenment, is also marked by the feeling of land giving way to feeling for the state. Both the feeling for the countryside and the language of the countryside gradually retreated. It left room for a single language of the land, a "written language," which possessed less of the comfortable, the relaxed expression, but instead strove for the more definite, the immediate quality. Among the men of this people, wherever they were permitted to settle, a strong sense of the homeland awoke. Their language treasured and guarded the tone and the forms of the old home, even when around them the manner and the sound was already in the process of change. This was particularly so across the breadth of settlement. Now, as they moved toward a new culture, so did they move toward the language, and they soon made it their own. Generally, the old "dialect," and with it the biblical sound cherished from past ages, continued to remain within the homes and the congregation as a type of neighborhood language. But the new language, uniting with all others, finally made its way everywhere. An old possession became a new one, set into a new form. It is surprising how quickly, and to what extent, those who sought education came to acquire a real ability in their new tongue, some even leaving their own imprint on the nation's language. This could happen simply because no claim was made upon the soul and no inner struggle was demanded in this education, though here and there resistance arose to it, stemming from the fear of anything new.

The Entrance Into European History

All the more did the soul have to confront a third demand made upon it, to enter into the history of the countries, and to face the questions as well as the hopes which this set before its own life. Millennia were to be telescoped into decades in order to make this participation possible. Every new epoch in the existence of this people had set a twofold task: to give new expression to the old and enduring revelation, and to prepare access to new goals for the old and enduring way. In these two tasks, this people's existence had always renewed itself. The two are inseparable. To separate them, to face only the one and not the other, would be to misunderstand both. When the goal of gaining a new education, which would and should only be an aid for attaining both tasks, was considered the essential and decisive task, then the substance, the essence of this people's life was endangered. In the different epochs these demands could have varying accents, a stronger and weaker one. The special accent gives each epoch its special character. In the epoch which now commenced, a special emphasis rested upon the question with which history now faced this people.

Throughout the many, many days, the men of this people had dwelt in these countries without living in them. They had no share in the inner occurrences of these lands. They were neither permitted nor able to have such a share. Only the need or misfortune of these lands touched them and, beyond that, almost every land became a setting for persecutions which were visited upon them. There they had but a place, a byway for their existence, where they did not share life with the others who were there. In the peasant serf, the *globae adscriptus*, they had a comrade in the extension and development of life; but a distance rested between them. These men had their life within their congregations. Here their thoughts stirred and turned, here their sensibilities stretched forth, here their hopes gained enlargement, here an entry opened itself to the cosmic cycles, the mystical spheres. It was a world for itself, a world which preserved their life for them. Now a new world opened before them, a world that could receive them, or appeared to want to receive them. In the land in which they had sojourned, they were now also to *live*, to join in experiencing what it experienced, in joy and in sorrow. They were to enter the history of the land.

The New Concept of History and Nationalism

Their task was made easier by one thing. The concept of history at that time, in Western and Eastern Europe, even in America, had gained new content. It had become new, since history itself became new. The great French Revolution, whose mother had been the era itself, and whose father had been Jean Jacques Rousseau, achieved the great "re-evaluation" of historical "values." A past was rejected. The boundaries drawn by the past were to vanish. A path was to be prepared for one idea. The history which this people was to enter was different from previous history. It exhibited that difference in another, a special way; it gave a concept to life which contained an abundance of consequences and fate within it. This concept was that of nationality. It could be a beneficial genius, and it could become an evil genius. It was able to change the idea of the people and of the state and with that also the idea of history. It wished to change the meaning of history, and the result was generally for the worse. But nationalism, too, in the beginning, before it joined with romanticism, guided man's vision to what was promised and what was yet to be.

Every revolution, in its evolution, is slow and quiet; the outbreak alone is sudden. This people had shared little of the experience of the gathering storm; it was not able to make its inner preparations. The new time came for it almost overnight, and with the suddenness of a new day. Only gradually, however, could it become aware of the new day, could it understand that for it, too, the "liberty and equality" which had been proclaimed had meaning. This people had not yet been able to confront the definite questions which the executor of the Revolution, Napoleon, set for them when he called a parliament and then a Sanhedrin of its congregations. The questions were manifold; they dealt with faithfulness, hope, home, inheritance, commandment, congregation. All of them were based on the one question: Was this people prepared to enter the lands and their history and to find its future there? Out of the answers that were given, an inner uncertainty sounds, something uncomfortable. It could scarcely be otherwise; the men who were to speak here for a people and for a time, had not yet been able to penetrate the full meaning of the problem. The time span had been too short; indeed, they probably faced the issue in disbelief.

But then, when a growing generation became more familiar from day to day with a newness that had entered life, the promise took a wider hold of the mind. Henceforth they would live in the lands where the fathers had sojourned, as upon shifting sands, that now became, for many, the expected and the longed-for. They would become citizens of the states and do everything now implied by the word "citizen." They would share in the work, so that everywhere the new would become reality; in this they would find the task and attain the happiness of their time. Like the history around them, so would their history, the special one, also be renewed.

These hopes awoke almost everywhere. At times they spoke louder than the great, the ancient hope, than the one, the constant expectation. At times, the ancient hopes seemed to have found expression in the new hopes. The new education which was acquired together with its language, the culture which was made one's own, was also to serve the realization of the ancient hope. Many thought themselves to be standing before the entrance to a messianic time.

Only the few grappled with all the questions the new *Weltanschauung* awakened, the questions concerning the sense of the mystery and the revelation. An outer silence encompassed the inner movement, the inner striving. Unobtrusively, the intellect that thinks in distances and in generations battled for its way. But while the few, in silence, sought out the mystery of the commandment, the many, almost all, were concerned with the questions regarding the new meaning of history. They were oppressed by the unrest of the streets, and voices of the day strove to answer them. The near and the changing was the field of thought; they approached everything, everywhere. They maintained the foreground, while the distances and generations remained in the background to which the depths rise.

It could thus appear as though the existence of this people was now merely a political one, one that was only timely, as though this people changed amidst the mutable. Sometimes it threatened to be this in actuality. The decades seemed to force back the millennia, as if the powers of rebirth could be vanquished by the creations of the day. But the forces of rebirth managed to sustain themselves. To this new epoch, in its threefold aspect—that of a new way of viewing the world, of new areas of culture, of new spheres of history—they gave true meaning and value. The difficult test, one of the most difficult in the life of this people, was passed. The power of expansion and the strength of resistance found one another and created new forms of existence.

Moses Mendelssohn

In the life of Moses Mendelssohn of Dessau the commencement of the new epoch is characterized. Within himself, in a life that was quiet yet became ever-more audible and recognizable, he brought together the power of self-affirmation and of resistance, of the will toward what is fully grown and what is in the state of becoming. He was able to achieve this through his personality, which was molded in the pursuit of this task. His personality demonstrated a new possibility, a new form, a new manner of grasping existence. He did not found the new epoch nor even pioneer it. But he deeply impressed upon his contemporaries and upon those who came after them, that new days—questioning, giving, demanding—were approaching them; they would have to respond, but they would also receive. He became an example, speaking to many men within and without, who hesitantly and gropingly searched for an avenue to the encounter. He became the certainty of a time still in the realm of uncertainty.

That a man such as Mendelssohn was granted to the beginning of the epoch, was a blessing that only a later time could fully comprehend. Mendelssohn did not have the genius of Judah Halevi, nor the great mystery of Moses ben Maimon, who had had to give answers to similar problems. In one respect these earlier men had an easier task; they stood in the middle of an epoch. Mendelssohn also did not have the grand quality of thought and intuition granted to Baruch Spinoza. No genius like Spinoza's dwelt in him; genius only possessed him at times and in certain hours. Insofar as one can judge today, he did not even struggle with himself. He said of himself that he had not been born for heroism. But he, the insignificant-looking man, had a great, enduring, courageous faith in himself. He had the simple courage that becomes a matter of course, which never and nowhere sought to demonstrate itself, but which proved itself always and everywhere. He never wanted to publicize himself, but one felt that he was there. He had that which the best of his people and this people itself in its best days had, that naïveté of maturity which comes when naïveté, the wonderful gift of childhood, does not end with childhood, but fulfills itself in ripening years. He stands at a commencement, and only beginnings are revealed in him. But in his being, in his humanity, there is already fulfillment. His personality is his most individual accomplishment; one is tempted to say that it is an historical achievement. But alongside it stand the achievements which made him a teacher. He solved the problem of the new education and its new language; he then became the teacher of the congregations of this people in the domain of the German language, a role he assumed particularly by undertaking to translate the Bible into German.

The manner of Mendelssohn's translation is not to be compared with the originality of the old Greek translation, the Septuagint. The Septuagint, as the first translation of a complete literature, stands on a level of its own. Nor can Mendelssohn's translation be placed alongside the riches of the Aramaic Bible translations, the Targum, or even next to the majesty of the Roman Bible, the Vulgate. It also has no place alongside the force and poetry of the German of Luther's translation, or the English of the King James Version. But it stands as a significant beginning, permitting the Bible to speak to the people of the Bible in a new language. Like every genuine Bible translation it seeks to account for the fact that the Holy Scriptures speak in every language and in every age. There is an admonishing word that sounds out of it. This too was heard. A religious, moral, intellectual inheritance, a possession of humanity and for humanity is to be made to live, is to be given contemporaneousness. Almost every generation after Mendelssohn attempted a new German translation of the Scriptures. In this, too, the humanism of this people evidenced itself; every humanism is ultimately a will to the present, not to the past.

One problem did not yet present itself to Mendelssohn, that of personal participation in the history of the states. His life ended before the onset of the great revolutions which brought these questions before the men in his congregations. True, he had come to know the state in the form which preceded the states created by the revolutions, the absolute state of the new mercantile system, the precursor of the absolute state of the production system. He lived in Berlin by special permit, in the capital city of one of the strongest of these states, and there he created the special form of his life. He was permitted to contribute to literature and to philosophy—but not to the life of the state. To each of these states the men of the congregations were, as they always had been, objects of financial interest, and now of economic plans. They did not have to fulfill duties within the state; they were only to be used. Out of duties, rights might have arisen, but objects are profitable, or unprofitable, instruments are useful or useless. None of them had true freedom of activity. Thus Mendelssohn, too, did not yet live in the state; he only dwelt there. He lived in the suprastate of the scholars and the educated, the true "kingdom" of this time; here, he was a citizen, here duties approached him, here he became assured of his rights. On this level, too, the problems emanated which now became the essential content of his life. He who had strong roots in the ancient heritage, whose personality had grown out of the deep ground, lived as a man within the atmosphere of the "Enlightenment" and within its outlook on the world. He, and therefore within him his inseparable ancient heritage, had been led into this new world which he now loved ardently. Between that which had grown within him and that which had come to be, between the millennia of his being and the decades of his new existence, a harmony had to be achieved in which both, each in its essentials, would keep their true tone. This integration had to be achieved for his own sake, so that it might attain both inner existence and a way within the new age. It had to achieve both, for he could not conceive of himself without his people. His thought could not turn to the most ultimate questions, if, in them, his people did not stand before him. His own existence could not be without that of his people, but neither could it unfold itself without the new world into which he had entered.

The Problem of Reason and of Revelation

All of this, for him, stemmed from the problem of the given law and of the knowledge and morality developing from it. Which is the law which enlightens and guarantees and, with that, also obligates and unites? Is it that discovered by reason and through which reason itself is disclosed? Or is that which was revealed to this people out of the mystery, the "law of Sinai," which grew within this people and gave it the power of continual renewal. The answer to this double question became his life's work once he had made a place for himself in the new world of the Enlightenment. Only in this task did he, who until then had gone his way almost unconsciously, learn to understand his special way. He now became clearly aware of himself and of his purpose. Fortunate is the man who is granted such true awareness.

The answer which he gives is not new; in much, it is reminiscent of earlier thinkers. But it is given in a new manner, in a new form of expression. After his time, philosophy was to find other patterns. His life had ended before the French Revolution, which brought about the new state, and the development of his philosophic method had already reached its goal when that great revolutionary of philosophy, Immanuel Kant, pointed out new ways. Here, too, Mendelssohn stands at a beginning. He was the first to pose the old problem in a new time, and those who came after him learned in their new times from him, even when they went beyond him.

The answer which he strove to give is that the law of reason and the "law of Sinai" come together within humanity. The former had been given to everyone, to grow in all, to become a power within all, and a light for everyone. The other has been assigned to this one people as a special dowry and as a special task, so that, for the sake of everyone, it might preserve a special strength and a special light until the end of days would be fulfilled. Thus the Enlightenment must rise for everyone and shine for all. This people can always approach it to live freely and joyfully within it, without ever turning away from itself, or worse, leaving and abandoning itself. The framework of its task is the "law of Sinai," just as the Enlightenment, in a sense, is the framework of the task for everyone.

This people's thinkers, in earlier and later days, answered differently. They had searched for the foundation of all law, and of this people and its distinction, in the ultimate mystery. They wanted to penetrate to something deeper. But what Mendelssohn said not only stirred sober consideration, but, in part, led this people, surrounded by something new which at times oppressed and at times enticed it, to testify before itself and the world of its duty and its right to exist. Mendelssohn had accomplished this in his days. The man who never desired public life or distinction, nonetheless, gave testimony, his own strong testimony. The purity and the steadfastness of his being were great proof. He became a testimony for his people. He seldom spoke of himself, though everything he says speaks of him, even his philosophy. There is a philosophy—as there is a theology—which is detached from its teacher. Such a philosophy or theology and its creator each have a life of their own; painfully, or antagonistically, they are kept apart. But this man was himself in everything, as Spinoza had been before him, who took his way to a new age too. It is unnecessary to say how much this other one towered above Mendelssohn in the power of intellect. But they are alike in their authenticity, in which purity and steadfastness became one.

Mendelssohn and Lessing

It was therefore highly meaningful for Mendelssohn that one of the most noble men in the German lands, Lessing, gave him his friendship. In Lessing, whose like has seldom been seen, that which was purest and strongest within the new age was brought home to Mendelssohn. Doubts ceased when one thought about Lessing. Mendelssohn could now believe in this age completely, because he could believe in this man. The confidence that had stirred within him now grew strong. Living human proof had been given it; now, it could not be shaken or changed. Mendelssohn's people also felt it, far and wide. They too had experienced something rare. A man's vision had probed them deeply in order to understand them. He had done so with that sympathy, with that love without which there is no understanding, without which the essential, the particular can never be grasped. Rarely did this people have the hope—and rare was the experience—that men would help it selflessly. But its soul always sought for understanding, and this had been granted by Lessing. Those near at hand knew it, and those far away sensed it. As long as the soul lives in this people, from generation to generation, it will think of Lessing gratefully. In dark hours, it will see in him the rays of a light; and where, at times, it can scarcely hope, it will be comforted.

The New Economic Life

Through Mendelssohn and through Lessing, many within the congregations—some happily, others reluctantly—recognized that a new era was knocking at the door. The French Revolution came and shattered walls wherever it penetrated. A new climate forced itself in, and everyone had to breathe it whether he desired to or not. One could almost see a boundary line between two areas of this people: the East, where the walls still stood and which had not yet been reached by this human testimony; and the West and center that had been opened to the new. The two were divided, or at least apart; but their congregations looked toward one another, sometimes out of their hopes, sometimes out of their suffering. They remained congregations of this people and they wanted to remain such for all time. In the West and in the East they prayed together and for one another. In the words of the ancient prayer: "Thou, Guardian of Israel, guard the remnant of Israel, so that Israel be not lost which still says: 'Hear, O Israel . . .' " •

There, where the new era had come or seemed to be approaching, the voices became more audible and urgent—voices from without and from within. They met one another. Soon the very manner and form in which they expressed themselves were no longer what they had been before. Almost within the span of one generation a change had been initiated. In retrospect, one is filled first with amazement and then with respect as one becomes aware of how, at that time, the men of these congregations became students in order to learn everything that would enable them to understand the days then commencing, in order to possess the ability to make a place for themselves in those days. An old trait, intellectual industry, could prove itself. Soon they were able to stand on their own as participants in a new approach to the world, within the changed culture, within the newly developing history of the state. Therefore, their great task now was to take a firm stand even here and remain upright.

In addition to this cultural development, the economic sphere also expanded at that time. Both the Enlightenment and the Revolution brought change and eruption. Although the economic realm reaches into what is uniquely human and seeks to determine it, the human, too, should enter the economic in turn, to order it, to ennoble it. From this

• See *The Authorized Daily Prayer Book*, ed. J. H. Hertz, p. 184.

point of view, no mere coincidence, but rather an inner relationship, now brought about the fact that, in Central and Western Europe, the so-called emancipation of the peasants and of the Jews shared the same days. Both peasant and Jew had been the *globae adscripti.* The earliest beginnings of humanism and religious revolution had permitted the historical hour to bypass them both. History, after all, is much less a history of victories and defeats than it is of comprehended and of uncomprehended opportunities.

But now the days and space changed also within economic life; and as the powers and breadth of scientific technology unfolded, human forces and claims also came to life. The one made demands upon the other, so that a new slavery might not develop, a slavery of technical science and of industry. The social commandment, by which the human element enters economy and technical science, began to speak, softly at first, but then ever louder. Once its law, its injunction, and its hope had rested within this people alone. With the Holy Scriptures, it had entered here and there into other spirits and temperaments. Now it became universal, just as everything which has been revealed within this people is destined to be. The ancient commandment marched from land to land, and like any true commandment it was also a prophecy. Men became fighters; more and more they found those who joined them and who followed them. The history of the peoples is often, in a variety of ways, a war of ideas and interests. Often, again in a variety of ways, particularly when possessions are enlarged, it is a war of the human and of the economic. Both conflicts, fundamentally, are a "war between belief and unbelief."

Thus entry into the history of these lands now meant entrance into this battle. In it, also, this people's claim for right and place was to legitimatize itself. In many of its finest sons the soul could now find new enlargement, and much that had been repressed could free itself. Belonging to one particularity or another could enclose a narrowness and a paltriness, a narrowness of horizon, a paltriness of concepts. A child of this people cannot exist for long without breadth of spirit; if perhaps the parents could do so, the children or grandchildren could not. They will need something greater and great. So it recurs in the history of this people. It cannot be surprising then, to mention an example, that among those who found themselves in one of the German or Italian states, many enthusiastically followed the call for a greater Italy or a greater Germany. But it was spirit of the old spirit, will of the old will, when many surrendered themselves to the great social idea which promised to unite the lands and to make the peoples one.

The Battle for Social and Economic Justice

In the striving for the right form of social life, demand and teaching very quickly turned toward one urgent matter: Creation and its product, effort and reward, work and ownership were to remain unified. No one, somewhere or somehow, was to step between them in order to take for himself that for which another had sweated. The worker was to possess and dispose. The fight for a better social system, for a truly social community, thus had to include the rejection of trade and those who traded.

This people had first been led into trade and then forced into it. It now appeared in the sight of the world, and to many who had left this people too, to be a people of traders. It is always difficult to view the totality and the reality from the outside. And it was particularly difficult in the case of this people, which was scattered everywhere. It was not easy to find—there, where the eye first glimpsed the peddler—also the thinkers and scholars, the mystics and dreamers, the men of longings, and the men of visions who were there as well. It was difficult to recognize how someone might be both in one, a man of trade and a man of intellect. The revolutionary of social philosophy was a son of this people, a descendant of generations of intellect. Karl Marx, while growing up outside this people, did not see it, and in rejecting trade, he also rejected his people.

The ways and methods of trade themselves were then changing, some quickly, others gradually. Everyone had to learn them again. Walls fell, and broader paths became visible. In some of them, energies which had previously been held back could extend; they could find and create areas here and there. The drive for colonization, the pioneer spirit which had lived for ages within this people, could come to life in a new fashion. Another heritage of theirs, an economic patience which does not shun any effort and is not afraid to try anything, proved itself. One saw the great planners, above all, the princes of finance, and particularly that one dynasty whose proud and faithfully true self-confidence traveled from capital city to capital city, at that time. Among those who arose, there were, then and later, also those who were ignoble; they surrendered the presence of millennia for the insecure decades. Here, too, the men of endurance and the men of the day showed themselves distinctly.

Yet even within the old and narrower areas there was now activity, often viewed enviously by the world outside. New possibilities were recognized by many within the congregations. They saw that the time of slow and deliberate motion had come to an end. They became aware that the manner of locomotion had not changed appreciably since the ancient days. Now, in quick development, it all changed. They understood that the economy would have to follow after the new and, perhaps, might even have to precede it. They also saw how the machine, through one invention after another, speedily brought into existence an abundance of products which waited to be transported to consumers. They also saw how money itself took a quicker route and constantly brought into existence new money and new types of money.

As a whole, they scarcely gained full insight into the new before others did. But in that one narrow area in which economic activity had been permitted them and had become an inherited habit, the new pattern forced itself upon them in a stronger, more immediate way. Moreover, something personal entered into this, for this financial newness seemed to be a part of the new freedom which they now wanted to win. The surrounding world, on the other hand, first came to see the new developments as they were manifested by this people.

Often, it believed and wanted to believe, that those to whom and through whom this newness had come were to blame for it. Old prejudices found nourishment here, new ones a fertile soil. Undoubtedly, it was not always prejudice that spoke here. Injustices were practiced. Some of the children of this people practiced the sin of usury and hurt their people. But, to view the sequence of the generations and the many areas in which this people lived, is to be confronted—despite one here and there—with an almost touching honesty. Despite many detours the way constantly led upward. Confidence was given and was returned, and it was only seldom disappointed. One could breathe pure air among this people. Moreover, something deeply human was also often revealed. These men worked untiringly, and they did not do so primarily for themselves. For the sake of their children and their children's children, they took all of this upon themselves so that they might live in a freer, more spacious world, where something loftier could be practiced with greater ease. The life of the little man was given a touch of greatness through this. He served and labored for the spirit. He carried his burden for the days to come.

The New Developments in Religious Life

Though the economy changed and filled this time with promise or despair, though it entered and went forth from the homes, it nevertheless did not essentially determine the existence of this people. This had been true in the years in which it had maintained itself, often under oppression, and it was so in the time which entered now, bringing and demanding change. Not the economic—no matter how strongly it affected everything—but the intellectual and the religious were the foundations of this people's existence. In the last analysis, everything depends upon this people's aridity or fertility in these areas. For that reason so much, indeed, almost everything, depended upon the fact that an answer was being sought for the two great questions posed by the times, that of a special history within the emerging, general configuration of the peoples and states, and that of religious and intellectual certainty within the newly forming *Weltanschauung*.

For a long time, many permitted these questions to pass. They did not want to hear them; perhaps they could not. The one group would or could not, for they would or could make their place only within the familiar thickets of the past. They forgot or did not know that one can continue to dwell within the past for a while, but that one cannot live in it permanently. The others would or could not hear these questions, for their only interest lay in the universal culture they were now attaining. They wanted to receive everything from it. They forgot or did not know that culture can be a companion for a stretch of the road, but never a leader. Only those who heard these questions and opened themselves to them, in order to struggle with them, established the existence of their people anew and marched forward with it on mankind's way.

Something difficult, yet encompassing, was required here. The two questions and the two tasks rising out of them could not be separated if both of them did not want to become one-sided and, with that, insufficient. The problem of history and that of belief, that of the way and that of the basic standpoint, can never be separated, let alone divided, for this people. Only one who knows where he stands, where he has his certainty, will know where he must go and what he must choose. And only he who knows that the way lies before him will know what the basic position, from which alone the way gains direction, will mean for all days. History can be understood only when one has penetrated into faith, and one can understand faith only when one also grasps history. There arose then from the banks of the Rhine, to the Danube, reaching to the Vistula, men who experienced this through a union of intuition and investigation. They gained an ever-clearer insight of this double necessity and a constantly clearer vision of the totality which unites them. They belonged to the generations that followed Mendelssohn, and there is much of him in them. Yet they were different, at times completely different from him. They belonged to the time following Kantian philosophy, and, above all, following the great Revolution which has engendered a cultural crisis. A renaissance in all of its depth and breadth can be recognized in these men, though each of them had his individual features, and they often seemed to oppose one another. These men were the proof of this rebirth and then became its guarantee, drawing out of the old strength, and creating a new strength.

They had been set into a time of transition. Days came and went, and no one knew what was passing and what was enduring; circles became dislocated and often it was not known what was the center and what the periphery. Roads crossed, and it was often difficult to see a clear direction. Far and wide this was experienced, and fates and periods depended upon the direction in which men turned. The men of this people found more of a problem than did other peoples, for in every thinker, in everyone who strove outward or was driven outward, stronger and more encompassing powers now struggled with each other, whether or not the individual was aware of this inner conflict. The decades, approaching him slowly or quickly, strove to displace the millennia out of which he had grown—whether he wanted them to or not. Not just the problem of what to do with his days or what was to be his fate, but his very existence was at stake. His historical personality was threatened. It is therefore understandable that many who could not rediscover the true way walked a mistaken way, or that they sought detours and therefore lost their direction.

A man of the old enclosed sphere, who neither then nor later was required to fight, or a younger man who was spared this fight because the older one had waged it for him, found it difficult to understand this time which either searched and could not find the right way or thought it had found it, and ceased to search. The people also rarely understood, although they were engaged in a similar, if not as far-reaching a controversy. Here, in the souls of these members of this people, in this Western domain, in this time of transition, the decades fought with the millennia. What mattered in and for every soul was whether the millennia were pushed back at times and finally displaced, or whether they won their way in order to permeate the decades, to establish them, to ennoble them. A restlessness with its waywardness, more, an excitement that does not permit rest, becomes evident to one who witnessed this time. An inner uncertainty that can also become an outer one becomes evident. Often, the step was unsteady, without self assurance.

The Response to Transition

When centuries, with their elemental feelings, with their organic forms of thought, are pushed back—either through events that break in, or through quick developments that fulfill themselves—the internal balance is damaged. The normal, ancient, and proven form of coming to terms between the individual I, which has its years and decades, and the total I, which has its centuries, is diverted. How much more must this become evident here, where the centuries had widened into millennia. These men themselves were not always aware of it, but it was still so. The coming to terms—more or less demanded by everyone—between that which had come into existence and that which was in its beginning, had been interrupted in its process. An old, internal balance is lost; the new one has not yet been won.

A lack of balance—or even of proportion—quickly draws down upon itself the glances of surrounding people; smiles, jokes, and mockery are evoked. Members of this people then became the butts of jokes and ridicule. Jokes and ridicule may be harmless, at times even friendly, and occasionally this was true. Often they arise from thoughtlessness which acts and does harm, without realizing that it harms. They were also often the means employed by the enemy and the villain, and became devices of disfigurement and caricature. They did not point to weaknesses and shortcomings in the manner of genuine satire, but invented distortions. It is no wonder that counterjoke and countermockery came to life. As far as can be seen, the counterjoke did not let itself be drawn to the low level of the villainous. Ultimately, it could not descend to evil because it never completely forgot the duty and the responsibility that belong to all.

Though it may be simple to show this special character, it was not transition only which had to be endured throughout several generations, and which not all could endure. These men also had to stay strong enough to meet the disappointments, both without and within, which accompanied the change; and not all of them were able to do so. The decades tell of the tired who lost courage or who failed; they tell even more of the fearful who ran away. This was no flight via a detour, taken so that one might return, as the Marranos had once done in Sepharad. It was not the kind of flight which meant that one remained within this people. It was a strange flight which led many astray, and removed them from what was desirable in their history. Fearfulness, springing from everything, was the mother and a belief in the new destination was the father of the concepts which justified flight; a culture that had gone romantic could always be ready to grant its blessings to such a venture. This was no flight before oppressing foes; it was flight from oneself, a flight from the millennia and out of the millennia into actual or into imagined decades.

The Holy Scriptures relate a moving flight which reaches into what is innermost and deepest in man: the flight from God. Moses tremblingly backed away from the path to which God called him; he was filled with apprehension. But the voice of God was stronger, and he followed it. It is told of the Prophet Jonah that he fled to Tarshish to escape the task entrusted to him by God; but God brought him back that he might do what God had commanded, that he might hear what God had promised. How moved and excited the Psalmist must have been to write: "Whither shall I go from Thy spirit? Or whither shall I flee from Thy presence?" (Ps. 139:7)

Much of this also took place within the men of this people who, at that time, in these and other ways, were in a sense fleeing from the presence of God. They left the great faithfulness for the little loyalties; they fled from the serious, the categorical commandment to friendlier, easier commandments; they turned from the one, great, enduring idea to changing and shimmering thoughts or to a never-changing thoughtlessness. Then they deserted or rejected the faith and the forefathers. Without doubt, there were tragedies; but perhaps even more comedies were enacted. It is difficult to pass the same judgment upon all, and it is also difficult to judge all harshly. After all, life itself is at times something of a flight.

How much pleasanter is it to turn one's gaze toward those who stood firmly or came to be firmly established in "a wavering time." Surely there must have been hours of uncertainty and of crisis in the souls of these men, hours during which they wanted to flee from God. But somehow they were able to find the enduring way or to rediscover it. They then held to it, and in it, discovered and rediscovered themselves. During their days and nights they may well have experienced what Solomon Gabirol, the Sephardi, felt when he let his poetry exclaim: "I flee from Thee unto Thee, O God." Gabirol probably built upon the sentence in the Psalms, and also probably desired to elevate the climax of Plotinus' teachings (whom he considered a master), the *phyge monupros nonon*, the "flight of the one to the One," of the "spirit to God." Gabirol gave voice to something which Plotinus had not heard, the voice of "I" which knows itself to have come out of the "I" of all I's.

The men and women who recognized and prepared the enduring way in this time of assimilation also heard this voice. In their time, out of their inner need, they hearkened to it, to this voice which brings back to God him who flees from God. Centuries lie between them and Gabirol, just as there are many centuries between him and the Psalmist. But to someone who takes in the reverberations, there penetrates, in all the changes of tone, a unity, a sameness. If one may say so, this people maintained its identity through its experiencing, its suffering, its learning, and its belief, with its questioning and searching and hoping. The people and the belief preserved their distinct personalities; times could only pass them by or enter them.

Almost suddenly, after all the unrest and the wavering, the observer sees standing before him a certainty—a certainty with all the clarity conveyed by it, a security of finding one's way with all of the confidence which it instills. The millennia have broken through; the old powers of growth have made their way to the surface once again; the time of rebirth is here. To someone who compares two or three generations, this appears as a miracle. Across the land of the Ashkenazim who had to meet this test at that time—a test for their own sake and for the sake of all—the call of the Prophet Isaiah seems to sound: "This is the way, walk ye in it" (Is. 30:21). The call was heard as if in wonder; and it was received as if in wonder; and it was carried along from one language to another. A different, a new time commenced, one that has only begun. It is our time, the one in which we stand.

The "Science of Judaism"

An abundance of voices now sounded forth; for many questions arose, one attracting another and that attracting still others. The mind of Europe itself was giving birth to many philosophies and sociologies, and to many teachings concerning the state and community. The outward-looking, the searching, seemed to be confronted with many points of departure; many directions presented themselves. The men in the congregations, the constantly questioned among humanity, now felt themselves to be questioned from all sides. Many answers were pronounced, often contradictory answers. But there is a harmony in them, for the reawakening process is revealed in everyone, this continual striving for the existence of this people.

The minds fought for and sought to recognize and to possess four things: the coming into existence of history and of this people; the meaning of religion and of this people; the way of righteousness, which was to become the right for everyone and thus also for this people; and the strength of the idea of Zion, of the "end of days" and its Messiah, in which all will unite, in which Zion and the earth will be one, and thus this people will be one with mankind. It is a fourfold search but in its basis, as in its goal, it is a striving for one thing. It is the search for the great line in history through which the manifold becomes a unity, the ways become *the* way. Only when this people sees that great line does it find itself. This time also saw the rich results of individual research, the harvests and seeds of what was called the "Science of Judaism" (*Wissenschaft des Judentums*). Respect for the particular, reverence for the obscure detail, was an ancient tradition among this people. One realized that intuition itself is preceded by effort, and that effort must follow intuition. Moreover, a new philosophy, the inheritance of humanism, was now teaching its new methods, and these were applied to the ancient, familiar material. Much of what one had known, one now came to know anew. A great meaningful work was achieved in selflessness and in untiring dedication. Men of the Eastern Ashkenazic area and of Italy joined and worked together with those of Western Ashkenaz. Here, too, the observer who looks back upon this is amazed and filled with admiration as he stands before so much that so few achieved.

The Printers Romm

Great names stand out when one turns to survey the individual areas. But there is one name, whose significance really belongs to later decades, that deserves particular mention; it is indicative of something completely characteristic of the *Wissenschaft des Judentums.* It is a name embracing much that yet remains anonymous—*Haalmanah vehaahim Romm,* The Widow and the Brothers Romm, the great Vilna publishers. Their name is mentioned with the deepest respect and with deep gratitude. A group of men worked together here, remaining almost hidden, desiring to serve: editors, printers, proofreaders; all scholars. They strove to publish critical new editions of this people's classics, particularly the Talmud with its commentators, but also the prayer book, the *Siddur*, with its variants. Another publisher, the publishing house in Rödelheim, must be mentioned. Besides the *Siddur*, it published a scientific edition of the *Mahzor*, the prayer book for festivals—and this too is a chapter of the great history of the *Wissenschaft des Judentums.* Something from the days of the humanistic revival once again lived in this people.

And yet, as great as this scientific achievement is, it is an expression only of something far greater. The men of whom it tells came to be confident in themselves, and they helped many others to attain this confidence. They experienced and came to know the birth of their decades out of the millennia, and they gave scientific or artistic form, at times both, to this knowledge. All of them, each with his talent and in his way, wanted to and had to answer the question that arose within them, the many-sided question: Who are you, and through what did you become what you are? For whose sake and for what purpose do you live? The question of their existence raised itself and could not be denied. They spoke the ancient word of Israel in their modern understanding: "I will not let thee go, except thou bless me" (Gen. 32:27). History had attained rebirth, new life. The soul became aware of itself, the spirit recognized the path leading from the former to the present.

The epoch commenced with that fourfold understanding which basically was one: that of history, of faith, of righteousness, and of hope. Each spoke in a manifold voice. Yet all has to be heard together, as a unity, if the meaning of that time is to be understood. And this must be kept in mind: All of this, as it makes a vital appearance in science and in literature, was ultimately the expression of a great experience, experienced also by those who did not live through it. The rebirth had come.

History demanded the most immediate answer (which implied personal decision) in relation to a double question. First, the question concerned something constantly reappearing in history, something internally identical in it: Is there a constant element that operates within history throughout all the changes of times, by means of which history is determined and the gift of renewal endures? The question concerned an enduring, creative strength, out of which every single personality could draw that which would place it into total history and self, and which would enable it to achieve something particular, something special. This question also concerned the accidental which, of necessity, is subjugated to the process of change. This people asked itself such a question first through its prophets and then through its teachers, its poets, its thinkers, its mystics—whenever it thought about itself and wanted reassurance of itself.

There was also a second question, speaking always with complete immediacy in its days: Could, and to what extent could the self meet and join worlds that had come into being, or contemporary situations? This question always arose when this people was surrounded in whole or in part by a state or culture that all or many of its members wished to join. Such a situation existed in Persian, Hellenistic, and Roman times, and, to a certain extent, during the Arabic time. Now the question was more problematical, more pressing than ever before, for now these men were approached not by something existing, something established, but by something in the process of becoming, something revolutionary. This people was supposed to participate in its development and growth. A clearly visible transformation came about. Everyone experienced it and felt himself gripped by it, almost encircled by it.

There is an inner connection between these questions. The latter, concerning the entry into other worlds, can only be answered if the former question, concerning what endures within history, finds a clear answer. The inner question, which is at rest in peaceful and unhurried days, makes a peremptory appearance when the other question, that of the relationship with a new world, urgently manifests itself. What must continue to exist throughout all change? What is the enduring something which makes it possible—perhaps even necessary—for one to adjust to change? The questions are inseparable, though both were silent in areas such as Eastern Europe where the old walls still stood, or in Asia and Africa, which the new way of history had not yet reached. These questions were at home only in the areas which had been gripped by the revolution in one way or another, that is, Central and Western Europe and the growing United States of America. Here the struggle for the solution of the problems took place.

These questions were not imaginary ones, nor had they been solicited. Rather, one could almost say that they were set by the existence of this people; they addressed themselves not so much to reason but to will. If the head assumed that it alone should deal with them, the result was aridity, infertile thoughts and infertile decisions. But the majority of this people did not consider these questions only intellectually; it felt them to be truly basic questions of its own life. These people felt themselves beset by them from within; their very heart and will demanded an answer. It therefore came as a liberation to them when men "in a spirit dwelt" showed that there were ways of answering these questions, ways that this people now could take, ways which would lead on to future generations. Spirit and will found one another; and a new form of existence arose in order to create still other forms.

Leopold Zunz and Heinrich Heine

Many names could be mentioned of men who helped create the work of renewal, but above all, three must be mentioned, for they were the masters. Foremost, one stands who is in a class by himself, Leopold Zunz of Detmold. The more the gaze of later days turns to this man, the more he gains in stature. Often it is true that the force of personality lessens scholarly ability, or scholarly energy decreases the will of a personality. In Leopold Zunz, the unbending personality permitted ever-new strength to stream into scholarly labor, and unerring scholarship kept reinforcing personality. He was a man who permitted history to speak through the abundance of its facts. Most of the time, he himself withdrew into the background; at times, he was almost concealed. But if one seeks to find him, one quickly feels the force of his personality. At times, a pathos becomes evident. It touches us because it touched him. And it is always touching, for it is rare; it is never introduced consciously.

One cannot speak of Zunz without at least parenthetically mentioning Heinrich Heine. Zunz, in whom the renewal became a matter of personality, stood close to this poet. And Heine remained close to him, both because he could and wanted to remain close to him. Heine, too, had been one of those who had "fled from God." He was the only one of those who continued to possess significance and who attained greatness. Ultimately he "fled to God." He had fled from God to poetry. Its wondrous gift had been granted him, and it opened worlds of which he could sing and tell in a way no one else ever could. In poetry he found the mystery, but not the certainty of his life; yet the way, the certainty remained open to him. He had fled toward a Hellenism which he saw in the joyful, shining colors he himself had given it, as opposed to the dark somberness in which the generations out of which he had come seemed to look at him. He did not gain certainty but conflict; but through conflict, he attained a clearer vision, and ultimately learned to recognize the truth. He sought irony as a refuge; it was to force him to remain truthful. He walked many false paths, but was never tempted into falsehood or deceit. And in truthfulness, he ultimately found the way, the way to his self, his life, his faith. He "fled from God to God." He left and he returned.

It is extraordinary to behold these two men next to one another, comrades in age and comrades of an age, clinging to one another throughout the passing years and throughout the changing times. Zunz was probably the only person of those days whom Heine honored, and even worshiped without criticism or irony. Sometimes it appeared as if he clung to Zunz in hours of inner need. His soul reached up to Zunz. This is telling testimony about both men. It is also a testimony concerning the expanse of this people's soul, which is able to encompass so much and so many; indeed, without this encompassing grasp, this people would have no soul, nor struggle and work. Those who struggled, who, in a sense, made life difficult for themselves, were preserved for the good. Heine and Zunz struggled in their manners. Those who did not battle, to the right or to the left, were blown away like chaff by the wind of history. Many know of

Heine and perhaps only a few know of Zunz, but the two stand next to one another, and their hands reach toward one another.

Zunz was a man of comprehensive view, a man whose scholarship worked in terms of centuries; he was also a master of philology. He was a scholar who felt himself approached by every single day and spoken to by every single human being of all centuries. That which looked to him and called to him, the great and the small alike, was more to him than a job for investigation or a mere problem of scholarship. Everything, too, was, if not primarily, the life of his people. He hearkened to the voice of the life that knew how to endure; he examined the features of this life which demanded a future, and he could not turn his ear and eye from it. He wanted to show what sort of life it was: united in its abundance and manifold in all its separateness; changing in its days and yet always the same; never like anything else, and never limited to a rigid form. He wanted to present all of this, so that his people could find its way. He approached this people's life at times from this direction, at times from that, and it stood before him always in new meaning. It became his knowledge and his experience. Those whose leader he was to become were to have the same recognition and then the same experience, so that in those wavering days they could become secure. To a great extent, perhaps even more than he had hoped, his plan reached fulfillment. Many for whom he is just a name still derive both concepts and attitudes from him.

Heinrich Graetz

Next to Zunz in rank, as perhaps no one else of that time may claim to be, is Heinrich Graetz, a man of the land of Posen, in which East and West at that time met and looked at one another directly. Graetz is little more than two decades younger than Zunz. But these two decades span a decisive historical period, that of the Napoleonic era. For the one, Napoleon had been an experience; for the other, only a tale. Many differences in the overall approach of these two men, as of others in those days, may be explained through this. The one first experienced the world around him in a time when hope rose everywhere, when freedom rolled in, and the other, in a time of disappointment and of growing reaction. Zunz began to look around him in days of hope; his eye, seeking out the way, turned from the present to all that preceded it. The other, who had learned to see in days of disappointment, took the opposite direction in his searching and questioning. He let his gaze move from the beginnings, the earliest, most creative of all developments to everything that followed, until it reached his own days. But though the manners of thinking and feeling of these two show particular traits, they agree in the one thing that is all-decisive. Both strove to comprehend the life of this people, and it revealed itself to their love. Out of that revelation they gained the knowledge that their people's hope of renewal, that hope of all hopes, was justified. Both of them served this renewal of life. They investigated the parts and therefore came to know the whole. They knew of the whole and they constantly spoke of it. They served the unity of this people.

Graetz was one of those rare and happy persons who know from the beginning what they want and what their talents are. This knowledge, and the task which he so clearly recognized as his own, created an enthusiasm within him which, at times, reached explosive proportions. Without it he could not have undertaken nor fulfilled the task of being the first to present to the world a *History of the Jews* from the oldest times to the present. His enthusiasm awakened the enthusiasm of many within this people.

Jewish history appeared before Graetz confronting his soul and self like a drama—the greatest drama in humanity—stretching to "the end of days." He saw it reaching his own generation in all its totality and unity. His most profound thoughts were constantly reawakened by it. He could not indulge in the serenity adopted by so many in their attempts at scholarship. His basic concern was not for events and personalities alone, but for the existence of his people and for the meaning of all history. Here and there Graetz made some small mistakes, but he recognized what was decisive and essential for every age. He was always able to comprehend the totality. Through this, he became a leader in rebuilding his people's unity.

Zacharias Frankel

Between Graetz and Zunz, between them in terms of years and in terms of nature, stands a man who must be mentioned with them as the third leader of this day: Zacharias Frankel. He came from Prague, that wondrous city, where oppositions often dwelt next to one another. A sober realism and an enthusiastic romanticism lived compatibly in Prague and, not seldom, seemed to support one another. The congregation often appeared to be like the city. It is possible that this city and this congregation, often with their paradoxes, had taught the young Frankel to look for the blessing of the center, that center which maintains free access and an open gate. The center appeared to him as the direction toward which the history of this people continually seemed to return. The way appeared to be the way in which the centuries of Talmudic life moved; and it was the Talmud, above all, toward which his own drive for learning turned. Another possible influence on Frankel's thinking may have been the teaching of Hegel. Many in those days thought history itself gave this answer, that all movement of the spirit, all development always leads back to the center, to the synthesis.

Fundamentally, he was determined by his charisma, by his talent, which was nourished from the depths of his people. His thought appears in a simple, almost overpowering harmony, and it ruled his life in an almost effortless manner. In founding the Breslau Seminary much was granted to him; that which he had planned and begun became an undertaking whose fruition he saw. He was gifted in finding men and bringing them together. He found the man for the place and the place for the man, uniting men with one another in their common trust of him. He was the first to create—in a period of new methods and new demands for the *Wissenschaft des Judentums*—an institution that might create new life. It became a spiritual home and a "mother in Israel." Propitious events brought that day about. But what was decisive was the fact that the day had found the man and the result of the events was life.

Zunz, Graetz, and Frankel entered into the being of this people. Each of them, in his own way and manner, experienced this people's totality. Through history they sensed unity, for true life proves itself by remaining one life. They, therefore, experienced the old in the new and the new in the old. For them there existed no contradiction—let alone an antithesis—between the new and the old. The strength of rebirth was in them and was able to achieve new power through them. This strength had arisen, as if in secret, in personalities such as these and in those who joined them, and it gained its clarity from the many who descended from them.

Krochmal and Others

One cannot speak of Zunz, Graetz, and Frankel without mentioning other men who were their comrades and became teachers of all who would study: Nachman Krochmal of Brody, Solomon Judah Rapoport of Lemberg, and Samuel David Luzzato of Trieste. As Maimonides once had wanted to offer a *Guide to the Perplexed* in the realm of philosophy, so now Krochmal undertook to offer his *Guide*, in the vast field of his people's history, to those who could not find their way. He wanted to indicate laws and ways that governed this history. He was one of the great pioneers; he saw what others only later came to see.

For a long time, among this people, it had been customary to lose the author in his work, to forget the man and his personal qualities when one considered his achievements. Now Rapoport looked toward the personality and revealed the unity of personality and its creations. He was one of the great masters of method; with the discovering ability of great erudition, he uncovered the hidden and the concealed and added them together.

In a time when the genius of the "holy language," the language of the Bible, was disregarded or not understood, Luzzato rediscovered this outstanding source. He was a poet and could penetrate what has been learned and discovered to its depths, so that within it and then through it science becomes knowledge.

The Encounter with the New Philosophy

To have studied history and become aware of the basic forces at work in it, was to discover what religion, justice, and hope have to say in those changed days. The voice of history was heard only by someone who listened to religion, to justice, and to hope. But to some, this ancient religion, which had been set into a new historic frame, had something very special to say: It asked its questions of the student and demanded his answer.

A new situation arose, which voiced its claims in a twofold way. Old intellectual familiarity failed, old ways of answering no longer led to the goal. Originating from the given, enduring position, thought had to be led in another direction, in order to meet something twofold which the time had evolved.

The first confrontation which could not be evaded, which was presented to religious thought then, was the new philosophy which was fashioning its systems, particularly in Germany. The Enlightenment, which had actually been more interested in creating a style of thinking than a system, had undertaken to supply belief with reason by guiding it away from mysticism. The new philosophy wanted to do more than that. It did not want to attempt only what previous centuries had tried, to make religion legitimate through philosophy or philosophy through religion. Philosophy now sought to be the ultimate perfection of all thought and all belief, the fulfillment of all religion and all humanity. The question, whether one religion or another led to truth, no longer existed; instead the questions were: Religion or philosophy? Half knowledge or complete knowledge?

Christianity was proclaimed to be the straightforward and certain way to the apex, to philosophy. The religion of this people Israel was assigned to a realm of lesser importance by philosophy—by a discipline of thought which at that time presented itself as the final, the absolute—not by a belief which till then saw Christianity as salvation and redemption, but by philosophy. An intellectual system which claimed to be *the* system assigned Judaism its place. *Philosophia tanta causa finita.* A changed and basically different situation surrounded the Jew. Judgment seemed to have been passed by a final and properly relevant court.

Here too—particularly here—this was a critical time, a time of decision. Some thought to bid farewell to the ancestral house of faith, even as they continued within the congregation of the faith. But, out of the totality, a voice speaks, telling how this people Israel, in lands of new freedom and of new problems, gained anew the brave and great will for its religion. In the strength of the rebirth there grew pious knowledge of self; and in it, there grew the strength of the answer.

The new word arose and began to speak, lightly and quietly, with many voices. Sometimes it turned to a wider circle, sometimes to a narrower one. It always grew out of the deep feeling for a task that had now been set, different than before, but just as meaningful. An early possession of this people, the sermon, now entered into a different era. Using new forms and new language, it strove to gain expression for the old and enduring content. On the whole, in the men who gave these sermons, one confronts a strong sense of duty. As small as the congregation might be to which they spoke, they knew themselves to be responsible for the entire heritage of this people and for the task they all shared. They endeavored to let the dignity of their faith appear before their group and before the people in whose midst they now lived. At times the individual attempt is deficient, at times clumsy and touching. But as a whole it is something great; the rebirth which had arrived is revealed in it. There is a luster here that touches even that which is small.

Behind the many, there stood the few, giving and helping, those "men in whom a spirit dwelt," the few, or the single ones in each generation. Each sought his own way, but together they form a significant sequence. Rarely is one of them merely a student; but each belongs, whether he realized it or not, to his predecessor. They are the men in whom the new religious thinking received its character, its determining line. The line led to new religious thought, and then led beyond it to thinking without end, arising out of the faith. They were the thinkers of their time, for they strove to receive within themselves something of the eternal and encompassing, and at the same time their thoughts plumbed the moment into which they were set.

Solomon Ludwig Steinheim

First among them, chronologically, and perhaps also in terms of rank, was Solomon Ludwig Steinheim of Bruchhausen, who was born five years before Zunz. Like many of the thinkers of the old Sephardic world, he was a physician, and in what he writes an Eros of healing often reveals itself. He seeks to lead his people to a healthiness of thought and to a well-being, as the straight and definite way to the summit which was to be climbed.

There was also something of a poet in Steinheim. He knew what discloses itself in "experience and poetry." Mendelssohn thought he had solved the problem of revelation and of reason in the reality that his harmonious personality revealed, and perhaps he had, in his own manner. But this unavoidably recurring problem now appeared before Steinheim. He saw that in revelation the eternal, the beyond, enters the human sphere; and that the human moves within the spheres of the eternal, the beyond, by means of reason. Reason and revelation can thus meet.

When Steinheim, in his time (which alternated in turning to an exclusive rationalism or romanticism), expressed the problem in other words, he also expressed, in his way, its meaning for thought in general. He saw clearly that this people's insight into its religion, its very nature, and therefore also its existence, depended on never losing its sense of revelation. To clarify the problem, one could say that in the face of all mythologies (including philosophy) and attempts, in the name of the state, to deny the men of this people rights, Steinheim gained a solid position, through his understanding of enduring revelation, which made possible the presence of self-confidence, and future development. Yet he did not want merely to hold his own against all the logicians of history, but against the all-embracing logos itself. Revelation thus became his answer, and reason seemed now to have gained a soul. There were probably only a few who understood Steinheim completely in his time, but later days repaid him with understanding. The most decisive fact here is that a man such as Steinheim could arise such a short time after Mendelssohn. He too is testimony that the rebirth had come, and in him too rebirth gains new power.

Samson Raphael Hirsch

Different, completely different, yet belonging to Steinheim inwardly, was a man who followed him and who would, perhaps, not have done what he did without him: Samson Raphael Hirsch of Hamburg. In him, too, we recognize the rebirth. He had a strong sense of individuality and by its strength he was able to arouse conscience. In his people he saw the great, world-historical individuality confronting him. If Steinheim had learned to understand his people by striving to comprehend revelation, Hirsch entered into the understanding of revelation by immersing himself in this people. A turn toward the special kept determining his thinking and, in many ways, his striving. He presented the particular task which this people, in those changed days, more than ever then, was to keep constantly in view, the task of its historical uniqueness. A uniqueness which always, in every stage of its existence, throughout all the changing events, had maintained its certainty. He recognized the new age and its culture; he neither hid from it, nor did he lose himself in it. With all of his predilection for the particular, which marks him so specifically and at times might seem almost a peculiarity, he nevertheless spoke the new language without any hesitation or wavering. This language was to help him reveal the soul of the Bible's words, to present the enduring sense of every commandment to the man of his days. He thus led into serious contemplation even those who did not tread his path.

Abraham Geiger

Next to Hirsch stands Abraham Geiger of Frankfurt. He is different too, but like Hirsch, he rose out of the rebirth and became one of its powers. For Geiger the essential and the decisive question deals with the enduring and the unchanging within this religion. This is his focal point. But, at the same time, he wants to discover that which, in each age encircles the focal point or strives toward it. The *Wissenschaft des Judentums* aimed to reveal this. Constantly taking and giving, he turned to it, and it must be grateful to him for many discoveries. But more important, Geiger was seized by the major task presented by religious life in a time of change. He wanted to make it possible—through new expression, through new forms in communal prayer—that the new certainty, and the joy of that certainty, could be possessed. This striving has often been labeled with the many-meaning and misunderstood word "Reform." What was striven for can be understood only if the original, linguistic meaning is once again given this word. Form was to be refashioned: form, which in so many ways was bound up with earlier times and which now threatened to turn into formlessness, was to be newly developed into the expression or the symbol of the idea. True reform, therefore, cannot exist without a lively understanding of the enduring. In a sense, reform presupposes the conservative trait. Without it, a finished formlessness quickly turns into a becoming formlessness. There is formlessness of lost form and formlessness of exaggerated form. Just as conservatism would petrify without reform, so reform without something conservative would become a shell without content. Every emphasis is different. That which has become receives more emphasis, but the will is the same. In Geiger, the will remained firm, particularly, since the rebirth of the religion became a power within him. He sought, therefore, to speak of revelation, in the new language, to the congregations of religion.

Joel, Steinthal, and Hermann Cohen

After Steinheim, Hirsch, and Geiger came others, different from them and different from one another, but alike in what was innermost and basic. Rebirth was in all of them, and they wanted to give testimony of the revelation which had come anew to this people. All of them thought to give new endurance to the existence of this people, each in his manner, each according to his lot.

Among the men who could be named here, a glance, cast back a century, rests on a few in particular. With all their particularities, with all their differences of ability, their thoughts were joined in moving toward the same significant direction. They began by looking toward religion from the vantage point of philosophy, and they came to see philosophy from the vantage point of religion. The deeper they penetrated into philosophy, the surer they became of their religion. The mysterious which there, in philosophy, was and had to remain the boundary, became their focal point, the fulfillment and guarantee of thought; in a sense, it became the Holy of Holies. From it, from religion, they could now survey everything, and they could gain the ultimate certainty for their philosophy.

These men achieved this position in various ways. Manuel Joel of Birnbaum in the land of Posen, was one of the first to gain an understanding of the specialness of the Sephardic philosophers before Spinoza; out of this, the particularity of his religion was disclosed to him. Heymann Steinthal of Gröbzig in the land of Anhalt (where Moses Mendelssohn was born) had journeyed to the spiritual foundations of the ancient language, and sought out its philosophy. There he created a path that led to the depth of the biblical word, to where revelation seeks to rise in the soul, and to the voices in his religion in which the inexpressible is heard. Above all of them, in the following generation, comes Hermann Cohen, from Coswig in the land of Anhalt. He was completely unparalleled in his power and breadth. He was truly a teacher of teachers, a teacher for the present and for the future. When the world of philosophy, the world of Plato and Kant particularly, seemed to surround him and to permeate him completely, his religion was reborn through his quality of genius, of naïveté. He received the dynamism of philosophy in the stronger dynamism of his religion, and it became his final harvest, a strength rising out of the renewed old strength through him.

Whoever contemplates these days, in which religion searched for its people and people searched for their religion, in which the religion of this people awakened and rediscovered itself in new life, will hear a clear harmony. He becomes aware of a rhythm, almost of a rhythmic law. Future days will understand this even more clearly.

The struggle to understand the meaning of this people's history and the striving for new religious expression were constantly connected with the fight for justice. It was a battle, constant in many lands, for this people's rights in the new state. But this particular battle for rights took its strength and gained its conscience in the great battle for the right of everyone, for the realization of social justice within humanity. That which might appear special, thus won its universality and its religious significance, and its legitimacy as well.

Many who stood within this people or came out of it (Karl Marx, in particular) were so completely filled by this great idea that the sense of this people's particular right was quickly confined and ultimately displaced. But in them, too, generally without their knowledge, a special power moved, excited, and conquered the spirit. It was the power which had lived in this people as in no other people; it was this people's original power from the days of Abraham, the ever-reborn power which comes from the divine commandment of justice. This people would not and could not live without the eternal law. When its prophets, its poets, its teachers, its questioners, each in his speech and in his manner and in his time, attempted to proclaim the entrance of one single justice of the eternal, unending, and absolute into the spheres of the terrestrial, the transitory, and the finite, they kept in mind the domain of human existence and of communal life. The constantly enduring task, the firm, immovable, unending way and goal—these they believed God had commanded; these were the guide of history.

Moses Hess

The longing for the great justice which bridges the peoples and unites them, and makes each people truly a people; and the longing for the right of this people amidst the peoples, are qualities which cannot be reduced fundamentally. In this connection one special person must be mentioned: Moses Hess of Bonn. Something special existed in this man: a sort of pious searching that saw the goal and knew the way, but still strove to find the paths that would lead to that way. Even in the natural sciences with which he was always deeply concerned, he was one of those intuitive persons who know before they see. Above all, part of the inheritance of the prophets lived in him, the "inheritance of the congregation of Jacob." His was the deep moral longing, the longing for the great justice, for the one justice for all peoples and for all among all peoples—for this people too, wherever it might live. He viewed the present from the future, *sub specie futuri*; this, too, was an inheritance from the prophets. Unlike others, whom he joined in the social task, he did not want to determine the future from the present. This explains the clarity of his vision for many of his people. His hope looked into the land which had been promised to the patriarchs and to their children. In the soul of this man there dwelt the complete and constant faithfulness which clings not only to yesterday and to today, to what was and is, but which clings to what will come, to the true future. In him the time of rebirth evidences itself too.

It appears in all of those to whom the great right spoke first through an immediate beginning, through the challenging first task to achieve rights for the men of this people, where they lived. The fight for rights, for the one and unshakable right, became their life's honor. It was religious dignity, and was even deemed by some to be the essential aspect of their religion; their belief became a belief in the rights which God had granted all. In this fighting belief they found the fulfillment of their life, of life in the congregation, in the state, and in humanity.

Gabriel Riesser

Here, too, the essential features are most clearly recognizable through a historical personality: Gabriel Riesser of Hamburg. His soul was given to the idea of right. It was said of him that "the right had become his temperament"; one could add, his religious temperament. Such words of praise could be applied to many others as well. This people desired to exist for the sake of the right. Longing received a new tone, will gained a new sound, the sense of justice gained a new language. In the lands in which men fought for the freedom that grows out of right, the children of this people entered the ranks of the fighters. They stood there for the sake of the land in which they lived and for the sake of their fathers' belief, out of which they drew their life. New faithfulness rose out of the ancient faithfulness. Wherever faithfulness called, the children of this people raised their heads and listened.

Then, as both before and afterwards, there existed faithful and unfaithful states. This people never repaid faithfulness with faithfulness, and it answered every faithfulness with its own unwavering faithfulness. Right was demanded that it might be faithful as free men. It knows from its ancient covenant that there is an uprightness in the right, an uprightness in righteousness. A verse in the Book of Deuteronomy speaks, and is exactly reproduced in the ancient translations of Greek, Aramaic, and Latin: "Justly [in righteous manner, uprightly], justice shalt thou follow" (*Juste, quod justum est, persequeris* [Deut. 16:20]). The existence of this people is founded upon this injunction. The best among this people recognized this when they fought for the rights of their people and for the rights of all human beings.

The Great New Hope: Herzl and Zionism

The threefold experience of history, religion, and justice, reborn, and striving for an ever-new awareness, was permeated and entwined with one theme, that of the great hope, the Messianic certainty. It was drawn together by this belief in the surely established goal, for the sake of which history can be demanded, for the sake of which history is worth possessing or, if necessary, enduring.

In those days of rebirth hopes appeared here and there, rising and setting. Events had been believed; they came and they went. Some assumed that ways had been discerned, and then it became evident that they were not true ways. Disappointments raised their voice and drowned out what had previously sounded within the heart. The most oppressing loneliness of all, loneliness amidst humanity, at times could take hold of the temperament. But searching for the testimony of this time, whether in that of a simple piety, or a seeking intellectuality, one always encounters—in spite of everything—the great confidence in an attainable future. Without it there is no genuine confidence in God, that confidence which is completely different from what has been named "optimism." It contains more of a heroism of the soul than optimism. Often there came thoughts when one felt deserted, deserted by the great and the lesser. But one did not feel lost as long as one did not lose oneself. These are the voices of that time. They can be heard in all the directions in which experience, contemplation, and searching moved. The one hope endured.

In it, a call was heard—a call that never ceased to be sounded in all hopeful days, even when it spoke softly—the call emanating from Zion and leading toward Zion. Moses Hess put it into words. And in the congregations in the South of Europe, close to the ocean, the longing worked in a wondrous way upon men, causing them to arise and go forth. In later days, the great poet Agnon, who gave a new sound to the Hebrew language and discovered anew the poetry of the mystery and of the wonder, told of them. But such emigration remained an individual event, an episode. Through one man, in whom a contemplative imagination became will, strength of action, and power of movement, through Theodor Herzl, the reawakening of the longing for Zion became an all-embracing force. Theodor Herzl was a man of Budapest, one of the strong Eastern outposts of the culture of the Western Ashkenazim. He let the word of Zion become a clarion call. He awakened many, in the West and in the East; he taught them to sit up and listen, to look out. Out of the strength that was stored in him, strength streamed into others. Out of the old "consolation," a new consolation had arisen for him. It became consolation for many in days which often seemed inconsolable; it became the consolation out of which strength emerges.

Who will dare forget this man? He is remembered, though events turned out differently from what he had surmised. He did not stand merely between eras, nor does he stand just between realms. He is one of those in whom rebirth revealed itself. From where he stood he gathered his experience, and from this particular point saw the life of his people. He belongs in the sequence of these men of the rebirth; he joined them, even when he himself was not aware of it. Without them, he would not have become what he did become; without them, there would not have been the movement that emanated from him. He too was an individual, a special person among them; and he too spoke an individual, a new language, and spoke it out of a rare clarity of thought, out of a rare devoutness of pure will. He was one of those who were able to give a new meaning and a new strength to the existence of this people.

The time of the great rebirth is not yet closed. Reawakened in all areas, the strength reached into the East and into the West. Moreover, in the years between two world wars, it came to unfold a new, rich, and meaningful life in the land of Ashkenaz itself—just as the time of the Ashkenazim drew to a close, as once the time of the Sephardim had ended. Many names of those who have passed on and those who are yet alive could be mentioned in gratitude. Those who are yet to come, those who will be able to survey the whole way and the continuing influence of what existed there, in their time, will tell of them. Will there be formed, out of this rebirth, a history of the spirit of the Ashkenazim in other lands, the lands of their immigration? Will the Ashkenazim of the West and the Ashkenazim of the East rediscover one another there, in a great encounter, so that out of the new union, out of a newly won unity, a strength of history may grow upon new soil?

America's Promise

Seeds had been sown into many new soils in the meantime. In the quarter century before the First World War, America had again become a place of promise for this people through the great immigration of Eastern Ashkenazim. The many who thus, year after year, sought their place in the new world, had left an area into which the revolution for human rights had not yet penetrated. They were now received by a land which had begun its history with a revolution in the name of human rights. They came out of a world of traditional and community piety in which the old way of their religion blew into every door and window and enfolded everyone in every street. Now they were to live in a land of individual piety, in which everyone selected the manner of his religion, in which religiosity was not present from the beginning, waiting for him and then surrounding him, but in which each had to prepare a place of his own. It was a new world; they had traveled across the ocean. With honesty and uprightness they affirmed the new way of the new world, even though, at times, a love arose here, a romanticism there, which turned to gaze longingly at the bygone past.

Through the broad stream of immigration, America became the homeland for millions of the children of this people. Never before did so many of this people live within a state which—an inheritance of its English origins—guaranteed every individuality, and yet became and remains an encompassing domain with *one* language, *one* culture, *one* law, *one* purity, *one* viewpoint, and *one* loyalty. Upon these millions, into whose homes the prosperity of this land entered, upon whom there rest only the easy, personal burdens, history has placed a great deal of responsibility. This responsibility is moral and spiritual, and it extends in particular to the old totality of which they are a part. As human beings we cannot select for ourselves merely one portion of a responsibility; responsibility is always the one and complete responsibility. Life leads the individual—and history leads the communities and the totalities—to confront their responsibilities. One of the greatest men of America, one of the greatest men of all times, the emancipator of the slaves in his land, called to his contemporaries: "You cannot escape history." Neither may we. Will its voice be heard? Those who are yet to come will hear the answer.

Developments in Eastern Europe

In the congregations of Eastern Europe, from where, year after year, men had started their journey to the New World, in all of these years, and even before them, a new strength had begun to develop out of the old strength. Old thoughts became contemporary, the ancient tongue renewed itself, a new generation grew up. It was not a revolution, the revolution had taken place previously. No new principle was established; no new point of departure was chosen. But the spirit widened in order to gain new experiences. A new sense of joy entered.

Things were understood differently than before, and different things were said.

The old Hebrew language, which had never left this people and had never stood still within it, began to stir itself anew. In all epochs it had re-formed itself. The old meaning of words gained new sense and new sound; out of the old form, new forms arise. The language kept re-experiencing itself. In the new era, the circle around Mendelssohn had come to experience this and had tried to mold what had been experienced. In the new awakening within the Eastern area, all of this now became stronger and even more alive. Three men, above all, must be praised here: the thinker, Asher Ginsberg, who named himself Ahad Ha-am, a man of Skwira in Podolia; Micah Joseph Berdichevsky, the searcher, from Meshilosh in the often tested and proven Ukraine; and the poet Chaim Nachman Bialik, also from the Ukraine, from Rady. Bialik, and with him others, at that time made the community of Odessa a central point of this new reality from which splendor and strength emanated. These men, so different and yet so alike, and many who followed them, prepared the way for the language in its renewal. They achieved this both for a present which had come to be and for days which were approaching. What will a day to come yet say? Into the old folk language, the "Jewish-German," or "Yiddish," that had once been brought along from Ashkenaz, there also entered a new sap that filled its trunk and boughs. It is one of the warmest, liveliest folk languages, rich in the forms and sounds of expression; it laughs and cries and sings and mourns in its own manner and in the manner of the land in which it lives. Like every folk language it has its provinces; it unites with the sounds and the forms of its home territory. There is one man that stands above all others here; Mendele Mocher Sephorim from Kopyl in White Russia (where Lithuania, Russia, and the Baltic lands meet one another). Others descend from him, and they gratefully named him their "ancestor." Will these descendants have descendants now that the old soil, the soil of the old, extensive, dwelling and living together, the soil from which this language gained its vitality, has been destroyed or has passed away? Only later days can give an answer. But, as always, the spirit will remain; so will this spirit which created its prose and its songs out of this native language.

Arthur James Balfour and Zionism

Time marched on in hasty, almost precipitate events. Hope rose upon the horizon, salvation here, fulfillment there, just as once a prophet of the return from the Babylonian Exile had said: "The sun of righteousness [shall] arise with healing in its wings" (Mal. 3:20). The faith that a new word would go forth from Zion, a word to this people among humanity and to humanity itself sent forth its healing rays. "Zion, wilt thou not ask about the peace of those who are bound unto thee?" Judah Halevi had once sung, questioningly, but also knowingly. Now this confident question sounded anew.

That which had been seen and sought a generation earlier by Theodor Herzl penetrated to one statesman. A statesman is one who turns from the idea of politics, so that politics can become an instrument of the idea, rather than someone who stands within politics, is surrounded by it, and, from it, looks about for an idea which could be made to serve politics. As long as the old power of gratitude lives within the Jewish soul and gives it life, the name of this statesman, Arthur James Balfour, will never be lost or be forgotten. He grew out of a people which had always been the people of the constant revolution. It is a people capable of the constant, conservative revolution because it always possesses or comes to possess again that moral, artistic gift: the ability to have time, the ability to take a step backwards and to survey that which came to be and that which will be. It was always prepared to accept a new principle if the day for it seemed to have arrived. This statesman thus freely chose an idea which had come to him, and a principle which it contained. He stated it as a matter of self-affirmation; he absorbed it into his understanding and will. Certainly, in his actions he had his own people in mind; but just as certainly, he had that people in mind into which he had now thought himself. Thus that "Declaration" entered history which, in the name of history, demanded a secure "national home" in the ancient land of the patriarchs for the men of this people whose dwellings trembled or seemed to shake.

In this Declaration this people found a new foundation; a new principle had been established, and, like every genuine principle, it proved itself creative. In other words, a possibility had now been given for this people to be creative upon a special soil. In the great work of preparation, which thinkers of this people called "providence," a new task was now set. This is all a man can expect in history, nothing that is complete, nothing already fulfilled is given to us, the children of men. What is given is only a possibility, the possibility to fashion anew a path that leads to God's commandment and, with that, to create something new, to be creative in what is new.

At that time, out of the congregations of Eastern Europe, first of all, and then out of the congregations of other countries, men set out toward the land of the fathers, in order to find the land and to find themselves: the young, who matured with the task; and the old, who became young again in the task. Hard work awaited them, and hard work created new enthusiasm. Thus began something unique in human history; the children of the old colonies founded by men from the ancient motherland, and of the colonies of those colonies, left their homes to enter that ancient motherland in order to colonize it, in order to be colonists of its restoration. A social order was created in which there were no differences of class and in which no one within the land was to feel himself excluded. That twofoldness which the prophet had promised—and therefore commanded—was fulfilled: "[He] hath made her wilderness like Eden, and her desert like the garden of Him-Who-Is; joy and gladness shall be found therein, thanksgiving, and the voice of melody" (Is. 51:3).

The Nazi Terror

But soon other voices sounded forth out of the world of Europe, striving to submerge all else, voices that served untruthfulness, that praised crime and jeered at righteousness. States disregarded their duties of faithfulness toward their citizens. Houses of prayer, in which faith, righteousness, and justice had been proclaimed, were burned to the ground; congregations, in which reverence for God, humanity, philanthropy, and a feeling for the total society had been nurtured, were dismembered; hundreds of thousands, children of this people, human lives containing a soul, were destroyed. And those that committed this knew what they committed. And the powers which practiced every crime created the readiness for new crimes. They stretched forth their hands—in the name of peace—to powers in whose midst right and righteousness dwelt. The peace was profaned; and a profaned peace brings an even worse destiny than a breach of peace. War always follows it, a worse war than that caused by a broken peace. The Second World War thus developed, and when it came to an end, the victors undertook the task of expiating the profaned peace through a labor of pure peace. In a sense, they wanted to reconsecrate humanity. The United Nations was to be the foundation for that task, so that a sanctuary of hope might be built. Will this come to be? Is this the commencement of a humane epoch, an epoch at the beginning of which the affliction of this people stood as "a sacrifice for many"? Those who come later will hear the answer.

The State of Israel

The gate to the United Nations, a gateway of a commandment and of a hope, opened itself to the State of Israel. Three years after the World War, the "homeland" became a state. It is still in danger. It is threatened externally, as a smaller state is often threatened by larger ones. It can also be threatened internally; every state is often threatened by a Satan, a "hinderer" who denies morality, the Satan of *raison d'état*, political reasoning which is prepared to justify anything one wishes to do, which pardons nothing in the opposition and everything in itself, which flees into excuses and in the process loses its way. There is an inner rebelliousness which hides itself under many cloaks, yet the state of this people can also be the state of the "covenant," of the commandment of God.

Two questions arise to transfix him who is filled with the love of the ancient land. The lands of the children of Ishmael surround the territory of this state, and a new national consciousness has awakened within them. They are united with vast areas in Asia and almost all of Africa by the same faith. In that faith, missionary zeal is constantly active. What will this mean for the State of Israel in their midst? Will that time return which brought so many blessings, in which Ishmael and Israel met one another spiritually, in which spirit joined to spirit, in which both enriched one another and enriched humanity?

And the other question: Which voice will finally be decisive in the state, that of the enduring covenant, the pledge, the commandment? Or that of the coming and going day which promises something of utility? This people can never be permitted to look only at itself. It has life only when it looks outward, when it sees itself within humanity, when it holds to itself for the sake of humanity and to humanity for the sake of itself. Its confidence, including its confidence in the land of the patriarchs, is founded upon the greater trust. Therefore, it also has hope here.

The Cold War Between East and West

There is yet another question that presents itself. It, too, can only be answered by confidence. Question and confidence are even more encompassing here, and they carry the fate of this people to distant reaches. Will that which has been separated, separated in humanity, and also within this people, will it yet unite? This is the question today, and the today's doubt and hope seek to give the answer. In the years after the wars, the division between East and West deepened. Since the days in which the Old World was settled by tribes, and shepherds became farmers, there has always been such a division, even though forms and boundaries change. Nations penetrated the West from the East and then from the West to the East; but in the end they returned to where they had come, and the former boundaries endured.

Are these boundaries drawn by nature—which was there before history and which often seeks to determine it—from the very beginning? Are feeling and will different in both places, and have they created different types of thinking and hoping? Often a line between North and South was also engraved in history; but the real separation remained between East and West. Will this continue? Will it continue to be true that "East is East, and West is West, and never the twain shall meet"? A static aspect of the millennia seems to exhibit a persistent power here. It seems to endure within itself despite the centuries. Will the individual strength of the great, dynamic ideas within humanity prove to be stronger? Will a new epoch commence for it, and, with that, will a new formulation of the task commence for this people?

This question reaches even further. For there is more in the old antithesis between East and West at this time than two philosophies confronting one another. Added to this are the philosophies rising out of the effects of the machine—that tool of tools—upon communal life. Starting from the effect of the machine, these philosophies desire to lead to a system of justice governing communal life. The system which established its fortress in the East had its origin in Western thought. It received its first and determining format, like a messianic gift, through a son of this people, through Karl Marx. It then drew strong and compelling powers from the Russian soil. The Russian land, from ages past, had encouraged the growth of a deep mysticism which was to bring redemption to all and which, as so many mysticisms, encouraged the desire to belong to one's own and special group. A strange mixture of an ever-renewed missionary zeal and a tenacious desire to be exclusive could thus form itself and create its dogmas. These dogmas were to hold everything together by establishing limits for faith. Will the dogmas win, or will it be faith that wins? The history of religions, and also of philosophies, constantly reveals a struggle between faith and dogma. The desire of faith to point out the paths emanating from it struggles with the dogmatic desire that wishes to believe that the goal is reached, that, henceforth, everyone is to be conscious of what has been established.

A question arising from this all-encompassing problem directs itself particularly to this people. Within the vast Eastern areas, whose portals are now closed, a part of this people lives. They are men with characteristic traits, congregations with valuable traditions. What will they be able to give, what will they want to receive, when days come, in which it is permitted to reunite what has been separated? The history of this people is a continual account of the reciprocity by means of which the diverse, ultimately the separated, segments of this people, willingly or unwillingly, enrich one another. The dynamism of its power to live and of its strength for resistance keeps gaining new impetus in this way. Will it prove true in this case?

Question after question confronts one who seeks a glimpse of the future of this people, no matter which the direction. But this is what history is here: it is a history filled with questions. It can take this form, and perhaps must do so, because it is founded upon the one, the great certainty. Throughout the flux of happenings, this remains one and complete. There cannot be a time, no matter how bright, that is certainty; and there cannot be a time, no matter how dark, that can shake the certainty. Instead, question after question may approach, and the attempt can constantly be renewed to open the doorway to the answer. Amidst all hopes and all disappointments, the hope endures.

The Righteous and His Faith

This people looks back upon more than three millennia of history, and, in them, upon a task. It never ceased to possess this, its history, for it constantly became aware of it again. It never ceased to form its history, for it kept grasping the task anew which it set. The way leading through the millennia is thus clearly recognizable for one who looks back; he sees how the grandchildren live in the forefathers and how the forefathers live through the grandchildren.

Throughout these centuries, varying days, days full of strength and days full of weakness existed. There were days in which this people lived its own destiny, and there were days in which it stayed far from what was related to it. But the greatness of this history lies in the fact that this people constantly returned to itself; it placed itself ever anew upon the ground of its existence. It regained its self-respect, for without self-respect, this people could not live. This people returned to the commandment of God, in which the promise dwells. This people can only be a people in relationship to God. It can only find itself when it seeks God; when it is distant from God, it becomes estranged from itself. It can only have strength in its life when it "enters into the covenant with God"; nearness to God is the foundation and the condition of existence here. Let us speak with the prophet: This people "shall live by his faith" (Hab. 2:4).

The prophetic word speaks of the "righteous," the *zaddik.* It is difficult to translate the word *zaddik* so that all of its meaning is conveyed. It designates one who, wherever he stands, knows that he stands before God. He is therefore serious about the revelation of God, the commandment, and the hope; it could be said that he is serious about God. In this manner, he learns to take himself seriously as an aspect of ultimate truth. Righteousness is the necessary beginning for this; in this respect, the translation of *zaddik* as "righteous one" makes good sense. Righteousness demands honest, unyielding self-examination, and for that reason it would never want to walk along enwrapped solely in itself. Without goodness, it can never find its way. This righteousness is the first and often the decisive test of the right, basic position of belief. If this test is passed, the ability exists to pass other tests. Only "the righteous" will be firmly established, he "shall live by his faith."

There is an ancient, confident belief that this people will never lack "righteous ones," these *zaddikim*, altogether. There may be very few of them, perhaps only "thirty six," as the poetry of an ancient legend dared to say; but through them, the strength for life would be preserved for this people. Every generation, it was hoped, would have them as its own, each born because of it and for its sake, all of them comforters for all times. They must come into being ever anew, for there is neither inheritor nor successor for any of them. They are often scarcely known, scarcely considered, scarcely seen. They dwell somewhere, in silence, in narrow places, these *zaddikim*; but around their life, observed or not observed by the many, there is a splendor that shines forth. Each in his own manner, the "thirty-six" righteous ones are the guarantors of life in every generation. Some of them may not be learned, but in each rests the great understanding, and he "lives by his faith," through his *emunah*. He lives creatively through his *emunah*. Again, the full wealth of this word, *emunah,* cannot be translated completely. For out of the root of the one word something threefold has arisen which remains one: truth, faithfulness, and belief. Through them, the *zaddik*, the righteous one, lives. And where he lives there is life. Through the *zaddikim*, the centuries were joined spiritually within this people.

This people's faith had entered the world as something revolutionary, taking hold of the soul and through it all intellectual as well as social areas. It demanded a completely different attitude toward life, one maintained constantly. A completely different principle was now to be valid everywhere and at all times; a completely different yardstick was to be applied to everything. It was a revolution that, initially and primarily, had to take hold of this people and had to take its effect within it, in order to fashion it into a special people, into this people. This people could only survive within the world and the changing times as long as its strength revived in rebirth, the sequence of epochs. Movement was always demanded, and on occasion its beginning brought a shock with it. In a sense, this people was always to be underway. Only a people with a belief filled with faithfulness, a belief which showed the firm foundation of the way that every generation had to choose anew, a belief which set ever-new tasks and offered ever-new vistas—only such a people was able to cope with such a history.

This people has to have the courage for the ever-new task, this courage to be "underway." If it keeps the great faithfulness in which something of the ultimate truth discloses itself, this *emunah*, it will possess this courage. Faithfulness unites all and everything here, the men and the times, that which is different and that which is separated; its power is stronger than the power of boundaries and of days.

The Tension of Jewish History

The history of this people is also a history of boundaries, of eras that divided it deeply, of domains and areas that created manners, of spheres of history within the one history. At times there existed a tension between the parts, but the parts never broke apart. In the end, the tension had the strength to create strength. The unity always endured.

It will endure, and blessing will stream from the whole to the parts and from the parts to the whole, as long as there are beings here who exist, and constantly arise again, who "live by their faith," so that the faith lives through them. Rabbi Simlai, who hearkened to both East and West, has said that the summation of all the commandments is that "the righteous shall live by his faith."

Everything declares itself in faith which, as certainty and experience, from the very beginning, had its earthly place within this people: the certainty of the covenant of God, of human freedom, of the revelation, of the reconciliation, of the soil and the community, of the readiness and the renunciation, of the will to Torah, to the message, to the contemporary and the coming, to work, and to the Sabbath, and the certainty of the gift of prayer and expectation. Faith appears as something manifold, but is one. In this totality, in this unity, and through this unity and totality, this people lived generation after generation, for the sake of the generations—"from Egypt even until now" (Num. 14:19). Thus, thus alone, will it continue to live.

"From Egypt even until now." Until this time, in which mankind is once more changing, its parts striving to separate, this people, participating in or drawn into everything, is yet to remain within its individuality in order to recognize and fulfill new tasks. Until this time, when once again focal points shifted or were displaced, when this people came to experience all the displacement in itself, it held fast to its own enduring focal point. Until this time, when the New World, which had become great, became the land of most of this people, and when in the Old World, nations were awakening, a new life had grown for this people upon the soil of the Promised Land. Until this time, when there arises, among peoples and religions, an almost undreamed of understanding for this people and its religion, and also a previously unknown adversary, this people is to be prepared and work willingly that "righteousness and peace may come together." Until this time, when mankind searches for itself and yet cannot find itself, this people is to cling fast to the fact that it has its existence in humanity and for the sake of humanity. "From Egypt even until now."

Moses once pleaded with God for his people that had gone astray: "Pardon, I pray Thee, the iniquity of this people according unto the greatness of Thy lovingkindness, and according as Thou hast forgiven this people, from Egypt even until now" (Num. 14:19). When this people prays for forgiveness year after year on the Day of Atonement, it utters these words. He who considers the future of this people finds these words forcing themselves to his lips and into his heart.

What will a later generation see when it looks about? What must it recognize, what may it recognize when it looks at itself? These are questions which the generation that lives today must address to itself, just as they were addressed to every previous generation, whether it heard them or not. Every generation by choosing its way, its present way, at the same time chooses an essential part of the future, the way of its children. Perhaps the children will turn from the eternal way, but in this, too, they will be determined by the direction of their parents. The responsibility to those who follow after us is included in the responsibility to ourselves. The way of the children, whether accepting or rejecting the direction, emanates from our way. Ways bind, wind, and wander.

Nevertheless, ever again a child is born; an individual, a promise of the likeness of the image of God; the great miracle within humanity is reborn. With the birth of a human being the whole problem of humanity is raised anew. The great possibility, the message to humanity, the annunciation of the confidence that must never end, is brought anew into life through the child. It always re-enters humanity in the sequence of the generations, and in history.

When people or peoples assume that they can fit history into a personally fixed pattern, they delude themselves. They want to make things easy for themselves. Responsibility in which freedom turns to freedom is so much harder. But all strivings and endeavors to bind history are in vain. An inheritance cannot be fabricated, let alone forced; it can only be assumed by a freedom that has the ability to build on it. The work of the clever and the mighty, who think they have established a lasting inheritance, breaks down so much easier, generally, than the work of the simple and the insignificant. The shrewd think they are securing the future; and one day, often very near, they or those who follow them stand before ruins. The question is raised, and many questions join in it: Is an inheritance possible, that can endure from generation to generation, not in its forms, but in its power (for the nature of form is change), that remains in its blessing, in order to endure any fate? When this people raises this question, it raises the question of its existence.

In all of the declines of history in which humanity apparently destroys itself or seems to refute itself, one thing surely endured and experienced renewal. That which was searched out and formed by the spirit arose out of ruins and beyond ruins; it wandered from land to land. It could speak to men everywhere; it could engage them in dialogue. The history of these rebirths encounters the works of the spirit —and in the spirit, in its best and ultimate forms, lies an essential part of the actual history of humanity. What would humanity be without it? Would it exist without it? The many things the tool built, the tool then destroyed in many ways. That which spirit has fashioned is indestructible. It endures, even when it is rejected. In the Bible, the word "spirit" has the sound of holiness. The spirit comes from God, and in it, too, man can sanctify himself.

The Encounter With God

One thing leads still higher, to something even more encompassing than the encounter with man's spirit. It is "nearness to God," the meeting with God. It is the greatest aspect of human existence. In it, "man gains his world, his eternity, in the span of an hour"; such is the daring expression of an ancient teacher. Thus, in an all-encompassing piety, the Psalmist prayed: "But as for me, the nearness of God is my good" (Ps. 73:28). Previously, this man of prayer said: "Whom have I in heaven but Thee? And beside Thee I desire none upon earth" (Ps. 73:25). This nearness is this people's inheritance through which alone it could and will endure, on whatever ground it may live. This people's true history is a history of encounters with God. It has this history for its own sake and for the sake of humanity. It bears it and is borne by it.

Every people is a question which God addresses to humanity; and every people, from its place, with its special talents and possibilities, must answer for its own sake and for the sake of humanity. Any people cannot, may not, be without humanity or beyond humanity. Humanity cannot be without all peoples nor beyond any people. God questions humanity through the peoples. Humanity lives only through these peoples, those that have come into being and those that are in the process of becoming. Every people is thus responsible for the fact that humanity exists. For the sake of a responsibility which it has before God, through the question which God poses, a people exists, just as the individual exists only when he is conscious of responsibility and finds his life in it. A man and a people are thus a question of God; or, as the wonderful image of an ancient teacher dared: they are a resignation made by God. Beyond all of the special questions, stands the one question which is life itself, the question from God.

Jewish Existence

This people Israel developed and grew in one millennium and formed the question that rests within it. It has kept arising ever again, through rebirths, in new epochs, for more than two millennia now. Through its prophets, its poets, its teachers, its righteous ones, Israel was able to learn how to listen to the question which God addressed to it. Its question proved, in Israel's experience, to be the deepest of all questions which live within and form humanity. This people's hope is, therefore, the greatest of all hopes; it is the great expectation to which the way of all ways leads. The iniquity of this people is, therefore, deeper iniquity than any other. And offenses against this people signify more than other offenses. Both need "God's reconciliation." This people is "a covenant for the nations," a law for the peoples.

On the "Day of Judgment" and the "Days of Penitence," this people knows, in its prayers that lift it anew to God, that it stands in court before God. The sin within this people reverberates through these prayers. Only because atonement is in God's hands, can this people appear before God. The prayer continues: "A court also sits in judgment on the nations." These words seem to express the question to the nations: "What have you done to My people, to this Jewish people?" But the reverence in which all, the peoples and the nations, may find themselves united, penetrates these prayers too: "So be it: Grant reverence of He-Who-Is our God, to all Thy creatures, and honor of Thee to all whom Thou hast created; and all creatures will revere Thee, and all creatures will bow before Thee; and out of them will come *one* covenant, to do Thy will with a perfect heart."* The great expectation speaks here, the hope for the reconciliation in which all reconciliations join together.

* See *High Holiday Prayer Book*, ed. M. Silverman, p. 11.

The Great Readiness for God

The great task of dark days, and the greater one of bright hours, was to keep faith with the expectation. Man waits for God, and God waits for man. The promise and the demand speak here, both in one: the grace of the commandment and the commandment of grace. Both are one in the One God. Around the One God there is the concealment. He does not reveal Himself, but He reveals the commandment and the grace. And He, the Eternal One, has given mortal man freedom of will and has shown him a goal for his will. But the ultimate remains concealed from man. Thus the prophet announced the word of God: "For My thoughts are not your thoughts, neither are your ways My ways, saith He-Who-Is" (Is. 55:8). The great reverence was exalted in this, and it always clung to this, even when men assumed that God's thoughts were their thoughts, and when men dared the supposition that their ways were God's ways. The mystery surrounds God. He is not the revealed God, but He is the revealing God. Wherever the great reverence lives in a man and the great readiness for God rises out of it, there and then, man is near to God.

Men near to God existed in this people in all its days. They are this people's "holy ground." This people is sustained by them alone. Through two sentences of Moses, this people declared itself for God and for itself by becoming conscious of God and of itself: "Hear, O Israel: He-Who-Is our God, He-Who-Is is one. And thou shalt love Him-Who-Is thy God with all thy heart, and with all thy soul, and with all thy might" (Deut. 6:4–5). The first sentence tells of the great reverence, in which the certainty of the belief dwells; and the second, of the great readiness, in which man declares himself for God. That God is our God, is the promise, the grace, upon which the commandment is founded. To love Him thy God, is the commandment out of which new grace flows to men. The man who fulfills the commandment has encountered God. These two sentences are not just sentences, they are the history of this people. This history, after all, is the history of encounters with God. Whoever wishes to see, sees this.

Man and the Mystery

We live in a clearness surrounded by mystery. This, our earth, courses around its sun, one of the many myriads of stars. Are there, upon any of these stars, beings like ourselves? Beings descended from a mother and father, who desire to live on through their children, beings who search and roam, who get lost in their days between birth and death, who doubt, who fear, who hope, who sin, and who can yet be reconciled?

Whatever the case, we are these men upon this earth. It is our home, and its circumference includes us. Upon it, we are born, generation after generation; and upon it, we die, grave after grave. For the earth exists in many years, and we, in but the few. It existed before us, it will exist after us. It carries us and reaches out to us. It holds fast to everything upon it by the strength of its attracting power.

But a miracle exists upon it, exists in human beings who live upon it. The miracle leads outward and upward and is stronger than everything terrestrial. It is the miracle of the spirit, of the created human who becomes creative, fashioning within the fashioned.

It is a miracle of the thinking human being. The spirit of men who dwell upon the earth, upon this star, travels into the All and takes up its foundation there. There, man cogitates. He takes space and time, which embrace all the stars, and makes them his tool. Comparing and measuring, investigating and counting, contemplating that which has come out of the thoughts of a higher power, he determines passage and duration. He recognizes the rule of the law, the constantly returning sanction of the enduring. A great definiteness, a great clarity appears before him; and he moves forward, from definiteness to definiteness, from clarity to clarity. He stands in the All and walks in the All. Such is the miracle of the thinking spirit.

But a greater miracle reveals itself to him here. For behind every certainty there stands a concealment, behind every new clarity a new mystery is revealed. All the certainties, all the concealments, and the searching spirit itself that traveled out into them, all are embraced by something unfathomable, by the miracle of all miracles. Behind all of them, above all of them, and beneath all of them is the great mystery which is beyond space and time, which exists through itself and which exists through everything that is. No man's mind has fathomed it or will be able to fathom it. But reverence, that reverence without which love does not live and faithfulness does not endure, may approach it. And it hears the voice out of the mystery: "I AM THAT I AM, thy God."

And another great miracle is within the human being upon this earth. It is the miracle in which the artistic spirit awakens. This spirit does not gaze outward but gains perspective. It steps back to view a totality, to hear a totality, to understand a totality—this totality in which the particular receives meaning and gains its place and its right. Thus, man also stands above the earth, above its constant change. He takes his position in the higher domain, that of ideas. Seeing, or hearing, or pondering, he wants to grasp a unity, a totality, a harmony there where he sees lines beside lines, hears sounds beside sounds, where he experiences thoughts beside thoughts. He, earthly man, has lifted himself above earth. He, the created man, begins as if by a miracle to be creative. Clarities, certainties approach him; and through him they appear to the days which come after him.

But here too the concealed once again emerged behind the definite; the mystery stood behind every clarity. Something which existed behind the presentations, behind the appearances, a unity, a totality, a harmony had opened itself; and behind it, in the hidden, a still wider totality, a more comprehensive unity, a deeper harmony, was surmised. Appearances were merely a reflection of an infinite mystery which had revealed itself. The reverence without which the truly artistic cannot exist could sense this. To it also, out of that unfathomable, the word sounded: "I AM THAT I AM, thy God."

Still another miracle exists, which develops and can then grant even greater power to the others: the miracle of the moral in the human being. The moral is the great contradiction of everything which earthly existence seems to indicate. Everything upon this earth bespeaks a battle of all against all, in which one being, in order not to be conquered, strives to conquer another. Existence upon earth seems to be an existence of self-seeking; self-seeking appears as the "natural." The other man is either the subjugated or excluded one, or he is the enemy. Now the great miracle fulfills itself within the spirit: men discover their true selves in selflessness, so that they begin to understand themselves. In the "thou" they discover the "I," and the other man becomes their "other one," placed near them, entrusted to them. A definiteness, a clarity has entered into being, into life. Now, not the drive for the desires of the hour directs or oppresses man; but something steadfast, enduring, a strength out of the strength of the law has come to exist within him, like a miracle. It is there to make him strong, to lead him, to order his life. Now there is something creative within him; he can form his self, he can give shape to his life. He, the created man, can become a creator. He can be free inwardly, free by reason of the commandment. He is allowed to be more than the earth upon which he was born and upon which he dies. The great commandment, which never ceases and never changes, this miracle—it renders it thus for him. This miracle of morality makes him truly man.

The Task

When man thus forms his life, he begins to create community. He is not only born into community as if by fate, but he has now been called to the task of molding it. He stands within it as a figure of freedom. The encounters between the "I" and "thou," the "we" and the "you" attain the possibility of good. He, the created man, creates freedom and peace. Human beings enter and depart, generations come and go, but the commandment endures; ever new, everywhere, it brings men together, toward peace, toward the peace of the community.

What was confused becomes definite; clarity pre-empts what had been confused. The man of this earth works for something to come into being which this earth itself does not give.

Thus the mystery again stands behind the clarity here. The certainty can only ascertain itself by drawing upon it. That which comes from the earth, which presents itself as "the natural," contradicts the creative power within human beings. It contradicts the fact that man rises above the earth by heeding something within himself which is above the earth, that is, the commandment, thus forming freedom within himself and community around himself. The earth does not answer when he asks for the fundamental reason. It only shows him battle and subjugation, the force which rises and then crumbles into itself. Perhaps it presents reasons of utility to him, for the sake of which it pays to act right, in peace and within the community. But useful things only possess their limited moment, in which they assume definition. Sooner or later they break apart and speak to displace one another or to destroy one another. Where is the fundamental basis for the commandment which endures, for the freedom and the community which endure? This is only revealed out of the mystery. The commandment has its roots in the mystery, out of which it gathers its strength, in order to give the mystery its meaning upon earth. Around the clarity there is concealment, the concealed around what it conceals; but from concealment comes the answer in which there is certainty and from which confidence emanates. The reverence learns this and meets the other, this higher world. The distant reaches become the nearness, and man hears the word: "I am He-Who-Is thy God. Thou shalt . . ." The "Kingdom of God" which has been promised to man and has been assigned as his task, has approached him.

And now, what of this people, in the midst of peoples that are upon this earth, with them on one star amidst stars? Around every people, each in its way and each in its place, there is something hidden. But around this people there is more of the mystery than there is around others. Here there is mystery rising out of the eternal mystery. When the poets and the prophets, the teachers and the thinkers who arose from this people's midst, came to think about their people—each in his time and in his way—they contemplated the unending worlds, the harmony of the spheres, the "heavens which declare the glory of God." Then they spoke of their people, of its way and its hope, of the commandment which it must follow in order to encounter peace. Only one whose soul has opened to the great mystery which dwells in all, whether he stands within or sees from without, will be able to understand the reason why this people is to exist and why it does exist.

Every people can be chosen for a history, for a share in the history of humanity. Each is a question which God has asked, and each people must answer. But more history has been assigned to this people than to any other people. God's question speaks stronger here. Many peoples turned toward the commandments of idols, and, in that, they lost the history which had been promised them. The word of the One God penetrated this people from its beginning. When the commandment of God awakes in man, freedom also opens its eyes; and where freedom commences, history begins. A difficult task was assigned this people in its history. It is so easy to listen to the voices of idols, and it is so hard to receive the word of the One God into oneself. It is so easy to remain a slave, and it is so difficult to become a free man. But this people can only exist in the full seriousness of its task. It can only exist in this freedom which reaches beyond all other fredoms. Its history began when it heard the word, rising out of the mystery, and emerging into clarity: "I am He-Who-Is thy God, who brought thee out of the land of Egypt, out of the house of bondage" (Ex. 20:2).

This is the basic foundation and the goal, this is the revelation and the expectation. And confidence then approaches the soul of man, so that the best within him will enter there, where the nearness to God, the encounter with God, will become new truth. Only the reverence, in which alone is belief, can hear such a thing.

Man lives within the universe and within history. This people understood that history and universe testify to a oneness, and reveal a totality and order. One word has dared to be the one expression for that which keeps everything together: "covenant"—"the enduring," the covenant of the One God. It is the covenant of God with the universe, and therefore with the earth; the covenant of God with humanity and therefore with this people contained in it; the covenant with history and therefore with every one within it; the covenant with the fathers and therefore with the children; the covenant with days which were and therefore with days which are to come. "As true as My covenant is"—this was the word of the Eternal One heard by the prophet when he thought about his people in a time of oppression and dark destiny, and certainty entered him. The question of all questions, that of the entrance of the eternal, the unending, the one, into the domain of the many, the terrestrial, the passing, this question in which the searching, the thinking, the hope of this people has always lived, in which it once grew and in which it was ever reborn—this question itself possesses the answer: "As true as My covenant is."

This people traveled through the history of humanity, century after century, millennium after millennium. Its very history became divine guidance for it. Once Moses and the children of Israel sang this song to Him-Who-Is, and said: "Thou in Thy love hast led the people that Thou hast redeemed" (Ex. 15:13). And confidence, whenever it looked backward or forward, then said: "Once they sang unto Him-Who-Is; so will they yet sing unto Him-Who-Is."